D0930600

a short introduction to english usage

a short introduction to english usage

J. J. LAMBERTS
Arizona State University
Tempe, Arizona

McGraw-Hill Book Company

New York St. Louis San Francisco Düsseldorf Johannesburg Kuala Lumpur London Mexico Montreal New Delhi Panama Rio de Janeiro Singapore Sydney Toronto

To: *L. M. Myers*

a short introduction to english usage

Library of Congress Catalog Card Number 78-159309

07-036083-9

1 2 3 4 5 6 7 8 9 BPBP 7 9 8 7 6 5 4 3 2 1

This book was set in Times Roman by Progressive Typographers, and printed and bound by The Book Press, Inc. The designer was Richard Paul Kluga. The editors were Robert Fry and David Dunham. Sally Ellyson supervised production.

contents

Preface *xi*

1. **"Good" English** *1*
   - The Problem of Correctness *2*
   - The First Grammarians *4*
   - The Beginnings of English Grammar *5*
   - Grammar as Function; Grammar as Taste *9*

2. **Approaches to Usage** *11*
   - The Linguists *12*
   - "Levels" of Usage *13*
   - Surveys of Usage *14*
   - Dialects *17*
   - Status and Status Symbols *20*
   - "Believable" English *23*

3. **Phonology—The Sounds of English** *25*
   - Phonetics *28*
   - "Organs of Speech" *30*

Articulation 33
Types of Articulation 34
Stops 36
Fricatives 39
Liquids and Glides 42
The Phoneme 44
Vowels 50
Diphthongs 55
Conclusion 59

4. Pronunciation *61*

Pronunciation and the Dictionaries 64
Stress 66
Some Phonetic Processes 76
Language Change 77
Sound Change 78

5. Special Problems *81*

Assimilation 84
Dissimilation 86
Syncopation 87
Epenthesis 89
Excrescence 89
Intrusives 90
Backing 92
Palatalization 94
Labialization 98
Vowels and Diphthongs 101
"Bad" Pronunciation 107
Foreign Words 115
Conclusion 121

6. Morphology—The Forms of English Words *123*

The Morpheme 125
Parts of Speech 127

7. Nouns *129*

Plurals *130*
Mutation Plurals *131*
Weak Plurals *132*
Zero plurals *133*
Path, etc. *135*
Inverted Plurals *136*
Foreign Language Plurals *138*
Compound Plurals *142*
Genitives *144*

8. Pronouns *149*

Personal Pronouns *149*
Person *150*
Number *152*
Gender *154*
Case *156*
Comparatives *167*
Accusatives *168*
I, we, us *169*
Them *170*
Who, whom *171*
Genitive *174*
The *-self* pronoun *176*
Indefinite Pronouns *177*

9. Verbs *181*

Inflectional Forms *181*
Present *183*
Third Person Singular *186*
Present Participle *187*
Preterite *189*
Past Participle *190*
"Strong" and "Weak" Verbs *191*
Weak Verbs *192*
Strong Verbs *199*

Strong Verb Classes *204*
Class I. *Write* *204*
Class II. *Choose* *207*
Class III. *Sing* *208*
Class IV. *Bear* *215*
Class V. *Break* *216*
Class VI. *Take* *217*
Class VII. *Blow* *218*
Anomalous Verbs *220*
Conclusion *230*
Auxiliaries *234*

10. Modifiers ***251***

Comparison *254*
Absolute Adjectives *261*
Dangling Comparison *262*
Adjectives and Adverbs *263*
Degree Words *268*
Past Participles *271*
Dangling Adverbs *272*

11. Connectives ***275***

Prepositions *277*
Conjunctions *280*
Tautologies *285*
Paired Connectives *286*
Conclusion *288*

12. Derivation ***289***

Affixes *294*
Prefixes *295*
Problems *302*
Inflammable *302*
Irregardless *302*
Disinterested *303*
Suffixes *303*
Back Formation *311*
Conclusion *313*

13. Syntax *315*

Agreement *316*

Genitives *318*

Objects *320*

Demonstratives *321*

Verb Congruence *322*

Reference *327*

Relatives *329*

Antecedents *331*

Collectives *332*

Word Order *338*

Negation *339*

Multiple Negation *345*

Anacoluthon *349*

Word Index *359*

Subject Index *377*

preface

A Short Introduction to English Usage lays no claim to being an encyclopedia of usage or even a dictionary of usage. It is simply an introduction. What it seeks to do is give the reader an awareness of the way that English usage works. If he understands that, he can fill in most of the important details for himself. The chief object of this book is to bring to the user of English a fresh way of looking at "good" and "bad" in speaking and writing—to give him a feel for usage rather than to burden him with opinions about it.

Underlying the problem of usage is the fact that language changes. We find it hard to believe that the English we speak and write has not always been pretty much as we have learned it, that it is even now in a slow but constant state of change. Yet whenever groups of people have become separated from each other by geography or occupation or social standing or other such reasons, in time the members of the respective groups have begun to speak and write differently from each other. Presently each comes to think of the other's language as "wrong." We have of course a kind of language which is used in our schools and in most of our books and magazines and news media. We regard it as "right." We shall discover, however, that any such "right" and "wrong" are likely to result from the merest of accidents. Often, as we shall see, the language of some people is typical of an early stage in a particular change while that of others represents a late stage.

It is clear that English grammar has a bearing on the problems of

English usage. Of this we are reminded again and again as we see grave sins being levelled against nouns, verbs, pronouns, and other features of the language. In fact our school-books and schoolteachers take it for granted that there must be a link between the two even though they neglect to spell it out. We shall take the next step. Throughout this book then it will be assumed that any usage may be described in grammatical terms, that is, as a physical happening. Like any scientific description, a description of language must be impartial; and therefore we must be prepared to find that a grammatical "rule" itself has no scruples about usage.

Most of the usage problems that this book is concerned with are matters of pronunciation or of word forms. Such things are always open to public inspection, to be sure, but the general reader seldom knows what to look for or how to evaluate what he sees; in fact, he is often hobbled by half-truths and fragments of folklore about language. For that reason the treatment of each set of usage problems is preceded by a short discussion of linguistic theory. Readers who have done some work in modern linguistics will immediately recognize a descriptive model here. Anyone who is more at home in another grammar need not feel obligated to follow it and should be able to make his own adaptations quite easily. But a descriptive approach is within the competence of the untrained reader, and it is the kind of grammar that one can walk into and out of, which is all that such a study of usage requires.

No apology is made for leaving vocabulary to its own devices. The old saying, "style is the man," holds true nowhere more strikingly than in one's choice of words. On the other hand, there is no aspect of language where whim and fashion enjoy more freedom. As a result, one picks his way item by item. For that reason we have dictionaries and usage guides.

Usage studies themselves are anything but unique. We have had them with us for hundreds of years, and it is a poor library indeed that cannot offer the reader a choice of a dozen or more. The better-known ones are typically catalogs of items, which are listed in alphabetical order. Since the person who consults such a handbook is usually interested in one specific item, the alphabetical order is a great convenience. Some of the better known ones are: H. W. Fowler, *Modern English Usage* (London, 1926); George P. Krapp, *A Comprehensive Guide to Good English* (Chicago, 1927); Bergen and Cornelia Evans, *A Dictionary of Contemporary American Usage* (New York, 1957); Roy H. Copperud, *Dictionary of Usage and Style* (New York, 1964); *Fowler's Modern English Usage*, revised by Sir Ernest Gowers (London, 1965); Wilson Follett, *Modern American Usage* (1966). Naturally all the unabridged and collegiate dictionaries belong in such a list since all of them have something to say about usage. There has been a great deal of discussion on the subject of dictionaries; but in general the wider the audience the dictionary addresses, the less specific its usage labels are likely to be. Finally we have innumerable handbooks for writing courses in colleges and high schools.

Anyone who takes a serious interest in usage should become familiar with Sterling A. Leonard, *Current English Usage* (New York, 1931), and a companion study, Albert H. Marckwardt and Fred G. Walcott, *Facts About Current English Usage* (New York, 1938). The authors were not so much interested in providing a lexicon of usage as in producing a source book, whatever its limitations. In the normal development of things, much of what was blasted as revolutionary in 1931 has long since become déjà vu. But it remains a model of methodology, and it demonstrates clearly that we cannot possibly look for unanimity in matters of usage. *Teaching English Usage* (New York, 1946), Robert C. Pooley, was an effort to transmit to teachers, especially those teaching at the elementary and secondary levels, some of the insights that systematic language study had brought to light. The real contribution of this book was that it gathered and put on display what scholars had been saying for some twenty or thirty years. Any perceptive teacher could have sensed that something was afoot, but Pooley got it all in one place. Nor can one ignore Martin Joos, *The Five Clocks* (New York, 1961). Joos passes over practically all of what we regard as the specifics of usage and focuses instead on the several kinds of social situations and the "style" that each demands. It should be mentioned that while many usage guides are directed to the production of what Joos calls the "formal," if not the "frozen" style, *A Short Introduction to English Usage* is principally concerned with the "consultative," and less often the "formal."

A list of usages is by its very nature selective. Our dictionaries of usage are intended for people whose language is on public exhibition—editors, authors, public speakers, and secretaries to a certain degree. Fowler and Krapp for instance offer hints on pronunciation to speakers of English; Copperud on the other hand narrows his scope to journalists. This book is likewise selective. It has no intention of arming the reader with a catalog of cautions; instead it offers him a broad sampling of typical pronunciations and grammatical constructions in order to demonstrate how usage operates. The specific purpose is not to inform, but to sensitize; not to transmit a body of facts, but to instill an attitude. Each of us after all needs to decide for himself whether he can live tranquilly with this or that usage or whether he should turn it in for another one.

Setting up or making a plea for a uniform model of English is farthest from the intention of this book. Dreary as the world sometimes is, think how dreary it would be if all of us talked alike. But the nature of man being what it is, there are those who feel a high calling to keep the language "pure." We have other things to worry about.

The best hope is that the reader may become aware of some of the varieties of English in order to be able to appreciate them—and even, sometimes, its "errors" and "corruptions."

Acknowledgments

Among those I wish to thank are Houghton Mifflin Company for permission to quote Winston Churchill, *Their Finest Hour;* F. N. Robinson, *Chaucer;* and several lines of verse from James Russell Lowell and John Greenleaf Whittier; also G. & C. Merriam Company for permission to quote the *Third New International Dictionary;* Random House to quote the *Random House Dictionary* and to the editor Jess Stein for this and other acts of graciousness. My thanks and appreciation also to various persons who read all or part of the manuscript at some stage of its development: Raven I. McDavid, Jr., Martin Joos, Philip B. Gove, Owen Thomas, Michael Shugrue, Freeman B. Anderson, Robert C. Pooley; among these my colleagues at Arizona State University: Thomas Ford Hoult, John Higgins, and especially L. M. Myers. May I also thank those at McGraw-Hill who had a part in directing this book from manuscript to print: Frederic Hills, Robert Fry, David Dunham, Sally Ellyson, and Georgia Kornbluth.

J. J. Lamberts

I

good english

Since every discussion about English usage has managed to offend someone, and since it is inconceivable that there will ever be a discussion that does not, there is possibly good reason to wonder why anyone should want to venture into the morass once again. Some matters, however, from their nature draw disapproval, whether they are handled wisely or stupidly. That goes for bringing up children, practicing one's religion, and supporting political candidates. Consequently some people have gone heirless, godless, and voteless. But short of spending a lifetime without uttering a spoken or written word, a person cannot avoid making a commitment to what he considers acceptable and right in language.

Our classroom instruction is likely to give us a picture of language as a body of rules from which we deviate every time we become careless or inattentive. Actually few things slow up talk or writing so much as the conscious awareness of a "rule." Our use of our language, whether spoken or written, is almost entirely automatic. The basic habits were established when we were infants, some of them even before we could talk. As we grew older the habits were reinforced and expanded; sometimes they were modified. Now and then earlier habits were "corrected," either for a set period of time or permanently. We think of language correction as the exclusive domain of the school mistress, but it can be carried out fully as well under the authority of a playmate or drill sergeant or employer or spouse. The end product bears no direct resemblance to "correct" in the school-book sense, but the effects on language practices are often profound.

To put it another way, our manner of speaking and writing results from certain choices that we have learned to make as users of English. Making the choice of a word or construction is easy enough. Explaining the choice, however—or even being aware that there are choices—scarcely anyone can manage. At best we volunteer a few grammatical terms and ask lamely, "Let's see, what *do* I say?" As the Duchess reminded Alice: "Take care of the sense and the sounds will take care of themselves." Which is precisely what all of us do as we acquire mastery over language; we ignore the language itself and devote our attention to what is being said. Very small children are still learning language, and consequently they embarrass their parents by making frank remarks about the way guests or visiting relatives talk. By the time we have mastered language we have also sensed that it is bad manners to seem to notice the way the other person talks, and the height of rudeness to call attention to it. But sometimes the manner of talk or writing is so unusual that it interferes with the message itself. Then we have a problem in communication, specifically a problem in usage. We may also think of it as a problem in correctness since the entire question of usage centers on that.

THE PROBLEM OF CORRECTNESS

Why should language correctness be a problem? Can anything be simpler than drawing up a list of expressions about which we happen to have noticeable feelings, negative or positive? Actually there are at least a thousand and one things that are simpler. The *what* of language completely overshadows the *how,* as it should, and for that very reason few persons are able to offer more than a sketchy inventory of the expressions they regard as objectionable. *Ain't,* as we should expect, figures conspicuously, thanks to a great body of written and spoken folklore on the subject. *It don't, you was* also earn mention, but the ability to produce a list of more than twenty expressions sets one apart as a person with a professional interest in the subject: a schoolteacher, perhaps, or an editor—sometimes a lawyer or a clergyman. Who would guess, for instance, that there are people who harbor a silent but passionate loathing for words like *hopefully* or *ongoing* or *facetious* or *fellowship?* The brand on *ain't* and *you was* is deep and conspicuous. There is no way to guess, however, which expressions one's dearest friends detest. The only clue is a chance outburst like: "If those fellows mention that stupid word 'dialog' again, I'm going to vomit!" But what could have brought that on?

It would be most pleasant if everyone could be sensitive to the same expressions that we are, and to the same degree. Much of the instruction in our schools proceeds on the assumption that this is already the situation, except for patches of waywardness which can be cleared up with diligence, grammar workbooks, and federal funds. The idea is vigorously supported by anxious parents.

Common sense will tell us that the idea is altogether unrealistic; uncomfortable as the realization makes us, usage is really a highly individual matter—almost a lonely one. After all, why should one person be greatly attached to a word like *vouchsafe,* and why should someone else, equally well educated and equally moral, develop a nervous twitch whenever he hears or reads it?

The study of correctness in English speaking and writing has had plenty of attention during the past two or three centuries, as the production of dictionaries, handbooks of usage, and innumerable magazine articles by amateurs and professionals will bear witness. In general the material takes one of two approaches. The first of these is the authoritarian, the other the empirical.

The authoritarian approach is the older of the two. It is associated in the public mind and in fact with the study of grammar and is frequently identified with it. Basic to this approach is the assumption that a clear distinction exists between "good" English and "bad" English, and further, that certain people by virtue of their training and occupation are able to perceive the distinction wherever doubt arises. Editors of dictionaries, teachers of English, and especially teachers of grammar are simply presumed to know all of the answers. A reputation like this is difficult to disclaim; sometimes disclaiming it is imprudent. Journalists especially imagine that the golden gift has been bestowed on them, that they bear a responsibility to identify and enforce "good" English.

Although it has always stood in the shadow of the authoritarian approach, the empirical has had its adherents from earliest times. Its present forms, however, have had to await the development of many of the sciences we presently take for granted, especially the various social sciences. There are empiricists who seem to question the overt existence of "good" English, a most unsettling suggestion to those who depend on an orderly universe. Yet in practice the language of the empiricists can seldom if ever be distinguished from that of the authoritarians. They simply take one more step. In other words, their question is not so much "What is 'good' English?" as "How do we determine what is 'good' English?"

THE FIRST GRAMMARIANS

As an independent discipline the study of language is extremely old. The Greek philosophers devoted much of their time to it, in effect laying the foundations for our present-day school grammar study. They started with the idea that Greek was the only real language in the world—since the rest of the human race consisted of barbarians who communicated in subhuman noises—and that an understanding of the relationships within their language would spontaneously open up to them the nature of their world and of their universe. The idea seemed logical, and if it worked it would save endless time and money that would otherwise get frittered away in scientific explorations and experiments. The nearest analogy in our time is the crude popular notion that we can discover the unknown merely by feeding data into a computer. Plato discussed the question in his dialog *Cratylus,* but no one has ever been sure whether Plato was in earnest; he may have been playing an obscure joke on his fellow philosophers. At roughly the time all this was going on in Greece, in India the grammarian Panini was completing the great grammar of the Sanskrit language. There is a world of difference between the grammar of the Greeks and that of the Sanskritists; we may be confident that if our contact had come by way of India rather than by way of Athens and Rome we should be looking at grammar in an entirely different manner today. To Panini and his colleagues Sanskrit was a sacred language: by means of this language they could preserve hymns and prayers with absolute precision. A person who depends on a grammar of his language to get him to the next world—not a common occurrence, it must be admitted—is likely to take it far more seriously than someone who thinks of it as an intellectual plaything or as a device for avoiding work. By and large the study of language in our schools and in our culture leans toward curios and knickknacks, the kind of thing that always manages to stimulate more interest than a careful and systematic study of the language itself. It surprises many people to discover that there actually exists a science of language. The science is called linguistics. Modern linguistic science had its beginnings in the last half of the eighteenth century, a few decades after the beginnings of modern chemistry.

The specific thing that people identify as "language study" can vary enormously, but the word *grammar* comes to mind immediately, and far too many of us look back on our elementary school encounters with it as an uninspired rummaging for prepositional phrases and adjective clauses. Year after year it came to an end around the middle of February, mainly because the teacher had become hopelessly bogged down in the subjunctive. Regardless of what miscellaneous material might find its way into an English grammar course, by chance or by whim of the teacher, the sturdy backbone of grammar study consisted of an unremitting quest for nouns, verbs, adjectives, pronouns, and so on. The student who had learned to identify these without fail thereupon presumably came into possession of two great blessings. First, he could write well; and second, he always used "good" English. There have been people who questioned this assumption. Indeed, they pointed to brilliant authors who knew nothing whatever of grammatical terminology, and students on the other hand who could diagram sentences like lightning but who were all thumbs when it came to composition and whose spoken English would embarrass a sharecropper.

THE BEGINNINGS OF ENGLISH GRAMMAR

The gigantic outlay of time and money and sincere effort committed to teaching grammar in our schools should after all these years have produced tens of millions of persons who never blanch at the sight of an empty page. But how many people consider themselves perfectly competent to compose a letter or report or other piece of writing? How many of them pass the paper to someone else to "look over," as they say, "for grammatical errors"? Most of them prefer to phone or mail a tape, and if these alternatives prove unworkable they dictate a letter and hope the stenographer has done her homework in spelling and sentence construction. Furthermore, how many people wonder what a split infinitive is and worry whether they may have been splitting infinitives unaware? Involved in our uneasiness about writing and our anxiety about correctness are two considerations which are really nothing more than a priori assumptions. First, something needs to be done; second, the study of grammar will do it.

Where did this idea come from? Surely not from the people who invented grammar. They would have dismissed it as rank nonsense. The Greeks engaged in grammar as a form of mental gymnastics, and the Sanskritists as a religious obligation, both endless miles away from what we have made of it.

But between the beginnings of grammar and the present time lie several stages of development. The solutions which people employed in order to meet each of the particular problems seemed natural enough at the time, and the wisest among us would have conducted himself pretty much as they did, given their information and outlooks.

The first such stage involved the transition of Latin from a spoken to a written language. The transition went on over a long period—several centuries at least—but at the end of it the people who needed to read and write Latin thought of it as a foreign language. A similar development has taken place and is still going on in English. For instance, a piece of writing like the Declaration of Independence, which is about two hundred years old, sounds quaint, but we readily understand it. Shakespeare's plays and the King James Bible, which represent English of a century and a half earlier, sometimes offer us real difficulties. We need to look up words and many of the constructions have to be explained in the notes or commentaries. The English of Chaucer, 200 years earlier still, is to most of us a foreign language and has to be translated. Now few people need to read Chaucer unless they want to, and they are under no obligation whatever to write or talk the way Chaucer did. But Latin had been established as the language of the medieval Christian church, and in order to carry on the affairs of the church the clergy learned Latin as a matter of course. For natives of the countries under Roman domination it had been easy at first; as time went on, however, more and more constructions needed to be memorized. Luckily for all, while Latin was still a living language several scholars had composed grammars of Latin, modeled on the Greek concept, but serviceable nevertheless. During the time that people had been speaking Latin it had been for them an elaborate set of habits, just as English is a set of habits for us. When it became a dead language the grammars remained as descriptions of what speakers and writers of Latin had done when they employed their language. Presently these descriptions came to be regarded as sets of "rules." Ignoring a minor rule could get a person the reputation for being stupid; ignoring a major one could result in being misunderstood. The cleric or scholar who prized his reputation learned all the rules and put them into practice. Since Latin remained the language of the church as well as of all scholarship throughout the Middle Ages and well into the Renaissance, people continued to memorize and to follow the rules.

The next stage in the development centered on the realization that English was a language in its own right. We take that for granted. On the other hand, we condescend to such varieties of English as Pidgin or Gullah or some street dialect. But for centuries the men who wrote and read Latin accorded English the same kind of condescension, in spite of important literary works like Beowulf and Chaucer's poetry. As late as 1545 Roger Ascham, schoolmaster to Queen Elizabeth I, supposed that he needed to apologize for writing in English rather than in Latin, because Latin would have been, to use his own phrase, "more easier."

The third stage followed shortly after the second and focused on a concern about correctness. In Latin and Greek there had been models to follow and if an author composed an essay or poem or drama or epic he could quickly determine whether he had been treading in the footsteps of the masters or simply pursuing his natural bent. Much of English literature had been growing up wild, so to speak. It is obvious that the Beowulf poet and Chaucer and many others were familiar with the classical modes, and yet they were guided largely by their literary instincts. Toward the end of the seventeenth century, realizing that English was indeed a full-fledged language, writers began to voice the need for a standard. John Dryden answered this need, so he said, by translating what he had written from English into Latin and back into English; strange as it may seem to us, that was because he was sure of his footing in Latin, but not in English. There ought to be an easier way. On the pattern of what had already been accomplished in Italy and France and Spain, eminent writers called for the establishment of an academy which could sit in judgment on neologisms in order to keep English "pure." Setting up such an academy was something that required royal authorization, but just about that time George I ascended the British throne. He was a German from Hanover, and he usually spoke French. That did it for the academy.

The fourth stage was a phenomenon chiefly of the eighteenth century, though it continues to flourish; it had to do with the notion of "universal grammar," that is, a set of generalizations which applied in some measure to all languages. European scholars supposed that these generalizations came out more strikingly in Latin than they did in other languages, but whatever validity there was to the idea resulted from several matters that had nothing to do with the inherent qualities of Latin. For instance, Latin had been in use far longer than any of the contemporary languages. All the scholars wrote and read it. It served as a linguistic medium of exchange for educated Europeans—Englishmen, Poles, Germans, Italians, Swedes, or anyone else. Also it was a dead language and that meant that no one would go switching signals in the middle of the game. It all depended on rules. A person wrote bad Latin because he had forgotten or neglected a rule. It was as simple as that. If the application of Latin grammar resulted in wholesome Latin, then a study of English grammar—so the argument went—should unfailingly bring about "good" English.

One of the manifestations of English life during the eighteenth century was an intense interest in grammar. Extraordinary shifts in population had come as the result of colonial expansion, the Industrial Revolution, and outbreaks of the plague. Englishmen who migrated to London from Yorkshire or Lancashire or Devonshire became uneasy about their manner of talk; that was true also of native Londoners who had suddenly amassed fortunes but found themselves snubbed by London society because of their uncouth utterance. The obvious solution: learn grammar. The best-known grammar of the time appeared in 1762 under the title *A Short Introduction to English Grammar,* written by Bishop Robert Lowth. Its opening declaration was: "Grammar is the Art of expressing our thoughts by Words." One might have wished for a clearer note, but those who encountered the statement supposed that they knew what grammar was and they did not ask questions. The book lived up to its advertisement: it was short. It ran to a modest 186 pages, printed with ample spaces and copiously wide margins, most of its substance given over to identifying nouns, verbs, adjectives, pronouns, and such like. Coupled with his description of the parts of speech—simply a direct transfer from Latin grammar—were Lowth's own comments on various expressions. A scant decade earlier Samuel Johnson had published his celebrated *Dictionary* in which he freely labeled words "low" or "vile" or "barbarous." Lowth exercised greater restraint, yet there were words and expressions which to his mind failed to make sense or which represented irregularities. This was the eighteenth century, and people believed in order.

By a word juggling operation of which they themselves were unaware, the grammarians of the period drew a false analogy between Latin and English, supposing that what happened in one language automatically happened also in the other. That was because they were investing the word *grammar* with two distinct meanings. In Latin an incorrect expression could be remedied by applying Latin grammar, for an expression was either Latin or non-Latin; it was either grammatical or nongrammatical. But the difference between "I saw it" and "I seen it" is not a difference between English and non-English; which means that if we call one grammatical and the other nongrammatical we are giving the terms other meanings than they had in Latin grammar. The person who says "I saw it" does so not because he has been taught a rule but because he belongs to that part of the English-speaking population which habitually says "I saw it." Moreover, he will say "I saw it" under all circumstances, even when he is half asleep, or drunk, or stoned. Carelessness or slovenliness has nothing to do with it. In fact, the only time such a person says "I seen it" is when he does so intentionally, to condescend to someone or to mock him.

GRAMMAR AS FUNCTION; GRAMMAR AS TASTE

The issue becomes more clear when we distinguish, as we should, between "grammar as function" and "grammar as taste." The idea of "grammar as function" turns out to be puzzling for many speakers of English since we do not encounter many nonfunctional constructions, especially in speech. We generally understand most of what other people say. The language habits that all of us employ are so firmly ingrained that it takes deep concentration to break a sentence out of its accustomed order, to put the words for instance in alphabetical sequence or some other arbitrary arrangement. That is why someone who has spoken English all his life may go for weeks without ever thinking about putting together the sentences he is composing. In other words, he has no difficulty with "grammar as function." But the person who has been brought up to speak another language, who thinks in another grammar than that of English, may well produce non-English constructions like: "My pen not writes; she not has of the ink," or "The out of the pasture having run calf has the farmer in the barn up locked."

Over against this we have "grammar as taste," and that involves habits of an entirely different order. As a rule the utterance is completely understandable, but certain features of it identify for better or worse the social standing of the speaker or writer. A more precise name for "grammar as taste" is "usage." Accordingly we shall from now on distinguish consistently between grammar as function and grammar as taste. The first we shall call simply "grammar" and the other "usage." It will be important to have the distinctions clearly in mind, because we shall be speaking quite regularly of one in terms of the other; that is, we shall be describing problems of usage in terms of grammar.

2

approaches to usage

In the popular mind, and this includes the opinion of most well-educated people, there is a picture of the kind of English we "should" use. It goes by various names: "good" English, standard language, acceptable grammar, correct usage, and all the possible permutations of these terms, and perhaps many more beside.

In daily life we take standards for granted. Is there a standard by which one can gauge the correctness of his language?

Until the turn of the present century, most Americans, if they thought about it at all, supposed that there was. The only really acceptable variety of English was that of the well-educated, chiefly from the northern and eastern sections of the United States. This stands to reason. The prestigious American colleges and universities were situated in the Northeast, and their influences percolated downward, sometimes at fourth and fifth hand, even to the humbler teacher-training institutions. Furthermore, Noah Webster, a New Englander, had taken it for granted that his New Haven speech could serve as a worthy model for the Republic. Whenever there was a question, people consulted *Webster's,* and that ended all doubt. Nor should anyone overlook the vast power and prestige of the great publishing houses of the country, situated largely in Boston and later in New York. Above all this was the fact that the settlers in the Northeastern states were the first speakers of English to settle in the new land, and their way of speaking and writing represented to later arrivals the way Americans typically spoke and wrote.

For these reasons American English has from its very beginnings manifested a remarkable homogeneity.

But maintaining such a style of language as a standard offered difficulties. It soon appeared that new words and expressions which identified artifacts and practices of recent development were making their way into the language, that new pronunciations were becoming fashionable, that new constructions were gaining increasingly wide acceptance. Were these corruptions? Many guardians of the language supposed they must be and sought to warn the public of the horrid consequences that would attend the introduction of such changes. But even an offhand look at the history of the English language makes it plain that in the course of only ten centuries virtually every feature of the language has undergone some change. Carrying this to its logical conclusion—assuming, of course, that every change is a deterioration—we should conclude that the English language must now be corrupt beyond hope of redemption. As we know, it is fully serviceable not only for ordinary communication but for the creation of a powerful literature.

And so by the 1920s a number of scholars had come to realize that the concept of a single monolithic standard of correctness needed to be rejected or greatly revised, that it raised more problems than it solved. Goodness and badness were not to be looked on as characteristics of the words themselves or of the phrases or constructions, as Dr. Johnson and Bishop Lowth and their contemporaries had supposed. Some of the later grammarians went even further and confused the entire issue with moral goodness, a confusion still fondly nurtured by persons who rely on their convictions rather than their information. Only the blessed angels know how many youngsters must have supposed that their use of *ain't* or *it don't* was nothing less than the first step down the primrose path.

THE LINGUISTS

The application of the empirical approach to the problems of English usage is a by-product of an entirely different enterprise. Among the grammarians of the 1920s were such anthropologists as Franz Boas and Edward Sapir and Leonard Bloomfield. They were linked to the older traditions in grammar, and their training had included a competence in Latin, Greek, and Sanskrit. But as anthropologists they had made excursions into various American Indian languages, where they had encountered linguistic concepts utterly unlike anything they had previously taken for granted. From these discoveries there emerged a picture of human language as a complex of social behavior characterizing a particular group of people. By extension of this idea, certain varieties of English itself might be regarded as typical of subcultures of the English-speaking world—regional and social dialects. Meanwhile the base of higher education in America continued to expand; by the close of World War I people were no longer framing their high school diplomas. College graduates made up a tiny fraction of the total population, but the number was inching upwards. At the same time the importance of a single cultural center began to decline and regional usages to increase in importance.

The tidy division into "good" and "bad" English rested on a subjective basis; it could scarcely endure a systematic study. That consideration had not really bothered anyone—there seemed to be no way of looking at the language except through traditional grammar as Bishop Lowth and his successors conceived of it. But by slow degrees a science of linguistics was growing up. It had attracted only scant notice in America. Before 1900 nearly all the important work was conducted in Europe and it was overwhelmingly the product of German scholarship.[1] By the 1920s, however, several Americans had made important contributions to the literature of linguistics. By 1925 the new school of "structural" linguistics had been born, and the scientific study of language presently began to command attention as an important social science. World War II made extensive use of language and communication skills as linguists put into practical use the so-called "Army method" for teaching scores of languages, familiar and exotic. With government encouragement and subsidy, American linguistic science presently overtook and soon outdistanced all its rivals abroad.

"LEVELS" OF USAGE

American linguistic science, to the extent that it is unique, came to birth largely in the study of the sounds of languages—phonology—because that

---

1 There were exceptions. William Dwight Whitney (1827–1894) was professor of languages at Yale and compiled a grammar of Sanskrit that is still in use. He was an editor of the 1864 edition of *Webster's Dictionary,* and editor in chief of the *Century Dictionary and Cyclopædia* (1889–1891). Major John Wesley Powell (1834–1902), a geologist who led an exploring party through the Grand Canyon of the Colorado (1870), was responsible for pioneering work in the study of American Indian languages.

seemed the most plausible place to begin in dealing with Indian languages. Soon the linguists branched off into other aspects. In fact, the early investigators were remarkably catholic in their concerns, regarding themselves competent to deal with all phases of linguistics. In consequence some of them also took another look at the problem of usage. Their contribution was the doctrine of "levels of usage," which achieved the status of dogma immediately.[2] The underlying assumption was a simple one: there are three social classes or levels—upper, middle, and lower—and corresponding to each there is a characteristic mode of using English. It does not call for extraordinary powers of observation after all to discover language practices typical of people from the professions, from service occupations, from ordinary labor. But built into the levels assumption was still another assumption, namely, that the language of the well-educated serves as a standard—in other words, as the kind of language by which speakers of other varieties ought to check their own and which they should unfailingly strive to emulate.

In the period following the 1920s the levels interpretation began to come under question, and later it came under attack. It is no longer taken seriously. But it is a truism in the history of scholarship that a theory does not need to be valid in order to generate study and research. It needs merely to supply a different starting point.

SURVEYS OF USAGE

Once the old "good-bad" dichotomy had become clouded with doubt, usage scholars began to wonder about the origin of the rules under which language had been judged good or bad. It is interesting to note that much of this inquiry developed at the University of Wisconsin and at the University of Michigan, both geographically bordering the area which had exercised such a durable hegemony in these matters. At the University of Wisconsin the researches of Sterling A. Leonard, with the assistance of Robert C. Pooley

---

2 S. A. Leonard and H. Y. Moffett, "Current Definition of Levels in English Usage," *English Journal,* 16 (1927), 345–59, and George Philip Krapp, *The Knowledge of English* (New York: Holt, 1927), Chap. 6, speak of levels of usage as an established explanation. Leonard and Moffett refer to the preface to the *Oxford English Dictionary,* written in the early 1880s by James A. H. Murray. Usage is discussed, but there is no mention of levels of usage. The levels interpretation unquestionably grew out of scholarly discussions and correspondence carried on during the mid-1920s.

and others of his institution along with H. Y. Moffett of the University of Missouri, accumulated incontestable evidence that the "rules" had often been set down arbitrarily by the eighteenth-century grammarians. The shock of this discovery has long since worn off, but during the early 1930s Bishop Lowth was roundly damned as the villain of the entire enterprise. The eighteenth-century rules rested on opinions about usage which important persons of the period had entertained. The next question appeared to be: what opinions do their counterparts in the twentieth century have about usage? Leonard compiled a list of 230 expressions regarding which there had been differences of opinion. A number were hyperfastidious; others were marginally subliterate. The entire list he submitted to 229 persons who had consented to serve as judges—among them several of the most distinguished American authors, editors of leading publishing houses, businessmen, eminent linguists, teachers of English, and teachers of public speaking. They were instructed to label the various expressions as they themselves reacted to them: "acceptable," "disputable," or "illiterate." What could have been more innocuous? Public opinion polls had not yet come into vogue, and people knew very little about sampling techniques. The results were tabulated and the various expressions listed as they had been ranked. The sponsor of the study was the National Council of Teachers of English; when the study was concluded in 1931 the council duly accepted the report. It was published some time afterward under the title *Current English Usage*. A great outcry sounded from many quarters, and one outraged newspaper editor declared that the English language was, in his own word, "imperiled." Leonard and his associates had merely determined what various prominent people actually thought of these usages; no teacher was under obligation to give them out as divinely inspired. Every usage scholar worth his salt might guess that the situation must be pretty much as Leonard had reported it, but a hunch and a survey are completely different matters.

After being out of print for nearly thirty years, the original Leonard study has recently been reprinted. The basic data, however, have been available in a monograph called *Facts about Current English Usage*[3] by Albert H. Marckwardt and Fred G. Walcott, at the time both of the University of Michigan. As we only too well realize, what is proper in speaking may not be acceptable in writing, although the distinction was not indicated in Leonard's report. Starting with the 230 expressions, Marckwardt and Wal-

---

3 *Facts about Current English Usage* (New York: Appleton-Century-Crofts, 1938).

cott set about to determine whether and when and where these usages had appeared in the publications of reputable authors; in other words, to assess their standing as literary English. Almost anything will turn up if a person looks long enough and hard enough. At times, indeed, reputable authors seem more tolerant of "incorrect" usages than the grammarians, or than even the educated public.

The quantitative approach has an attractive plausibility. One of its most vigorous exponents was C. C. Fries. While his reputation rests on his contributions to English grammar, he was likewise interested in English usage and characteristically distrustful of flat statements. To his mind a mathematical formulation was the only valid means for describing divided usage. A number of such descriptive statements appear in his *American English Grammar*.[4] Another instance of the quantitative or percentage statement is to be found in Margaret M. Bryant's *Current American Usage*.[5] Miss Bryant served for a number of years as chairman of the Committee on English Usage of the National Council of Teachers of English. The study incorporates many of the reports which first saw the light in magazines published by the council. The appeal of this approach is also reflected in the usage treatment of the *American Heritage Dictionary*[6] which has centered a good deal of its publicity on its "usage panel," consisting largely of journalists, some college professors, and a few politicians—about a hundred panelists in all—whose opinions on specific usages have been rendered in mathematical percentages. How much reassurance one can take from the information that 50 percent of the panelists accept a split infinitive is open to conjecture.

By one means or another the early investigators of usage hoped to be able to transfer the study of usage out of the highly subjective approach that had characterized it ever since the eighteenth century. Could the whole thing be set on a reasonably objective footing? Studies like those of Leonard and his successors proved to be of limited help in establishing a standard of usage, although the scholars engaged in the work unquestionably supposed that some kind of standard would ultimately develop out of their efforts. There were outbursts of impatience at the slowness with which their ideas were winning acceptance, but they never intended to be iconoclasts, to behave like Scythians in the Garden of the Muses. Some adjust-

4 *American English Grammar* (New York: Appleton-Century-Crofts, 1940).
5 *Current American Usage* (New York: Funk & Wagnalls, 1962).
6 *American Heritage Dictionary* (Boston: Houghton Mifflin, 1969).

ments would have to be made, to be sure: a few borderline expressions were long overdue for admission to the canon of good usage, and a number of hard-and-fast rules might profitably go by the board. But why should this unsettle or disturb anyone? Investigators of usage had simply looked at items of information that had been lying about in plain view for heaven knows how long. Leonard had put on paper nothing more than what nearly any person with a pair of functioning eardrums could have discovered for himself—for instance, that people with an honest claim to being well educated said things like "Go slow" or "It's me" or that they sometimes put prepositions at the ends of their sentences. And anyone with a paid-up library card could check the *Oxford English Dictionary* or Otto Jespersen's *Modern English Grammar* to discover for himself exactly what Marckwardt and Walcott had found. But when we are dealing with language it is no great trick to ignore anything we do not want to see and hear. All of us do it.

As the study of usage continued, the "standard" which had appeared to be so substantial and so obvious during the 1920s grew gradually more and more elusive. The three-level classification for explaining and especially for classifying varieties of usage continued to flourish in the textbooks, complete with schematic diagrams, but it proved far less productive than should be expected. Although the intermediate level was mentioned again and again, under a variety of names, no one seemed able to identify any expressions that were characteristic of it. Finally, in the late 1940s, John S. Kenyon explained why.[7] There was no such level. In place of the three usage levels of the 1920s Kenyon proposed two "cultural levels," as he called them: standard and nonstandard. Other differences depended not on the social standing of the user of English, but on the specific use to which the language was being put at a particular time.

DIALECTS

During the late 1920s the "dialect" approach to usage study began to win serious though widely scattered attention. It labored under a handicap from the very start, chiefly because many people had already made up their minds about dialects. They thought of them in relation to economic distress or to life in a social or cultural backwater. Under no circumstances ought the lan-

7 John S. Kenyon, "Cultural Levels and Functional Varieties of English," *College English,* 10 (1948), 31–6.

guage of polite conversation or of great literature to be thought of as a dialect.

But even before the anthropologists of the 1920s began to make public what they were discovering, it was becoming apparent that grammar was far more widespread than the language scholars had supposed. The old fiction about languages that had "no grammar" along with the fiction about languages that had vocabularies of seventy words had been discredited by the linguists. Languages spoken by people who knew nothing about plumbing or even about writing turned out to have grammars just as complex and just as elegant as Greek or Latin or English or German, or any language, in fact, with a highly developed literature. The grammars could not be dismissed as inferior or crude; they were simply different. Suppose one carried this line of thought a step further: what about nonliterary and nonschoolroom varieties of English? Dared one assume, for example, that English is something that people actually say and write, and not what someone thinks they ought to say and write? About the latter there was no shortage of information; it had been piling up ever since the seventeenth century, thanks to the labors of grammarians over these three centuries. Even Leonard and his colleagues, for all their apparent intrepidity, had played it safe; their surveys had been addressed to some of the hot spots of usage, not to any broad spectrum. If anything, they were hoping to spread the tent of respectability over a number of expressions that the fastidious stylists had excluded.

Dialect study had little or no interest in usage problems as such, although from its very nature it could scarcely evade them. With American English as its subject matter, dialect study began at the exact moment when someone observed a feature in American utterance that differed from the corresponding expression in the homeland. Within a relatively short while there appeared lists of expressions, bearing heavily on the unusual and the grotesque, chiefly on names for things. The compilers seldom took pains to conceal their distaste.

Systematic dialect study, however, is only about a hundred years old and had its beginnings in Germany when an enterprising scholar mailed postcard questionnaires to thousands of schoolmasters all over the country. From the answers he received he was able to construct a detailed map of the principal German dialect areas. His successors in various countries improved on the techniques for gathering information, including the painstaking training of field investigators and the preparation of lists of items to be sampled. Actual work of collecting data for a linguistic atlas of the United States was begun in 1930. The original project concentrated on New

England, and the *Linguistic Atlas of New England* was published in 1939.[8] Since that time the other states have been surveyed, either completely or in part. The expense of publishing such specialized materials, however, coupled with the limited interest they generate, accounts for the fact that outside of a few books, a number of magazine articles, and a substantial library of doctoral theses, most of the information remains stored in filing cabinets at such universities as Michigan, Minnesota, and Chicago.

Dialect items taken simply by themselves may seem incongruous, especially if they are unusual—*cain't* as a pronunciation for *can't,* or *swang* as the past tense of *swing,* or *goober* in place of *peanut*—and yet if these items are spread out on a map to show where they are in common use, certain highly systematic features come to light. A dialect map maker can draw a line around the area in which a particular feature occurs, or he can draw a line separating two contrastive features. It should not surprise anyone to discover that the distribution of these dialect features follows closely the settlement history not only of individual localities, but especially of the country at large. A broad band, for instance, extends westward from the New England states, encompassing New York State, Michigan, Wisconsin, Minnesota, and the northern regions of Pennsylvania, Ohio, Indiana, and Illinois. This makes up a single large dialect area, reflecting a westward movement of population from the early settlements in New England.

Now the principal thing that such a dialect survey reveals is the nature of the early settlement history, in other words, the language deposit which the early settlers left behind. All of this may seem like a lot of labor to confirm the obvious. Yet it offers a vivid demonstration of the manner in which language differences operate; why, for instance, a native of Michigan or upstate New York will regard *dove* as perfectly normal English and *dived* as bookish; why, on the other hand, a native of southern Ohio or Missouri will regard *dived* as normal English and *dove* as either bookish or simply odd. It demonstrates also that the language of the unlettered and untraveled manifests greater differences from locality to locality than the language of the literate and highly mobile.

From the very nature of dialect investigation, its contribution to usage study is relatively limited. The number of items comes to somewhere between 800 and 1,000 at the outset, and few of them have any real usage

---

8 Hans Kurath, ed., *Linguistic Atlas of New England* (Providence, R.I.: Brown University Press, 1939–43); also Hans Kurath, *Handbook of the Linguistic Geography of New England* (Washington: American Council of Learned Societies, 1939).

relevance. What a person calls an earthworm or a dragonfly seems to have precious little bearing on his social standing, and the same presumably applies to the name he gives to a stone fence or a frying pan.

A major contribution of the *Linguistic Atlas* project is its specification of the substantial differences in the way Americans use their language and the degree to which these differences relate to geography. What the textbooks have dismissed as "bad" English may in actual fact be nothing other than regional English—used in everyday life by millions of competent and educated people. The distinction between "good" and "bad" English is often the difference between the idiom of New York and Chicago over against that of Memphis or Houston. To generations of schoolteachers who have accepted the language of New York and Chicago as "good" and that of Memphis or Houston as "bad," any questioning of such "standards" proves gravely disturbing.

More than one wag has defined a language as a dialect backed by a strong army and navy. A dialect may be considered prestigious for a number of reasons—none of them linguistic—for instance, because it is prevalent in a center of commerce and culture and political power, as London and Paris. It may also owe its prestige to the influence of one or more great universities—Oxford and Cambridge in England, and in this country Harvard and Yale. It is interesting to speculate what might have been the nature of American English if the first important centers of learning in the United States had been, say, Texas Christian and Southern Methodist Universities.

The United States, regardless of the supposed influence of television, radio, and other diffusions of the human voice, is becoming and will continue to become increasingly multidialectal. More and more people are clinging to their regional pronunciations; all radio and television have done is make the fact more apparent. And the *Linguistic Atlas* surveys have given dialects scientific status of a sort by identifying them with specific labels.

STATUS AND STATUS SYMBOLS

During the period when the usage specialists of the 1920s were putting their money on the notion of three social levels, the sociologists were still a decade or more from any systematic investigation of social stratification. Middletown was being studied for the first time in the late 1920's; Elmtown, Yankee City, and the others appeared later. The older European concept of class had pictured social standing as an "across-the-board" affair, and people took it for granted that royalty was always royalty, no matter how straitened by circumstances, and conversely that commonalty was destined to remain commonalty, no matter how exalted. It was an idea that Shaw toyed with in *Pygmalion:* would a guttersnipe really be a lady after she had learned to speak "proper English" and had mastered society manners? Shaw managed to be quite ambiguous about the whole thing. The play, we must remember, was written some years before the first shot of World War I was fired, and it mirrors the attitudes of its era; we would do well not to read our own attitudes into it.[9]

The usage specialists who followed the "levels" concept of the 1920s were charged, perhaps with warrant, of depending more on their data than on their better judgment. Once a writer or speaker had been admitted to the assembly of the elect by virtue of education or distinguished authorship or other qualification, could he be relied on to produce "good" English under any and all circumstances? It was assumed that he could be. So this was once again an across-the-board affair; again there was an upper class. Nothing had been changed except the standards for admission.[10]

Henry Ford used to remark about his Model T automobile: "You can have any color you want, as long as it's black." American society is supposed to be something like that—all one vast middle class. While American society has no hereditary aristocracy and no hereditary proletariat, it does have people who command a higher social standing than others. This is true of the society as a whole, and also of the composition of various groups within the society. Relative rank within a group is something that present-day sociology deals with under the term "status." The term has become familiar enough in everyday language that all of us have some conception of what it covers.

Status can be looked at in a number of ways, as being "achieved" or

---

9 There is the story of the Princess and the Pea, and also the story of Cinderella. In the first story the true princess comes in disguise, but is found out. She is so sensitive that a single pea hidden under a great stack of mattresses keeps her awake all night. Blood is sure to tell; once a princess, always a princess. Americans typically find the story amusing, but unreal. Cinderella makes better sense. She shows up at the right place at the right time and pleasant things happen. But for those who want to see it, the old idea of social class is in plain sight: Cinderella is the only one who can get her foot into that glass slipper. Only princesses—born princesses—have small feet. You can be at the right place at the right time and still lose—if you weren't born a princess.

10 A treatment of class differences in British usage, a good share of it tongue-in-cheek, appears in a collection of essays edited by Nancy Mitford under the title *Noblesse Oblige* (New York: Harper & Row, 1956). It is here that the terms "U" and "non-U" as applied to language first came into general view. What is spoken of as "U" language, as distinguished from "non-U," is the language of the British upper classes, on the whole a "blood aristocracy."

"ascribed," for example. Achieved status is the standing a person acquires chiefly by his own efforts—by studying, saving his money, working hard, and sometimes simply staying out of jail; but as we realize, in some social groups it is the opposite of all of these. Ascribed status consists of the standing conferred upon a person, often as the result of accidents over which he has had no direction, like being born into a rich or highly educated family. There is also "subjective" and "objective" status. As the name suggests, subjective status indicates a person's own private estimate of his standing with respect to the group; objective status what others in the group think his standing is. There may be wide differences.

By reason of the complex lives we lead, most of us represent not simply one but a number of social groups. As a result we do not have *a* status; we have a variety of statuses, depending on the situations in which we operate and the roles we play in them.

The phrase "status symbol" has been rendered familiar through its use by both amateur and professional sociologists, referring to an item or activity by which a person seeks to indicate his status (subjective), or by which others gauge it (objective). We may in fact picture our language as a single enormous status symbol. A usage one person may regard as correct (subjective status), another will regard as grossly incorrect (objective status). This means further that a person moving from one social situation to another often experiences a change in status. Thus it makes a world of difference whether a woman is attending a reunion of her college sorority or a reunion of her relatives; there may be significant differences in what is considered "right" language. Normal talk at a sorority reunion quickly runs the risk of sounding snobbish or hypercorrect at the family gathering. A characteristic of ascribed status is that the person is obviously accepted as being "at home" in a group, that others may even copy or imitate him. Schoolteachers are often struck by differences in language practices a child manifests in the classroom and on the playground. In the classroom the teacher provides the model since she is "at home" there; on the playground the model may easily be a boy or girl completely lacking any of the conventional linguistic graces but thoroughly "at home." Unless our own contacts are exceedingly narrow, we find ourselves time and again in circumstances where, despite the "purity" of our speaking and writing practices, we are clearly outsiders. A familiar comedy situation is the distress of a middle-aged female reference librarian at a lunch counter, flanked by a squad of burly furniture movers. A particular situation may permit us to modify certain characteristics of our language, and the degree to which we do this depends on whether we elect to become identified with a particular group or to preserve our separateness through the integrity of our language. This happens wherever a special "language" exists, as, for instance, in the military service. Some recruits sound like career army men before they draw their basic issue; others continue to sound like civilians to the very day they are mustered back into mufti.

What all this means is that we cannot take for granted a single overall correctness, appealing as the idea may be, but that there are just as many "correctnesses" as there are status-relevant situations. How "correct" one is depends partly on his choice and partly on his linguistic sensitivity. In one situation he makes no effort whatever to join in; in another he seeks overtly and covertly to conform. The characteristic style of "black" speech of which white people have become increasingly aware in recent years is a striking example of a "correct" variety of English within the larger speech community.

"BELIEVABLE" ENGLISH

To state it briefly: "good" English in any given situation is the kind of English that certifies a person's competence to deal with the subject he is speaking or writing about. It is believable language. And for every person it is to some degree unique. A physician is believable and is using good English when he talks like a physician; a desk clerk at a motel is believable when he talks like a desk clerk. Neither has any business trying to sound like the other on the assumption that the other uses "better" English.[11]

Of course such an explanation lays open to question the "standards" by which our school-book instruction has been governed. There are those who look on any such outlook as an open invitation to linguistic barbarism. They imagine that the barriers are being let down and the rules trodden underfoot, that anyone can write or speak as he pleases. But this is like sup-

---

11 In the course of World War II a battery of tests indicated that I had the mechanical aptitude to become an aircraft instrument specialist, and as a result I spent most of nine months learning to service aircraft instruments. My tour of duty in this capacity with my own squadron consisted of changing one airspeed indicator on one Piper Cub. It was done acceptably, but I was transferred to keeping a set of records because I could type; a former bread truck driver took my place servicing instruments. Later it dawned on me why. He "talked like" a mechanic; I made no effort to try. He was believable; I was not. A short while after this I was transferred again, this time to become editor of an Air Force publication, a role in which I was presumably altogether believable.

posing that the only alternative to King George III needed to be chaos. Actually there never has been a time when a person could not say whatever he pleased. He could even use any or all of the taboo words, as long as he was prepared to pay the penalty. It could be costly, and it still is. Using the "wrong" expression can mean outright social disapproval, or it can mean misunderstanding, or it can result in heartbreaking delay in getting acceptance from one's peers.

By tradition our schools have been committed to something called "good" English, which, if we get right down to it, is merely classroom English[12] which includes no expressions that might trigger a frown of disapproval from an English teacher. Such English, however, serves only to show who "belongs" in that particular situation. Ultimately one becomes identified with an occupation or some clearly defined activity and he adopts the language appropriate to it. A used automobile salesman begins to sound like a used automobile salesman; the salesman for luxury automobiles develops an entirely different pronunciation and vocabulary. Neither one any longer depends on his schoolroom English. Those preparing to engage in the various professions are required to spend more time in classrooms and commonly have gone well beyond voting age before they step into the "outside world." In consequence they absorb more of the classroom style, and this may make us think of their language as "better."

It would stagger human capacity to consider all the expressions on which users of English have been known to disagree; consequently this study addresses itself to a limited number of them and tries to show how typical differences operate as well as how they have come to exist. Some usages are regarded as nonstandard, as the kind of expression a person would not knowingly use in writing or speaking to an educated person. They are identified as such.

From time to time grammar rears its head. But grammar is a means to an end, not an end in itself. Knowing grammar, and only that, does not solve any usage problems, regardless of what we have been led to believe. The most we can ask of any grammar—and there are several of them—is that it should enable us to identify the problem, describe its appearance, and possibly explain how it happened to become a problem.

---

12 It is assumed that elementary school teachers speak correct English. Is it perhaps that elementary school teachers have been trained to adopt a characteristic style of speaking, especially when they are discussing English, and is it this style which the public has come to regard as unusually correct?

3

phonology—the sounds of english

Any subject that we are able to examine scientifically needs to "come apart" into a number of smaller fields or areas so that specialists can look at it in detail. This is true of chemistry, of history, of theology—in fact, thousands of subjects. It is true of human language, for individual languages have always been assumed to come apart at specific places, sometimes called "levels." For this reason language scholars have customarily divided their subject matter into specialized areas—four of them as a rule—under such formidable names as phonology, morphology, syntax, and lexicology.

The first of these, "phonology," deals with the sounds of a particular language or dialect, specifically the manner in which the sounds are produced, transmitted, and perceived. "Morphology" relates to the forms of the individual words, including the classification of their inflections, their affixes, and the various compounds into which words may be combined. "Syntax" has to do with the relationships between words in a sentence, but also in smaller units like clauses and phrases. "Lexicology" deals with the vocabulary, with the choices of words open to us.

Often it is not what people say that upsets us; we may react even more strongly to the way they talk—the "how" rather than the "what." Certain expressions we consider mispronunciations. Depending on how deeply we reverence the language and how kindly we feel toward the speaker, we may "correct" him, we may resolve to bear with his weaknesses, or we may resolve to avoid him as much as possible. But not all pronunciations that differ from our own are necessarily unfortunate, regardless how commonplace they are. Radio and television announcers, for example, have been trained to pronounce *news* to rime with *muse* rather than with *moos,* even though the latter prevails over most of the United States. Side by side with it we have a pronunciation like that of British *shed-yewl* in contrast to our own *sked-yel.* Few Americans would pronounce it that way; we should probably be irritated by an associate who used that pronunciation. We should not, however, hold the same attitude toward an Englishman, and perhaps we might tolerate it for a short while in the speech of a colleague just returned from Great Britain after living there for three or four years. On the other hand, to pronounce *character* with the stress on the second syllable, like *reactor,* is a grave error. Yet in Shakespeare's time it was a standard pronunciation, as appears from the metrical pattern:

> *See thou Character. Give thy thoughts no tongue.*
> —*Hamlet,* I.iii.60

And so we explain one variation by geography and the other by history.

But what of the person who pronounces *picture* as "pit-cher" (instead of "pik-cher"), or the one who puts the stress on the second syllable of *theater,* as in *creator,* or who rimes *grievous* with *devious?* The pronunciation editors of *Webster's Third New International Dictionary*[1] do not recognize the first pronunciation at all; the second they consider questionable and label "sometimes," and the third they call "substandard." Are we justified then in assuming that these usages result from an impaired or defective or depraved taste? Possibly so, but it may be unwise to correct the offender on that basis.

It would spare us much anguish and awkwardness to be able to depend on English spelling as a guide to acceptable pronunciation. But English spelling is unbelievably inconsistent as those who have relied on it have discovered. We look with mild amusement and even pity on phonetic spellings, especially if the writer has been creating them as he went along. We call them misspellings. But a single spelling of a word like *lead* or *read* or *wound* or *live* can indicate two distinct pronunciations. Scores of well-educated persons have discovered to their chagrin that *misled* does not rime with *fizzled.*

---

1 *Webster's Third New International Dictionary of the English Language* (Springfield, Mass.: Merriam, 1961); also referred to as WNI3. Where there is a significant problem, reference is made as well to the *Random House Dictionary* (New York, 1966), indicated as RHD.

In an ideal spelling situation a single alphabetical symbol corresponds consistently to a distinctive sound in the language. In that respect English is anything but ideal. There are languages which boast such an advantage, to be sure, but it has often been achieved at a high cost—a shattering revolution, or an oppressive dictatorship, or an embarrassingly late arrival of mass literacy.

Until almost the beginning of the twentieth century the editors of dictionaries of English fostered the belief that there is really one and only one way to pronounce a word. The idea has proved to be remarkably long-lived. In order to indicate such pronunciation they resorted to a system of diacritics—macrons, breves, circumflexes, tildes, single and double dots below and above letters—which still flourish in a few of our commercial dictionaries. One alternative to using diacritics has been to respell the words, using regular combinations of the standard 26-letter alphabet. Another has been to supplement the standard alphabet with additional characters. This practice has long been followed by both amateur and professional phoneticians wherever special type faces were to be had. Among the distinguished amateurs who had access to a print shop was Benjamin Franklin, one of the first to employ the symbol 'ŋ.' The most recent such augmented alphabet to attract widespread attention has been the Initial Teaching Alphabet (ITA), designed for the purpose of teaching elementary school children how to read. About a hundred years ago several European phoneticians developed what is known as the International Phonetic Alphabet (IPA) which continues to be widely used by phoneticians and which constitutes the basis for the great variety of phonetic alphabets now in use. The development of this alphabet rested on the assumption that the use of a limited set of symbols would enable a phonetician to transcribe accurately any sound in any language whatsoever.[2] In recent decades the science of phonetics has been advanced to such a degree that undergraduate college students routinely conduct operations beyond the dreams of the most practiced nineteenth-century phoneticians. Electronic devices enable us, of course, to do fantastic things with sound, but as the result of fuller understandings of the nature of human speech we have neither the need nor the impulse to be so technically minute. In fact, many language specialists now at work in this country, particularly those engaged in studying American English, make use of a relatively uncomplicated phonetic alphabet that can be produced by an ordinary type-

2 The complete International Phonetic Alphabet is reproduced in a number of places, among them the *Encyclopædia Britannica,* sv "Phonetics," and the *Random House Dictionary,* sv "Phonetic alphabet."

writer to which perhaps half a dozen special characters have been added.

With a few hours of instruction a moderately bright elementary school pupil can learn how to handle a phonetic alphabet. The problem is not so much gaining control over a special alphabet as it is discovering what goes on in conventional and unconventional speech. Language is a physiological activity, produced by certain organs of the human anatomy. As a rule, speaking calls for amazingly little physical effort; even frail people seem able to talk for hours without manifesting fatigue. Because it is so easy, we are able to completely ignore the processes involved. Indeed we usually experience some surprise and a measure of self-consciousness when we begin to examine them objectively. But such an examination will enable us to realize the extent to which our social judgments rest on seemingly trivial variations in the movements or positions of parts of the throat and mouth.

PHONETICS

All languages except dead ones consist basically of sounds and arrangements of sounds. The study of such sounds, either in general or in relation to a particular language, is called "phonology."

Much of present-day phonology is in the realm of theory, dealing with over-all patterns rather than with specific sounds. An important and immediately practical aspect of phonology is the consideration of the speech sounds themselves, that is, their production, transmission, and reception. This is called "phonetics." Since we can think of language with respect to source, medium, and goal, we consider that there are three subdivisions of phonetics: articulatory, acoustic, and auditory. Most of our present concern will be with articulatory phonetics, but more of that by and by. "Acoustic phonetics" deals with the transmission of the spoken language from source to goal. Usually it goes directly from mouth to ear, as in a face-to-face conversation or a lecture. It may involve transmission across some distance in space, as by telephone or radio, and it may involve a delay in time, as by means of a tape recorder. This phase of acoustic phonetics is considered a branch of physics, and for reasons easy to understand the Bell Telephone Laboratories have staked out much of this field for exploration by their own scientists and engineers. But acoustic phonetics may also consider the sound itself, especially the way it sounds to the hearer. Another branch goes by the name of "auditory phonetics," and it relates to the receptive mechanism, specifically the human ear. Little of the human ear can be observed in actual operation without damaging its incredibly delicate parts.

Most of the exploration has been undertaken by anatomists and neurologists. The latter have been trying to find how a mechanical impulse is transformed to a neural impulse. As a rule we take little active interest in auditory phonetics, except when we happen to find our hearing impaired through cold or allergy, or when we become potential customers for hearing aids.

The actual production of speech sounds is called "articulatory phonetics" and it is concerned with the way in which human beings originate certain characteristic sound waves. As the name suggests, it deals with articulating mechanisms, with those "moving parts" of the body which we use in talking. There are a number of such parts, most of them visible to the eye or palpable to the tongue or fingertip. With the aid of a small mirror and preferably a flashlight, one can study the way the tongue moves about in the mouth; he can also put his fingers into his mouth and notice the texture and firmness of the tongue. It seldom occurs to anyone to take this trouble; we correctly assume that the tongue will be there if and when we want to examine the vocal apparatus. This explains why so few people know anything about speech production. A century ago Alexander J. Ellis complained of this ignorance, even among phoneticians:

The consequence is that writers being unaware of the mechanism by which the results are produced, were constrained to use a variety of metaphorical expressions which it is extremely difficult to comprehend, and which naturally have different meanings in the works of different authors. Thus sounds are termed thick, thin, fat, full, empty, round, flat, hard, soft, rough, smooth, sharp, clear, obscure, coarse, delicate, broad, fine, attenuated, mincing, finical, affected, open, close, and so on, till the reader is in despair.[3]

In informal, nonscholarly discussions about language it is not unusual to hear certain speech sounds described as "broad" or "thin" and even less accurately as "hard" or "soft." Within recent years there has been developed a system for describing speech sounds acoustically. It is also possible to describe them in articulatory terms. Whether a person hearing a speech sound finds it easier to describe the way it sounds to him or to place his speech organs in the exact position for reproducing it is difficult to say. Neither one is easy. Small children seem capable of imitating speech sounds with remarkable ease, but the ability is lost about the time the child gains complete control over his speaking habits.

---

3 Alexander J. Ellis, *On Early English Pronunciation* (London: Kegan Paul, 1874), Early English Text Society, Extra Series, No. 2, p. 24.

"ORGANS OF SPEECH"

There is a phrase "organs of speech" which is based on the idea that speech is a function of a number of bodily organs, comparable in a sense with respiration or circulation or digestion. In that sense, however, we really have no organs of speech. Important though the production of language may be, the speech function is biologically a secondary consideration, in fact, a function superimposed on the organs used.[4] Any organ that ceases to operate presently becomes diseased and atrophies, but "organs of speech" are just as healthy in deaf-mutes and Trappist monks as they are in the excessively wordy. The "lower animals," as we think of them, have similar vocal mechanisms, yet they merely bark or mew or neigh or moo or baa or bray.

Significantly, many of our words having to do with language center on that most versatile of speech organs, the tongue. The word *tongue* is itself a metaphor for language in a phrase like "tongues of men and of angels." *Language* and *linguistic* come from the Latin word *lingua* 'tongue' and *gloss* and *glossary* from Greek *glōssa,* also 'tongue.' Much of the body besides the tongue is actively involved in speaking, with still other parts standing in reserve, to fill in if necessary. An instance of this is the esophageal noise—really a controlled burp—which people learn to employ after their larynxes have been removed by surgery. More familiar, however, are the gestures of the head or hand, and of course the sign language of deaf-mutes.

While we sometimes flippantly describe language as "the noises we make with our face," this happens to be an accurate description. Speech is basically nothing more than a musical tone which becomes modified by passing through a series of tubes and echo chambers.

In describing the physical production of speech we customarily start at the bottom, namely, with the diaphragm, a powerful sheet of muscle spanning the base of the rib cage. It serves to initiate the breathing action of the lungs. Lung air is normally exchanged about eighteen times a minute, the time for inhalation and exhalation being approximately equal. When we speak we greatly alter this rhythm, giving considerably longer time to exhalation. The diaphragm controls this rhythm by metering out the flow of air as needed.

The lungs themselves are a pair of sacs whose biological function con-

---

4 Actually our speech organs do much better at producing speech than we should expect from organs of digestion and respiration. Recent studies on the biology of language by Eric Lenneberg and others indicate that there is a "speech instinct," a special adaptation for communication that is characteristically and uniquely human.

sists of exchanging the oxygen and carbon dioxide of the blood stream. They are extremely fragile, but the rib cage, or thorax, shields them from external injury. The ribs themselves are somewhat flexible so that the chest expands and contracts when we breathe. The individual air sacs making up the lungs interconnect by a vast ramification of tubes which ultimately join at the bronchi, and these in turn attach at the trachea, familiarly known as the windpipe. The trachea rises out of the chest, passing directly behind the collarbone, and consists of a tube from 4 to 4½ inches in length, essentially a stack of rings of cartilage which prevent it from collapsing.

The larynx, popularly known as the voice box, is situated at the top of the trachea and at the bottom of the pharynx or throat. It acts as a valve which directs food into the esophagus and keeps it from getting into the lungs, not so difficult in most animals since their food and air passages are practically horizontal, but a tricky matter in human beings since both food and air passages are vertical so that gravitation speeds the movement of solids and liquids. Surmounting the larynx is a leaf-shaped cartilage called the epiglottis which automatically blocks off the air passage whenever food is being swallowed. When a person has had his larynx removed through surgery, a substitute air passage is provided by making an opening in the front of the neck. The throat is then connected exclusively to the food passage.

The other important feature of the larynx is a pair of bands of flexible tissue known as the vocal cords.[5] They can lock air into the lungs, thus providing a more rigid foundation for the arms when a person chins himself or lifts the front end of a Volkswagen. To hold the breath one closes the vocal cords very much as he closes the lips. The vocal cords can be held together with great compressive force so that no air can escape between them.

We may picture the vocal cords[6] as a pair of moist ligaments in the form of a V with its apex pointed toward the front of the larynx, set at roughly a right angle to the axis of the trachea. The cords are about ¾ inch long in adult men, about ⅝ inch in women, and proportionally smaller in children. The vocal cords join in a hinge; at the back they are attached to a pair of movable cartilages called arytenoids, and because they are movable

---

5 The term *cords* is a compromise. Phoneticians use a variety of names: *chords,* which they certainly are not, or *folds,* or *bands,* or *tissues,* or *membranes.*

6 A detailed description of the structure and operation of the human larynx may be found in the *Encyclopædia Britannica,* sv "Voice."

the cords swing apart or come together, either of which they can do with considerable force and suddenness. At their greatest angle of opening, about 30 degrees, air from the lungs passes between the cords completely unimpeded. The space between the cords is known as the glottis. When the glottis is narrowed, to an angle of about 5 degrees, the passage of air sets up a pulsation of the inner edges of the vocal cords and the result is a sound we call *voice.* It is this "fluttering" motion of the vocal cords that cuts the airstream into a continuum of rapid puffs, which is also what a fire siren does. The air pressure required to initiate and maintain the motion is surprisingly small. The musical pitch of the glottal tone depends on the frequency of the puffs, and as we know, this can be regulated with extreme precision. The cords also determine relative loudness of the speech signal by varying the amplitude of their motion.

Interrupting the flow of air by sudden closure of the glottis, or, more commonly, initiating a tone by a quick and almost explosive opening of the glottis, produces a unique speech sound known as the "glottal stop," which phoneticians indicate by a conventional symbol [ʔ].[7] The glottal stop is common in most dialects of spoken English, but since our writing systems have no characteristic symbol to represent it,[8] and since it makes no difference to the meaning of an utterance in English whether the glottal stop does or does not occur, few people even realize that such a sound exists. Most speakers of English produce it with the sharp onset of any word we think of as beginning with a vowel. It occurs in the familiar grunts of affirmation and negation that for want of better symbols we spell "umhuh" or "unhuh." More precisely we should perhaps write [ʔmhm] and [ʔmʔm]. When air is sucked very rapidly into the lungs and is then interrupted by an abrupt closure of the glottis, the resulting sound is a hiccup, conventionally but inaccurately written as "hic."

In the production of speech the larynx discharges its function by emitting a musical tone. This tone can be interrupted by brief or longer moments of silence, can be raised or lowered in pitch, can be increased or decreased in volume. Other modifications are brought about by means of a complex arrangement of chambers and passages within the head and neck which serve as resonators. One of these is the throat or pharynx, another

---

7 In discussions of phonetic matters it is the usual practice to enclose phonetic data in square brackets: [ ].

8 In some languages the glottal stop is an important speech sound and in writing it is often indicated by an apostrophe: ['].

the mouth itself, and still another the nose, which, as every viewer of television commercials has long realized, is not merely a slender tube connecting the back of the mouth to the nostrils, but a cavity of fairly impressive dimensions, branching off into other cavities known as sinuses. These resonators fill out the glottal tone with a multitude of unbelievably tiny echoes, setting up the unique harmonic pattern of the individual voice.

ARTICULATION

Certain parts of the human anatomy, both fixed and movable, are employed in the act of speaking. The lips, jaw, tongue, and teeth are so readily visible that they scarcely require description. Another important element in the production of speech is the roof of the mouth, called the palate, a thin layer of bone covered with a thin layer of tissue. It does little more than keep food and air from getting into the nasal passages. Infants are sometimes born with an incomplete closure of the palate, a malformation known as "cleft palate." It can be remedied by surgery, or in extreme cases covered by an artificial palate, but if left untreated, as it occasionally is, the person will have a characteristic sniffling manner of speech.

Toward the front of the palate, running directly behind the upper row of teeth, is a small, firm ridge of tissue known as the alveolar ridge. It happens to be important in the formation of several speech sounds in English, though not necessarily in other languages.

The palate itself we distinguish into the hard palate and the soft palate, the reason for the names being obvious to anyone who troubles himself to run a forefinger back along the roof of the mouth. At one point the firmness gives way, namely, at the front edge of the soft palate. It may be prudent to discontinue the exploration at this point since touching the soft palate with the finger causes a gagging sensation and is one of the tried and true methods of bringing on vomiting in emergency. The soft palate terminates in a fold of soft tissue called the *velum,* a Latin word meaning 'curtain,' immediately related to the English word "veil." The name is not at all fanciful since the velum can be raised or lowered in order to open or close the passage of air into the mouth. The familiar "Say 'Ah'" from the throat specialist is his way of getting a patient to raise his velum and reveal the back of the throat. When a person closes his lips and puffs his cheeks full of air, he needs to lift the velum to the back surface of the upper pharynx to prevent air from escaping through the nasal passages; dropping it releases the air outward through the nose. Between syllables of the words *shipment, submerge, catnip,* and *kindness* one can detect the characteristic movement of the velum as it goes to relaxed position.

The *uvula* is a small dangling tip which forms the extreme end of the velum. It is likewise flexible and in a number of European languages it is trilled to produce an *r* sound. In gargling with a mouthwash, a person simply vibrates the uvula rapidly. Some years ago when tonsillectomies were more the vogue than they are now, surgeons often snipped off the uvula as a routine part of the operation; this macabre mutilation has now been abandoned.

We take the tongue for granted, but without it human speech as we know it would be impossible. The tongue consists of a bundle of muscles capable of an incredible variety of movements, some of them of dazzling rapidity. It can be flattened to the floor of the mouth, or the tip of it can be turned back into what we call "retroflex" position. It can spread out to close off the passage of air completely at many possible points of contact. It can accomplish such a contact with perfect accuracy time after time, in respect to both position and the degree of pressure applied.

The muscular structure controlling speech is situated very close to the central nervous system, as are the organs of sight, smell, and hearing. We seem to be putting forth little physical exertion when we talk, but that is because a typical muscular movement in speech is very small, from 1/100 inch to about 1/2 inch at most. But a staggering number of muscles are called into play; it is estimated that in speaking a sentence of a dozen words a man activates more muscles than he will use in chopping wood for a full day.

Types of Articulation

In speaking we produce a succession of vocal sounds which blend into each other yet which the listener is able to distinguish as acoustically different from each other. A sound as such is simply a complex airwave which has been modified by a specific arrangement of the position of several speech organs. All this has, of course, no connection with the letter of the alphabet or phonetic symbol employed to identify it. A mark of invincible ignorance in these matters is to persist in talking about "letters" and to identify them with sounds.

Presently we shall be taking up the problems of pronunciation, but before we do that we must pay some attention to the way speech sounds are made. For this we have objective data with respect to articulation, specifically the manner and point at which speech sounds are articulated.

The vocal cords, as we have already observed, originate a continuum of sound known as glottal tone, which can be modified in pitch and volume. The tone may also be interrupted by periods of voicelessness, sometimes a minute fraction of a second in duration, affording a basic contrast between "voiced" and "voiceless" speech sounds.

A closure of the speech passages which cuts off the sound is called a "stop." Stops may be made at any of several places in the mouth, from the glottis itself all the way to and including the lips, generally wherever a couple of articulating mechanisms can come together to completely block the expiration of air. A sound on the other hand that is not completely blocked but continues with some degree of modification goes by the general name of "continuant." In the sound system of English there is a basic contrast between stops and continuants. Continuants may be produced, for instance, by a partial closure or constriction of speech organs, setting up a noticeable air friction. This may or may not be accompanied by glottal tone; such a sound is called a "fricative." Several types of fricatives are made by expelling the air through the closed or nearly closed teeth with a characteristic hissing or buzzing sound. These fricatives are sometimes further distinguished as "sibilants."

Some English speech sounds—all of them continuants—are made through the nose rather than the mouth. They are included in a larger class sometimes called "resonants." With the oral passage closed at some point, the velum is lowered, diverting the sound through the nose. Not unexpectedly such sounds are called "nasals." Then there are the soft and flexible articulators like the lips, the tip of the tongue, the uvula—and strictly speaking also the vocal cords—which may be set fluttering by a sharp burst of air, especially if the passage is partially constricted. Such sounds are called "trills." In most standard varieties of American English the trill does not occur as a regular speech sound. It may be used for special purposes, however. A trill made by the pursed lips is supposed to indicate a reaction to cold weather and for want of a better spelling is written *brr*. A variant of this, expressing disgust or disapproval, is written *faugh*. Sometimes an articulator—usually the tip of the tongue—makes a single rapid contact, as in a common variant pronunciation of *r* in *three* or *through,* or the *t* in many pronunciations of *water*. To distinguish it from a trill we call this kind of articulation a "flap." The difference between Spanish *r* and *rr* is flap as contrasted to trill articulation.

A full inventory of the possible types and points of articulation that phoneticians need to take into consideration is enormously involved and would be profitless for the present consideration of speech sounds. Whenever necessary we can indicate modifications of these basic articulations. But a difference in utterance which is conspicuous enough to be noticeable, and, more especially, conspicuous enough to irritate somebody, should be describable in objective terms.

Stops. Spoken English has two types of stops, one voiceless and the other voiced; the difference consists essentially of the absence or presence of glottal tone.

The sound customarily indicated as the first in the voiceless stop series is produced by a simple closure of the lips, and it can occur at the beginning, the middle, or the end of a word: *pill, upper, rap.* It is known as a "voiceless bilabial stop" and the conventional phonetic symbol is [p]. When the tip of the tongue touches the alveolar ridge and the sides of the tongue spread out against the inner surfaces of the upper teeth, the passage of air is blocked completely and the result is a "voiceless alveolar stop" as in *tip, utter, at.* The phonetic symbol is [t]. In some types of American English, most notably "Brooklynese," and in many of the languages of western Europe the tongue touches the back of the upper teeth, in which case it is properly identified as a "dental stop." The term "dental" is often used loosely in writings about phonetics to identify various speech sounds articulated in the locality of the teeth and the alveolar ridge. Speakers of English have either the alveolar or the dental stop articulation, not both.

The tip or point of the tongue may touch the palate anywhere along its length from front to back and a speaker of English will identify the sound as [t]. If, instead, the upper surface of the tongue, back an inch or more from the tip, touches the palate, the user of English recognizes an entirely different sound. This is called a "voiceless velar stop" and the phonetic symbol is [k]. In the English spelling system the sound is indicated sometimes with *c*, sometimes with *k*, sometimes with *q*, and sometimes with a combination of them.[9] The tongue can touch the palate in a number of places in producing the velar stop, the precise location being determined largely by the nature of

---

9 The Etruscans, whose civilization flourished in ancient Italy before the Romans took over, employed an alphabet which distinguished three stops, spelled respectively with *C*, *K*, and *Q*. The Romans, not especially imaginative in such matters, simply took over the Etruscan alphabet and along with it these three letters, any one of which would have been adequate. We have inherited the same letters with a few additional confusions that twenty centuries have made possible.

the sound that immediately follows it. The tongue makes a contact nearer the front of the mouth in a word like *keep* than in a word like *coop*. The reason becomes apparent when one pronounces the vowel sounds spelled *ee* and *oo*; the first seems to be made nearer the front of the mouth and the other nearer the back. The velar stop merely anticipates these positions. The voiceless velar stop [k] occurs initially, medially, and finally in English: *catch, liquor, sick.*

If the upper surface of the tongue is pushed forward a small fraction of an inch beyond the point of contact for the word *keep,* a speaker of English typically interprets the resulting sound as strikingly different from a stop. It closely resembles the alveolar stop [t], but it breaks off at once into a fricative. The difference between the pronunciation of the initial sounds of *keep* and *cheep* or of *cap* and *chap* illustrates this. The spelling *ch*[10] for the sound is thoroughly misleading in words like *child, riches, ouch,* but no more so than the *t* in *righteous* and *pasture*. Phonetically it may be analyzed as two sounds, [t] + [š], and a number of phoneticians accordingly write it as [tš] or in the older style [tʃ]. It behaves, however, like a unit sound in somewhat the same way that the ammonium radical (NH_4) behaves like a metallic element. We speak of such a sound as an "affricate." This one is called a "voiceless palatal affricate" and the phonetic symbol usually assigned to it is [č].

The stops [p t k] and the affricate [č] are spoken of as "voiceless" because there is no glottal tone or "voice" to accompany them. Corresponding precisely in point of articulation to the voiceless stops, and differing essentially by the addition of glottal tone is a series of "voiced" stops: [b d g]. They occur in words like *bee, robber, ebb; day, rudder, add; guy, beggar, egg*. Corresponding to the voiceless palatal affricate [č] is the "voiced palatal affricate" which is written [dž] or [dʒ], but most commonly [ǰ]. In the word *judge* it occurs initially and finally. The economy of the above arrangement ought to be obvious: by moving the vocal cords a minute distance we add voice and thereby create an additional series of sounds.

The production of the voiced bilabial stop [b] is characterized by a buildup of air pressure which is released by opening the lips. The air pres-

---

10 The ancient Greeks evidently had in their language a series of voiceless stops, phonetically similar to French [p t k], which they wrote as π τ κ. But they also had a series of "aspirated" voiceless stops, phonetically very much like English [p t k] in *pill, till, kill,* which they wrote as φ θ χ, and which ultimately developed into the sounds [f θ x]. When the Romans came to transcribe the Greek words into their own alphabet they simply indicated the difference by adding the letter *h* to the equivalent of the Greek aspirates: *ph, th, kh* (spelled ch).

sure, however, can be released in an entirely different manner, simply by keeping the lips closed and dropping the velum to route the air and the tone through the nasal passage. The resulting sound is not a stop but a continuant, described as a "bilabial nasal," with the symbol [m] as in *me, summer, am.* Corresponding in position of articulation to [d] is the "alveolar nasal" [n], as in *now, manner, inn.* English also has a "velar nasal" [ŋ], corresponding in position of articulation to [g]. It does not occur in initial position in the usual spoken English, but is found in names of persons and places, chiefly African and Southeast Asian, as *Nkrumah* and *Ngo.* Medially and finally it appears in words like *ringer* and *lung.* In conventional English spelling [ŋ] is written as *ng* in a word like *singing,* or as *n* before *k, c,* or *q,* in *think, zinc,* or *cinque.* In the speech of some Americans and Britons, often of irreproachable social and educational standing, [n] occurs in place of [ŋ], chiefly in the participial ending *-ing* in words like *runnin', jumpin', playin'.* Historical evidence suggests that [in] was probably the original ending, the [iŋ] being in fact a bourgeois overcorrection. Such a consideration scarcely tempers the concern of elementary school teachers or of mothers of the young, who enjoin their charges: "Don't drop your *g*'s," or "Be sure to pronounce your *g*'s." The truth is very few of us sound the [g] in this situation. The consonant combination [ŋg] occurs in *finger,* but not in *singer* (except in the speech of those who also call Long Island "lon guyland"). Some persons pronounce this consonant combination in the words *English* and *England,* others in one but not the other, still others in neither one. In the speech of most educated Americans [ŋg] as such does not occur at the ends of words. Where it does occur it is often regarded as a "foreign" accent. Nasal continuants in English speech are normally voiced. The unvoiced variants of [m n ŋ] would be transcribed as [ṃ ṇ ŋ̣] and are called "sniffs."

A schematic organization of the consonants of the voiceless and voiced stop series and of the nasal series appears as follows:

	bilabial	*alveolar*	*palatal*	*velar*
voiceless	p	t	č	k
voiced	b	d	ǰ	g
nasal	m	n		ŋ

Such a diagram has the virtue of demonstrating relationships with respect to point and type of articulation which are otherwise often obscured.

Fricatives. Side by side with the series of voiceless and voiced stops and of nasals are the consonants of the fricative series, voiceless as well as voiced.

The first consonant sound in this series is produced by touching the upper teeth with the lower lip and drawing back the upper lip. With the tongue flat on the floor of the mouth or drawn back a little, air without glottal tone is directed between the teeth and lip to produce an audible friction. This sound we identify as a "voiceless labiodental fricative" [f], as in *fee, offer, off.* At times there is bilabial articulation, which is to say, the sound may be produced with both lips, specifically following a bilabial consonant in words like *comfort, clubfoot, hopeful.*

We hear it said that German and Dutch and other closely related languages are "guttural," which means only that these languages happen to have one or more fricatives articulated at the palate or velum. In English the fricatives happen to be bunched toward the front of the mouth. Not only that, but the relative distance between the points of articulation is smaller; consequently speakers of other languages are likely to have difficulty with English fricatives more than with the other consonant sounds.

With the teeth barely opened, the tip of the tongue touches the opening so that air escapes all around. In the speech of some persons the tongue is thrust between the teeth. The resulting sound we identify as a "voiceless interdental fricative" and indicate it in the phonetic alphabet with the Greek letter theta [θ]. It is regularly spelled *th* as in *thigh, nothing, oath.* Of the present-day western European languages only English has the [θ] although Spanish has it as a variant of [t]. Historically it was present at one time or another in most of them, including French, whence our word *faith.* In their attempts to produce the characteristic English pronunciation, speakers of these languages ordinarily substitute either a stop or an adjacent fricative, so that *thin* and *nothing* become either *tin* and *nutting* or *sin* and *nussing.* The stop modification is associated with the idiom of some American ethnic groups and has generally been regarded as substandard, especially because of its actual or fancied association with the style of the Cosa Nostra. The fricative modification carries no such stigma and is even cultivated by persons trying to preserve or affect a Continental European accent.

When the teeth are closed and the lips drawn back the air escapes with a sharp hiss. This is the "voiceless dental fricative" [s] as in *see, essay, us.* There is also a "voiceless palatal fricative" [š], commonly spelled *sh,* as in *she, usher, ash,* though *ss* in *mission, ti* in *nation, ch* as in *chic,* and so on. The teeth are closed but the tongue is pulled with the tip curled upward; there may also be rounding of the lips. Many speakers of English achieve the same acoustic effect by curling the tongue into a lengthwise groove.

The only other fricative of the voiceless series that speakers of English commonly employ is the "glottal fricative" [h]. It has no localized friction other than that of the oral cavity in general. It is written *h* and occurs typically in *hay* and *ahoy*. In spite of the spelling, it is not sounded in final position, as in *Utah, yeah, oh.*

German, Dutch, Scottish, and some local varieties of Spanish have a fricative with velar articulation known as a "voiceless velar fricative." Phoneticians indicate it with the symbol [x] (which in conventional spelling is the equivalent of the [ks] combination), and it is spelled in various ways: Scottish *loch,* Dutch *dag,* Spanish *jota.* Because of its close phonetic relationship with English [k], the speaker of English in effect reverses what the western European does when he encounters English [θ], and for [x] he substitutes [k], unless by some lucky chance he has learned to produce [x]. This velar fricative was a characteristic sound in English and it remained until approximately the latter part of the fifteenth century. About the same time the introduction of printing brought about some standardization of English spelling. The *gh* spelling had indicated [x], and although the sound itself was lost, the spelling remained. The velar fricative [x] developed into a number of quite different sounds. In *laugh, cough, enough* it has become [f], in *drouth* (also commonly when spelled *drought*) it has become [θ]; in *though* and *through* [w], in *hough* [k], and in *light* and *sought* it disappeared altogether.

There is also a voiced fricative series in English. Identical with [f] except for voicing is the "voiced labiodental fricative" [v], as in *view, over, eve.* In the word *of* it is spelled *f,* and in some pronunciations of *nephew* with *ph,* otherwise it is consistently spelled with *v.* No other letter of the English alphabet is so consistently matched with a sound. In faulty imitation of ancient Roman practice, *V*'s and *U*'s are sometimes interchanged on cornerstones and other lapidary inscriptions: VNITED CHVRCH. Corresponding to [θ] is the "voiced interdental fricative" [ð] which is likewise spelled *th* and for that reason regularly confused with it. It occurs in initial position in a group of frequently used words: *the, this, that, they, there*—eighteen of them in all—but not *through.* Medially it occurs in *other,* finally in *bathe.* Identical in articulation with [s], except for voicing, is the "voiced dental fricative" [z]. It occurs in *zoo, hazy, ooze.* For certain historical reasons it is usually spelled *s* in medial and final positions, as in *easy, busy, laser, wisdom,* or *is, was, has, as,* and most plurals: *dogs, horses, noses, knives.* Identical with [š] except for voicing is the "voiced palatal fricative" [ž].

While the palatal [š] is relatively common in English, [ž] is not.[11] It appears principally in words of French origin, like *azure* or *pleasure*. It is sometimes final, depending on whether one pronounces *rouge* and *garage* with [ǰ] or [ž]. Both are heard in the speech of educated persons. The consonant does occur initially in *genre,* a word employed in discussions of literature and painting, hence pronounced exclusively with initial [ž]. In *gendarme,* which many Americans take to be what the French call a police officer, [ž] is the more usual pronunciation. Otherwise it appears principally in names like *Zsa Zsa, Gisele,* and sometimes *Jeanne.*

It would scarcely occur to us to question the occurrence of contrastive voicing, say, between sounds like [p] and [b]. We regard this as reasonable, and in general the contrast is strongly reinforced in our spelling system. Contrastive voicing in the fricative series we find more difficult to accept. It was a relatively late development in English, running to completion—or to its present state, at least—not much more than five hundred years ago. The basic contrast developed after English spelling had started becoming standardized, and consequently we have such curious doublets as *dizzy* and *busy,* one respelled and the other not. Furthermore, apart from a manuscript or two from the early fifteenth century, English spelling has never systematically differentiated between [θ] and [ð]. In Anglo-Saxon times the copyists employed two symbols, ð and þ, which were interchangeable. Following the Norman Invasion of A.D. 1066, the copyists began using the *th* more generally.[12] A person who has never paid attention to such matters is likely to be surprised to learn that the initial consonants of the words *thin* and *then* are not alike. The "minimal pairs" we have in English, that is, sets of words differing only in respect to a single contrasting sound, consist of *either* and *ether, thy* and *thigh.* It calls for a rare imagination to conceive of a sentence in which the two might be confused. The contrast between [θ] and [ð] is real but it does not happen to be a vital one in English. In fact, in the pronunciation of a word like *without,* the two sounds are interchangeable. The spelling contrast between [f] and [v], on the other hand,

---

11 In various counts made of the relative frequency of various English speech sounds, the consonant most used is [n], with [t] closely following. By contrast [ž] occurs only about 1/144th as often as either [n] or [t].

12 The symbol ð dropped by the way almost at once, but þ was retained as a scribal shorthand symbol. With a small *e* over it, it spelled *the;* with *t* over it, it spelled *that,* and so on. Until William Caxton set up the first printing press in England in 1476, printing of English books was done in Holland by Dutch compositors. Not having þ in their type fonts, they slipped in *y* instead. This was the origin of the *ye* in countless establishments trying to be antique: "Ye Olde Gasse & Oyle Shoppe."

was recognized in early times by English copyists, all of whom were familiar with Latin where the letters *f* and *v* (or *u* as they often wrote it) represented two different sounds. In unstressed words, the *v* may be the spelling for the sound [f], as, for instance, in the word *have* in a phrase like: "I have to be there." It is sometimes spelled *hafta* to represent illiterate pronunciation. The spelling may be illiterate, but the pronunciation certainly is not. Anything else would be an overcorrection.

While the Norman scribes employed the symbol *z* along with *s* and were generally responsible for introducing it into the English alphabet, *s* has been preserved in numerous spellings to represent either [s] or [z]. There seems to be little rime nor reason to the way it is used. A word spelled *use* has the sound [s] when it is a noun and [z] when it is a verb. But as a verb to indicate customary past behavior or activity [s] is standard, as: "I used to be a boy contralto." The words *was, has,* and *is* are sometimes written *wuz, haz,* and *iz* to give the idea of unlettered utterance. What an ironic commentary on our orthography that such spellings happen to be more phonetically valid than the acceptable ones.

The English fricative series, like the stop-nasal series, can be represented by a schematic diagram to indicate a similar instance of phonetic "symmetry":

	labiodental	*interdental*	*dental*	*palatal*	*(velar)*	*glottal*
voiceless	f	θ	s	š	(x)	h
voiced	v	ð	z	ž		

Liquids and Glides. There remain a few English consonant sounds which do not fit into any of the classifications thus far considered. Phoneticians of an earlier day enriched their terminology with metaphor whenever they ran short on precise information. As a result we still sometimes give the name "liquid" to the initial and final consonants of *lull* and *roar.* The term is far more poetic than scientific. Similarly, the initial consonants of *wet* and *yet* are called "glides." Present-day phoneticians have offered other and more precise names, but the older ones are still used, especially in nontechnical discussion.

The first consonant in the group is a "lateral" [l] and is variously identified as a "continuant" or "resonant." It occurs in *lee, alley, ill.* The articulation for [l] is much like that for [d], except that air, and therefore voicing as well, escapes past either side of the tongue, and usually both sides; hence the name. Pronouncing a word like *headlong* or *idly* aloud and very slowly will demonstrate the motion of the tongue from complete closure of [d] to the lateral articulation of [l]. In English [l] is ordinarily voiced, although immediately following a voiceless stop or fricative, as in *plate* or *slate,* it often has voiceless articulation. Many languages, among them Polish, Welsh, and Navajo, have a voiceless [l] as a regular speech sound. The usual spelling in Welsh words is *ll* as in the names *Lloyd* and *Llewelyn.* To Englishmen this sounded like [fl] and that is why the name *Lloyd* also developed into *Floyd* and why *Llewelyn* appears as *Fluellen* (*Henry V,* III, vi.)

The distinctive character of this consonant depends not so much on the type or manner of articulation, as it does on what we might call "resonance." This resonance itself can be approximated and often is, usually without intent, by children and by persons with defective articulation. In such cases [l] is often replaced by or coalesces with [w]. We shall observe this in more specific detail in relation to some of the developments that have occurred in the history of the English language.

Closely similar in articulation to [l] is the resonant [r] which occurs in *rye, eerie, air.* We are likely to think of these two sounds as being totally different from each other, and the difficulties that Orientals experience in keeping them apart strike us with some surprise. But phonetically the difference is often minute. The tongue tip touches the alveolar ridge to form the lateral [l], usually with light pressure, the area of contact barely exceeding a few square millimeters. There are several phonetic variants of [r], as most of us realize, including the flap or very brief trill characteristic of some British speech. Most Americans and Britishers bring the tongue into approximately the position for [l]. The tongue, however, does not make contact with the alveolar ridge; it is widened slightly so that the edges touch the inner surfaces of the molar teeth. With some speakers of English the tongue tip is raised, turning back, in fact, toward the palate. That is why it is sometimes called "retroflex," which means 'curled back.' In common with [l] the [r] is marked by a distinctive resonance. To help them produce a reasonable imitation of American [r], school pupils in western European countries are sometimes told: "Think that you are trying to talk with a hot potato in your mouth."

The remaining consonants in English are sometimes called "glides" because of the motion of one or another of the principal articulating mechanisms. Again the description is more poetic than scientifically precise. There is nothing that really resembles gliding. To produce the "palatal glide" [y] as in *you, beyond, eye,* the jaw is raised and the tongue lifted close to the palate, after which both tongue and jaw are lowered. Very little jaw movement takes place in words like *year, yeast, yip, Yiddish.* There is a slight retraction of the tongue. As we shall note by and by, the palatal [y] is phonetically identical, except for the positions in which it occurs, with the vowel of *sit* and also with the vowel element of *seat.* The sound which we indicate with [w] as in *we, away, owe* involves a momentary rounding of the lips and a retraction of the tongue so that the back of it nearly touches the soft palate.[13] Depending on which aspect one chooses to emphasize, it may be described as either a "labial" or "velar glide." Some phonologists distinguish also a "voiceless velar glide" [ʍ] as the initial sound of the *wh-* words: *why, what, when, where,* but not *who.* Others interpret it as [hw], which represents the way the words were actually spelled before A.D. 1100.[14] The question is academic for many speakers of American and British English who pronounce these words as though they began with [w]. Such practice may be deplored by schoolteachers, but it is seldom crucial. Few people are given an opportunity to be confused by utterances like "Weigh the whey," or "Which witch?" or "We'll wheel away."

The consonants [w y r] are also classified as "semivowels," which refers not so much to the type of articulation as to the manner in which they relate to other speech sounds. While they can and do function as consonants, they may also function as vowels, or in combination with other vowels as diphthongs.

THE PHONEME

The student of elementary Spanish marvels at the ease with which the dullest novice can pick up the pronunciation from the spelling. Words like *beisbol* and *nacaut,* within the fairly broad limits of Spanish pronunciation, correspond to our own *baseball* and *knockout.* On the other hand, it is pretty much anybody's guess how the word corresponding to 舌 sounds in one or another of the Chinese dialects.

---

13 A noticeable contact between the back of the tongue and the soft palate would of course produce the velar stop [g]. The distinction between [g] and [w] has frequently been all but lost, accounting for "doublets" like *warden, guardian; wage, gage; war* (from Old High German *werra* 'strife'), French *guerre;* German *Hag,* English *haw.*

14 The opening word of the Old English epic poem *Beowulf* is simply *Hwæt,* literally, 'What,' but it presumably meant 'Behold' or 'Lo.' The *wh* spelling was introduced through the influence of the Norman scribes. After all, the language already had *ch, gh, ph, sh, th;* and regularizing *wh* made it complete.

The explanation we commonly get or give is that Spanish is "spelled phonetically" while English is only partially so, and Chinese not at all. "Spelled phonetically" is really a lame way of saying that in the Spanish spelling system a distinctive character of the alphabet quite regularly corresponds to a distinctive sound in the language. No one can say that about English. Consonants and vowels run all over the place. We have scores of words pronounced alike but variously spelled: *ewe, yew, you,* for instance, or *sew, sow, so,* or *new, knew, gnu.* And we have letters and combinations of them that seem madly unpredictable in their association with sounds: *ea,* for example, in *hear, head, heard, heart, break, idea, create, beatify.* Apart from the general inconvenience and the emotional wrench resulting from having to accommodate ourselves to a different system of spelling, we would regard as fortunate a one-to-one correspondence between the characteristic sounds of English and the letters of the alphabet. In the present situation a phonetic system of spelling seems little short of utopian. But however impractical it may be to achieve in practice, the notation of a phonetic alphabet does make sense.

Under ideal conditions, a conventional writing system represents a kind of preliminary analysis of the language as expressed in the relationship between the sounds of the language and the letters of the alphabet. We assume that a language consists of distinctive sounds which can be recognized by both speaker and listener and that every typical speaker of English regularly makes a consistent contrast wherever such a contrast is called for. But in day-to-day practice that assumption needs to be modified. Each one of us has experienced, after all, the uncomfortable and sometimes downright embarrassing circumstance of misunderstanding what was said. Naturally we have assured ourselves that the speaker had slovenly enunciation; rarely would it occur to us that the speaker was remarkably clear, that we ourselves were slovenly in listening.

Language specialists, however, have realized for some time that the speaker not only speaks, but the listener listens, and each one participates actively in the transaction of communication. The listener supplies substantially more than a good eardrum or two. This can be demonstrated quite easily. We can remember having to strain to listen to some speaker, and we can remember also the feeling of physical fatigue later on. Ordinarily the act of listening is automatic, like breathing or chewing, or even like most of the talking we do. An automobile driver may switch from "automatic" to "manual" operation of some part of the vehicle, and in a similar manner a listener may assume control over his listening.

So far from being a package of neatly separated sounds, as clearly demarcated as the letters on a printed page, the language that comes delivered to the listener's ear is a torrent of vocal noises tumbling forth often at the rate of two dozen in a single second and then disappearing forever. The differences we have already noted with respect to type and point of articulation are merely a few of a tremendous number of possibilities—differences, for example, in loudness, in pitch, in duration, in tenseness, in nasality. Some of them are meaningful while others are meaningless. The variety of speech sounds which the human vocal apparatus can produce borders on the infinite. Some of the more skilled phoneticians can distinguish well over a million of them.

One of the more remarkable of the early phoneticians was a brilliant American entomologist named Samuel S. Haldeman who became interested back in the 1850s in the diversity of human speech and who thereupon undertook to devise a phonetic alphabet which would provide a unique symbol for each individual speech sound he had isolated, his method being to begin with a letter of the conventional alphabet—capital, lowercase, italic, or whatever came to hand—or a numeral and to invert it or turn it on this side or that or to chip off various projections, all for the purpose of indicating minute differences in articulation which he had identified and described. Before his work came to an end he had exploited the Roman and Greek alphabets and a fair part of the Hebrew. Opposite the flyleaf of the book a distraught printer tipped in a slip of paper to declare to the reader that he was washing his hands of all responsibility for the affair.

Haldeman was demonstrating a prodigious capacity for observation. Since in the mind of the general public any expertise in phonology is on a level with sorcery, phoneticians are expected to do superhuman feats. The public image of the phonetician has been modeled after the character of Professor Henry Higgins of *Pygmalion* and *My Fair Lady*.[15] It does not really help anyone to understand the language better to be able to detect all of the distinct sounds in the stream of speech. Except in his role as language scientist, the phonetician has no advantage over the lay person who distinguishes perhaps no more than fifty, and in fact he often finds his skill a distraction. The phonetician after all can devote his attention to the sounds as sounds for only a short while, invariably at the price of intense concentra-

15 George Bernard Shaw was profoundly interested in the work of the great British linguist Henry Sweet, obviously the model for Shaw's Henry Higgins. There is an instructive essay on Sweet in the preface to *Pygmalion*.

tion, and usually at the cost of hearing what the speaker is really trying to say.

We have the impression that as we learned to speak and understand our language we got the habit of paying attention to certain sounds and that these sounds constituted practically all there was to the language, or at any rate to the phonology of it. The truth is, we had to learn to ignore an even greater variety of features of the sound system. Even the briefest excursion into phonetics makes this evident. The novice in phonetics encounters a host of surprises, but at the same time he commonly experiences a sensation of vague discomfort as it first begins to dawn on him what there is to be heard.

We are aware of the language itself and of our commonplace habit-controlled reactions to it. Some training in phonetics demonstrates the great complexity of human speech. Such training also indicates that the two are not part of the same package—that our reactions to spoken language are automatic while our detection of phonetic data comes hard-earned. Is there—in our nervous system, perhaps—a sorting mechanism which noiselessly winnows out all except the barest minimums, which reduces the continuum of speech to its ultimate essentials and discards or ignores the rest? The realization that this was precisely what happened every time a human being came into contact with a spoken utterance was a breakthrough of major significance in the history of language science. In one form or another the general idea had been considered early in the twentieth century, but Edward Sapir in this country and Prince Nikolai Trubetzkoy in Hungary, working independently of each other, came to essentially the same conclusion during the mid-1920s. Sapir had been making an analysis of the language of the Nootka Indians of British Columbia, employing the services of a native informant. It puzzled Sapir that his informant insisted on a distinction in sounds in Nootka which to Sapir sounded identical, at the same time remaining oddly unresponsive to "obvious" differences between certain sounds in English. Sapir realized that he and his informant were reacting differently to certain sets of sounds as the result of their respective language backgrounds. Sapir's explanation is called the "phonemic principle."

The manner in which the principle operates is not especially difficult to understand, but what commonly disturbs people is the realization that all of it goes on smoothly and quietly within their nervous systems without even the barest hint of its operation.

To illustrate it, let us consider the voiceless alveolar stop [t] as it occurs in English. We have indicated that it is generally produced by contact of the tongue tip with the alveolar ridge, though in some varieties, "Brooklynese" and some western European accents, the contact is with the backs of the teeth. Speakers of English who come from Pakistan and India bring the tongue into contact with the hard palate some distance back of the alveolar ridge. We sometimes refer to these habits as regional differences in pronunciation, or "accents."

If we listen closely, however, we notice more subtle distinctions. Initial [t] in a word like *too* or *tie* is regularly "aspirated," which is to say, a brief puff of air intervenes between the consonant and the immediately following vowel. In French there is no such aspiration, and a person wishing to speak French in even a modestly convincing manner needs to observe this feature. Also, in English if the sibilant [s] precedes [t] as in *stew* and *sty,* the aspiration is greatly reduced or entirely disappears. In a number of languages—Mandarin Chinese, for instance—an aspirated and an unaspirated stop are regarded as distinct sounds; a speaker of English reacts as though they were the same. In the speech of a native[16] user of English the positioning of the aspiration is entirely automatic; one variant occurs in one position and the other occurs in another, and for that reason we call them "positional variants."

Between vowels or between the syllabic consonants of words like *letter* or *bottom* we have several variants. In the speech of some highly educated Americans of advanced years and of Britishers generally the stop is aspirated. In the speech of others it is unaspirated, and is phonetically identical with the [t] of *stop.* Most speakers of American English, especially of middle age and younger, do not aspirate [t] at all, but voice it so that *latter* and *ladder* sound exactly alike, or to use the technical term, they are "homophones." In the northern dialects of the British Isles and in parts of the eastern United States, conspicuously "New Joisey," the glottal stop [ʔ] is often a positional variant of [t], as in *bottle* or *butter.* In final position, in a word like *cat* or *bit,* the stop may be aspirated, though usually only in stressed speech. More commonly, especially before a pause, the tongue maintains a momentary contact with the alveolar ridge with the result that the stop is said to be "unreleased." Sometimes a small child will ask its

---

16 "Native" in our popular vocabulary often refers to a semicivilized member of an African or Australian or Southeast Asian tribe. In linguistics the term is completely colorless. A native speaker of a language is someone who has learned a language by being exposed to it from the time he was born.

mother, "Did you say *can* or *can't?*" and the mother will become cross, not realizing that the youngster still needs to respond to the unreleased final stop as a characteristic positional variant in the mother's speech practices.

It is significant that we do not recognize these differences until someone calls our attention to them and even after that we find it difficult to keep them in mind. Ever since we came into contact with language we have been trained to behave as though the variants were exactly or very nearly alike. An individual speech sound, like the [t] taken all by itself within a larger utterance, is known as a "phone," that is, a phonetic unit—the smallest unit into which language can be analyzed. When we listen to a person speaking we are not aware of the phones at all, but instead we respond to the "phone types," the sounds like the different varieties of [t], which bear some phonetic similarity and which we have been taught to regard as identical. Such a phone type we call a "phoneme."

One of the difficulties here is that the phoneme is not an objective thing but an operational concept. The phones are the only reality. The phoneme is an interpretation which the listener applies to a specific item in the stream of speech. Because the phonemic principle exists we can understand each other; without it human speech would be far too complicated to be intelligible.

Simply stated, as speakers we produce phonetic material, that is, phones. As listeners we sort it out into phonemes. There is, as we have suggested, no simple sound that we can classify as a "pure" alveolar stop—or "pure" anything else, for that matter—since the adjacent sounds invariably color the character of any sound. That is the reason we speak of "positional variants," for which the more precise term is "allophone."

A phoneme we may describe as the sum of all the allophones which the speaker of a particular language regards as identical, as sounding alike. For the voiceless alveolar stop there are four or five readily identifiable allophones, and a number of others that a highly trained phonetician would pick out. Phonetic data we customarily enclose in square brackets: [t]; in fact, in a very precise phonetic transcription the recorder needs to indicate to the very limits of his perceptive powers such features as aspiration or relative tenseness or laxness, not to mention features that are predictable from the environment in which the sound appears. In a phonemic transcription, on the other hand, predictable features, and even features of free variation, are omitted as being taken for granted. The usual practice is to enclose phonemic data between virgules, also called diagonals: /t/.

Now in view of all this, it becomes apparent that Spanish spelling is not really phonetic at all, but phonemic, because an exact phonetic spelling could be misleading. The Spanish word *nada* 'nothing' we should expect to be pronounced as it is spelled [nada], and some speakers of Spanish do say it that way. But many of them instead say [naða] since in medial position [ð] is commonly an allophone of Spanish /d/. Ask the speaker of Spanish whether this sound more closely resembles the initial sound of English *day* or English *they* and he will immediately indicate *day*.

Just as the speaker of a language automatically supplies an aspiration here and a lengthening there and a nasalization somewhere else, the listener automatically reverses the process, ignoring the aspiration here and the lengthening there and the nasalization somewhere else, thus sorting out the thousands and thousands of possible allophones of the language into the three or four dozen phonemes to which he typically responds.

Each language has its unique set of phonemes. The range of possibilities, however, is so stupendous that there are probably no two languages out of the three or four thousand presently spoken that make use of the same set. Even different dialects—social or regional, and certainly historical—of the same language may not have the same phonemes; that is an important reason why they are dialects. And so in learning to master a new language we not only need to control the production of the speech sounds, but we must learn to hear the individual phonemes for what they are. The speaker of English fails to recognize the /rr/ of Spanish because English does not make a phonemic distinction between /rr/ and /r/. The same holds true for nasalization of vowels in French or the distinction between long and short vowels in German. Learners of a language commonly get the impression that it is easier to speak a new language than to understand the language when it is spoken. One reason is, of course, that they have not learned to sort out the phonemes.

Vowels

Most people have no problem here. Ask them how many vowels there are in English and they immediately answer: "Five—*a, e, i, o, u,* and sometimes *y* and *w*." The books say that. It demands only a little reflection to understand that these are not vowels, and not even letters, but names for letters of the alphabet. And furthermore, as we pronounce the names for the individual letters, we do not pronounce vowels, but diphthongs.

Identifying and isolating the consonant phonemes of English offers relatively few problems, since the essential contrasts that determine their status are obvious and, to a speaker of English, reasonable. Beginning students of phonetics usually find it hard to distinguish /θ/ from /ð/ and vice versa, but we know from experience that with patience and time the problem will be taken care of. The question whether the voiceless palatal affricate should be considered as two sounds /t/ + /š/ or one /č/ is interesting but not crucial. Even the spelling of consonants is reliable—spelling regularities far outnumber the anomalies—by as much as 50 to 1.

The status of the English vowel phonemes, however, has separated phonologists into several camps and has engaged them in lengthy and sometimes heated exchanges. How many vowels are there? By what criteria does one assume that a vowel has phonemic status? There is more to the problem than lining them up like eggs and counting them. English spelling has been a treacherous guide for most of the past thousand years. Elements of an earlier underlying system are becoming more and more obscured as time goes by and as the language changes. Indeed, the history of the vowel sounds in the regional dialects of the English language is complex beyond belief. And what we call English would be quite unrecognizable to a contemporary of Chaucer; even George Washington and Ben Franklin would find us difficult to understand.

Suppose we begin by collating a number of words with identical or similar consonant arrangements, but with differing medial vowels or vowel "nuclei," as linguists often call them: *sit, set, sat, shut, sot, should, showed, sought.* The same arrangements of consonants can accommodate several other nuclei as well: *seat, sate, sight, suit, shout.*

Conventionally the nuclei of the first group are called "short" vowels, and of the second group "long" vowels. Phonemic length of vowels is a fairly common feature in various languages, among them classical Latin, Anglo-Saxon, and modern German. When we speak of vowel length we mean simply that the sound of a long vowel is prolonged for a greater duration than that of a short one. How does this operate in English? We have been told that the vowel nucleus of *sit* is short while that of *sight* is long. The best way to test that is to pronounce the words. They are of equal length. But when we pronounce *sit* in contrast to *said* or *sight* in contrast to *side,* we notice that the nuclei of *said* and *side* are about twice as long in duration as those of *sit* and *sight.* In our school-book terminology we do not, however, speak of the vowel of *said* as a long vowel or that of *sight* as a short one; apparently the notion of long and short as applied to the English vowel system will bear another look.

Length does figure as a feature of English vowel pronunciation, but it is allophonic, not phonemic. Phonetically short vowels occur before a voiceless consonant, or before a continuant followed by a voiceless stop: *cat, can't* as contrasted with *cad, can; Burt, burnt, burst* contrasted with *bird, burned, burrs*. Long vowels occur before voiced consonants: *bad, give, rang*.

A different kind of contrast operates between the vowel nuclei of *sit* and *sight*. Regardless of how long one elects to hold it, the nucleus of *sit* remains generally unchanged in articulatory position or phonetic quality: it is still the same vowel directly after /s/ as before /t/. If, however, one slows up the pronunciation of *sight* in the same manner, a difference shows up at once. Immediately after /s/, in much of spoken American English, the vowel is approximately the vowel in the stressed syllable of *father;* immediately before /t/ it has approximately the vowel of *sit*. To put it another way, the nucleus of *sit* is a simple one, that of *sight* is complex.

Now obviously we are unable to describe vowel sounds with the same set of features that we use to describe consonants. All of them, for instance, are voiced. Contrasts in length or in nasal or oral articulation are entirely allophonic. There is no closure of any of the passages of the mouth or nose, and little if any constriction anywhere. Yet the vowels differ strikingly among themselves.

As a speaker of English pronounces the words *sit, set, sat* in that order, the only feature that changes consistently is the relative size of the mouth opening, in other words, the relative height of the lower jaw. The vowel of *sit* /i/ is produced with the teeth nearly closed; that of *sat* /æ/ with the mouth open, and that of *set* /e/ somewhere between the two, with the lips spread relatively wide.

When the lower jaw is in high position, as for /i/, but with the tongue pulled back and the lips rounded rather than spread, the result is the vowel of *should* /u/. With the tongue and lips in the same attitude but with the jaw lowered as for /æ/ the vowel is that of *sought* /ɔ/. The vowel of *showed* /o/ is somewhere between the two.

These relative jaw heights and tongue and lip positions give us a set of objective criteria for describing the simple vowels of English. We may say, in fact, that relative jaw height and tongue position are phonemic in the English vowel system. Accordingly we call /i e æ/ "front" vowels and /u o ɔ/ "back" vowels: /i u/ are "high," /e o/ are "mid," and /æ ɔ/ "low." This means that we can quite accurately identify the vowels in terms of their articulation, /i/ being a high front vowel, and /ɔ/ a low back vowel. While such terminology may be forbidding to a person being introduced to English phonetics, the terminology itself is relatively simple. Thinking of our everyday vowels in such technical terms is what causes most of the hesitation.

During the century or more that phonetics has been flourishing, phonologists have devised many varieties of schematic arrangements of vowel positions. They go by the name of "vowel chart," and are of interest mainly to specialists. But here we are concerned with identifying the vowel phonemes of English. Those we have thus far described may be organized schematically as follows:

	front	*back*
high	/i/	/u/
mid	/e/	/o/
low	/æ/	/ɔ/

Most speakers of English make a distinction between the vowels of *cat, cot, caught.* In general the vowel nucleus of *cot* is made further to the back of the mouth than that of *cat* and further forward than that of *caught.* It is described as a "low central vowel" and the symbol is /a/. In most varieties of American English it is the vowel of the stressed syllable of *father.*

In words like *but, blood, son,* and also in many words that may be unstressed, like *of, was, does, us,* there occurs a vowel that we describe as "mid central" and indicate with the symbol /ə/. It is also sometimes spoken of as a "neutral vowel" since it is the kind of sound that comes out when the mouth is about halfway open and the tongue somewhere between front and back. The sound itself, apart from any phonetic considerations for the moment, serves as a "hesitation sound" in the speech of many people, and for want of better spelling is commonly written as "Uh, uh, uh," and sometimes "Er, er, er," the latter chiefly in dialects where /r/ is dropped.

We call most of the phonetic symbols by their alphabet names. As mentioned earlier θ is called "theta" and ð is called "edh" /eð/—an Anglo-Saxon name for an Anglo-Saxon letter. Where it occurs we call ŋ "eng" and g we call "gee" with the initial consonant of *good.* The symbol æ is called a "digraph," ɔ is usually "open o" and ə is called "schwa" /šwa/, from the Hebrew.

If we add the two central vowels, the chart of the English simple vowel phonemes appears as follows:

	front	*central*	*back*
high	/i/		/u/
mid	/e/	/ə/	/o/
low	/æ/	/a/	/ɔ/

An obvious characteristic of this arrangement is its neatness, or "symmetry," analogous to that of the stop series and the fricative series. There appears to be an omission, namely, in the high central position. Many language scholars have been convinced that phonetic symmetry requires a vowel in this position and consequently they have set up a "high central vowel" /ɨ/ popularly known among phonologists as "barred eye." There happens indeed to be a sound in English—the vowel of the stressed syllable of *children,* or *just* (as in "Just a minute"), and of a rather common pronunciation of words like *silver, sister, dinner,* etc. Naturally we run into frequent attempts to "correct" it, under the impression that the speaker is saying *sulver* and not *silver.* The sound /ɨ/ is extremely widespread in the unstressed syllables of words like *waited, mitten, chorus.*

Some phonologists, as may be expected, see no reason to assume that there needs to be a ninth vowel phoneme, mainly, as they see it, because it happens to fit a hole in the pattern. Others regard it as a phoneme in good standing and hear it everywhere. There are also phonologists who contend that three low vowels cannot possibly account for all the sounds that occur in their own personal dialect, especially in words like *pass, ask, rather,* where the vowel is less "fronted" than that of *cat* and less "backed" than that of *father.* The phonologists who maintain this represent the speech of the southern states.

An inventory of phonemes is simply an approximation of the speech of millions of users of English. It indicates which vowels they differentiate in their speech, though it does not indicate the precise nature of the differentiation in each instance. While the question of "barred eye" or the question of a fourth low vowel—sometimes called the "Confederate vowel"—may seem trivial and academic to nonspecialists, they are items which point the way presently to a larger and more adequate understanding of the nature of language. This organization of the simple vowel nuclei offers a reasonable phonemic spelling for a number of English words, many of them already spelled "correctly": *get, met, yet, yes, put, mar, bar, fit, skin, grit, spilt, prim, milk, window,* and so on.

Diphthongs

The number of actual phonemes that a language employs may vary. Some languages have as many as sixty, some as few as twenty. English is somewhere between these extremes. English happens, however, to have an unusually full assortment of vowel phonemes—possibly as many as ten in the speech of some users of the language. Many languages have far fewer. Sanskrit, Tagalog, and Arabic manage with three; Navajo with four, classical Latin and Japanese with five. But in actual practice things are not quite so uncomplicated. While Navajo, for instance, has only four simple vowels, a vowel can be long or short, it can have high or low pitch, it can have oral or nasal articulation, a total of thirty-two possibilities. In Latin a vowel could be long or short, in addition to which there were a number of diphthongs.

Compared with English, the vowel system of Spanish is simple and virtually austere. As a result speakers of Spanish encounter difficulty making themselves understood in English. A typical problem is the pair of sentences: "Pablo bit Carmen" or "Pablo beat Carmen." A speaker of Spanish hears them as pretty much alike, if not identical; he may be able to observe a difference if he listens closely, but it is hard for him to remember which is which. We explain this by saying that the vowel nuclei of *bit* and *beat* are in phonemic contrast in English, but not in Spanish. At best they are in free variation. Practically all speakers of English sense a contrast here, but what is the nature of it?

Following an old tradition we call the vowel nucleus of *beat* "long *e*," suggesting that if someone sounded the vowel nucleus of *bet* long enough he would presently get the vowel nucleus of *beat*. The speaker of Spanish has no problem hearing the distinction between *bet* and *beat*, although logically he should if the assumption were true that the vowel of *bet* is a "short *e*" and that of *beat* a "long *e*."

In considering the simple vowel nuclei we noticed that the nucleus of *sit* is a simple one, a high front vowel /i/. We noticed furthermore that the nucleus of *sight*, or *site*, is not simple, but complex, consisting in the speech of many Americans of a low central vowel /a/ plus a high front vowel /i/, that is to say, a "diphthong" /ai/. A provisional transcription then of the two words shows *sit* /sit/ contrasted with *site* /sait/. Few phonologists would argue that the nucleus of *site* needs to be analyzed as a simple unit, say /i/ plus length or some such thing. The assumption that this is a diphthong is found, in fact, under the most transparent of disguises, in the explanatory matter at the front of all the newer dictionaries. By an accident of spelling the word *shout* has a vowel nucleus spelled with two letters, consequently it is not difficult to claim diphthongal status for it. Careful listening will indicate that in the speech of many Americans, especially from the North and East, the diphthong consists of /a/ plus a high back vowel /u/, hence a diphthong provisionally written /au/ and a transcription of *shout* will be /šaut/.

It is not simply a coincidence that one diphthong ends in a high front vowel and the other in a high back vowel; many, if not most, of the English diphthongs consist of a vowel plus /i/ or /u/. In older phonological studies the diphthongs are often written *ai, au,* and so on. The result, however, is a relatively complicated statement and it is now the general practice to assume that the vowel nucleus of any syllable consists of one vowel at most. In place then of /i/ and /u/, phonologists employ the semivowels /y/ and /w/. Phonetically the difference between /i/ and /y/ or between /u/ and /w/ is negligible, but /i/ and /u/ are articulated as vowels and behave as such, while /y/ and /w/ are articulated as consonants. And so *site* may be transcribed as /sayt/ and *shout* as /šawt/.

Side by side then with the simple vowel nuclei like /i/, /e/, /æ/ and the rest, we have what phonologists call "complex nuclei," consisting of a simple vowel and a semivowel. To explain the English "long vowels" as complex nuclei takes care of a number of questions; certainly most of those we shall encounter. There are other explanations. In fact, the more up-to-date commercial dictionaries employ a system, or systems, that the general reader can comprehend with some ease. Furthermore, each of us has developed his own personal system, never written down, by which he automatically sorts the barrage of phones into a neat arrangement of phonemes. How he does this is something the psychologist has to worry about; how the end product of his sorting operation looks is something the phonologist speculates about.

We have observed that English spelling—in its nobler moments, at least—tends to be phonemic, particularly with regard to the simple vocalic nuclei. Words like *slow, win, tent, best* are already phonemically spelled. But difficulties arise when we undertake to deal with words like *beat, bait, boat, boot, bite,* and *bout*. There is quite a bit of jaw and tongue motion in the vowel nuclei of some of them. In comparing *bet* and *bait* we discover the nucleus /e/ in both, but in the latter there is also a palatal semivowel /y/, yielding the complex nucleus /ey/. The phonemic transcription of *bait* is simply /beyt/. Similarly *boat, bite* and *bout* are rendered as /bowt/, /bayt/, and /bawt/.

What to do with *beat* and *boot* raises some questions. On the analogy of the other complex nuclei, *bit* and *beat* ought to be transcribed as /bit/ and /biyt/; similarly *boot* should be /buwt/. It would be unrealistic to pretend that many persons hear the nucleus of *beat* as /i/ + /y/ or that they hear the nucleus of *boot* as /u/ + /w/, and for just this reason a number of phonologists have taken their leave at this point and have offered some other explanation. The others assume that we are not concerned with what a person hears but what he responds to. Then it becomes a question of whether we are dealing with phonetic or phonemic items. Phonetically the evidence may seem shaky, but it remains an explanation that many scholars regard as the most satisfactory. Others find it a less than moral way of juggling facts in order to make them fit a neat pattern.

Given nine simple vowel nuclei and the semivowels /y/ and /w/, we have some twenty-seven possible nuclei. No speaker of English has all of these; his speech would be far too complicated. While a combination like /u/ + /y/ looks strange, most of us have heard it in certain local pronunciations: *push,* commonly /puš/, may be /puyš/, and *bush* may be /buyš/. It may be explained as an allophonic variant of /u/ before /š/. There are great numbers of such variations, most of them involving only a few words. But we also encounter variations that are more widespread. All of us have heard the silly line with which people torment teachers of public speaking: "How now, brown cow." In much of the country the vowel nucleus is /aw/ and we should transcribe the phrase as /haw naw brawn kaw/, but in other areas /æw/ is regular in these same environments, so that a proper transcription reads, /hæw næw bræwn kæw/. That is to say, every occurrence of /aw/ in one speech area corresponds to /æw/ in the other one. In a general way we associate the /aw/ diphthong with the Northern speech area and /æw/ with the Midland.[17]

---

17 For many years it was generally taken for granted that American English could be divided into three principal dialects: New England, Southern, and general American. Following the researches of Hans Kurath, a new picture emerged. Closely associated with the settlement history of the United States we have three broad dialect bands extending east and west across the land, called Northern, Midland, and Southern. Northern includes all of New England and New York, the northern half of New Jersey, the northern tier of counties in Pennsylvania, the northern half of Ohio, Indiana, and Illinois, and the states north of them. Southern includes most of the old Confederacy. Midland lies between the two. These dialect boundaries are only approximate and include, of course, many subdialects. And west of the Mississippi the lines become extremely hard to follow. A good treatment of the Kurath division appears in W. N. Francis, *The Structure of American English* (New York: Ronald, 1958), as Chap. 9, entitled "The Dialects of American English." The chapter was written by Raven I. McDavid, Jr., one of Kurath's close associates in this work.

A phonetician ordinarily finds the differences in the way Americans speak fairly noticeable not only because he has been trained to listen to the sounds as sounds, but because such differences have meaning for him. The nonspecialist dismisses the other person's speech as difficult to understand. He may perhaps notice that such a person "talks differently" without, however, being aware of what accounts for the difference.[18]

Our various regional dialects exhibit their most striking differences in their treatment of diphthongs. It is possible that no single diphthong is common to all speakers of American English. Several appear, however, to be more widely distributed than the others, including /iy/ *mete,* /ay/ *mite,* /uw/ *moot,* and /ow/ *mote.*

Some languages, like Japanese and Spanish, show a preference for a syllable construction consisting of consonant plus vowel—symbolized as CV. Typically an English word like *motorboat* becomes *motobotu* in Japanese. Other languages, like English and Mandarin, seem to prefer a "closed syllable"—CVC or (C)VC which may be extended to (C)VCVC. This is apparent in many words that we ordinarily think of as containing simple vowels: *see, say, do, by, no,* which actually contain the semivowels /w/ and /y/: /siy/, /sey/, /duw/, /bay/, /now/.

While representations of *go* and *see* as /gow/ and /siy/ seem reasonable, words like *flu* and *ski* usually call for a second look, yet we presently realize that they are actually /fluw/ and /skiy/. In fact, adding the semivowels /y/ and /w/ takes care of all of the high and mid vowels in stressed syllables. But there remains a "residue" as a small list of words which have one of the low vowels /æ a ɔ/ in final position. Apparently words like *baa, bra,* or *law* /bæ/, /bra/, /lɔ/ constitute an exception. To be sure, not many words fit this category, but those that do merit an explanation. Phonetically the vowel nuclei of *baa* and *law* are longer than the nuclei of *bat* or *loss,* suggesting that vowel length is phonemic here. But once we introduce phonemic length, we shall be over our heads in other problems. For this reason many phonologists get around the issue by means of another semivowel /h/, which they can do with some consistency since /h/ otherwise occurs as a voiceless aspirate only initially and medially. Why not assume that the lengthened vowel is an allophone of /h/ in final position. Accord-

18 In Dallas I tried to call an old friend whom I had not seen for a number of years. When I called his office a young lady informed me that he was at "the fire," or that was my impression of what she said. I wondered whether Dallas had some kind of institutional fire when I realized that she was speaking Central Texas, that what I had heard as /fayə/—or possibly /fæyə/—would in my own speech by "the [Texas State] Fair."

ingly the words *baa, bra,* and *law* may be phonemically transcribed: /bæh/, /brah/, /lɔh/.

Complicated as all of this may seem, it does not yet account for all of the features of the pronunciation of English. There are certain regional and social pronunciations of American and British English in which /r/ follows a vowel of the same syllable in words like *sir, bird, learn, heart.* In the more usual American pronunciation *heart* is heard as /hart/, but in some varieties of English speech the /r/ is lost. The result should be simply /hat/, the familiar word *hot.* This is not the case. Instead the vowel of *heart* is long while that of *hot* is short, but, of course, if we extend it to phonemics we once again confront the problem of phonemically long vowels. Previously we have dismissed length as allophonic, as the difference between the nuclei of *sat* and *sad:* /sæt/ and /sæd/. Just as the /iy/ of /biyt/ is in effect a compromise, so a contrast can be expressed for *hot* and *heart* in an *r*-less speech community by /hat/ and /haht/.

Historically the dialects with /r/ maintain the original pronunciation as the spelling clearly indicates. But someone who says /bəhd/ and /ləhn/ for *bird* and *learn* has every right to consider his own pronunciation as basic. Where he says /haht/ another person says /hart/, indicating that /haht/ and /hart/ are in contrast as dialect differences. To be consistent, therefore, /r/ is also to be accepted as a semivowel. Such an explanation is not without problems, as one may suppose, but for our present limited purposes it is a satisfactory one.

It is thus possible to consider the complex nuclei of English as consisting of any of the nine simple vowel elements plus /y/, /w/, /h/, and /r/, making possible a total of forty-five possible combinations. Evidently all of them do occur, although some are relatively rare. The word *push,* already referred to, has at least three widespread variants: /puš/, /puwš/, and /puyš/. Even more familiar are the variations of the word *wash,* where all of the semivowels appear: /wɔhš/, /wɔwš/, /wɔyš/, and /wɔrš/. Then we also find /a/ in place of /ɔ/ in some regional varieties.

CONCLUSION

It should be obvious that there is really no limit to the study of phonology. For our present purposes, however, it will serve as an instrument; and at this point we need only to be familiar with the characteristic speech sounds of the language and the manner in which they are produced. After all, what are the differences in speech that mark "wrong" from "right"?

In performing activities like walking, running, playing golf or tennis—and even eating—we are accustomed to relatively large anatomical movements. By contrast the insignificant differences in the position of the organs involved in the several speech sounds appear much too small to account for meaningful differences in sound. That is because we commonly underestimate the fantastic dependability of our speech organs to respond with exactly the sound we want to make. To be sure, we have done some practicing. By the time a normal child is five he will have spent four or five thousand hours rehearsing speech sounds over and over as an essential part of learning to talk.

We also underestimate the sensitivity of our hearing. The eardrum, or tympanum, consists of a membrane about 1/2 inch in diameter, capable of such complex motions that it can respond to all of the various tones and pitches and harmonics produced by a symphony orchestra. Stories are told of more than one conductor who stopped the orchestra in rehearsal to inform a single member of the violin section that a string was out of tune. Orchestra conductors have the same kind of ears as other people; the difference lies in training, and presumably any one of us could learn to do the same thing. The human ear is so sensitive that it can detect a wave of sound with the amplitude of a mere one-hundredth the diameter of a hydrogen atom, if anything so small and feeble can be comprehended. It can distinguish a time difference of three hundred-thousandths of a second elapsed between the instant a sound reaches one ear and the instant it reaches the other. This capacity makes stereometric hearing possible and explains why we can turn to precisely the direction from which sound is coming.

The ear has only one function, and that is to hear. And this it accomplishes with dazzling competence

4

pronunciation

We can speak of a standard only when we have something reasonably homogeneous to be measured—a standard viscosity for motor oil, or height for kitchen sinks, or width for bed sheets. Some things exceed the standard and others fall short of it, but the standard remains nevertheless. In matters of social conduct and behavior one cannot establish a rigid standard by legislation or decree, but it is relatively easy to discover what members of various social groups typically do when, for instance, they communicate with one another, or earn a living, or carry on warfare, or mate. We listen or watch or ask questions. Narrowing this down, we may assume also that there exists a standard variety of English which will be typically employed by all persons who have occupied themselves for a minimum of one year by attending an accredited liberal arts college. This may not be a particularly realistic assumption, and for that reason we seldom make it. After all, the social group it represents is far from homogeneous. On the other hand, we take less of a chance in making the assumption of this group than in making it of the entire population of the United States, regardless of age or education. Yet it was a workable assumption three or four generations ago, when the college population was comparatively small and those enrolled in college were seriously committed to the study of law or medicine or theology or other trustworthy academic pursuit, when those graduating from college might be looked upon as faithful guides in manners, morals, and utterance. The editors of our recent "collegiate" dictionaries face an unresolved situation here. Indeed a usage or perhaps style of language characterizes in a general way those who are attending or who have attended college. The usage and the college-educated segment of the population, however, do not correlate evenly. Many college graduates—some with advanced degrees—speak and write with no regard whatever for the "genteel" conventions in language. And there are also those who by formal academic standards are uneducated, but who never embarrass themselves by either spoken or written word.

All of us have discovered that we communicate most easily with those who use the English language pretty much the way we ourselves do. Within that group there happens to be a normal way of speaking and writing, with the result that we rightfully regard it as a standard for members of such a social group. The usages do not have to be identical for everyone, and they seldom are; one person may, for example, say /mawntən/ and another /mæwntɨn/, or one may say /æprɨkat/ and another /eyprəkɔt/. Now as long as no one notices, and especially as long as no one calls attention to differences like those between /mawntən/ and /mæwntɨn/ or between /æprɨkat/ and /eyprəkɔt/, these variant pronunciations are all standard. Our dictionaries list variant pronunciations on precisely that basis. But if for some reason a person comes to associate a pronunciation like /mawntən/ with the characteristic language of his own social group and /mæwntɨn/ with that of the outsiders, we have the makings of a difference in usage. Few of us spontaneously notice such things; someone else—usually a teacher or "usage authority"—has pointed them out to us and has given us a clue to their social significance. If a person has no strong feelings of attraction or distaste regarding those who say /mæwntɨn/, for him it is merely a variant. Suppose now that someone appears who speaks of a /mawntiŋ/. Suppose further that this person has an untidy appearance, that he manifests grossly repellent table manners, that he is obviously unreasonably ignorant. It will be for purely nonlinguistic reasons that the members of a social group may shun or reject the person himself, but at the same time they will identify his manner of speaking as substandard. There is nothing phonetically "wrong" with a pronunciation like /mawntiŋ/ to indicate a topographical elevation; after all, when it is spelled *mounting* this pronunciation has a number of acceptable meanings. But if a pronunciation like this for *mountain* is something that members of a social group regularly associate with those they regard as their social inferiors, then to such people it is substandard.

The converse is also possible. One can try too hard and identify himself as a social climber. His language we call hyperstandard.

By tradition our schools have concerned themselves with the plight of the speaker and writer of substandard English, and we suppose that if we have done away with certain pronunciations and constructions we shall thereby do the person a valuable service. We are likely to forget that the speaker of a particular mode of language expresses his integrity in this manner. To the speaker of the kind of language which many educators—and teachers of English notoriously so—regard as substandard, the language of the educators themselves is affected and unreal. Such a person rejects the "standard" of the educated not because he is ignorant or predelinquent but because his instincts assure him that "real people" do not speak this way at all.

None of this makes any sense if we regard language as a simple matter of active production and passive reception, that is, if we think that the speaker or writer does all the work and the listener or reader provides nothing more than a pair of warm eardrums or moist eyeballs. Any understanding of the phonemic principle ought to clear up such a narrow and limited picture. The significance, however, can be missed quite easily. It is this, namely, that each of us lends the stream of speech his own subjective interpretation, which includes breaking up this continuum and sorting out the phonemes. Whether anyone else goes through the identical analytical procedure we have no idea; we assume that millions of other speakers of English must do it because they appear to understand English very much as we do.

In sorting out this flow of talk into phonemes, or performing an analogous operation in reading a stretch of writing, the human brain conducts an incredibly brilliant operation. Yet this is still only a limited part of its activity. Simultaneously it carries on other sorting operations—with fundamentally different procedures—at various levels, including a screening of usage items. These usage items are the characteristics that give language its social relevance, that identify the speaker or writer as a "right person" or "wrong person."

The "knowledge explosion" in linguistics has come about to a great degree since and because of the invention of recording devices, especially the tape recorder. In studying language we are not confronted with an actuality like a solution in a beaker or a layer of sedimentary rock or a set of attitudes common to the residents of a metropolitan suburb. Instead, language is something that is either happening at a particular moment, or capable of happening, and therefore constantly on the verge of change. The tape recorder has enabled us to put a "hold" on the transitory speech event and to examine it closely at our convenience.

PRONUNCIATION AND THE DICTIONARIES

For most of us the problem of pronunciation remains largely academic. We may perhaps record some interesting pronunciations, and occasionally "correct" an especially outrageous one. But some people live with pronunciation as a fact of life—public speakers, actors, teachers of speech, for instance—no one quite so crucially as the pronunciation editors of various commercial dictionaries. How are they to indicate pronunciations in a way that the nonspecialist will understand?

There is a tradition, still remarkably viable, in which the conventional spelling of a word is preserved by whatever means available. The newer dictionaries no longer use it and have not used it since the beginning of the present century. It may be seen in bargain "unabridged" dictionaries offered at unbelievably low prices in food supermarkets—actually reprints of very old editions of standard commercial dictionaries. The tradition also continues to flourish in the pronunciation of proper names in many editions of the King James Bible. Irrelevant orthographic features are spoken of as "silent letters," and others are marked with an assortment of diacritics. As a result of more accurate observation of phonological data, dictionary editors have not relied on the standard spelling for some seventy or eighty years, but they have never been able to completely abandon the various marks above and below the vowel symbols. Anyone familiar with the history of such matters, however, will have observed a transition toward a phonemic spelling and a deliberate discarding of redundant diacritics. The most radical change, although it may not seem so, has been the practice of employing one symbol, or uniform set of symbols, for one phoneme or set of phonemes. The editors have had their eye on the International Phonetic Alphabet[1] but have stopped short of adopting that, working out instead a modification which looks like a compromise between tradition and probable trends in phonological notation.

The simple vowel nuclei are indicated as follows by the more recent unabridged dictionaries:

---

1 The Funk & Wagnalls *Standard Dictionary* employed two sets of symbols—the conventional diacritics and also a modification of the IPA. During the late 1930s and early 1940s some tentative attempts were made to promote the IPA, presumably with the expectation of ultimately adopting it to use in the various dictionaries. G. & C. Merriam published *A Pronouncing Dictionary of American English* (Springfield, Mass., 1944) which used the IPA throughout and which was edited by John S. Kenyon, author of "Guide to Pronunciation" in *Webster's New International Dictionary of the English Language,* 2d ed., and by Thomas A. Knott, general editor of Webster's *Second.*

	WNI3	*RHD*
/i/	i *tip*	i *if*
/e/	e *bet, bed*	e *ebb*
/æ/	a *mat, map*	a *act*
/ə/	ə *humdrum*	u *up*
/a/	ȧ *father*	ä *art*
/u/	u̇ *pull, wood*	o͝o *book*
/ɔ/	ȯ *saw, all*	ô *order*

Both dictionaries also distinguish a low back vowel. WNI3 indicates it with *ä* as in *bother, cot,* but adds: "Most American speakers have the same vowel in *father, cart.*" RHD indicates it with *o* and gives as key words *wander, yacht, astronaut, box, cough.*

Diphthongs, or "long vowels" in popular usage, are indicated as follows:

	WNI3	*RHD*
/iy/	ē *beat, nosebleed*	ē *equal*
/ey/	ā *day, fade*	ā *able*
/ay/	ī *site, side*	ī *ice*
/ɔy/	ȯi *coin, destroy*	oi *oil*
/uw/	ü *rule, fool*	o͞o *ooze*
/ow/	ō *bone, snow*	ō *over*
/aw/	au̇ *now, loud*	ou *out*

Here obviously the dictionaries have clung more closely to tradition. WNI3 in a parenthetic note regarding the diphthong /ay/, which both dictionaries continue to indicate with the symbol *ī*, observes, "Actually, this sound is ä + i or ȧ + i."

How far to go beyond such matters is a problem dictionary editors cannot altogether ignore. No editor can possibly hope to record all the current pronunciations that are in good standing, much less note the localities where they prevail. But neither does an editor dare to ignore the fact that there are differences. WNI3 goes to some lengths to explain various features of East Coast pronunciation; RHD is concerned with the character of various diphthongs consisting of a simple vowel plus /r/, a phenomenon that phoneticians often speak of as "*r* coloring." Even with limitations like these, the present-day dictionaries are taking vastly greater pains to acknowledge actual pronunciations than their predecessors did.

STRESS

Discussions about language are likely to give the unfortunate impression that words are really just so many discrete units. Now in many languages, English among them, an utterance will come apart at specific places, corresponding with considerable consistency to the spaces we insert between our words in reading and writing. There are exceptions. In spoken English we are likely to encounter a word division like *a nother* in place of the conventional *an other* or *another* in an expression like "I read a whole nother chapter while I was waiting for the dentist." More common, however, are phrases like *do not, are not, have not* in which the vowel element of the negative particle began to disappear several centuries ago and which have now collapsed to *don't, aren't,* and *haven't.*

Listening to a child as he learns to talk, one often gets the impression that he is learning words one by one. Much of the evidence available on language learning suggests instead that he begins almost at once to deal in sentences; often by the time he is sixteen months old he has acquired some control over the basic sentence types of his language—the statement, the question, and the request (or command). When he has reached five or six years he will perhaps be doing some reading, since this is the time when he is commonly confronted with the written mode. This is now not a connected discourse but a series of separate letter combinations to indicate words, each one of which he masters as a separate reading item. As a result we get a characteristic wooden diction in which every word is given equal emphasis. For example:

> Jack and Jill went up the hill

In normal adult speech the first, third, fifth and seventh syllables are spoken more distinctly than the others, partly by raising the musical pitch, partly by increasing the volume. A small child reading the material for the first time would be inclined to give every syllable equal value. We assume with good reason that the youngster has learned to read "normally" when he begins giving material like this the same kind of contrastive stresses that he uses for ordinary speaking. Much of our poetry has a rhythm in which stressed and unstressed syllables are contrasted in a relatively simple pattern which is repeated over and over again. This we call *accent* or *beat* and it coincides to some extent with the stress patterns of day-to-day speech.

A two-syllable word in English will have one syllable in which stronger stress is contrasted with weaker stress in the other: *ab*-sent, *broth*-er, *cro*-cus, *dark*-ness. Where the stress falls on the first syllable, as it most commonly does in English, the pattern is "trochaic." But it may also fall on the second: a-*bout,* be-*lieve,* com-*pose,* dis-*grace,* and this pattern is called "iambic."

A simple alternation of strong and weak stresses fails to account for words of three or four syllables, and even of many phrases only a few syllables in length. In words like *aggravation, benediction, catastrophic, deposition,* there is an alternation, but the third syllable receives stronger stress than the first; the fourth in each of these instances has a heavier stress than the second. A different pattern appears in words like *alligator, benefactor, category, desultory,* where the first syllable receives heaviest stress and the third syllable less heavy. Since the vowel bears the stress in any syllable it is a common practice to indicate the degree of stress with an appropriate mark over the vowel. Strongest stress is known as "primary" and is marked with an acute accent /´/ over the vowel; weakest stress we call "weak" or "no stress" and we distinguish it with a breve /˘/ or no mark at all. In present-day English speech it is not uncommon for the syllable to be lost altogether. We indicate "secondary" stress with a circumflex /ˆ/ and "tertiary" with a grave accent /`/. All four of these stresses are to be found in running speech, but whether for all levels of stress the difference is phonemic or whether it is stylistic, either partly or altogether, has been discussed by phonologists without any clear agreement among them.

To be sure, contrastive stress does occur in many words. It constitutes a minimum difference between a number of nouns and verbs, and in that sense it is presumably phonemic in words like *cónduct* and *condúct, dígest* and *digést, óbject* and *objéct.* Dictionaries have customarily followed a practice of placing a diagonal stress mark after the stressed syllable: *mon'key.* This practice has also been adopted in the Revised Standard Bible, which has meanwhile discarded all other diacritics. When dictionary editors find it necessary to indicate not only primary but also secondary stress, they commonly employ a lighter stress mark for secondary stress: *mon' key shine'*. WNI3 is the first of the commercial dictionaries to make a break with this style, and in keeping with a system the International Phonetic Association has used for a century, primary stress is indicated by a raised vertical mark before the syllable and secondary stress by a lowered mark before the syllable: *'mon key,shine.* As long as commercial dictionaries remain committed to using any kind of diacritics, stress marks on vowels will be out of the question. On the other hand, unless one is very insistent on finding four levels of stress, the IPA system is workable. Weak stress is indicated by absence of any stress mark.

With the lowering of the degree of stress, there also occurs in English a regular change in the quality of the vowel nucleus itself. Conventional English spelling conceals the extent to which much of our speech is actually unstressed. A sentence written:

What do you want?

would be almost unrecognized by a speaker of English if uttered:

/hwât dùw yuw wánt/

especially if each word were pronounced separately and distinctly. This would be much more likely:

/wədəyəwánt/ or even /wəǰəwánt/

In the unstressed syllable we typically have a loss of distinctiveness of the vowel, which is "centered" to /ə/.[2] This change from a front or back, high or low articulation, to the neutral vowel pronunciation is characteristic of English, and the phenomenon is known as "gradation." What happens to the word *atom* will illustrate the principle. In its base form in English, /ǽtəm/, primary stress falls on the initial syllable and the vowel of the second syllable is neutralized to /ə/. Add a syllable like *-ic,* for instance, to make *atomic,* and the stress moves down to the next syllable /ətámɨk/. The vowel of the first syllable has been neutralized and the second has a distinctive vowel quality. A further addition, as in *atomistic* /æ̀təmístɨk/, moves the stress down still further and once more rearranges the relation of the neutralized and the distinctive vowels. Any attempt to overhaul English spelling will need to take into consideration this behavior of English vowels under conditions of stress and reduction of stress.

The degree of contrast between the stressed and unstressed syllables is decidedly greater in English than in many languages. The user of English tends to render any unstressed vowel as a mid-central vowel and unless he is carefully instructed he will carry this practice over into languages like

2 "Barred eye" /ɨ/ is commonly an allophone of /ə/ in unstressed syllables.

German or French or Spanish. In fact, when speakers of those languages try to mimic the speaker of English, they neutralize all less stressed vowels and diphthongize the stressed ones wherever possible:

/kòwmə sə yâhmə ùwstéhd/

We have plenty of evidence to show that this stress contrast has been developing over the course of a number of centuries. In Anglo-Saxon the verb inflections for past tense and past participles of what we call "regular" verbs were invariably syllabic. At the time of Chaucer—about 1400—the vowel had presumably become neutralized, though in the English spoken in London the syllable was still pronounced, especially in poetry. In certain varieties of regional speech, including that of the north of England, there was already some loss or "syncopation" of the vowel. By the time of Shakespeare it was normally lost, but for metrical purposes it could be restored, although it must have had an archaic ring to it:

Looke with what courteous action
It wafts you to a more removéd *ground.*
—*Hamlet,* I.iv.33–34.

A few syllabic *-ed* endings actually survive, principally those with religious or poetic overtones: *agéd, blesséd, curséd, belovéd;* also *learnéd,* particularly in reference to scholarly organizations known as "learned societies"; and some miscellaneous words: *dogged, crabbed, crooked.* But the tendency toward syncopation is so strong that it sometimes engulfs other words by analogy. Thus *naked* and *wicked* may be pronounced /neykt/ and /wikt/ in nonstandard usage. *Misled,* already referred to as the past participle of *mislead,* sometimes becomes an entirely new—though nonstandard—verb: "I have been misled," pronounced /mízəld/. These are probably "spelling pronunciations," a phenomenon we shall note in detail by and by.

Lowering of stress has also affected several score monosyllabic words—chiefly pronouns, auxiliaries, and connectives. The degree of informality undoubtedly determines which words may be reduced and the extent to which this is carried out. In unstressed environments the vowels may be "downgraded" to /ə/ or /ɨ/; those of some words are completely syncopated.[3]

3 John S. Kenyon, *American Pronunciation,* 10th ed. (Ann Arbor, Mich.: Wahr, 1951), pp. 105ff; Otto Jespersen, *Essentials of English Grammar* (London: George Allen & Unwin, 1933), pp. 47–49; A. C. Gimson, *An Introduction to the Pronunciation of English* (London: E. Arnold, 1962), pp. 240–242.

A word like *have* in "I could have gone" would seldom be rendered as /hæv/, which might be regarded as hypercorrect. Not uncommonly it would be /ày kúdəv gɔ̀n/ and in very rapid speech /ày kúdə gɔ̂n/. This is often written *coulda* to represent the speech of an illiterate or ignorant person, just as *going to* is written *gonna.*

Some contrastive stress undoubtedly occurs in all languages, otherwise it would be one long dreary buzz, but English goes further than most of those we ordinarily encounter in the extent to which a number of successive unstressed syllables are permitted to collapse. In some phrases such reduction is required—*going to* as an expression of future time may actually be a hypercorrection when given the full pronunciation since /gónə/ appears in most styles of spoken utterance, except the highly formal. The same consideration holds true for phrases like *have to, couldn't have, want to, did you, let me* and scores besides. If spoken at the typical conversational rate —from four to seven syllables a second—these reductions are perfectly normal. Any slowing of the tempo, however, demands that the individual words be sounded and the reductions reversed. Failure to observe this basic distinction is likely to make the speaker sound stupid.

Such further lowering of stress in the vowels of unstressed syllables in English, and with it a neutralization and syncopation of the vowel element, seems to be less a condition than a development. Even now it is bringing about certain changes in the language which have escaped general notice. We come face to face with the results of it when a hapless speller renders *corrupted* as *crupted* and *succumbed* as *scummed.* In spoken English names of familiar places regularly fall victim: /klrǽdòw/, /ɨlnɔ́y/, /kèlfɔ́rnyə/, /èhrzównə/, /flɔ́rdə/, etc. Some years ago John Davenport gave the name Slurvian[4] to this kind of pronunciation, and he cited typical forms like *Yerp* (Europe), *Murcan* (American), *harr* (horror), *plight* (polite). The very worst that can be said for such reductions is that they are inelegant; every indication seems to show that communication goes on unimpaired. Certainly not one person in a thousand notices /smént/ for *cement,* /gráǰ/ for *garage,* /srǽmɨks/ for *ceramics,* or even /rlíǰəs/ for *religious. Spirit* becomes /spírt/, but this pronunciation has a long and distinguished history. A monosyllabic pronunciation is the only one that will fit into a proper scansion of the word in most of Shakespeare's plays, and a spelling *sprit* is attested by the *Oxford English Dictionary* from as early as 1447 to as late as

4 John Davenport, "Slurvian Self-taught," *New Yorker,* 18 June 1949, p. 29.

1782. Reductions like these occur only in familiar words, of course; we should scarcely expect to find them in words like *fuliginous* or *propaedeutic* or *vaticination,* unless we happened to be on terms of easy association with people who used them casually and fairly often in ordinary conversation.

The vowel of the unstressed syllable of words like *rabbit, horses, waited, Alice, spinach* is phonetically closer to /i/ than it is to /ə/ in the speech of many users of English, and consequently some phonologists assume that this variant is best transcribed by ɨ. The distinction is not phonemic; it makes no difference in meaning, and scarcely any in style, whether a person says /rǽbɨt/ or /rǽbət/. Some centuries ago when English spelling was more free than it is now, the scribes of the period normally indicated the vowel with *e*, just as we do now, but in the west of England there were many instances of *u* in the writing and in the east many instances of *i*, suggesting that the distinction may have been geographical also. There is little agreement among phonologists about whether /ə/ or /ɨ/ happens to be a feature of any present-day regional pronunciation. Unstressed vowels in the speech of most of us are evidently pretty much of a mixture.

But closely related to all of this is the question of the final syllable of words like *happy, money, nicely, easy.* This is an unstressed syllable, or having tertiary stress at best, so we should assume that the vowel will have been reduced to /ə/ or /ɨ/, which means that /hǽpiy/ or /mə́niy/ and the rest cannot be defended with any consistency. Chances are understandably remote that anyone except a pedant or an incurably curious person is going to consult a dictionary in order to learn how to pronounce the final syllable of *happy,* but such a circumstance does not give a dictionary editor license to ignore it. Presumably the user of the dictionary already knows what a *girl* is or what *sand* is, yet the lexicographer defines both words with as much studious effort as he bestows on words like *adiabatic* or *bahuvrihi.*

The more recent desk dictionaries have dealt with the problem as follows:

American College Dictionary (1947)	hăp′ĭ
Webster's New Collegiate Dictionary, 6th ed. (1949)	hăp′ĭ
Webster's New World Dictionary (1953)	hap′ĭ
Webster's Seventh New Collegiate Dictionary (1963)	'hap-ē
Standard College Dictionary (1963)	hap′ē
Random House College Dictionary (1968)	hap′e
American Heritage Dictionary (1969)	hăp′ē
Webster's New World Dictionary (2d ed.)(1970)	hap′ē

These solutions are not entirely satisfactory. The *i* spelling encourages very literal-minded persons—and there are such—to pronounce the vowels of both syllables of a word like *silly* exactly alike. Linguistically it makes an interesting trick, but the result in the speech of most of us is not English and scarcely merits encouragement. The *ē* spelling suggests, on the other hand, that the vowels of both syllables of a word like *easy* are identical, in spite of E-Z spot removers and E-Z scalp emollients. Many phonologists transcribe the unstressed syllable as /ɨy/, which accords reasonably with what many of us actually say.

A television set or performance is ordinarily referred to in America as a "TV." Till now the expression has preserved a measure of stress on both syllables, /tìyvíy/. The spelling *teevee* is also rendered occasionally as *teevy* and that suggests a development within the foreseeable future to a pronunciation /tíyvɨy/, already regular in compounds like *TV dinner* or *TV snack,* but less common as an independent form. There seems little likelihood that the industry will be able to stem this usage, any more than the telephone industry was able to prevent people from calling a telephone a phone.

A number of words normally ending with the /ə/ of an unstressed syllable have a variant /ɨy/ which we regard as substandard and old-fashioned. The development to /ɨy/ is a normal one, but there seems reason to believe that these forms have given way before the pressure of "spelling pronunciation." *Extra* and *soda* have been with us for a long time and are thus sometimes written *extry* and *sody* to represent folk speech. Names of flowers like *begonia* and *petunia* become /bəgównɨy/ and /pətúwnɨy/. Ailments like *neuralgia* and *pneumonia* and *diarrhea* become /nəræ̃ljɨy/ and /nəmównɨy/ and /dàyəríy/. The latter word has its stress on the last syllable and consequently has its full vowel quality, like *idea,* which becomes /àydíy/, except in places where it is stressed on the first syllable, /áydɨy/ or /áydeh/. As a result of this process, many names of women have familiar variants: *Amanda, Mandy; Annetta, Nettie; Matilda, Tillie; Martha, Marty; Miranda, Mirandy; Rebecca, Becky; Sarah, Sally.*[5] A variety of sausage attributed to the Italian city of Bologna, the nearest English equivalent of which is /bəlównyə/, has undergone much the same kind of phonetic treatment to become *baloney* /bəlównɨy/, or, commonly, /blównɨy/. Unlike the other words in this group, the pronunciation is not regarded as old-fashioned, although it is considered informal.

---

5 Loss of the initial syllable in some of these names results from a different linguistic process known as "apheresis" (cf. p. 300).

The meaning of an English phrase depends in part on its stress pattern. Where a noun is preceded by an adjective as modifier, the noun receives the primary stress: *nìce dáy, gòod shów, fàt chánce, hàrd wórk.* If the modifier itself is a noun, the stress falls on the first word: *dóghòuse, óil wèll, áirplàne, fíg lèaf.* Sometimes these last are explained as compounds; after they have been hyphenated for some time they may come to be written as single words. There is very little logic to guide the earnest seeker in this area; over the course of time certain practices have become established, even though they often appear contradictory. One simple rule has no exceptions: the elements of a certain compound cannot bunch too many letters of the same kind, as in *beeeater* or *skiinterest* or even *knockkneed.* Such compounds are written with a hyphen or as two words. But since English syntax makes it possible for many words to operate as more than one part of speech, the same combination of words can have two entirely different meanings, depending on the placement of stress: *bláckbìrd* or *blàck bírd, Whíte Hòuse* or *whìte hóuse, bádmàn* or *bàd mán, sléeping bàg* or *slèeping bág.*

Expressions which have become set phrases with specialized meanings often reduce the vowel of the final syllable to weak stress and a neutral quality. *Forehead* has long been pronounced as /fɔ́rɨd/ or /fɔ́rəd/ or /fárɨd/, the /fɔ́rhêd/ variant having come in as a spelling pronunciation. Spelling pronunciations like /bréykfæ̀st/ and /kə́pbɔ̂rd/ for *breakfast* and *cupboard* do not display one's learning. *Clapboard* is less familiar; the "approved" pronunciation is /klǽbərd/. *Waistcoat* is a British word and it is pronounced /wéskət/; this pronunciation is also encountered in the United States. A spelling pronunciation, however, is common in both England and this country.

Certain "rules"—established not by higher authority, but by long and honored practice—govern our pronunciation, and while we may be unaware that they exist, let alone be able to summarize them, we sense when they have been violated, usually realizing vaguely that "something is wrong." There are suffixes, for instance, which may be reduced in some words, but not in others. Thus an adult male who does not damage things when he comes in contact with them can be described as a /ǰèntəl mǽn/; a male adult in general may be referred to as a /ǰéntəlmən/. The final syllable is similarly reduced in *Frenchman, Englishman, Dutchman:* /frénšmən/, /íŋglišmən/, /də́čmən/. British *postman* /pówstmən/ is often regarded as a literary expression in this country; we call a mail carrier a *mailman* /méylmæ̀n/. Words with a /mən/ suffix are: *fisherman, countryman, alderman, clergyman, journeyman, nobleman, penman, husbandman, seaman, police-*

man, plowman, merchantman, infantryman, longshoreman. The /mæ̀n/ or /mæn/ suffix appears in later coinages: *handyman, businessman, airman, medicine man, superman.* Usage with respect to *cameraman* and *hangman* appears to be divided. The *-ful* suffix likewise has stressed and reduced forms. *Sinful, beautiful, awful, merciful* and others in which the suffix has a metaphorical meaning are pronounced /sínfəl/, /byúwtəfəl/, /ɔ́fəl/, /mə́rsəfəl/. The literal senses, *mouthful, cupful, handful,* are /máwθfùl/, /kə́pfùl/, /hǽndfùl/. A similar distribution appears with the *-land* suffix, primarily in geographical distributions. *Holland, midland,* and *island* are pronounced /háln̩d/, /mídlənd/, and /áylənd/, but in compounds like *Disneyland* and *cloudland* the suffix is pronounced /læ̀nd/. Those that have been in long and frequent use may be recognized by their pronunciation: *England, Iceland, Greenland, Scotland, Ireland, Maryland.* On the other hand, *Thailand* and *Basutoland* and the like generally retain the vowel quality of the final syllable. *Newfoundland* has in common American usage two reduced syllables, /núfəndlənd/, although the local population call it /nyúwfəlæ̀nd/. *Nobody* and *somebody* have both the stressed and the unstressed forms: "Nobody, but nobody, undersells Gimbel's," where the form is /nówbâdɨy/. In ordinary conversation /nóbədiy/ and /sə́mbədɨy/ are usual; the name *Peabody* is similarly reduced in some localities. On the other hand in *everybody* and *anybody* the full vowel is retained.

English has not one but two basic stress patterns, corresponding broadly to the two "vocabularies" which make up its lexicon. By historical relationship English is a Germanic language with close affinities to Dutch, Flemish, German, Danish, and Swedish. In its earliest recorded form it was the language we call Old English, or more familiarly Anglo-Saxon.[6] Among the features which characterize the Germanic languages, in contrast to more distantly related languages like Latin and Greek, is a "fixed stress," as distinguished from the "movable stress" of the related non-Germanic languages. All of us have lived with it, but few of us have noticed how it operates. For instance, in certain words—usually the ones relating to

6 Anglo-Saxon is properly the name given to the people of several Germanic tribes that dominated England from the middle of the fifth century till the Norman Invasion of 1066. Their language was always called English, even by Alfred the Great, King of the West Saxons. The term Old English is applied to the language spoken and written from 450 to 1100; Middle English from 1100 to 1475; and Modern English since 1475. The names were bestowed by Henry Sweet; he called the language we speak New English but it never caught on. The abbreviations used to designate the several periods are: OE, ME, and MnE.

matters of everyday concern—the stress of the word always remains on the "root" syllable, regardless of how many prefixes or suffixes may be attached. A syllable like *-lieve-* /líyv/ may be expanded to *belíeve, disbelíeve, disbelíeving,* and even a superlative like *disbelíevingest* to describe the ultimate skeptic. Another such root word is *stand* with compounds like *withstánd, understánd, misunderstánding.* In contrast to the fixed stress of Germanic or "native" words in English is the movable stress of the "borrowed" vocabulary which the English language acquired from Latin and Greek, often by way of French. These words began to enter the language soon after the Norman Invasion of A.D. 1066 and continued to come in for some centuries afterwards. Cognate with English *stand* is the Latin form *-stant-* which occurs in words like *cónstant, substántial, instantáneous, substantiálity.* Or the Greek root word *phon-* which linguists have found especially useful: *éuphony, phóneme, phonólogy, phonométrics.* In words like these, the more syllables are added, the further the stress recedes to the end of the word.

Speakers of English are not aware of the complexity of the stress pattern of their language till someone points it out to them. Most of them handle this mingling of stress patterns with little difficulty. There has been some remodeling over the course of the centuries, it is true. A few words taken in at an early date have become naturalized in accordance with the native stress: *revíve, revíval, revívalist; allów, allówance, allówable; attráct, attráctive, attráctiveness. Capital* has drawn *cápitalist* along with it; we should expect /kəpítəlìst/, a British pronunciation.

Most of the familiar English words of two or more syllables have their stress on the first syllable, which is as a rule the root syllable: *bútton, hándsome, yéllow, hópeful, píllow, wálrus.* In French the stress is more commonly iambic, the stress falling on the final syllable, but scores of words that were originally French have long ago fallen into the English pattern: *béauty, détour, géntle, náture, cértain, nátion, mádam.* A shift from various original patterns to the English stress pattern continues, though it is proceeding rather unevenly along geographical lines. We observe a tendency in the speech of various persons, particularly those from the rural South, to stress the initial syllables of words like *cement, insurance, umbrella, police, museum, idea.* Intimations of "correctness" are involved, and those who adhere to the older and more widespread pronunciations frequently regard the innovators as "wrong." Conversely, in some words the stress has been moved to the initial syllable while nonstandard speakers stress the second syllable, for instance, *théater* in standard English but *theáter* in a less acceptable variant; or *míschievous* in standard English but *mischíevious,* with the addition of a syllable, in nonstandard speech.

For a variety of reasons the pronunciation of certain words has never settled on a single stress pattern, and educated people have been able to use either pronunciation without discrediting themselves: *obligatory, formidable, acclimate, automobile, Byzantine, harass, adult, address, applicable, abdomen, combatant.* It calls for a special kind of aplomb to live serenely in the presence of divided usage, which probably explains why a list like this is relatively short. Most users of English shun the luxury of free choice in such matters.

SOME PHONETIC PROCESSES

Early in the present century a Polish oculist named Lazarus Ludwig Zamenhof put together an artificial language which he called Esperanto. The name in the language itself means "hope," and it was Zamenhof's dream that his language might bring together people of every nation all over the world within the federation of a common tongue. Apart from its vocabulary, which is borrowed from a number of European languages, Esperanto is relatively easy to learn, for all verbs and nouns and modifiers are completely regular.

In contrast to such a rigidly regular "artificial" language as Esperanto, the various "natural" languages like English and Turkish and Swahili have a general regularity to them, otherwise it would be impossible for anyone to learn them. An English-speaking child who has mastered the pronunciation of the fricative /ð/, for instance, can count on being able to use it in words like *the, them, these, those,* whenever he has occasion to use the words. Such a feature is regular; it will not change during Lent or during periods of high barometric pressure. Most of the noun plurals in English are regular, and so, in spite of appearances, are the verb tenses. But tucked away in odd corners of every natural language are curious irregularities that the native speaker defends with all his heart. Undoubtedly much of our attachment to the wretchedly erratic spelling system of English stems from some such sentiment.

To an extent beyond anything we realize, we nurture irregularities, large and small, that serve no linguistic function as such, but which operate with terrifying effectiveness as social gauges. In an artificial language everything is regular and a person needs a willful stupidity in order to get himself into difficulties. In a natural language there are snares and pitfalls everywhere; a person cannot utter ten syllables without giving out a substantial amount of social information about himself.

LANGUAGE CHANGE

A fundamental axiom of language study can be summarized in just two words: "Language changes." This should be obvious from the existence of a subject like etymology in which we trace the changes in the meanings of various words. But to the person encountering etymology and etymological principles for the first time, everything seems hopelessly haphazard. Regarding etymology Voltaire is said to have quipped: "Etymology is a science in which the consonants count for very little and the vowels count for less." So indeed it may have seemed in his time. Voltaire died in 1778 and it was in 1786 that Sir William Jones delivered his celebrated paper suggesting a relationship between Sanskrit and Latin and Greek, so giving a tremendous impetus to scientific etymology and providing it with a systematic basis.

So far from being haphazard, language change is remarkably regular. We assume, in fact, that every change can be identified and classified, though not necessarily explained. Nobody knows why languages change; we simply know that they do, and that nothing will keep them from changing.

The English language has been changing during its long history. There have been profound changes in its phonology, and although many of the sounds we use in present-day English appear to have been in use also in Old English, the organization of the sound system was quite different. Compared to English of the present, Old English had a highly complex inflectional system. Where syntax today is largely a matter of word order and of connectives, that of a thousand and more years ago depended primarily on the endings of verbs, nouns, adjectives, and pronouns. Most changeable, of course, has been the vocabulary. The study of each of these subjects has its own procedures, governed by rules of its own.

Now whenever a language changes, a difference presently comes about in the way different people talk, simply because a language change does not affect all the speakers of a language, and least of all does it affect all of them at the same time. There is, for example, a major dialect boundary which runs east and west across the United States, north of which the word *greasy* is typically pronounced as /gríysiy/ and south of it as /gríyziy/. We can describe the medial consonant of the one pronunciation as voiceless and the other as voiced, applying completely neutral terms to the distinction. We can also explain that the Northern form is constructed on the noun base /gríys/, and that the Southern form has developed analogically with *easy* /íyziy/. In tracing the history of the pronunciations we can show that Shakespeare spelled it *greazie* (*As You Like It*). But which of the two is "correct," or "right," or "standard"? Or can it be that both of them are?

That we can deal thus with differences in language, discussing them in neutral terms, often troubles those who believe that we have a moral obligation to take sides from the beginning. Any kind of language feature can be described and explained, we must remember, even though we feel no compulsion or even mild inclination to adopt it. In the case of the two pronunciations of *greasy,* there are so many people who use one and so many who use the other that we cannot judge on the basis of sheer numbers. And we can scarcely judge on social standing or education. Here we simply conclude that this is "divided usage." Some language changes, on the other hand, cut off small groups of the population from the main body of it, and then the kind of social prestige these people manifest determines whether the language feature is to be regarded as standard or otherwise.

The language itself is always perfectly neutral. Usage never is.

SOUND CHANGE

A familiar pronunciation difference that we encounter in the United States at large is a distinction between the diphthongs /aw/ and /æw/. The first we commonly associate with the speech of Midwesterners, and the other in a general way with the speech of Southerners. Although such things cannot be determined with as much certainty as we could wish, we assume that both are developments going back to an earlier stage in the language when there was only one diphthong, probably /aw/. Just when certain speakers of English began to produce the /æw/ diphthong we do not know. It hardly matters. But there are those who feel we should be concerned, and they advance theories that have to do with diet or humidity or atmospheric pressure, evidently hoping to keep the same thing from happening again. The change was simple and clear-cut, and it affected all occurrences of this diphthong. Such a change we call "isolative," since it does not depend on sounds preceding or following. Not all occurrences of /aw/ necessarily become /æw/ when such a sound change operates, for over against isolative changes there are others called "combinative" in which sounds take on the coloring of other sounds preceding or following. In most of southern Canada and also in eastern Virginia and eastern South Carolina the /aw/ diphthong remains /aw/, except before voiceless consonants, and in this environment it becomes /əw/. *House* then becomes /həws/, and the expression *down and out,* in which most Americans have /aw/ in both *down* and *out,* is pronounced /dáwn ən ə́wt/.

Such reference to sound change makes it seem a common occurrence, and a capricious one, as though someone might wake up in the morning and discover that all his short vowels had mutated between the time he went to bed and the time he got up. That does not happen. The sound changes we encounter run their course over a period of decades and often several centuries—usually several successive lifetimes. A change affecting all the diphthongs in English began in northern England in the fourteenth century and ran to completion in the eighteenth century. It is known to scholars as the "English Vowel Shift." So gradually did it operate that not till 1874 did anyone become aware that something had happened.[7]

At any given moment in history we have in current use several centuries of the language. There is the speech of the grandparents who could at one time converse with their own long-deceased grandparents and at the other end the speech of the grandchildren who will ultimately be able to converse with their still to be born grandchildren. For a person now aged 70 or 80 such a span of generations could easily reach back to the time of the American Revolution.

Yet even within the relatively short span of a single lifetime a person will be aware of language change, although he never identifies it as such. When we are young, say eight or ten, the speech of older people strikes us as stately and dignified. As we grow older, in early middle age, the speech of older people has come to seem less dignified, but meanwhile we discover that young people are using what impresses us as an increasingly depraved form of English. This is true not only of vocabulary but even of pronunciation and occasional sentence constructions. When we ourselves have become pensioners, we shall have caught up with the older folk, who now sound surprisingly normal when they talk. But we shake our heads over the future of the language if it is to be left to the tender mercies of the youngest

---

7 The first scholar to notice that a language change had occurred was Alexander J. Ellis (cf. footnote 3 in Chapter 3). Some thirty-five years later Otto Jespersen provided the name: the English Vowel Shift.

generation. At any given time all the then-living generations can understand each other; the real and subtle language changes that are occurring, however, we commonly interpret as deteriorations. Actually, however, they are nothing more than normal language changes. It seems incredible that someone may once have been troubled over our own use of the language, wondering where it would all lead someday.

5

special problems

Words like *fatal, blessed, vermin, common, circus,* and *vinyl* as spoken in ordinary conversation have the identical vowel in the unstressed syllable, that is, the neutral vowel /ə/. Till recently our commercial dictionaries indicated this sound in a number of ways, one of the more common practices being to italicize the letter and to mark it with a breve [˘]. In words like *beggar, better, elixir, motor, picture,* and *zephyr* it was the usual practice to superscribe the letter with a tilde [˜]. This gave nervous persons all the encouragement they needed to conclude that they "ought to pronounce all the letters": /féytæ̀l/, /blésèd/, and so on. Such pronunciations which pay overscrupulous attention to the spelling and which go above and beyond the standards of normal linguistic decency we call "spelling pronunciations."

Spelling pronunciation marks a person who knows how English words are spelled—a minor token of literacy, after all—but who shows off this knowledge by conspicuously aggressive pronunciations over against those of the rest of the population which he dismisses as "careless" or "slovenly." It is an intimidating form of snobbery, and relatively few people feel prepared to withstand it. But it is a false and insecure snobbery. Fiction writers occasionally employ it to caricature the speech of the social climber.

Many spelling pronunciations are in themselves harmless, and over the course of time a good many of them have attained preferred status. *Perfect* came into the language as /pǽrfìt/ and that was probably the way Chaucer and his contemporaries pronounced it. He spelled it *parfit;* later the grammarians introduced the current spelling in order to make the word look like Latin and ultimately the present pronunciation prevailed. *Vittles* was respelled to *victuals, det* to *debt, doute* to *doubt,* but spelling pronunciations never caught on. *Comptroller* was a misguided effort to respell *controller,* and although /kəntrówlər/ is still standard, the spelling pronunciation /kâmptrówlər/ is common and stands a good chance of displacing the other. *Theater* was spelled *theatre* or *teatre* when it was first adopted into English, the latter indicating that in the French fashion the initial consonant was /t/. The stop has long since given place to the fricative /θ/. Similarly, names like *Matthew, Thaddeus, Bartholomew, Dorothy, Martha, Katherine, Elizabeth,* and *Theodore* have the shortened forms *Matt, Tad, Bart, Dot, Marty, Kate, Bet,* and *Ted,* reflecting the time when the *th* spelling symbolized the stop /t/. The full forms were subjected to spelling pronunciation, presumably as being more dignified, but the nicknames have been left untouched. Thomas is an exception; so is the Thames in England and Canada. The Thames in Connecticut is gradually becoming /θéymz/.

Solecism, a designation for a language error of any kind, is a scholarly word more often encountered in print than exchanged in conversation. Historically only /sáləsìzm/ has any justification, but most persons looking at the word assume that it ought to be /sówləsìzm/, which is a usage that more recent pronunciation guides have come to acknowledge as standard. This guessing at the pronunciation of unfamiliar words has introduced /dáwr/ in place of /dúwr/ for *dour,* /béyd/ in place of /bǽd/ for *bade,* /ráybɔ̀ld/ in place of /ríbəld/ for *ribald,* /dáyəs/ in place of /déys/ or /déyəs/ for *dais,* /párlyəmənt/ in place of /párləmənt/ for *parliament. Clothes* has been /klówz/ in respectable circles for hundreds of years, but /klówðz/ keeps coming back because of the spelling. The same may be said of /ɔ́ftən/ side by side with /ɔ́fən/ as a rendering of *often.* Words like *Christmas* /krísməs/, *listen* /lísən/, *thistle* /θísəl/ and others like them are unaffected since they are more commonly spoken than read. The unstressed vowel of words like *sailor, senator, advisor, tutor* may receive secondary stress, along with a self-conscious /ɔr/ pronunciation of the final syllable. Such a phenomenon is the reverse of the lowering of stress and vowel quality that occurs with the gradation—or "downgrading"—of vowels to /ə/. What occurs here is an "upgrading" from /ə/.

It is a cliché among British fiction writers that speakers of London Cockney "drop their *h*'s." But we do pretty much the same thing in the case of a word spelled with initial *h* in an unstressed position, as "He had his hat in his hand." In a multisyllabic word, the first syllable of which is unstressed and spelled with initial *h,* we often have divided usage: *hotel, historical, humane, heretical, hysterical.* Since the indefinite article *an* is employed in words beginning with a vowel—or vowel sound, as *an hour, an honor*—*an* is justified on phonetic grounds in phrases like *an historical novel, an hysterical woman, an hotel,* but only if the speaker regularly pronounces these words with no initial /h/ whatever. Understandably the pronunciation of /h/, long lost from words like *vehement, annihilate, forehead, vehicle,* is a spelling pronunciation wherever it appears. In the same way it is a restoration in *historical* and *historian,* but so general a restoration that the *Oxford English Dictionary, Webster's Third New International Dictionary,* and the *Random House Dictionary* do not so much as recognize another pronunciation. The spellings *an historical* and *an historian* do occur as relics from the time before /h/ was restored. This has no phonetic justification, very little historical justification—and only social reasons for remaining in existence at all. In the eyes of many users of English it is useless snobbery. In words like *herb* and *homage* one does as he pleases and will have good company in either case.

Spelling pronunciations of *hiccough* and *epitome,* to rime with *off* and *home,* as well as of nautical expressions like *boatswain* and *forecastle,* must be set down as instances of simple garden-variety blunders.

A few British words retain their earlier pronunciation in England but have been done over in the United States as a result of zealous spelling pronunciation. *Ate* /éyt/ is etymologically /ét/ but this usage has become substandard in the United States and appears to be losing ground in England. In Noah Webster's *Blue-backed Speller* the words *date, hate, fate,* and *grate* are rimed, but not *ate,* suggesting that the pronunciation may have been standard as late as the first third of the nineteenth century. *Clerk* /klə́rk/ generally remains /kláhk/ (or /klárk/) in England; as a proper name it is usually respelled. *Suggest* remains /səǰést/ in England, but is commonly /səgǰést/ in America. Transplanted place names have received uneven treatment. *Worcester* (spelled *Wooster* in Ohio) is an example of an earlier pronunciation preserved; *Berkeley* on the other hand has been remodeled.

Draught as in *draught beer* turns up as /drɔ́t/ in the utterance of those who visualize /drǽft/ as being spelled *draft.* The brewers and the advertising community have the interesting option of using the *draft* spelling consistently or of giving birth presently to an entirely new word pronounced /drɔ́t/, related perhaps to *drought.*

ASSIMILATION

"Assimilation," as the name indicates, is the process or act of making several unlike things similar or alike. We speak of assimilating food; it means that beans and potatoes and the cooked flesh of animals have been turned into bones, sinews, and cholesterol. We also speak of assimilating outsiders or foreigners into a culture; it means that they acquire various postures and attitudes and reactions, and presently become indistinguishable from any other members of their new culture.

Assimilation in language means that one sound begins to resemble some other sound, either partially or completely. Every contrast that exists between speech sounds can be affected to some degree by assimilation. When vowels adjoin the nasals /m n ŋ/ they are usually nasalized in English, especially when there is a nasal before and after the vowel nucleus: *among, nine, mean, name.* Voiceless consonants between vowels are likely to become voiced, especially when they occur in unstressed syllables. As is apparent from the spelling, words like *is, was, has, as* at one time ended in voiceless fricatives, and the voicing that has taken place is assimilative. Such voicing is especially likely to occur when a stressed syllable follows the fricative. For instance words like *lúxury* and *éxecute* have medial /kš/ and /ks/, but with a shift in stress, as in *luxúrious* and *exécutive,* the medial consonants are voiced to /gž/ and /gz/. As a secondary result we sometimes hear the hypercorrect /lə́gžəriy/. This phenomenon, to be discussed later, is called a "back formation."

Although an individual sound is usually regarded as an item that can be isolated, in normal speech there is some shading from the sound immediately preceding and the one immediately following; in fact, in a phenomenon called "umlaut" the sound causing the change is merely anticipated and does not adjoin the sound affected. Such shading is normal. The expression "careless speech" has a reproachful ring to it, suggesting something we ought to avoid, yet few things can prove more distressing than the "careful" speaker, the person who produces every vowel and consonant with exaggerated precision.

Assimilation occurs, as we have suggested, in the manner of articulation. A voiceless sound can be voiced next to or near voiced sounds, but a voiced sound may be unvoiced in voiceless surroundings. In English such unvoicing took place before *to* in several set combinations: *have to, has to, used to, supposed to:* /hǽftə/, /hǽstə/, /yúwstə/, /səpówstə/, all of them expressions of obligation or habitual action. These are quite different from *have two* or *used two* in: "We have two Siamese cats" or "Clarabelle used two eggs in the pudding." Occasionally someone enunciates *have to, has to* and the others as though they were *have two, has two,* and the rest. This is not a mark of careful speech at all, but a hypercorrection, in fact, a spelling pronunciation.

Assimilation also takes place from one point of articulation to another. In the word *grandpa* there are three medial consonants: /ndp/. Both /n/ and /d/ are alveolar, one a continuant and the other a stop; likewise /d/ and /p/ are stops, one alveolar and the other bilabial. First /d/ assimilates to /n/, becoming /n/, which in turn partially assimilates to /p/, becoming a bilabial nasal /m/, and the result is the familiar /grǽmpə/. An even more complex development goes on as *going to* /gówiŋtə/ becomes *gonna* /gónə/, the form most speakers of English employ in un-self-conscious talk. There are at least three intermediate stages which may be used depending on the relative formality or informality of the situation. In representations of vulgar or uncultivated speech words like *seven, eleven,* and *captain* are sometimes respelled as *seb'm, 'leb'm, cap'm.* Persons from all levels of society use them informally, but if these assimilated pronunciations appear in slow or measured speech they sound distinctly uncultured. The word *sentence* undergoes several kinds of assimilation. It may be /séntns/ but also /sénəns/ and /sénˀns/ with the glottal stop as a variant of /t/. The reporter who hears a public figure use the pronunciation /ìnənǽšənəl/ has no choice but to spell it *international,* a courtesy we accord public figures but sometimes withhold from obscure or unpleasant ones.

Unstressed monosyllabic words, referred to above (pages 69–70), not only undergo downgrading of the vowel and complete loss, but the consonants are subject to assimilation. The connective *and* may be reduced to /n/ in a phrase like *here and there* /hîyr n ðéhr/. Between labial consonants it becomes a labial /m/ as in *top and bottom* /tâp m bádəm/; between velars it becomes /ŋ/ as in *dog and cat* /dɔ̂g ŋ kǽt/. Advertising people appear to have some intimation of such a development. In former times the ampersand & was a symbol for *and,* but now it gives the impression of awesome dignity as *Abercrombie & Fitch, Beagleheaver & Son, Montgomery Ward & Co.* H. W. Fowler used it throughout his *Modern English Usage*[1] as did the editors of *Time* during their earlier decades of publication. *Time* has long since abandoned it, and it no longer appears in the second edition of Fowler.

---

1 *A Dictionary of Modern English Usage,* 1st ed. (London: Oxford, 1926); 2d ed. (London: Oxford, 1965).

The current trend toward *'n'* seems aimed at a relaxed and folksy style: *sun 'n' rain wear, fun 'n' fixin's,* and the unphonetic *Dog 'n' Cat Hospital.* Even *Hansel 'n' Gretel* is not unheard of—an absurdity to anyone familiar with German.

Negative words are likely to appear in unstressed positions in the sentence—by far the greater number of them with the verb auxiliary—and in consequence they have been subject to a variety of assimilations. The familiar *can't, didn't, wouldn't* represent principally the loss of an unstressed vowel. In *shan't* and *won't* (the latter formed on *woll,* an alteration of *will*) the /l/ has also become assimilated. Before a nasal /n/ the sibilant /s/ is often assimilated, as in the pronunciation /bínəs/ sometimes heard for the word spelled *business.* In the same manner *isn't* and *hasn't* have assimilated forms /ínt/ and /hǽnt/, both of which have presumably become identified with *ain't,* or appear to have done so. *Doesn't* develops in like manner to /də́nt/ so that a speaker intending to say "it doesn't" may seem to his listeners to be saying "it don't."

DISSIMILATION

Sounds tend to resemble each other and to become identical or similar through assimilation, but they may also tend to become unlike, especially when the same sound is repeated at too brief an interval. Is it possible that our vocal apparatus automatically balks at repeating certain sounds and just as automatically selects others instead? This tendency toward making sounds unlike is called "dissimilation." Dissimilation in English affects the consonant /r/ more generally than it does any other, and /l/ occasionally. It is not a conspicuous language feature, but there are some words it frequently affects and these may be regarded as usage problems.

Belfry, which we associate immediately with one bell or more, had nothing to do with bells when the word was coined. It was an item of military equipment with a German name which was taken over by the French, modified somewhat, and passed along to the English who heard it as *berfrey* and almost immediately altered it by dissimilation to *belfry.* By any rule of etymology *mulberry* should be *murberry;* the French word for *mulberry* is *mure.* There is the French word *quatre,* 'four,' which is respelled in *catercornered* /kǽtərkɔ̀rnərd/ 'four cornered,' which is dissimilated to /kǽtɨkɔ̀rnərd/, in turn spelled *cattycornered* and then subjected to the ultimate cuteness in the spelling *kitty-cornered*

The /r/ in an unstressed syllable is often lost through dissimilation. The development is phonetically quite different from the "dropped /r/" in the speech of many Americans living along the Eastern seaboard and also that of many Englishmen. So *reservoir* becomes /rézəvɔ̀r/, *thermometer* /θəmámətər/, *caterpillar* /kǽtəpɨ̀lər/. In *governor* the usual development is /gə́vənər/. Side by side with this is *governess* where there is no dissimilation, and *government,* where there is loss of /n/ by assimilation to the neighboring nasal /m/. We also have *February* /fébwerɨy/ which then becomes /fébyɨwèrɨy/ as an unintentional rime with *January* /ǰǽnyɨwèrɨy/; *library* becomes /láybèríy/. *Surprise* and *particular* may be heard as /səpráyz/ and /pətíkyələr/ from speakers of standard English. There is also sporadic dissimilation of /r/ in words like *secretary* /sékətèrɨy/, *performance* /pəfɔ́rmənts/, and *interpret* /ɨntərpɨt/.

Dissimilation of /l/, though relatively rare, has occurred in the word *colonel* /kə́rnəl/. The spelling is military and for that reason reflects tradition. *Fulfill,* though commonly /fùlfíl/ or /fəlfíl/, has a variant /fərfíl/, partly as a result of dissimilation and partly on the analogy of words having a *for-* prefix.

The word *business* /bíznəs/ not infrequently has a dissimilation of the fricative to a stop with the pronunciation /bídnəs/. The name *Amabel* 'lovable,' a variant of *amiable* and often "clipped" to *Mabel,* has two bilabial consonants /m/ and /b/, and by dissimilation becomes *Annabel.*

SYNCOPE

The Greek word *katahedron,* after passing through Latin and French, has emerged as our English word *chair.* Greek *eleemosyne* followed a similar route and emerged in English as *alms.* The verb *had* is derived from a now lost Germanic original which in at least one of its forms must have quite closely resembled Gothic *habaidēdun.* And of course *had* is reduced even further, to a single phoneme, in words like *I'd* or *he'd.*

If this process goes on everywhere and if it affects every language, ultimately all human utterance ought to collapse to a single monosyllable, or to nothing at all. Naturally there are headshakers who feel convinced that this will surely come to pass unless we mend our ways and enunciate more clearly. But nothing so disastrous has happened in the thousands of years human beings have been talking. In fact, the supply of words is increasing at a headlong rate.

Words do become shortened in time, and the shortening of a word by loss of an unstressed element, usually a vowel, is called "syncope" or "syncopation." Some instances of it we have already noted (pages 69–70 and 85). A thousand years ago English nouns and verbs and adjectives had a system of inflections, which were generally a full syllable in quantity. Most of them disappeared completely; nearly all the others became syncopated at an early stage of the language. A word like *day's* in the language of A.D. 800 was written *dæges* and would have been pronounced /dǽyes/; by A.D. 1100 or earlier it would have become /dǽyəs/, and by A.D. 1400 it had become /dǽyz/, representing a complete loss of the unstressed syllable. Syncope of inflections of English nouns and verbs has proceeded irregularly. After consonants the *-en* inflection of verbs is still regularly syllabic in the few words where it has been retained. After semivowels the unstressed vowel has been syncopated, as in *grown, blown, lain.* Syncopation often occurs when an unstressed vowel immediately follows an *-en* inflection: *taken away* /tèyknəwéy/.

Unstressed vowels in other than initial or final syllables are also often syncopated. As a misguided reaction to this the vowel is sometimes "restored" by spelling pronunciation, the result being regarded as a nonstandard usage. *Interest* and *interesting* are /íntrəst/ and /íntrəstìŋ/ in standard English and have been so for a long time. Similarly *business* is /bíznəs/, *valuable* is /vǽlyəbəl/, *superintendent* is /sûwprìnténdənt/, *several* is /sévrəl/. To add a syllable to these words or to words like *diamond* and *emerald* may be interpreted as a self-conscious effort at correctness.

Syncopation of the vowel in unstressed prefixes and other elements at the beginning or end of a word has become widespread in current English in all areas of society, among the educated and uneducated alike. For that reason it can no longer be regarded as an emblem of untidy diction. The development has been mentioned briefly in another connection (page 70). The fact that such pronunciations have become part of the language has little more than passing interest except as a demonstration of the basic orderliness of language and of its systematic development. This kind of syncopation has undoubtedly been in operation in English considerably longer than we should suppose. As a result, by the time someone has called it to the attention of the public and sounded the general alarm, it is no longer an option but the normal pronunciation of a significantly large number of the speakers of English. We need to bear in mind that such a development is in keeping with the general pattern of the language; any attempt to stop it or divert it or reverse it will certainly bring about unanticipated and usually unfortunate side results.

EPENTHESIS

"Epenthesis" is a linguistic process essentially the opposite of syncope in that it consists of inserting an unstressed vowel between consonants where it does not etymologically belong. It is not a common phenomenon in English; it is considered nonstandard.

In words like *calm, palm,* and *balm* the /l/ has been lost following a back vowel and before /m/. It remains, however, following a front vowel in words like *film* and *elm*. Not infrequently an epenthetic vowel appears in pronunciations like /fíləm/ and /éləm/. *Athlete* and *athletic* are pronounced /ǽθəlìyt/ and /æ̀θəlétɨk/, such pronunciation more often by those with an occupational interest in the subject itself than by those who use the words casually and occasionally.

In some other instances there is at least a hint of analogy at work. *Arthritis* often becomes /àrθəráytɨs/ as though it were *Arthur-itis; disastrous* /dizǽstərəs/ is constructed on the word *disaster; evening* /íyvəniŋ/ may be constructed on *even,* or it may be spelling pronunciation; *umbrella* /əm-bərélə/ apparently borrows its rhythm from words like *number* and *lumber; rigmarole,* often /rígəməròwl/, is also spelled *rigamarole* as a variant, and follows the pattern of words like *ragamuffin* and *rig-a-jig*.

"Ease of pronunciation" would offer an engaging explanation, but many language scholars find this an evasion rather than an explanation.

EXCRESCENCE

An old farmer burst into a meeting some minutes after the proceedings had begun and discovered that those present were voting on an issue. "I don't know what yer votin' on, but I'm agin' it," he shouted. Now it would scarcely occur to us that *agin',* or *again,* represents the original form of the word and that, strictly speaking, *against* should be regarded as a corruption. In Old English a noun could be given adverb function simply by adding genitive *-s* to the noun. In the somewhat archaic style of Shakespeare it was possible to say:

> *Pray to the gods to intermit the plague*
> *That* needs *must light on this ingratitude.*
> —*Julius Cæsar,* I.i.58–59

The word *needs* can be translated by the somewhat more contemporary phrase 'of necessity.' In the same manner *mid* became *mids, while* became *whiles, among* became *amongs, one* became *ones* (respelled *once*), *two* (cf. *twain*) became *twice, three* became *thrice.* The list used to be a good deal longer, but a number of old-fashioned words have dropped out of the language.

Evidently it was on the analogy of words like *first, most, last*—all of which may also be used semiadverbially—that *agains* acquired final *-t* to become *against. Amongs* became *amongst,* a form which occurs occasionally in American English, but far more often in British. *Whilst,* similarly constructed from *whiles,* is an everyday word in England, but scarcely ever heard in America. Except for phrases like "betwixt and between" or a cliché like "betwixt the devil and the deep blue sea," the word *betwixt* from an older *betwix* is rare in this country. An "excrescent" *-t,* as it is called, has appeared in words like *across, once, twice, close, wish, attack* in some varieties of American English, but such forms are commonly looked on as being substandard.

If consistency had anything to do with it, we might argue that *acrosst, oncet* /wə́nst/, and *twicet* /twáyst/ deserve a place in the sun. This is where the machinery of usage operates deftly. The "right" people know the "rule" that permits them *against, amongst,* and *whilst* but stops short of *acrosst, oncet,* and *twicet.* Similarly, while *peasant* from French *paysan* maintains an excrescent /t/, *varmint* is borderline; *orphant* from *orphan,* and *sarmint* from *sermon* are regarded as archaic or uncultured.

INTRUSIVES

Here and there we encounter mildly improper verses exploiting the rime of *dance* with *pants.* At first sight this looks dubious, if not impossible, as a rime. But it is a typical "ear rime," one that needs to be read aloud.

When a nasal consonant, for instance, is followed by a fricative produced at the same point of articulation, an "intrusive" stop frequently appears between the nasal and the fricative. In a word like *dense* the final *ns* is commonly pronounced as [nts], thus homophonous with *dents.* There seems to be little social importance associated with the presence or lack of intrusive stops in one's speech. They may occur in words like *French, strange, attention, Kansas, comfort, length, warmth, lymph.*

Intrusive stops have also appeared in other surroundings. Before the final *-le* in words like *thimble, tumble, tremble, gamble* we have an intrusive /b/. *Thimble* is etymologically related to *thumb,* from Old English *þūma;*

tumble has an antecedent *tummelen; tremble* is derived from Latin *tremulāre;* and *gamble* comes directly from the word *game.* One who played games was a *gameler. Thunder* has an intrusive /d/; the German equivalent is *Donner. Sound* as in *sounded* has also an intrusive /d/; the word is derived from Latin *sonāre. Drown* has developed into *drownded* by the identical process; but *drownded* and *drownding* are considered substandard. Shakespeare spoke of *swoonded* for *swooned.* The process has been around for a long time; sometimes the developments are acceptable and sometimes they are not. *Chimney* becomes *chimley* partly by dissimilation and partly by analogy with the *-ly* words. *Chimbley*—a substandard form—has an intrusive /b/.

There is also an intrusive /r/ in many dialects of English, specifically those sometimes referred to as "*r*-less," and although the general manner in which it is developed differs from the way intrusive stops have come about, we recognize it immediately in words like *idear* and *Cuber* for *idea* and *Cuba.*

In current English there is a "linking *n*," which at one time involved a number of words, but is now limited to the distinction between *a* and *an.* Before a consonant we use *a*; before a vowel we use *an: a grape, an orgy.* Until two or three centuries ago "linking *n*" operated also in the pronouns *thy* and *my: my nose, thine eyes.*

English has of course many words with final unstressed /ər/: *brother, mother, father, sister;* all the "agentives": *worker, maker, talker, idler;* all the comparatives: *bigger, sweeter, plumper;* and scores of miscellaneous words: *jigger, figure, sugar, motor, liquor.* In the pronunciation of persons from *r*-less areas, final /ər/ is spoken as /ə/. Furthermore, in all the areas where English is spoken, *r*-less and otherwise, there are many words with final /ə/: *idea, Florida, Martha, Cuba, poinsettia, Rita, Paula, lava, melodrama.* In some local speech the list also includes words like *fellow, yellow, window, shadow, potato,* which are rendered as /félə/, /yélə/, and so on. Analogous to "linking *n*" then is a "linking *r*" in the so-called *r*-less speech areas. In these localities, like those in which /r/ is retained, the /r/ is regularly pronounced before words with an initial vowel: *brother-in-law* /brə́ðərɨnlɔ̀h/. On the other hand, *Brother John* is pronounced /brəðə ǰán/. Not all *r*-less speech communities are consistent in this. It is typical of New England and much of England; far less and sometimes not at all in the Southern states. And so, since final /ə/ automatically and regularly becomes /ər/ before words with initial vowel sounds (and sometimes before a pause), words like *idea* and *Cuba* are given the same final syllables as *better* and *brother*. That is, we should expect *The idea of it* /ðɨy âydíyər əv ìt/ but *The idea makes sense* /ðɨy àydíə mèyks sênts/. Contrary to the general impression, people like former President Kennedy do not regularly say *Cuber* or *idear*. These variants occur only before words beginning with vowels and sometimes at the end of a sentence. Elsewhere they are *Cuba* and *idea*. Characteristically, we notice pronunciations that are unfamiliar or that are different from our own, and pay no attention to the familiar ones. Those who pronounce *Cuba* and *idea* consistently as /kyúbə/ and /àydíyə/ do not observe these same pronunciations when they are used by others and thus fail to notice the *r*-less pronunciations before consonants.

Many people pronounce an intrusive /d/, very likely the outgrowth of zealous "schoolmastering" at the elementary and secondary school levels, in unstressed words like *in* and *on* when they appear before words beginning with a vowel. We have already observed that a word like *and* is commonly reduced to /ən/ in a phrase like *Jack and Jill* /ǰǽk ən ǰíl/. Such a reduced form is also possible before a word with an initial vowel: *eyes and ears* /âyz ən íyrz/. Out of respect for conventional spelling the teacher may insist on restoration of the /d/, so that we have /âyz ənd íyrz/. So far no harm has been wrought. But the user begins to add /d/ to other words ending in /n/, with the result that we get expressions like *On every occasion* pronounced /ànd évrɨy əkêyžən/ or *In our time* as /ìnd áwr tâym/. It may even occur within words: *imaginary* as /ɨmǽǰəndèhrɨy/.

BACKING

"Backing" is the name given to a sound change in which the pronunciation of a vowel is shifted for one reason or another from front or mid to back articulation. Backing in English has usually been a combinative development.

Initial labial consonants are phonetically related to /u/ and /w/ and have consequently been responsible for some instances of backing. *Father* originally had the vowel of *cat;* the same is true of *was* and *wall* and *water*.

The most important and widespread type of backing is that of /ȅ/ to /a/ before /r/. As such things go, it is four or five centuries old, and perhaps even older, but its acceptance into the various dialects of the English language has been most erratic. Several British names like *Berkeley* or *Hertford* or *Derby* have simply been respelled in America to *Barkley* or *Hartford* or *Darby* in order to preserve the pronunciation. On the other hand *Berkeley* and *Derby* in America have been subjected to spelling pronunciation and are regularly /bə́rklɨy/ and /də́rbɨy/. To pronounce them otherwise on the grounds that it would be more correct or that the English do it that way or that it has historical justification is snobbery. Some words have been respelled: *star, far, Harry.* By assimilation the name *Henry* developed a variant *Herry* which presently became *Harry.* The quality of the vowel varies from /hériy/ to /háriy/. The names *Clark* and *Sargeant* have been respelled; *clerk* is /kláhk/ in much of England, and by spelling pronunciation /klə́rk/ in America; *sergeant* has not been respelled and retains the back vowel both in England and the United States. The spelling of *heart, hearth,* and *hearken* is ambiguous; the pronunciation of the vowel is regularly /a/, although an older /hə́rθ/ survives here and there in cultivated usage and occasionally in poetry. *Earth* is regularly /ə́rθ/, but in some speech areas a back vowel may occur.

Not unexpectedly, several words have developed double forms. *Parson* and *person* now have separate meanings, but go back to the time when the clergyman was the only educated "person" in a locality. *Varsity* and *university* refer to the same institution; *varsity* has been carried over from a generalized British usage to a specialized usage in this country. *Varmint* and *vermin* refer roughly to the same kind of animal. The original form is *vermin* from Latin *vermis* 'worm.' Those acquainted with the literature of the Middle Ages know very well that worms formerly came in many sizes. Structural stresses permitting, they could be as much as a city block in length, could snort blue flames and vast quantities of dark smoke, and could become airborne with little difficulty. Vermin are now thought of as being small and virtually indestructible household pests like ants and flies. The word *varmint,* which has not only the backed vowel but an excrescent /t/, is a regional word, and is applied to predators like coyotes and foxes and skunks, especially in linguistically informal contexts.

The pronunciation /sártɨn/ for *certain,* /sármən/ or /sármɨnt/ for *sermon,* /búk làrnɨn/ for *book learning,* /tárnəl/ for *eternal* are regarded as substandard. The pronunciation /əmárɨkə/ for *America* has some regional currency. President Harry S. Truman used it in his public addresses after he had taken office as President. The "good" English people made considerable ado about it, seeing the English language once more in jeopardy. To avert disaster, Mr. Truman graciously modified his diction to "school of speech" pronunciation.

PALATALIZATION

Assimilation to each of the semivowels /r y w/ is a phenomenon of English and each produces its characteristic effects. That of /r/ we have identified as "backing"; that of the palatal semivowel /y/ is called "palatalization." The sounds that have resulted and which we therefore call "palatal" are /š ž č ǰ/.

Palatal consonants in the English language developed at different times and in somewhat different situations, although the semivowel /y/ is regularly involved. A word like *cheese* was part of the Anglo-Saxon vocabulary, although it came originally from Latin *caseus* from which our word *casein* is also derived. Several other words came into English from Latin during the early period, among them *chalk* and *chest*. Side by side with them were native Anglo-Saxon words like *child, cheek,* and *choose* and also a number of French words adopted after the Norman Invasion, among them *cherry, chair,* and *chain,* all with initial /č/. Sounds like this one have been in the language for so many years that there are no problems.

English also took over from French a number of words at an early stage of the Middle English period (Between 1100 and A.D. 1475), including several with a rounded high front vowel /ü/, as in French *fortune, nature, virtue.* English had no such vowel; it had been a phoneme of Old English, but the vowel system had been remodeled and could no longer accommodate the sound. In English of the time there was a high front vowel /i/, but it was unrounded; there was also a high rounded vowel /u/, but it was a back vowel. If producing these features simultaneously constituted a problem, a person could do the next best thing by putting them one after the other: first a fronted and then a rounded vowel. That is what happened. The diphthongal system of English had by this time begun to assume something of its present arrangement and the result from French /ü/ was a diphthong /iu/, or, more accurately, /yuw/. Thus *fortune* would be rendered /fɔ̀rtyúwn/, *nature* /nǽhtyúwr/, and *virtue* /vìhrtyúw/.

We have observed that when the palatal variant of /k/ is fronted beyond a certain point, the speaker of English recognizes another sound, the palatal affricate /č/. Likewise, when /t/ is assimilated to the palatal /y/, the result is also /č/. In a phrase like *hit you* /hít yùw/, for instance, the development in rapid speech is /híčə/. As long as the words adopted from French maintained the characteristic French iambic stress pattern, it seems likely that they continued to be sounded as though they were French, but once they began conforming to the English trochaic pattern, palatalization set in. *Nature* had become /néytyùwr/[2] and presently developed to /néyčər/. Other words that followed this same general phonetic change were: *picture, future, virtue, actual, century, suggestion, Christian. Courteous* is sometimes pronounced /kə́rčəs/, though more often /kə́rtyəs/ and even /kə́rtɨyəs/. *Virtuous* and *righteous* not uncommonly maintain the unpalatalized forms /vɨ́rtyuwəs/ and /ráytyəs/ and the reason is that they are restricted largely to pulpit utterance. *Courteous* has carried on an older and more conservative pronunciation because of the social situations in which it is typically employed. *Literature* in student diction is likely to undergo sundry indignities, as, for example, a reduction to /lídəčər/. In the utterance of its more staid practitioners the opposite extreme is represented in /lítərətyùwr/. Such care is rarely bestowed on the pronunciation of *legislature,* which is seldom anything except /leǰɨslèyčər/, not surprising if one has had dealings with legislators. *Culture* is ordinarily /kə́lčər/ in referring to preparations in which bacteriologists propagate bacteria, also in compounds like *agriculture* and *horticulture.* The same pronunciation is often used for a phrase like *mass culture,* especially where the reference is patronizing. In speaking seriously and reverently of the arts and letters one may use and hear /kə́ltyər/, but /kə́ltyùwr/—sometimes mockingly spelled "cult-yure"—is usually a hyperstandard variant. *Amateur* is usually /ǽməčər/; an unpalatalized variant /ǽmətər/ may be an attempt to straddle between the relaxed but usual pronunciation and the very correct /ǽmətyùwr/ in view of those to whom it is often applied.

By a development closely parallel to the one above, /d/ became palatalized to /ǰ/ as the result of a following /y/. The number of words in which it appears is relatively short; among them *soldier, verdure, graduate.* The /dy/ unpalatalized pronunciation often occurs in *verdure* and *graduate,* but also in *grandeur* and *educate.* In words like *individual* and *cordial* either /dy/ or /ǰ/ is possible. A /ǰ/ pronunciation, however, in *immediately, tedious, India* is regarded as British or a deliberate imitation of British pronunciation. In characteristic American speech this is so rare as to be a curiosity; instead there is likely to be an unstressed medial vowel: /imíydɨyətlɨy/, /tíydɨyəs/, /índɨyə/. *Indian* appears to have followed much the

---

2 At the time this change took place the diphthong was probably /ah/ or /aə/. What we call the "English Vowel Shift" was in operation during the Middle English period, but it would have had no effect on palatalization.

same development as *India.*[3] *Idiot,* sometimes spelled *ijjit* in local color fiction to represent /íǰət/, seems to be recessive, if indeed it was ever common.[4]

Directly following /s/ the palatal /y/ causes palatalization to /š/ in words like *ocean, special, fission.* The /š/ also distinguishes words like *patient* and *nation,* in fact, all the words with final or medial *-tion.* A word like *nation* was originally Latin but was taken over into French very early. As part of the English vocabulary acquired during the Middle English period the words were originally spelled *pacient* and *nacioun,* indicating that the pronunciation was either /sy/ or /š/. The present *t* spelling had nothing to do with the pronunciation. It was introduced during one of several periods in which Latin lore was enjoying a revival in England. To their great delight the copyists discovered that many English words were—or seemed to be—related to Latin originals, and as a result scores of words that had achieved fairly rational spellings on their own were made to conform to an obsolete Latin orthography with no concern at all for the way they happened to be pronounced.

At the time that *sugar* and *sure* came into English from French, the initial consonant was not /š/, but the cluster /sy/, but it then became palatalized to /š/. Several things have happened to *sumac,* which has been rendered as /súwmæ̀k/ but also /šúwmæ̀k/ and even /šúwmèyk/.

The /sy/ remains unassimilated in the verb *associate;* when the word is used as a noun it is palatalized to /š/ as /əsówšət/. This form also occurs in attributive use as *associate pastor* and *associate professor.* A word like *propitiate* is more often read than uttered and would therefore be less subject to palatalization than more familiar words.

The American pronunciation of the words *issue* and *tissue* is quite regularly /íšùw/ and /tíšùw/ or with reduction of stress /íšə/. British usage commonly prefers /ísyùw/ and /tísyùw/ which some speakers of American English use, although these pronunciations may be regarded as fastidious.

Before /uw/, corresponding to an older and still fairly widespread /yuw/ in England and parts of the United States, there is little palatalization of /s/. In British usage, words like *superman,* and *suitable* have the /yuw/

---

3 In *Tom Sawyer* Mark Twain selects as his villain an aborigine named Injun Joe, reflecting a pronunciation that must have been widespread a century ago. It seems not unreasonable to assume that the general attitude toward the Indian, and also toward a person like Jim in *Huckleberry Finn*—regularly identified as a "nigger"—was responsible for such phonetic reduction. Currently both pronunciations are much out of favor as instances of unpleasant ethnic associations.

4 Rudyard Kipling, *Captains Courageous* (New York: Century, 1897), p. 77. The *Oxford English Dictionary* cites *idget* (vulgar) and *nidget* (archaic).

nucleus in the stressed syllable, but in these words and others like them the initial cluster of the stressed syllable is commonly /sy/ and not /š/.

The phoneme /ž/ has come into English in a few words like *garage* and *beige*, derived from French, and in French-type feminine names like *Gisele, Gigi, Zsa Zsa.* Otherwise it regularly develops from palatalization of an earlier /ž/. In words like *vision, confusion, decision* the /y/—spelled *i*—has brought about the palatalization. The same situation applies in the words *brazier, crosier,* and *hosiery.* In a word like *azure* an early pronunciation would presumably be /ǽzyùwr/ and palatalization would develop this into /ǽžùwr/ or /ǽžər/. A similar development took place in *pleasure* and *measure* and *exposure.* In self-conscious speech this might be rendered as /plézyùwr/. Words like *usual* and *usury* may have either a self-conscious /yúwzyùwəl/ and /yúwzyəriy/ side by side with the everyday /yúwžəl/ and /yúwžəriy/.

The development of a word like *easier,* if it had followed the normal pattern, would have been /íyžər/, but through the strong presence of the positive form *easy,* the comparative has remained /íyzyər/ or /íyziyər/. *Version* and its derivatives, like *conversion, aversion, diversion,* are ordinarily pronounced with /ž/. Pronunciation with /š/ is characteristically British; when it occurs in American English it is usually in a studied utterance.

The bogey of "careful pronunciation" proves especially frightening to many people in the matter of palatalization. There is the suggestion, seldom uttered but often implied, that a person is more cult-yured and ed-yucated if he says /kríytyùwr/ than if he says /kríyčər/ for *creature. Critter* /krítər/ is, of course, completely beyond the pale. But the stuffiness of such diction is not so much the problem as is the lurking peril of overcorrection. When someone says /ríydyən/ and /gɔ́rdyəs/ and /mədyéstik/ for *region* and *gorgeous* and *majestic* it may be difficult to decide whether he is not very perceptive or is trying to play an obscure joke. *Massachusetts* is sometimes pronounced /mæ̀sətyúwsis/ or /mæ̀sətúwsits/ chiefly by speakers from the South and Southwest. *Verdure* is often rendered /və́rdyùwr/, but *virgin* as /və́rdyìn/ is misplaced humor unless the speaker does not know better. Nearly a century ago C. H. Grandgent[5] reported observing a classroom in which the students had been schooled in a highly affected pronunciation of words like *nature, fortune, educate.* He was scarcely surprised therefore when the students addressed their schoolmistress as /tíytyùwr/.

---

5 As reported in Kenyon, *American Pronunciation* 10th ed. (Ann Arbor: Wahr, 1951), p. 149.

LABIALIZATION

Following a vowel and immediately preceding a labial or velar consonant the semivowel [w] has developed as an allophone of /l/ in the speech of many persons. As a rule we associate it with the language of small children, although it is heard in the pronunciation of adults who have presumably carried it over from childhood. Thus words like *elm, film, pulp* are spoken as [éwm], [fíwm], and [pə́wp]; *elk, milk,* and *bulk* as [éwk], [míwk], and [bə́wk]. This "labialization" is also found in the last syllable of the word as in *little* and *bottle* [lítəw] or [wítəw] and [bátəw].

Conspicuous labialization of this kind we tolerate in small children, confident that they will presently grow out of it. In adolescents and adults we may find it annoying, like an infantile habit that should have been corrected. In such situations labialization is socially unacceptable and therefore "wrong," or "bad" English. Yet there are other situations, as we shall observe shortly, in which labialization is "right," or "good" English, and any deviation is "wrong."

Labialization of /l/ as a combinative sound change is still going on, but it has proceeded at an uneven rate at various times and places. This gives it rich social overtones and a situation in which one can fall easily into either substandard or hyperstandard usages.

Labialization took place some centuries ago following a back vowel and preceding a velar in a number of words, chiefly monosyllabic, like *walk, talk, chalk, yolk,* and *folk.* In *walk* the original /wálk/ developed into /wɔ́wk/, a pronunciation which is still fairly common, although a further development to /wɔ́hk/ is more generally prevalent. The words *yolk* and *folk* have simply become /yówk/ and /fówk/. But in more complex words, there have been several possibilities. In *catafalque*—not a problem word for most of us—either -/fɔk/- or -/fɔlk/- is standard. In most common present-day usage *falcon* and *balcony* are /fǽlkən/ and /bǽlkəniy/. Falconers themselves prefer /fɔ́kən/ and this pronunciation, like that of the family name *Faulkner* /fɔ́knər/, reflects the normal development of the word. *Falcon* as /fǽlkən/ is in part a spelling pronunciation and also a development from a form in which the vowel was /æ/ rather than /ɔ/. Since the word came into common usage as the name of an economy automobile this latter pronunciation has been reinforced as one we should anticipate from automobile salesmen. *Balcony* until a few decades ago had an alternate pronunciation /bæ̀lkówniy/, where the vowel would not have been labialized. There is some limited use of /bɔ́kəniy/, apparently analogical to *balk*

Balkan as a word in general currency is less than a hundred years old, consequently it is regularly either /bɔ́lkən/ or /bǽlkən/. *Volkswagen* most commonly occurs as /vówlks/, although many speakers of American English regularly say /vówks/. And others simply English the word as though it were *Folks' wagon.*

In the standard American pronunciation /l/ is not labialized following a front vowel and preceding a velar consonant as in *talc, silk, Wilkins, Kilgore, alcohol,* but occasionally there is labialization in *elk* and *milk.*

Labialization of /l/ before a labial consonant, that is /f v m p b/, involves a degree of lip-rounding in anticipation of the consonant itself. Here the assimilation has been highly irregular. In *calf, half, salve,* /l/ follows a low front vowel and precedes /f/ or /v/, and labialization has been complete. *Calve* is /kǽhv/ but is rare except in agricultural usage. The name *Ralph* has a traditional pronunciation /réyf/, occasionally heard in this country, though far more commonly in England; /rǽlf/ has the advantage of being backed by spelling. *Golf* among traditional players of the game may have the variants /gáf/ and /gɔ́f/; ordinarily those who have taken it up within recent decades say /gálf/ or /gɔ́lf/ and sometimes /gə́lf/, restoration of /l/ being largely a spelling pronunciation. In standard speech *gulf* has no labialization. Following high and mid front vowels and preceding labials, /l/ is sometimes palatalized and sometimes not. There is little or none in *elf, shelf, wilful, Wilfred;* in *self* and especially in compounds like *himself* and *herself* some labialization takes place in various parts of the country so that /hìmséf/ and /hə̀rséf/ are familiar variants. A parallel development takes place with respect to *twelve. Help* is ordinarily /hélp/, but /héwp/ and /hép/ are common in the South and parts of the Midland. The past tense of the verb is regularly *helped.* In the South there is a variant, generally nonstandard, stemming from an earlier form *holp* which may be either /hówlp/, but commonly /hówp/. *Alp, scalp,* and *pulp* show little evidence of labialization. *Bulb,* however, which is ordinarily /bə́lb/, may occasionally occur as /bə́hb/ in the South in the speech of persons from all levels of society.

In contrast to the irregularity and sporadic labialization of /l/ before /b p f v/, it is regular and apparently of long standing before /m/. Words like *calm, palm, alms, embalmer* in a few isolated speech areas appear as /kǽm/, /pǽm/ and so on, but ordinarily as /káhm/, /páhm/, and the rest. Spelling pronunciation has left its mark in this area, especially among public speakers who are distrustful of their diction. Thus among radio announcers and clergy a word like *psalm* often shows up as /sáhlm/ or /pesáhlm/ or /pizám/.

In all these words the restoration of /l/ is a hypercorrection. The family name *Holmes* is regularly /hówmz/ and /hówlmz/ is usually nonstandard. *Almond* is ordinarily /ǽhmənd/ or /áhmənd/ in standard English. Mass distribution of the nut has been accompanied by mass distribution of the word and the consequent spelling pronunciations: /álmənd/, /ǽlmənd/, /ɔ́lmənd/. In California, where a substantial part of the American production of almonds originates, the pronunciation is seldom anything other than /ǽhmənd/. *Salmon* is regularly pronounced /sǽhmən/; *salmonella,* however, is pronounced /sæ̀lmənélə/. It has nothing to do with fish, but is a form of food poisoning named in honor of a veterinarian, D. E. Salmon. *Balmy* /báhmɨy/ refers to the weather, but also has some application to persons of unstable temperament. The latter application arises from a confusion with an entirely different word, *barmy*—/báhmɨy/ in British pronunciation and along much of the Atlantic seaboard. The word is related to *barm,* an old word for 'yeast.' Excessive intake of yeast, specifically in the form of malt beverages, has been known to produce intoxication. To call a person who is drunk or simply euphoric /bálmɨy/ is not only an overcorrection, but plain error.

Labialization had already occurred in French in several words which were afterwards imported into English, among them *auter* and *sautier.* The grammarians restored an earlier Latin spelling, *altar* and *psalter,* after they had become English words. Since labialization in English does not occur before /t/, spelling pronunciation followed after a normal interval.

In a few words like *would* and *should* the vowel nucleus was /uw/ at a relatively early stage of the language, and in unstressed environments the labialization by /w/ presently accounted for the assimilation of /l/. We have written records in which the words are spelled without *l* as early as the middle of the fifteenth century. During the seventeenth century it was a common practice to write them as *wu'd* or *shou'd,* but the force of custom eventually eliminated these variants. *Could* in its original form had no *l* in its spelling. It acquired the present spelling with *l* some time after A.D. 1500 by analogy to *would* and *should* as an "inverted spelling."

In careful speech *almost* has the pronunciation /ɔ́lmòwst/, but in relaxed or rapid utterance /ɔ́mòwst/ is regular. Before the semivowels /w y r/ the /l/ is often vocalized in informal situations and even in the normal utterance of many well-educated speakers of English in words like *always* /ɔ́wèyz/ or /ɔ́wɨz/, *already* /ɔrédɨy/, *all right* /ɔráyt/, *million* /míyən/, *valuable* /vǽyəbəl/, *failure* /féyər/, *William* /wíyəm/, and so on.

Since in current English /r/ is phonetically closely related to /l/, we may anticipate some labialization of /r/. It does occur, to be sure, but only in pronunciations that are clearly childish or defective, as /wə́n/ for *run,* /wǽbit/ for *rabbit,* /fwə́m/ for *from.*

VOWELS AND DIPHTHONGS

Depending in part on who is doing the speaking and in part on who is making the analysis, the English vowel system is interpreted as consisting of somewhere between five and ten "pure" vowels—or simple vowel nuclei—and from two to four semivowels.[6] We have already observed that consonant and vowel sounds are affected to some degree by the sounds immediately adjacent to them. Sometimes the modification is quite marked, although the untrained listener is not likely to respond to it. Such changes or modifications can be described as regular developments arising from specific circumstances. Lengthening of vowels, for instance, before voiced consonants, or nasalization of vowels in the vicinity of nasal consonants may be identified and described as predictable phenomena. It would be pleasant if we could assume that all such matters can be reduced to inflexible rules and generalizations as they presumably are in an artificial language like Esperanto. But in a natural language like English we continually run into small bundles of exceptions which operate side by side with broad general developments. The exceptions have come about in a number of ways, usually as the result of dialect mixture, which in turn consists of a variety of holdovers from earlier patterns.

Although there are scores of examples, two words will illustrate this principle: *busy* and *soot.* As every schoolchild realizes, *busy* is not pronounced the way it is spelled. The present spelling reflects the pronunciation of a dialect of British English which at one time possessed enough prestige to support a literature and a spelling system of its own.[7] The accepted

6 Phonologists have been divided on this matter for many years. There are arguments for a "binary" interpretation of the English "long vowels" and diphthongs; there are also arguments for the IPA analysis or a modification of it. In fact, individual phonologists commonly make their own modification of the one or the other system. One clear advantage of the binary system is a practical one, namely, the fact that it can be adapted to an ordinary typewriter.

7 This was the dialect of the English West Midland, still spoken as the dialects of Manchester and Liverpool, known as "Mancusan" and "Liverpudlian." They are no longer taken seriously as literary dialects. A translation of the New Testament was made some time ago into the dialect of Liverpool, known as "Scouse," and there is available a guide to the dialect under the title *Lern Yersel' Scouse.*

pronunciation /bíziy/ is that of the dialect whose speakers have achieved or maintained enough prestige to establish a "standard" for speakers of English all over the world. Not many people say /búziy/ any longer. Those that do take a chance on identifying themselves with a cultural backwater. There is no reason to conclude from all this that a front vowel is better or more pleasing to the ear than a back vowel in such a situation—as in *pussy*—or that the people who say /bíziy/ are collectively wiser or more virtuous than those who say /búziy/. At one time in the past, two dialects were in competition, and English has preserved a characteristic feature of each. The predominance of one form of speech depends on a number of things, none of them linguistic, and all of them social or political or geographical.

Soot has three pronunciations: /súwt/, /sút/, and /sə́t/. It is not a word that calls up associations of elegance; in fact, an intimate acquaintance with soot suggests deprivation. The "right" people have electric heating or gas or heat pumps. The most common pronunciation both in the United States and in southern England is /sút/, and it assumes a personal experience with soot. Contrasted with this we have a down-to-earth pronunciation /sə́t/, but beside both of them there is /súwt/, which a person might use in making a scholarly reference or otherwise indicating detachment. Such developments of the vowel nucleus have parallels in other areas; these illustrate, however, the influence which accidents of economics and sociology bring to bear on our preference for one or another pronunciation.

In American English we have a dialect contrast in a small list of words having either /i/ or /iy/ as a nucleus, and side by side with it another list having /u/ or /uw/ as a nucleus. A descriptive generalization is possible here: words with simple nuclei tend to be old-fashioned and mainly colloquial while those with complex nuclei are socially preferred and characteristic moreover of the literary style. Some of them are actually differentiated by contrastive spellings: *sleek* and *slick; creek* and *crick, breeches* and *britches, gleam* and *glim.* The distinction between *sleek* and *slick* involves more in some cases than the social standing of the speaker; both have to do with a certain kind of smoothness, one concrete and the other figurative as well. *Breeches* represents a spelling pronunciation, but widespread, so that /bríyčəz/ is regarded as urban, referring to a style of wearing apparel; /bríčəz/ is more folksy and includes a wider range of garments, sometimes including feminine underwear. It is the only form that would be permitted in a comment like: "Ronald is getting too big for his britches." *Clique* is pronounced as either /klíyk/ and /klík/, though the latter is more likely to receive unfavorable comment from the purists. Naturally it has been confused with its homophone *click,* to which it is etymologically related, and students have been known to write things like: "This girl and I cliqued right from the start." *Been* tends more to divide along geographical lines than social. The /bíyn/ pronunciation has long been considered characteristically British[8] and Americans generally recognize it as such; /bín/ is characteristically American. The vowel has developed as a raising from /e/, in an older and not entirely obsolete pronunciation:

> *For of all sad words of tongue or pen*
> *The saddest are these: It might have* been.
> —Whittier, "Maud Muller"

The raising from /e/ to /i/ occurs before nasals in words like *English, England, enjoy, engage, engine, embrace* and a sporadic pronunciation, especially common in the Midland, of words like *pen* and *men.*

The pronunciation of a high back vowel, spelled *oo,* has engaged the interest of phonologists for at least three centuries. From the spelling one would naturally assume that the pronunciation ought to be "long *o.*" It seldom represents the /ow/ nucleus, except possibly in *brooch* /brówč/, but here spelling pronunciation is having its little day as /brúwč/, riming with *hootch, pooch,* and *smooch,* takes over. The simple nucleus /u/ occurs in a large number of words, many of them in very common use, most of them ending in a stop: *book, look, cook, took, shook, crook, good, hood, wood, stood, foot,* but *wool.* In a few the nucleus is /ə/: *blood, flood.* Also many have /uw/, most of them ending in a continuant: *goose, loose, ooze, gloom, fool, tool, proof.* Between the two is a long list of words in which either /u/ or /uw/ appears. The geographical and sociological distribution of one and the other is extremely complex; perhaps the only generalization that will hold any weight being that the old-fashioned pronunciation is commonly the one with the /u/ nucleus, while /uw/ appears in socially self-conscious usages. Many people employ the two pronunciations interchangeably, in some of the words. The list includes: *root, roof, hoof, hoop, coop, room,*

---

8 A few years ago my attention was caught by a graffito on the wall of a public convenience in York, England, which read as follows:

> The painter's work has being in vaine
> The shit house artist has struck again

Being is a variant which could not possibly occur in the United States. It represents the /iy/ nucleus, and also a very obvious spelling inversion with *ng* /ŋ/ in place of *n* /n/.

broom, sometimes also *moon, spoon, hoot,* and *food.*. *Hood* as a term to indicate a criminal is generally /húd/, a spelling pronunciation, but in Chicago and the nearby suburbs it is regularly /húwd/—a shortening of *hoodlum.*

The /yuw/ "triphthong," as it is rather inaccurately called now and then, in distinction from the /uw/ diphthong, occurs chiefly in English words which were adapted from French. Thus *bureau, viewpoint, muse, puny* (from *puis né* 'born later'). There are non-French exceptions: *Bermuda, Beulah, Kuhn, Fuchs, Cupid, Europe.* These are generally names of people or places.

The contrast between /yuw/ and /uw/ originally occurred following most if not all of the consonants of English. It remains in initial position, as in *use* (vb.) and *ooze.* It remains also following labial consonants: *fuel* and *fool; butte* and *boot; pure* and *poor; mute* and *moot;* sometimes following velar consonants: *cute* and *coot;* and following /h/: *hue* and *who.* A single contrast occurs following /g/, but so far as is known, not many persons observe it, or need to. The line from Keats' "The Eve of St. Agnes":

And threw warm gules on Madeleine's fair breast

offers relatively little trouble because scarcely anyone bothers to look up *gules.* A few do, and they discover (not very easily, it must be remarked) that it is the heraldic word for the color red, and a few of these may further learn that it is pronounced /gyúwlz/. The pronunciation /gúwlz/ would be spelled *ghouls.* The picture called up is interesting, but something other than what John Keats had in mind.

Following an alveolar consonant, however, the /yuw/ combination has been simplified to /uw/ in much of the United States, but unevenly, with the result that /yuw/ continues as characteristic of some regions and also as a socially preferred pronunciation in some segments of society, often as an adopted speech practice. Fiction writers in representing the not-quite-educated person have often had him saying *dook* for *duke, dooty* for *duty,* and *toon* for *tune.* Or a small boy may enjoin the other, "Sloot the flag, Herman." This stock caricature is actually very much like the *gonna, hafta, wuz,* and *uv* spellings—not to be taken too seriously.

An earnest effort to be "correct" is likely to lodge the speaker in trouble since usage in this area is treacherously contradictory. In the kind of speech often assumed by radio and television announcers, there is the word *news,* rendered /nyúwz/ in deference to a pronunciation required in the older dictionaries. On the other hand, *noon* has not been derived from

French and consequently it is always simply /núwn/, in spite of which countless announcers have brought us the /nyúwndèy nûwz/. And then there is also the hostess who with an air of elegance speaks of /nyúdəl syùwp/. It would appear that the reverse tendency is at work with respect to *coupon,* which should be /kyúpàn/ by any etymological considerations, but advertising agencies have promoted /kúwpàn/ with such vigor that the other is looked on as old-fashioned. *Percolate* has a strange variant /pérkyùlêyt/ as the result of an upgrading of the medial vowel, and possibly through analogy with *peculiar. Escalate* has become /éskyùwlêyt/ in hypercorrect English, perhaps by the same kind of upgrading.

The teacher in a high school English class was describing Sherlock Holmes's appearance. Along with the famous pipe and cape the teacher mentioned Holmes's familiar headpiece: "He wore a stalking cap. . . ." A student raised his hand: "I saw the movie on TV a couple of months ago and I thought his cap had a bill on the front and back." Millions of speakers of American English get no sense at all out of such an exchange. But there are several million of them who live in or near speech areas where the vowels of *cot* and *caught* have coalesced so that the vowels /a/ and /ɔ/ are not distinguished. The schoolboy who heard the phrase "stalking cap" was one of those people, and he supposed that his teacher had said "stocking cap."

Such a distinction as that between /a/ and /ɔ/ can be most confusing to follow. In a large part of the United States *on* is rendered as /an/, but in others as /ɔn/, and still others as /own/. Either /a/ or /ɔ/ occurs in *orange, sorry, foreign,* as well as in *cough, coffee,* and *office.* However, a person undertaking to mimic the /ɔ/ pronunciation on the assumption that he can make a simple one-for-one switch is certain to run into profound difficulties. Among the problem words are *clock, not, shop, sod,* but also *fog, frog, hog,* and so on. *Hog* often shows up as /hɔg/, for example, especially in the pork producing regions, and writers striving to achieve a rural effect are likely to use the spelling *hawg.* The pronunciation /hag/ is preferred in urban speech, especially in the North. *Dog* is almost everywhere /dɔg/ and local color writers spell it *dawg.* It actually is /dawg/ in parts of the Deep South. *God* has become /gad/ in most parts of the country, the older /gɔd/ being associated with oaths, spelled *Gawd,* and also with an unpleasant sanctimoniousness in the minds of many listeners. *Chicago* has either /a/ or /ɔ/ since both the pronunciations occur there, but as may be expected there is a good deal of fruitless discussion about which is "correct."

When a person attempts to remodel his pronunciation, he is likely to lodge himself in difficulties which make him sound at best peculiar and at worst silly. This is especially the hazard run by the person who has no training in phonology and whose idea of "improvement" amounts to a selective aping of items out of a "prestige dialect." "Broad *a*" is a notorious example. The vowel, phonetically between the low front /æ/ of *fat* and the low central /a/ of *father,* is characteristic of a number of speech localities, particularly New England, and it occurs in several words like *ask, pass, calf, laugh*—primarily before a nasal or fricative consonant. Zealous educators have transplanted a few of these items in far distant places; /ahnt/ for *aunt,* for instance, still flourishes in the schools of Minneapolis.

Typically the difficulty lies in trying too hard. The person who undertakes to employ what he regards as "broad *a*" usually assumes that it is a general replacement for /æ/, and consequently he puts the vowel where it has never occurred in any recorded dialect of English, past or present. Words like *cat* and *applesauce* then become /kaht/ and /áhpəlsɔ̀s/. In a compound like *bathmat,* the vowel of the first syllable may be backed, the second not, and so anyone who says /báhθmàht/ is trying far too hard. These are "hyperforms"—an insidious trap for the person trying to make an impression. The radio announcer wants, for instance, to say "Tenth at Grand" and it comes out /ténθ àht grǽnd/.

So far from being chaotic and unpredictable, the diversities of the various speech communities of English are in themselves remarkably orderly. In spite of occasional differences that seem considerable, the particular forms are generally intelligible. Most of the speech comes through directly, especially that of people whose speech we hear day by day. But where the language is significantly dissimilar we engage in "translation," whether we recognize it as such or not. That is to say, the person who ordinarily says /wɔ́hš/ for *wash* may be surprised the first time he encounters /wɔ́rš/ or /wɔ́yš/, but once he has become familiar with the variants, he makes the indicated "translation" automatically.

Whenever we engage in translating one linguistic form into another we are required for an instant to observe language as language, and this requires that we for a moment pass a social judgment. It may be approval; it may be disapproval. There are translations that we have performed so often and so routinely that we no longer pass judgment. Or we may have to do it all over again, as when we meet an acquaintance after a separation of a number of years and realize that we had forgotten the mannerisms in his language.

If all people spoke exactly alike, there would be no usage situation, and of course no usage problems. But no two people speak exactly alike and usage problems are a fact of life for us all.

"BAD" PRONUNCIATION

At a military installation in the Panama Canal Zone during World War II the office of the post chaplain was employed after hours as a sentry post. Late one evening the telephone rang, and the guard, a corporal from Atlanta, answered the call, here in transcription approximately as it sounded:

/čǽplinz ɔ̂fɨs gáhd spìykɨŋ/

The response has not been recorded.

Now as we realize only too well, there are many features of pronunciation which we regard as unconventional, and of these there are some we unequivocally disapprove of. Such pronunciations usually have recognizable associations with some regional or social group, or with some age or occupational or ethnic background, and on such bases we regard the pronunciation as "bad."

Generally the distribution of these features proves to be far more complex and contradictory than a first glance would indicate, and discovering this has been known to unsettle many people who embarked on a serious study of language. It explains also why professional language scholars usually deal more gently with these unconventionalities than elementary school teachers, journalists, mothers, and other custodians of private and public morals. In words like *huntin'* and *fishin'* we have what is erroneously called a "dropped *-g*." The spelling rather awkwardly indicates that in a single narrowly restricted position an /n/ appears where we conventionally encounter /ŋ/. But the replacement is only partial. In many places where /ŋ/ occurs, /n/ never replaces it, otherwise we should have frequent confusion between *sin* and *sing, thin* and *thing*. The list is long. The replacement seems in some cases to be a dialect matter, perhaps calculated, especially among elementary school pupils, and it arouses a predictable flutter of apprehension on the part of skittish parents and teachers who labor valiantly to "correct" it. As soon as the young person finds the /iŋ/ pronunciation socially more negotiable he discards the other, in spite of the correction and not because of it. But many of us have been taught to associate the final /in/ rather than /iŋ/ with the speech of the less educated. It is, of course, a feature of familiar or informal speech and it is fairly common—sometimes even exaggerated—in off-the-cuff talks by Presidents, educators, and others conversant with the more formal style. But in our minds it is the cowboy who goes "ridin' across the range," and if he did anything else we should brand him an imposter. It does not occur to us that the /in/ form may very well be the original and the /iŋ/, so to speak, a "corruption." Language features that we are instructed to dislike are commonly held up to us as corruptions and instances of decay, when, as we have observed, and shall observe from time to time, they are usually old-fashioned and nothing worse than that. So, depending on the situation, /in/ is out-of-date as contrasted with the now fashionable /iŋ/. But these considerations are secondary. That is not the way parents and teachers look at it. They become uneasy because they do not want their charges to be identified in the eyes of the public at large with the "have-nots." Things are never quite so simple as that, for there are some persons who regard the /in/ ending as standard—many of them well educated and with the best of social credentials, in this country and especially in England—and they in fact consider a too careful /iŋ/ ending a bit bourgeois.

But there are also those who overdo matters and who make themselves conspicuous by their hypercorrections. *Chicken* /číkɨn/ then becomes /číkiŋ/, *mountain* becomes /máwntiŋ/, *cousin* /kə́ziŋ/, *wagon* /wǽgiŋ/, *ruin* /rúwiŋ/, *fashion* /fǽšiŋ/. A little of this remains, but far less than there was several generations ago, evidently indicating that there is less alarm over the "dropped *-g*" than there used to be.

Side by side with the replacement of /iŋ/ by /in/, there occurs in many varieties of speech, though less frequently in that of the well educated, a development to /iyn/—actually an "upgrading" of the vowel nucleus—so that *hunting* and *fishing* are rendered /hə́ntìyn/ and fíšìyn/. Phonetically it calls for a more radical remodeling than the "dropped *-g*," and yet it seldom provokes unfavorable comment. Considerations like these illustrate some of the difficulties in judging one pronunciation rather than another to be incontrovertibly "bad."

It appears to be in the nature of pronunciation that even a few "defective" consonants will stand in the way of making us understood and especially of making us socially acceptable. Labialization of /l/ and /r/ is not unusual, yet a person aspiring to a position of leadership may find it a grave handicap since it is associated with hypocoristic speech, that is, baby talk. Difficulties in pronouncing /θ/ and /ð/ we associate with the foreign-born. Some decades ago it would have been cause for concern, but being a foreigner no longer carries the social stigma that it did four or more decades ago. Substituting /θ/ for /s/ we call a "lisp." Social attitudes toward lisping have varied remarkably over the course of time. Up to about twenty or thirty years ago a young woman could affect a lisp as a mark of coyness; in a young man it might identify a homosexual. Today it is apparently nothing more than a minor speech defect with few connotations. During the Restoration in England it was a stylish affectation among young men. In describing the Friar of the *Canterbury Tales,* Chaucer remarked: "Somewhat he lipsed for his wantounesse," giving the impression that around 1400 the lisp distinguished a sensualist.

Consonant clusters undergo a variety of simplifications, mainly by assimilation. When someone pronounces *through* as /θuw/, his speech may be taken to border on the hypocoristic, if not defective; yet /æst/ in place of *asked* /æskt/, or /fiθs/ and /siks/ for *fifths* and *sixths* /fifθs/ and /siksθs/ seem able to pass in all but the most formal situations. Applying our usual tests, we should be obliged to dismiss one as "bad" and approve the others as "good." Logic and consistency have nothing to do with it.

As we have indicated, our tolerance of individual difference in regard to vowels and diphthongs is far greater. Regional and social accents depend more than anything else on vowel and diphthong variation. Sometimes sounds fall together and this often happens before /r/. *Mary, marry,* and *merry* are homophonous over much of the United States, and there are few dialect regions in which there exists a viable distinction between *coarse* and *course,* between *oral* and *aural,* between *morning* and *mourning.* Every teacher of English composition has encountered instances of confusion between *are* and *our, card* and *cord, for* and *four,* or *they're, their, there.*

Now it stands to reason that, as such things go, a nine-vowel system might be relatively cumbersome. Most languages get along with far simpler systems. But since every language appears to have a few areas in which it seems to be needlessly complicated, it is possible that such a vowel system as we have performs that service for English.

That speakers of English typically and regularly employ a nine-vowel system is actually an assumption, and it rests on the conclusion of those who have made the analysis. They have listened to themselves, to each other, and to their colleagues, and practically all of them have the full complement. That is to say, this is an analysis of the language of the educated which has been made by educated people. Would a person from a different background—assuming that he had acquired the necessary training—come to the same conclusion? A few linguists have declared that nine vowels will not do; they have ten in their speech.

There is a kind of language, as we shall observe again and again, which the cultured and educated typically employ. We could call it "Establishment English" and a person born to privilege speaks Established English as his native tongue. One would suppose that people speak this language because they are educated; however, it is more likely that the converse is true, namely, that they have a built-in advantage for becoming educated because of the way they speak. Among these people may be the so-called "self-educated," more usual at the beginning of this century and earlier than they are now.

The familiar attitude toward the utterance of the uneducated, or the less-educated, or, more accurately, the never-will-really-be-well-educated, is that this language is slovenly or careless—to use two overworked terms—or in any event that it could be done much better. The listener is vaguely aware that it ought to come off more precisely, although he is at a loss to identify just what it is.

In the variety of American English perhaps arbitrarily identified as standard, the generally accepted inventory of vowel phonemes consists of the following:

	front	*central*	*back*
high	/i/	/ɨ/	/u/
mid	/e/	/ə/	/o/
low	/æ/	/a/	/ɔ/

Yet in the speech of many persons there exists little distinction, if any, between the vowels of the "low series" /æ a ɔ/ as contrasted with those of the "mid series" /e ə o/. How critical after all is such a distinction? That is to say, how much vital communication depends on the existence of these particular phonemic contrasts? Some contrasts, while they are indeed phonemic, nevertheless carry an extremely light load of significance. The contrast, for instance, between /θ/ and /ð/ is the same as that between /s/ and /z/, namely, voicing. While scores of words depend on the /s/ and /z/ contrast, very few depend on the one between /θ/ and /ð/. That is why an untrained person finds it so hard to notice the difference.

Disregarding the "*ask*-vowel," mentioned before as the Confederate vowel, and also a low back vowel in the stressed syllable of a word like *water* as pronounced in Philadelphia and along the New England coast, these two vowel series make three possible contrasts: /e/ and /æ/, /ə/ and /a/, and /o/ and /ɔ/. Of these three only the first has any significant number of "minimal pairs," that is, of words exactly alike except for this single contrastive feature. Many of them, like *head* and *had, send* and *sand,* cannot possibly be confused since they are different parts of speech and never occur in the same environment. A few of them, however, seem to be exceptions:

I felt tired so I *set* (*sat*) down for a spell.

My dog Palomar wants you to *pat* (*pet*) him.

All you could see at the pier was *nets* (*gnats*).

But it is exactly confusions like these that we stumble over again and again in conversations with certain of our acquaintances:

He always manages to get in *bad* (*bed*) with the boss's wife.

Context may make it clearer, but for the moment it can be puzzling.

It is possible that the high central vowel /ɨ/ is here actualized as /i/ in stressed syllables and /ə/ in unstressed ones. In view of such coalescences, we can set up a workable five-vowel system of American English:

	front	*central*	*back*
higher	/i/		/u/
lower	/e/	/ə/	/o/

Anyone accustomed to producing the contrasts made possible by the nine-vowel system finds himself cramped by a five-vowel system. Yet those who communicate in this manner do not sense any difficulty. It may appear sporadically among those with advanced educational attainments, but is more widespread among the less educated. These are the speakers of non-standard English, known technically as "Vulgar English."[9] Whatever its defects and deficiencies, the system does not keep its users from communicating and they do not even communicate awkwardly, as does a person with a distinct lisp or a marked labialization of /l/ or /r/. But when a speaker of standard English listens to a speaker of Vulgar English, he gets an impression of general muddiness. The latter, however, does not feel handicapped. It is like the position of a person who pronounces *pin* and *pen* exactly alike, and thousands of highly educated people do this. Where there is confusion he adds a modifier, tenpin, or common pin, or ball-point pen. We should, however, realize that the speaker of Vulgar English is likely to represent the speech of some geographic locality and frequently makes meaningful contrasts that may in turn be lost on the speaker of standard English.

---

9 "Vulgar" here is a colorless term with special technical significance. It refers to the "common people" as distinguished mainly from the scholars and other learned people. St. Jerome translated the Bible into the language of the common people and it has since been called the Latin Vulgate. In this sense *vulgar* is not to be regarded as derogatory.

The existence of this "dialect," if it may be called that, has been recognized from time to time. The idea, however, that we have not a debased or retarded or incomplete variety of English, but essentially another form of the language with an independent phonological system is something that educators do not gladly accept. It would be a good deal more reassuring to suppose that Vulgar English differs from its standard counterpart only in degree and that we can shortly bring the two together by nothing more radical than chinking in the gaps here and there.

Side by side with the pronunciation of Vulgar English we have a number of types of utterance which for one reason or another we regard as nonstandard. Commonly we dismiss them as "bad." But every pronunciation, standard or nonstandard, can be described in objective terms. And every pronunciation has some reason for existence. It is relatively easy to classify some pronunciations; deciding, however, whether they are socially acceptable presents a different problem and a far more difficult one.

Many of the considerations on which we make value judgments with regard to pronunciation have already been discussed, among them such matters as palatalization and labialization. In each situation the linguistic process is in itself perfectly respectable, for it has operated again and again in one language and another, and the results have been accepted by the best speakers of that language. But that is not always the situation. We have, for instance, in current English a divided usage in several words in which either /æ/ or /ey/ is possible as the nucleus of the stressed syllable. The words *status, data, stratum, granary* have both pronunciations, and for what it counts, the current dictionaries give the /ey/ pronunciation first. The option is free, but not entirely so. The pronunciation /stǽtəs/, for instance, cannot be regarded as "bad"; but among sociologists, who make status their business, the usual pronunciation is /stéytəs/. *Apparatus, gratis, ration* are also in this category, but, again for what it is worth, the dictionaries appear to prefer /æ/. WNI2[10] in these words preferred /ey/ and gave /æ/ a grudging second place. Must we regard the pronunciations with /ey/ old fashioned? Such things are extremely difficult to determine; despite samplings and surveys, if anyone managed to establish the data precisely, their usefulness would be ended, since a usage question has relevance only when a significantly large number of people cannot be completely sure of themselves.

10 WNI3 has based its choices of pronunciation on thousands of hours of tape recordings, chiefly of public figures, on radio and television. WNI2 relied on its consultants, a total of 114 public figures in education and government, who listed an average of 2.97 advanced academic degrees each.

That is why a dictionary which offers several options is more useful than a dictionary that gives only one. *Ignoramus* usually has /ey/ but there are those who pronounce it with /æ/. The same applies to *matrix.* *Patriot* divides along national lines; the Americans usually pronounce it with /ey/ and the British with /æ/. *Macron,* not a household word in any commonplace household, to be sure, has been threshed around by scholars for several generations; here again the British seem to prefer the nucleus /æ/ and the Americans /ey/. *Radio* and *radiator* almost consistently have /ey/ in the stressed syllable, but /æ/ enjoyed limited currency some years ago. Occupation, social standing, geography, nationality, history—all of these in a measure determine the choices we ultimately make.

Consistency is not altogether wanting here, but the general pattern is not distinguished by it. In day-to-day utterance we have clear boundaries between *rack* and *rake, mat* and *mate;* with *data,* however, the lines seem to disappear so that /déytə/ and /dǽtə/ are not two separate words, but one. While the distinction is phonemic, it functions on a social rather than a semantic level. The fact that one says /déytə/ rather than /dǽtə/ identifies him in the mind of certain persons as having linguistic taste and discernment. Others may regard him as a snob. No one can predict with any degree of assurance which will be which, especially when the preferred pronunciation of words like *status* and *apparatus* and *radiator* is governed by such whimsical considerations as frequency of use or point in historical time or geographical location.

And then there are pronunciations which, in the estimation of the better-informed, mark the user as somewhat less than alert. The word *Babel* (Genesis 11) has been pronounced /béybəl/ from of old, but those unfamiliar with Genesis commonly say /bǽbəl/ through confusion with an unrelated word, *babble.* *Babel* is not a common word; about the only occasion anyone has to use it is in singing the Christmas carol, "It Came upon the Midnight Clear." As a rule it is mispronounced there.

Such a contrast between the nuclei of stressed syllables operates in many words, and now and then a particular word causes people to write to usage authorities; consult dictionaries, both current and obsolete; and indulge in a good deal of uninformed bickering. Ultimately everyone wearies of the strife and it becomes bad form to bring up the question at all. This has happened to several words, among them *alternate, gaseous, drama.*

But hypercorrectness is always an interesting possibility. It serves to single out the person who is unsure of himself. Many times he takes refuge in spelling pronunciation—a notoriously treacherous solution. Consider the words which end in *-ine* or *-ile*. *Asinine* is regularly pronounced /ǽsənàyn/; *alkaline* may be either /ǽlkəlìn/ or /ǽlkəlàyn/; *feminine* is only /fémənən/; *margarine* may be either /márǰərìn/ or /márǰərìyn/; *gasoline* is only /gæ̀səlíyn/. Through words like *crystalline, Philistine, quinine, mezzanine, aniline* one threads his way with apprehension. As may be expected, there are some dismal misses:

> *When you see the sign*
> *It's* genuine.

Versatile in the United States is ordinarily pronounced /və́rsətɨl/; in British usage, however, it is usually -/tàyl/. *Mercantile* may be /mə́rkəntìyl/ or /mə́rkəntàyl/; rarely -/tìl/. *Juvenile* and *infantile* are commonly heard as /ǰúwvənàyl/ and /ínfəntàyl/, in phrases like *juvenile delinquency* or *infantile paralysis,* but also "morning after" reproaches like *juvenile behavior* or *infantile remarks.* The unstressed variants are also current. There appears to be no consistency in this pattern, which makes it a source of much confusion and hypercorrection.

And then there are analogical pronunciations. The principle of analogy involves the "ratio" formula of elementary arithmetic: *grape* is to *ape* as *grate* is to *x*. The *x* naturally turns out to be *ate* /eyt/ even though it was historically /et/. Unfortunately many people fall victim to a false analogy of some kind.

Mischievous, heinous, grievous, on the analogy of words like *devious, serious, tedious,* pick up an additional syllable to become /mìsčíyvɨyəs/, /híynɨyəs/, /gríyvɨyəs/. We associate such a development with persons of limited culture and education and so we dismiss it as a "bad" pronunciation. In other words, the analogy is an unauthorized one. On the analogy of *editorial, memorial, senatorial,* we hear *electoral, doctoral, pastoral* pronounced as /əlektórɨyəl/, /dàktórɨyəl/, /pæ̀stórɨyəl/. These are also considered incorrect. The form *gubernatorial,* of questionable etymological support, is now to the highest degree standard, but for a century after it was introduced there were those who insisted that it should have been *gubernatoral.* There were similar comments about *senatorial* and *presidential.*

Homogeneous /hôwmòǰínyəs/ often occurs in nonstandard utterance as /hòmáǰənəs/, clearly under the influence of *homogenized* (milk). *Escape,* pronounced /èkskéyp/, has been influenced by, *exclaim, excuse, excrete. Sherbet,* vulgarly rendered /šə́rbərt/, lends a doubtful distinction to every person named Herbert. *Siren*—not the kind that gave Odysseus and Orpheus trouble, but the kind police and ambulance drivers employ—is properly /sáyrən/; /sàyríyn/ has some historical antecedents but seems largely influenced by an unidentified Irene. In the pronunciation /rékənàyz/ for *recognize,* the speaker has analogically but improperly involved the word *reckon* with an assist from the principle of assimilation.

In a few words we encounter a phenomenon known as "metathesis," which, to put it simply, consists of reversing certain elements. In the early days of the English language *grass* was often pronounced /gærs/, *bride* and *bird* were confused again and again, and *ask* was /æks/, a pronunciation still lingering on in folk speech. *Pretty,* which in careful speech occurs as /prítɨy/, by the same process becomes /pə́rtɨy/ in less formal speech. *Children, iron, apron* often appear as /číldərn/, /áyərn/, /éypərn/. *Cavalry* pronounced /kǽlvərɨy/ has Biblical overtones; *perspiration* is sometimes /prèspəréyšən/, and analogy may also have been at work here. *Bronchial* and *larynx* as /bránɨkəl/ and /lárniks/ are nonstandard. *Nuclear* has been pronounced /núwkyələr/ so often by distinguished persons that this usage may ultimately become standard despite the heroic efforts of the purists.

FOREIGN WORDS

The English language has served for centuries as a nesting place for foreign words from all parts of Planet Earth, though the extent to which this has been significant is vastly exaggerated. American English contains a number of Indian words, for example—most of them place names. Yet it is safe to say that no Narragansett Indian would recognize the Massachusetts town of Cochichuate as his own, no Ojibway the Michigan city of Muskegon, and few if any Navajos would understand the usual pronunciation of Biklaibito in Arizona as a Navajo phrase. *Squaw, wampum, papoose, mugwump,* and *tobacco* have been thoroughly Americanized. A speaker of Arabic finds it hard to claim as his own words like *alcohol, mohair, sofa, coffee;* only with difficulty and some prompting does a Dutchman recognize *brandy, gas, yacht,* and *cookie* as words that were originally Dutch. To suppose that these are still basically Narragansett or Navajo or Arabic or Dutch is absurd.

When a word is taken into English, it starts becoming Englished at that very instant. The problem is to know how far the process has gone at any one time. Words like *gentle, beauty, mutton, nourish* may be recognized as French in a vague way since they have been thoroughly done over and the results have been accepted for hundreds of years. To pronounce them as though they were still French would be hyperpedantry. Other expressions, however, still have a good bit of French about them—*coup d'etat, laissez faire, garcon*—and only an ignorant person pronounces them as though they were English. *Garçon* comes out something like /gàrsúŋ/, which is not Parisian by a long ways, but quite wholesome compared to the /gárkàn/ tourists have been known to say.

Unlike the Swiss or Belgians, we Americans do not need to depend on our ability to use foreign languages in order to make our way in the world. Whether this is good or bad is for the moment beside the point. Neither do we find our language so impoverished that we need to resort to other tongues to express subtleties of which English proves incapable. The result of all this has been that our employment of languages, particularly German and French, often becomes a form of symbolic behavior.

In our folklore the German scholar is studious and analytical, given to such tepid forms of dissipation as stowing away liters of lager, playing plaintive songs on the zither, and hiking about the countryside in suede shorts known as *lederhosen.* Now if we think of ourselves as studious and analytical we will make sure that our conversation is larded with an appropriate ration of Teutonisms; which ones they are does not really matter. The fact that there are ready-to-hand English equivalents is completely irrelevant; words like *Existenz* and *Philologie* and *Mensch* will lend a scholarly aura to a conversation, and a word with an umlauted vowel is impressive. In our folklore the French people, quite by contrast, are regarded as worldly, possessed of a singularly unrepentant attitude toward various forms of sinfulness. Americans tend to think of Victorianism as normal, though they would like to identify themselves with French hedonism. Since worldliness covers a far broader spectrum than does studiousness, the number and variety of words used in English that are plainly French are greater than those that are plainly German.

The pronunciation of French words by speakers of English is governed by one simple generalization, namely, the more a word is used by Americans and Englishmen the less it ultimately sounds like French. The only way, in fact, that a word can pass itself off as academic French is to be virtually unknown to the general English-speaking public. Four words demonstrate how this relentless Englishing process operates: *coupé, menu, mayonnaise,* and *première.* In the early days of automobiles, the industry, what there was of it, wavered between assuming an image of elegance and catering exclusively to the incongruously named "carriage trade," or being "just plain folks" and wooing the mammon of the mass market. In the classification of horse-drawn conveyances a coupé was a pretty posh buggy. The word is still spelled *coupe,* its accent cast aside along the way, and for the last forty years it has been pronounced /kuwp/. If the word *menu* had remained exclusive and obscure it might still sound reasonably French, /məníw/ perhaps. The final *-u* was a rounded high front vowel and remains so in France. *Menu* made its first recorded appearance among speakers of English in 1837, but within the century, eating places had multiplied unbelievably and the proprietors needed a name for the lists of their offerings along with the retail prices. The corner saloon had its *free lunch,* but this needed to be more selective. *Bill of fare* was perhaps ambiguous, as was *program. Menu* was brief, conferred the kind of toniness even the dingiest beanery cook dreams of, and was all but impossible to misspell. It is commonly /ményùw/, sometimes /ményə/. *Mayonnaise* has also been subjected to the indignities of the food trade, as it is called on to stand in for less expensive spreads. It has fallen into the English stress pattern as /méyənèys/. For *premiere* several dozen variant pronunciations are current. Of them all /prímyèhr/ appears to be the most generally accepted, clearly a compromise between the Hollywood /prìmíyr/ and what sounds like French to those who have never been seriously exposed to it.

A la carte and *à la mode* prove difficult to deface completely, although the latter sometimes wavers between an Englished /æ̀ləmówd/ and /æ̀ləmə́d/. *Debutante, matinee, gourmet, fiancée* are also recognizably French; *éclair* would unquestionably become /íyklèhr/ almost instantly except that it has been protected by the stresses of the phrase *chocolate eclair. Negligee* and *lingerie* have preserved a /ž/, although /ǰ/ occurs in a "slightly marked-down" variant. *Lingerie* represents a compromise between the French nasal vowel and the English vowel: /lànžəríy/. *Coiffure* has done better than we should normally expect, but that seems to be because the expression *hairdo* offers the fainthearted a viable alternative. The usual pronunciation is /kwàfyúwr/ or /kwàfyə́hr/. *Hors d'oeuvres* has the genuinely vulgar form /hɔ̀rs dóvərz/ which an occasional well-intentioned hostess has accepted on good faith with disastrous consequences. The rounded mid-front vowel of *oeuvres* does not occur in English except as an allophone of /ə/ preceding /r/, as in *bird* or *girl.* As a result the most common rendering of the phrase is /ə̀hr də́hrvz/. It is as much as most speakers of English can manage.[11]

Words like *protégé, monsieur, milieu* compose a class by themselves. They are the property of persons who already possess a passable French, and while it is never considered good form on the part of a speaker of English to make the supreme sacrifice of pronouncing French as though it really were French, the words have been at best only lightly Englished.

Italian words like *pizza, andante, lasagna, mafioso, bravo* maintain their credibility as Italian words as long as they do not sound too blatantly English. A spelling pronunciation would be as fatal here as elsewhere, although the spelling is more dependable than it is in other familiar languages. But one scarcely worries about whether the stressed syllable is a simple nucleus or a diphthong, or whether the medial consonants make up a long consonant or a cluster. The pronunciation /píytsə/ does not sound English; it must be Italian.

Spanish words have been anglicized with an unusual earnestness, especially in the Wild West of the old days. The *vaquero* of Spanish became *buckaroo, juzgado* 'condemned' became *hoosegow, la riata* became *lariat.* But the Spanish of the Mexican restaurant is treated with some respect; foods like *tortillas, tacos, enchiladas, chili* are given at the very minimum the kind of pronunciation one would achieve after a year of Spanish in high school.

Some German words have been beaten completely into an English shape: *sauerkraut* /sáwrkràwt/; *dachshund* /dáksənt/ and even a spelling pronunciation of sorts, /dǽšhàwnd/; *kindergarten* /kíndəgàrdən/; *weiner* /wíynìy/. Others have maintained recognizability as German: *Weltschmerz, Umlaut, Sprachgefühl.* The German system is enough like English that it calls for little strain to remodel a word. The extent, however, to which the remodeling is done depends on whether the word is most used in the kitchen or the lecture hall.

Before /m/ or /n/ in a word having French origins, a vowel written with *e* is pronounced as /a/ in words like *ensemble, encore, entourage, entente, entree.* In certain others the speaker is given an option between /e/ and /a/: *envoy, envelope, centigrade, centimeter.* In still others /e/ is regular: *centipede, entry, engagement.* Anyone who pronounces *ensemble* with /e/ is

11 The /vr/ cluster of French suffers wretchedly on the lips of users of English. During World War II an important city in the invasion of Normandy was Le Havre, which Americans and British to a man pronounced as Lee Harve /lìy hárv/.

not trying hard enough, while anyone who pronounces *centipede* with /a/ is trying altogether too hard. The fundamental rule in usage, including pronunciation, is: Do well enough, but never too well—which is sometimes paraphrased as: Quit while you're ahead. *Endive* with /a/ is for many listeners a case of doing too well. After all, it is only a salad green. With words like *envoy, envelope, centigrade* every man is on his own. How does the listener respond to another who speaks, for example, of /ánvəlòwp/? Is he impressed by the speaker's sophistication or irritated by his presumptions? The choice is not between right and wrong, but between appropriate and inappropriate, in other words, a well-tempered sense of situation.

The names of cities and other geographical designations pose special problems. As a rule they defy etymology and logic. Chances are overwhelming against any outsider who can score perfectly on clusters of names like: *Waltham, Quincy, Gloucester,* or *Greenwich Village, Houston Street, Gramercy Park,* or *Desplaines, Goethe Street, Devon Avenue,* or *Buena Park, La Jolla, Los Angeles*. Every locality has at least one place name to bewilder the outsider. Near Phoenix there are Spanish names by the score; so there is also the little old lady from the East who lends her best Spanish pronunciation to Baseline Road, one of the highways in South Phoenix. Much of language is intended to distinguish the insider from the outsider. Nothing, of course, makes the distinction more radically than household words employed within a family.[12] Place names are the common property of the people of the community.

Foreign place names are indescribably tricky. We speak of Paris and Rome and Geneva and Copenhagen and Berlin and The Hague. They are all anglicized. We are not permitted to anglicize Quito or Buenos Aires or Iquique. To say /pàríy/ or /rówmà/ or /žənéhv/ shows that one is trying too hard. It is not necessary to go the full distance, to pronounce Milan as /mìláhnò/—merely stressing the second syllable will do—but /máylən/, as in southern Michigan, goes too far in Englishing. On the other hand, calling Florence /fìhrénze/ is an affectation. The thread between too little and too much is often hard to follow.

It is the pronunciation of Latin which serves as the classic example of

12 One evening I was visiting a young lady *en famille,* her mother and an older sister also being present. The mother suggested by and by that I might like a cup of coffee and the older sister went to the kitchen to prepare it. Some minutes later the mother asked how the coffee was coming along and the young woman answered, "It'll be ready in a few minutes. It's just started to puke." There was a muffled explosion of embarrassment by the mother but rich laughter by the young women. Obviously I could be "trusted" with a household expression.

right and wrong in these matters, since it illustrates the contradictions of English usage and the curious snares laid for the unwitting and the unwary. There is no conscious conspiracy. But it is part of the intuitive approach the "right people" have in such things.

We assume first of all—though somewhat tongue-in-cheek, to be sure—that everyone will have studied Latin at least through Virgil and will consequently have mastered the school-book pronunciation, which is really nothing more than an attempt to approximate the way Romans spoke their language at the beginning of the Christian era. It may be a guess, but it is a good one. Except for working out classroom exercises, however, or declaiming select passages from Cæsar or Cicero or Virgil, a person normally avoids school-book Latin pronunciation. The Germans have made it a practice to translate words from Latin and Greek into German, but when a word like *Prozess* 'process' slips through, the Germans treat it as though it were their own /pròtsés/. Such terms are usually scientific or philosophical. Church Latin, employed chiefly in singing anthems, medieval or modern, is generally the way an Italian would read Latin. The ability to employ this pronunciation with confidence identifies the speaker or singer as one who has the leisure for cultivating an intimate acquaintance with medieval writings, or one who possesses the talent for singing in a choir, Episcopalian as a rule, preferably "high church." On appropriate occasions one may impress his church Latin into service for quoting scripture (the Latin Vulgate, naturally), or for echoing some sententious passage from one of the church fathers. Legal Latin, the kind used in courts of law, is the only kind that many people ever see or hear. It is also the language of legislative assemblies and sundry mottoes. It proves most authentic when it sounds like English and not at all like school-book Latin. Thus *habeas corpus* /hèybyəs kɔ́rpəs/, *sine die* /sàynɨy dáy/, *e pluribus unum* /ìy plûrəbəs yúwnəm/, *cave canem* /kèyviy kéynəm/. The rule applies to all national, state, and academic mottoes rendered in Latin and goes back, of course, to the time before it occurred to anyone that there was a "correct" way to pronounce it, when Italians read Latin as though it were Italian, and Germans as though it were German, and Englishmen as though it were English. University and college campus Latin defies all systematic classification and only the person who has traveled the rocky road of academe its full distance can be aware of its contradictions. Campus Latin has recognizable antecedents in both school-book pronunciation and brash unblushing anglicization. Yet no one seems offended by the strange hybrids that come as a result. *Alma mater* is commonly given as /ǽlmə máhtər/, *magna cum laude* /mæ̂nyə kəm lɔ́dɨy/ may also be /mâgnàh kùwm láwdèy/ or a mixture of the two. No one but a university professor would dare to manifest such lack of sensitivity toward a language the last of whose native speakers died more than fifteen centuries ago. *Curriculum vitae* is also a strange scramble: /kərîkyələm víytày/. The effect, almost needless to say, is perplexing, but it serves to hold at a proper and respectful distance anyone whose academic credentials are not in proper order.

CONCLUSION

We consider phonology a science. We consider it that because by means of it we are able to handle objectively the data of speech. These data we can analyze and describe and record in precise measurements, like jaw height or duration in fractions of a second. Furthermore, these statements are subject to check and verification by any competent observer.

Phonology not only deals with objective data, but it offers a system of classification. Every science rests on some generalization or on some fundamental principle which makes it unique among the several sciences. It is in terms of such a generalization that the sound system of English may be classified in an orderly manner. The statement of the phonemic principle provided the unique premise for phonology.

In any natural science we must be prepared to deal with anomalies—items which do not conform to the general pattern we have set up. Common sense tells us that the pattern is valid, yet we cannot incorporate the anomalies into the pattern. These anomalies we can describe in phonological terms, just as we can describe the "predictable" features, and for that reason many people have assumed that they were the concern of the linguist, particularly the phonologist. Linguistics can indeed describe the irregularities, but as linguistics it has no way of accounting for them. Since this is commonly overlooked, we spend staggering amounts of time and waste incredible hours of teaching time on descriptive matters in the hope of explaining the anomalies. It is true, the linguist may seek to explain how an irregularity got into the language, but this he does by putting on another hat, that of the language historian. Other matters are almost exclusively the province of the social scientist. Some pronunciations have become archaic, which is to say, they have gone out of date. Such matters have to do with modes and fashions and belong to sociopsychology rather than to linguistics. Some pronunciations characterize a specific geographical region. These we identify as regional dialect features, and in order to explain them we need to know something about geography and demography and population movements. Still other pronunciations identify people with advantages of education or wealth or culture or social standing. This is the realm of social class, or, more accurately, of social status.

At best each of us can speak with assurance for his own age group, his own geographical area, his own educational and occupational accomplishments, his own social status. In the past it has been supposed that there was a "correct" pronunciation; but it was a pronunciation that had validity for only a small segment of the population and excluded most of the users of the language. It assumed that these people were "wrong" unless they conformed in every detail to the language practices of the linguistic elite, ignoring the fact that a person's speech is his integrity. Give him another manner of speech and he cannot but regard himself as an imposter or a fraud.

In spite of the communications explosion—the increase in travel and mobility, the vast school population, the demands on one's time by radio and television—the idea that we are nearing a linguistic unification in this country or anywhere else is totally unrealistic. It has never happened in the past and there is no reason to expect it now. Rather than seek to erase the differences in language, it makes more sense to learn what the differences signify and to enjoy them for what they are.

6

morphology—the forms of english words

Those of us who paid attention to our elementary school teachers eventually learned a number of memory gems like "A noun is the name of a person, place, or thing," and "A verb is a word that shows action or state of being."

This information was presumably of great value, but our instincts told us that it had absolutely no currency outside of an English grammar class. In games of skill or chance we found opportunities to negotiate what we had learned of mathematics in order to figure odds and averages. We could exploit what we learned in health classes, and we might even introduce extracurricular material. If the occasion arose, we were permitted to assume the roles of various historical characters from Sir Galahad to Jack the Ripper. But anyone who mentioned adjective or participle or passive voice at once automatically forfeited the companionship of decent American boys and girls. As a matter of fact, these terms were never so much as breathed in our classes in geography or social studies, and not even in literature, all of which—so the grammarians would have us believe—simply brimmed over with grammar. Out of a sense of duty some teachers might make diffident notations on our written compositions, and they might suggest that we use fewer nouns and more verbs, or more nouns and fewer verbs, but that seldom made the situation clearer. Nevertheless, so we were assured, the study of grammar would eventually help us write better.

A vital phase of this grammar study consisted of classifying individual words into grammatical categories, or "parts of speech." There were eight of them: noun, verb, adjective, adverb, pronoun, preposition, conjunction, and interjection. Some of the grammar books included a ninth, the article, but since the entire part of speech consisted of only three words most of the grammarians slipped them in quietly somewhere among the adjectives.

This feverish search for parts of speech came about naturally enough. A century or more ago, when members of the professions were fewer in number and when the textbooks written for them were harder to come by, it was not unusual to publish scholarly material in Latin in order to make it available to people whose native tongues ranged from Danish to Rumanian. It was assumed therefore that a young person entering a profession would have learned Latin and Greek with reasonable competence.[1] As a result most of the so-called instruction in English grammar was frankly designed to prepare a select group of young men, and an even more select group of young women, to read Latin and Greek fluently. We should not be surprised therefore to find that the categories thus defined turned out to be primarily those of Latin and Greek and rather incidentally those of English. In fact, the definitions are not much more than general clues to the Latin categories. As applied to English, they often overlap, a situation which has distressed many schoolteachers who imagine that since grammar claims to be a science, everything ought to fit neatly into its proper compartment.

The shortcomings of the old-time grammarians have been only too apparent. Their immediate successors, at least in point of time, were the structural grammarians. The structuralists never managed to free themselves from the idea that a person was not a true-blue grammarian unless he sorted out the parts of speech. But as scientific grammarians they could improve on the older generation by proceeding in a more orderly manner, by making the categories less leaky. In C. C. Fries' system[2] there is a large class of English words that can be distinguished by the presence of certain "determiners"—words like *the, this, that, some, any.* Those of another

---

1 We forget how recently a thorough competence with Latin was taken for granted. The real decline took place in much of the country between the two World Wars. About a hundred years ago a staple item in the reading of every American boy was the "Horatio Alger novel," with its hero, supposedly a poor boy, working his way to riches and recognition by diligence and the avoidance of harmful habits. Typically, however, the Alger hero had a few thousand dollars (temporarily in the clutches of the villain); he contrived almost uniformly to get on friendly and financially profitable terms with a Wall Street broker; and he had a serviceable education. A fifteen-year-old boy, temporarily down on his luck, might take a job teaching Latin at a small-town high school in order to earn his room and board. Alger's readers seem to have regarded this as normal behavior.

2 *The Structure of English* (New York: Harcourt, Brace, 1951), pp. 110–141.

class can be distinguished by "auxiliaries" which immediately precede them: *may, can, will, must. . . .* On the other hand, an important class of words may be recognized by a plural inflection, as that of *dog* and *dogs,* and another class may similarly be recognized by a tense inflection—as that of *walk* and *walked.* Not all words that are marked by determiners also take the plural inflection, and not all words that are marked by auxiliaries also have past-tense inflections.[3] Some of the newer grammarians take a wry view of the entire operation and suggest that there is nothing especially scientific about such a classification; the older grammarians know exactly what they want to sort out and conduct the search with the randomness of a "Wanted" poster in a post-office lobby.

Whether it is really important to classify every word with absolute precision is a question grammarians raise from time to time. We shall in any event be dealing with several operational categories which customarily go by names like *noun, verb, adjective, pronoun,* and we shall be using these names although they may be identified differently. To anyone able to speak and write English, they are certainly familiar by operation. In some instances they are familiar by name as well.

THE MORPHEME

Just as the concept of the phoneme is basic in the sound system of a language, so we have a corresponding concept called a "morpheme" in constructing words. Like the phoneme, it is an abstraction, but one that enables us to relate and classify many features of language.

If we examine, for instance, several words like *bullfrog, bullhorn, bulldozer, bulldog,* we immediately recognize a common element, *bull.* Each of these words can "come apart," so to speak, at the juncture of *bull* and the element that happens to follow. Thus *bull* constitutes a meaningful unit; we associate it with strength or bulkiness or just general clumsiness.

We can try a similar experiment on words like *frog, dog,* and for good measure *hog,* breaking it into the element *og* on the one hand, and *fr, d,*

---

3 Some grammarians get around this by setting up separate though overlapping classes: nouns and nominals, verbs and verbals, adjectives and adjectivals, adverbs and adverbials. G. L. Trager and Henry Lee Smith, Jr., *An Outline of English Structure,* Studies in Linguistics, Occasional Papers, No. 3 (Norman: Battenburg Press, 1951); James Sledd, *A Short Introduction to English Grammar* (Chicago: Scott, Foresman, 1959).

and *h* on the other. This does not work as well; every user of English realizes at once that it makes no sense. The *og* element by itself is meaningless.

Words like *cat, star, dream, heat,* we speak of as independent or "free" morphemes since each one can operate as an independent linguistic unit, and none of them can be broken down into smaller meaningful units. The same holds true for words like *run, take, keep, grieve,* or words like *pink, square, pale, large.* By convention we call the words in the three groups "nouns," "verbs," and "adjectives," respectively.

Many English words—in fact, most of those listed in the dictionary—can be broken into two or more meaningful elements. A word like *inflame* consists of the element *in-* which has the general significance of "putting something (or somebody) into something (or somebody)" plus the morpheme *flame. Flame* is a free morpheme in English since it cannot be broken down any further and can occur independently, but *in-* we call "bound" since it does not occur by itself, at least not in this sense. It makes sense only when it is attached to other morphemes, some free and some bound: *inform, inflate, influence, infuriate.* But there is also an *in-* which has a general negative sense: *infirm, inelegant, infrequent, inert, infidel.* They have the same phonetic shape, but not the same meaning, and therefore we think of them as separate elements. It may happen that the *in-* does not detach at all, as in *indigo, ingot, Indian.*

The first *in-* meaning "putting something (or somebody) into" has several other forms. There is *im-,* as in *imprison, immure, immerse, imperil,* and *il-* as *illuminate, illustrate, illusion,* and *ir-* as *irradiate, irrigate, irruption.* By tracing the history of the various forms we presently discover that the *in-* is the original and we account for the others by assimilation. Forms like *im-*, *il-*, *ir-*, are variants and we call them "allomorphs." Since this particular morpheme can appear in several allomorphic forms, we refer to it by its most typical form, enclosed in braces: {in}.

Side by side with the morpheme {in} with the meaning "to put something (or somebody) into" there is, as we have noted, a morpheme with the identical form and a set of allomorphs with corresponding shapes, but with a general negative meaning: *im-*, as in *immoral, immobile, impossible,* and remotely, *imbecile;* or *il-*, as in *illegal, illogical, illegitimate;* or *ir-*, as in *irreverent, irrespective, irreligious.* There may be confusion, as in *inflammable.* The usual practice is to assign numbers to morphemes that are phonetically identical, in order of linguistic importance or frequency of use. Consequently the negative morpheme would be designated as $\{in_1\}$ and the other as $\{in_2\}$.

It seems reasonable that a language consisting largely of monosyllables could only have a fairly simple morphology, while one in which a single word could be strung out to ten or twenty syllables would in all likelihood have an extremely complex morphology. In this respect English is moderately simple. Actually English has two quite independent morphological systems. The first, which we shall consider in detail later, is called "derivation," and it involves the patterns by which bound and free morphemes may be combined and by which a word can transfer from one part of speech to another. The second is called "inflection," and it involves the changes in form which indicate strictly grammatical relationships. This proves difficult to define or explain without seeming to talk in circles. Perhaps we can best approach it by looking at some of the words themselves.

PARTS OF SPEECH

Traditionally we speak of "parts of speech," assuming that every word in an English sentence could be assigned to one of some eight categories. Many grammarians prefer to distinguish the elements of a sentence by morphological elements that they have in common, and for that reason they call them "form classes." Some words—prepositions, conjunctions, and the like—have no morphology and not even much "meaning," as we ordinarily think of meaning. They carry out specific grammatical functions like connecting words or larger constructions, identifying nouns and verbs, and negating statements, and they are called "function words" and sometimes "structure words." In traditional grammar they had pat names like "adverb" or "conjunction"; present-day grammarians have never come to any kind of agreement regarding what they ought to be called.

In a general way the major form classes correspond to the categories we call "nouns," "verbs," "modifiers," and "personal pronouns." It is well to remember that the definitions to be found in the handbooks are on the whole pretty unreliable. For instance, "An adjective is a word that modifies a noun," or "An adverb is a word that modifies a verb, an adjective, or another adverb," or "A pronoun is a word that stands in the place of a noun." These are bad identifications. Like defining a cow as "a large four-footed beast covered with untanned leather," such a definition neither distinguishes the referent from other items having the same qualities, nor does it necessarily identify its fundamental characteristics. Each statement is true, to be sure, but only partly true. Many words, for instance, can modify nouns besides adjectives: *prison term, gas chamber, murder weapon; sinking sensation, broken record, injured expression; he man, she tiger; in group, through street, down staircase.*

Before a child has so much as been enrolled in nursery school he has already made some kind of preliminary analysis of the language, and without realizing it he has worked out categories into which various items fit. The youngster has no idea that he is doing this, and much less is he able to identify the categories, but he makes them operate effortlessly. Dictionary editors offer definitions for the words of the several form classes. *Webster's Third New International* gives the following for *noun:*

> **noun** \'naůn\ *n* -s *often attrib* [ME *nowne*, fr. AF *noun* name, noun, fr. OF *nun, non, nom*, fr. L *nomen* — more at NAME] **1 :** a word that is the name of a subject of discourse (as a person, animal, plant, place, thing, substance, quality, idea, action, or state) and that in languages with grammatical number, case, and gender is inflected for number and case but has inherent gender **2 :** a word except a pronoun used in a sentence as subject or object of a verb, as object of a preposition, as the predicate after a copula, or as a name in an absolute construction — see COMMON NOUN, COUNT NOUN, MASS NOUN, PROPER NOUN

Random House Dictionary defines *noun* thus:

> *Any member of a class of words that are formally distinguished in many languages, as in English, typically by the plural and possessive endings and that function as the main or only elements of subjects, as* deed, belief, writing, man, Ohio, whiteness. *Nouns are often thought of as referring to persons, places, things, states, or qualities.*

One suspects with good reason that the part-of-speech labels which editors assign to individual words are assigned as the result of a well-developed language sense rather than from frequent and painstaking reference to the definitions. A person needs to have a reasonably good working sense of the various form classes of his language, and then the names will make some sense. There is no record that anyone has ever learned much about his language from starting with the definitions and then working to the words they fit.

7

nouns

The English noun typically consists of a "base" to which may be added either or both of two inflectional morphemes, the first having the general meaning "more than one," and the second technically known as "genitive" (less accurately but more commonly "possessive"). The base form is identified with "singular number," which is to say that unless it is otherwise specified the word refers to simply one of anything; "more than one" is called "plural." The characteristic spelling form used for both morphemes is *-s*, although the genitive is written *-'s*. To identify them as morphemes we may employ the symbols $\{S_1\}$ for the plural and $\{S_2\}$ for the genitive.

Spelling books offer scores of rules about constructing the plurals, such as "Change the *y* to *i* and add *-es*." It is important to remember that these rules apply only to spelling and have nothing whatever to do with the pronunciation. When we come to examine the sounds of the plurals in sets of words like *cat, dog, horse;* or *truck, auto, bus;* or *cup, bowl, dish,* we discover a completely systematic arrangement or "distribution" of the plural allomorphs:

/kæt/ + /s/	/trək/ + /s/	/kəp/ + /s/
/dɔg/ + /z/	/ɔtow/ + /z/	/bowl/ + /z/
/hɔrs/ + /əz/	/bəs/ + /əz/	/diš/ + /əz/

The form of the allomorph is determined by the final sound of the noun base, which is to say, if the final sound is a voiceless nonsibilant, the morpheme is phonemically /s/; if it is a voiced nonsibilant, the morpheme is phonemically /z/; if it is a sibilant, that is /s, z, š, ž, č, ǰ/, the morpheme is phonemically /əz/ (and allophonically [ɨz]).

All of this applies to "regular" noun plurals, and if we may be permitted another hopelessly circular definition, a regular noun plural is one that conforms to the above pattern. New words added to the vocabulary of English or adapted from the existing vocabulary form their plurals in this manner, regardless of whether they come from French, Chinese, or outer space, as in *discotheque, wu-ts'ai, quasar.*

There are also some English nouns that we classify as "irregular." Compared to the total number of nouns in the English vocabulary, the list of irregular plurals is quite small, numbering not more than a few hundred at most. Some of them are employed with great frequency, and others, mostly because they are sheltered by academic obscurity, are scarcely ever used. The plural of *haniwa,* for example, a word of Japanese origin referring to a clay figure involved in ancient burial practices, is *haniwa.* Should such a word become frequently used, though the chances at the moment seem very slim, the plural *haniwas* may be taken for granted.

Irregular plurals serve no useful grammatical function and the inventors of artificial languages waste no time getting rid of them. Like irregularities in phonology, they can be described objectively in linguistic terms, and their historical development can usually be traced with considerable accuracy. But that does not explain why they occur. They exist for purely social reasons. Each class of irregularities corresponds to a different social background, making the irregular plural a useful status indicator.

The normal tendency of English morphology is toward complete regularity. Since earliest times this regularization has been going on, though at very different rates of change. At any given time there may be current in the language two and sometimes even more variants of an inflection. One of these will then be the older irregular form side by side with the newer regular one. To understand acceptable usage therefore, one needs to know exactly how far such regularization has proceeded in each specific instance.

PLURALS

There are some seven modifications or types of the irregular plural in English, each one reflecting a different historical development.

Mutation Plurals

First and most familiar is a cluster of household words: *man, men; woman, women; tooth, teeth; foot, feet; goose, geese; mouse, mice; louse, lice.* These are extremely old forms and all of them preserve a contrast that existed in Old English. It was never a large class of words, even in Anglo-Saxon times. A number of nouns still current on a homely level have now regularized their plurals, or otherwise we should have had pairs like: *book, beek* or more probably *beech; nut, nit; oak, eak; goat, geat; cow, ky. Night* is the older plural form; if the original singular had been preserved it would have been *neight.* In nouns that retain the irregular plural, the contrast between singular and plural consists of a simple vowel alternation, specifically from a back vowel in the singular to a front vowel in the plural. These are known as "mutation" or "umlaut"[1] plurals. The reason these particular plurals have been preserved is that children acquire them at a very early age, the plurals sometimes even earlier than the singulars. As soon as this pattern stopped being a viable one, words like *book, nut,* and *oak* succumbed to the pressure of analogy. The remaining words, being household words, frequently used, preserved their older plurals. The child learning the language in such instances acquires the plural along with the singular not as part of a pattern but as a separate item of information.

Thanks to the systematic extermination of all forms of biological existence that compete with our own, lice and mice are becoming uncommon, and it seems conceivable that the plurals of *mouse* and *louse* will have become regularized within a generation or two. Lice are now thought of almost exclusively as plant lice, and it is evidently for reasons of daintiness that gardeners and nurserymen refer to them as aphids. In metaphorical use, especially as applied to human beings, *louse* has a regular plural:

---

1 The word *umlaut* is familiar enough to students of elementary German who commonly think of it as the two dots over the vowels *a o u.* Umlaut is really a variety of vowel assimilation which occurred at an early stage in the history of the several Germanic languages, including not only High German, but Dutch, Scandinavian, and English. In the early plural of the word *mann* 'man' we can assume a prehistoric form **mann-iz* (see footnote 5). The /i/ of the inflection had the effect of fronting the /a/ by anticipation and then disappearing by syncopation. The result in Old English was *menn.* Essentially the same process occurred in German, but German writers adopted a practice of indicating umlaut by adding an *e,* as *Maenner* 'men.' Subsequently the *e* was reduced in size, then written above the vowel itself, and simplified finally to a couple of dots. In German names the older practice of using *e* is not uncommon: Goethe, Maetzner, Muench.

Hector is a louse and so is his brother. They are both louses.

This pattern appears to have had very little analogical attraction for other similar words. One exception seems to be *titmouse,* a small bird that could not possibly be mistaken for a mouse; nevertheless the plural is *titmice. Mongoose* has a regular plural. It lives in India where it enjoys considerable popularity because it kills snakes. It in no way resembles a goose. Mock plurals of words like *moose, caboose, papoose* are made up in fun; also of *house, spouse, blouse,* but they are seldom taken seriously. *Talisman, cayman, ottoman* have no relation to the base *man,* and they construct their plurals on a regular pattern.

Although these umlaut plurals are irregular, we can nevertheless describe the plural of a word like *tooth* as $\{\text{tuw}\theta\} + \{S_1\}$. The typical form of this plural is *base + vowel change.*

Weak Plurals

A second class of English words has dwindled down to two "live" forms: *child* and *ox.* A plural morpheme with the phonemic form /ən/ was at one time widespread in English, and it formed the regular plural for scores of words, among them *name, hunter, month, tongue, star, earth, heart, widow, swallow.* Plurals in German and Dutch commonly have this /ən/ inflection. The only word remaining that originally belonged to this class is *ox*; its plural is *oxen.* Since in our expanding economy oxen were replaced by mules and horses which in turn were replaced by tractors, few people are aware of ever having seen an ox. Oxen are thought of as semimythical creatures, like unicorns or griffins. In many places *oxen* is itself regarded as the singular form:

Lagan is as smart as an oxen and slightly better looking.

Where people recognize *ox* as singular, the plural *oxes* is fairly common and it will undoubtedly become even more so as time goes on. *Dummox,* analogical with *lummox,* but a respelling and restressing of *dumb ox,* has the regular plural *dummoxes.*

Child originally had a plural that was identical with the singular, like *sheep* and *deer.* There was also a small class of Old English words like the original forms for *calf, lamb, egg* which had a plural which was presently reduced to /ər/. This was then added also to *child,* making *childer.* After some time the other plurals in this class fell into the regular plural class, but instead of conforming, *childer* went on to add the /ən/ inflection, and with syncopation of a syllable it became *children.* The plural form preserves the vowel quantity of the original; the monosyllabic singular was involved in a sound change, accounting for the diphthongal nucleus. This plural has been preserved as an irregular form because, like *man, woman,* and a few others, it is used with great frequency, from the time of early childhood. In non-standard English it has acquired still another plural, /čilənz/, spelled *chilluns.*

Brother has the regular plural *brothers,* but in archaic language, especially where there are ecclesiastical or fraternal overtones, the form *brethren* survives. Here we commonly have mutation of the stressed vowel of the base, although /brəðərən/ is far from uncommon. By analogy a semiliterate *sistern* appears in "brethren and sistern," and this is usually regarded as humorous, although it had some literary standing 600 years ago. *Kine* as the plural of *cow* (Genesis 41:18 KJV) is likewise a double plural in which the /ən/ inflection is attached to a mutated base.

A few additional plurals having this characteristic pattern persisted as late as the time of Shakespeare: *eyen* 'eyes,' *hosen* 'hose' (Daniel 3:21 KJV), *shoon* 'shoes.' *Shoon* is occasionally used in poetry. The cartoonist Al Capp, creator of "Li'l Abner," has attempted from time to time to make *schmoon* the plural of *schmoo* in order to exploit puns like "When the schmoon come over the mountain," or "The Valley of the Schmoon."

The typical form of this plural is *base* + /ən/.

Zero plurals

In a small class of nouns the singular and plural forms are identical, and grammarians describe the plural morpheme as "zero" or "null" since nothing is added to the base to form the plural. A conventional symbol for "zero" or "null" is $\emptyset$, and the formulation is: $\{S_1\} = \emptyset$.

The principal members of this class are *deer* and *sheep* and also *swine* unless the reference is to unpleasant human beings. In this case the plural *swines* is sometimes used, especially in informal situations. *Horse* has an occasional zero plural, now generally archaic, its last domain being the military. Like words of the two preceding classes, these words are relatively common and they have been transmitted by word of mouth rather than as literary forms. Furthermore, they have been associated with farming. Until a generation ago the language of the farm and of the sea was strikingly conservative since farmers and seamen were largely removed from active association with other people, especially those in larger centers of commerce and culture. As a result agricultural and nautical language preserved forms that had gone out of use everywhere else.

When spoken of collectively, *bear, fish, elk, grouse, moose, bison, trout, bass,* and the like employ the zero plural:

> We bagged five *deer* and a couple of *elk.*

But the well-known story that Robert Southey composed for his grandchildren is called "Goldilocks and the Three Bears." That is to say, when these creatures are considered individually the regular plural is used. This is true especially of expanded forms, as in speaking of the Benevolent Protective Order of Elks.[2] Then there are: the Fraternal Order of Eagles, Lions International, Detroit Tigers, Chicago Cubs.

Plurals like *sheeps* and *deers* are common enough in spoken English, often passing unnoticed. But they are rigorously edited out of written English. The most celebrated occurrence of *deer* is perhaps:

> *O, give me a home where the buffalo roam,*
> *Where the* deer *and the antelope play.*

While *deer* has preserved the zero plural, its compound *reindeer* is often regularized to *reindeers.*[3]

Expressions of measurement, especially the nonmetric, usually have the zero plural principally in colloquial use and characteristically among the less educated. They reflect a construction current at an early stage of English and must therefore be considered archaic rather than corruptions: *six ton of hay, four pair of socks, a hundred foot of shore line.*[4]

---

2 The Moose Lodge, so called, is officially known as the Loyal Order of Moose. If the analogy to the Elks held, we should refer to more than one Moose as Mooses. This evidently does not happen.

3 Early editions and recordings of the song "Rudolph, the Red-nosed Reindeer," spoke of *the other reindeers.* In later editions this has been changed to *reindeer.*

4 In attributive constructions the uninflected form is standard: two-ton truck, eight-pound baby, five-act play, three-dollar bill, twenty-one-gun salute. The plural form would be regarded as incorrect.

Path, etc.

The word *path* /pæθ/ has as its plural *paths* /pæðz/. The allomorph consists of voicing of the final fricative of the base plus /z/ and occasionally /əz/. Several dozen words construct their plurals on this pattern: *calf, self, mouth, shelf, wife, thief, life, leaf, bath, house, wolf, half, knife.* Other words, though phonetically quite similar, do not: *myth, gulf, belief, laugh, grief, sabbath, oaf, cough, bluff.* The words in the first group are all part of the Old English vocabulary and present a holdover from a plural construction which was in operation in the earliest time of which we have any record. Most of them were in sufficiently common use to keep the pattern alive. Those in the second list are from non-English sources or otherwise they seldom appeared in the plural form at any stage of the language.

There are also some words which form their plurals both ways: *hoofs, hooves; scarfs, scarves; turfs, turves; sheaths, sheathes. Beeves* refers to more than one head of beef cattle; *beefs* refers to more than one complaint, usually delivered in a truculent manner. *Staves* are wooden poles with which people brained one another in olden times, or they may be sections of a keg or barrel; *staffs* are groups of like-minded people assembled for some specific purpose, like teaching a high school, advising a general, or publishing a periodical. It is sometimes said, not without conviction, that a cat has nine *lives;* several copies of a well-known magazine would be so many *Lifes. Cloverleaves* are to be found in clover patches and sometimes pressed between the pages of old books; *cloverleafs* at intersections of super-highways. The plural of *bath* is /bæðz/; in compounds like *bubblebaths* or *showerbaths* it is often /bæθs/. In these words the older form maintains its integrity in the regular uses of the various words, but in compounds and extended meanings the tendency toward regularization is strong. *Loaf, elf,* and *sheaf* are sometimes rendered with regularized plurals.

Cloth has the plurals /klɔθz/ or /klɔðz/; *clothes* as a separate development was formerly pronounced /klowðz/ and is still so pronounced from time to time, although this is regarded as a spelling pronunciation. As a result of consonant assimilation /klowz/ has become standard. *Chief* has the plural *chiefs. Kerchief* is a related word (from French *couvre chef* 'cover the head') and has a regular plural in /s/ but also a plural /kərčɨvz/. *Handkerchief,* a compound of *kerchief,* forms its plurals in the same manner.

The typical form of this plural is: voicing of the final fricative of the base + /z/ or /əz/.

Inverted Plurals

Words like *watches, couches, fitches* have both plural form and plural meaning since they follow the regular pattern. Some words, however, appear to be plural in form but are not specifically plural in meaning. *Riches* is an example. For example:

> *The ransom of a man's life are his riches.* —Proverbs 13:8 KJV
>
> *The crown of the wise is their riches.* —Proverbs 14:24 KJV

In Present-day English *riches* is ordinarily construed as plural, but a sentence like:

> *He lost his money and was down to his last rich.[5]

is nonsense. The word entered English by way of French *richesse* 'abundant means, wealth,' and presently became respelled according to the English pattern.

A number of words operate in this fashion, among them *alms, thanks,* and *pains*—not the kind one gives, but the kind one takes. *Headquarters, barracks, means* can be construed as either singular or plural. *Savings* and *wages* are also singular or plural: "These are unprecedented savings," or "This savings will be passed on to the buyer." *Wages,* though now most commonly regarded as plural, is singular in the familiar "The wages of sin is death." In contrast to such cereal grains as rye, wheat, barley, rice, and corn, the word *oats* is almost exclusively plural. *Oat* would perhaps be applied to the activities of a squeamish person out on the town who has "sowed a wild oat." *Athletics* may refer collectively to everything the physical education department promotes, but in reference to physical activity it is singular. Words with a plural form but a generally singular meaning further include: *mathematics, molasses, physics, stairs, shivers, shambles, measles, mumps, hysterics, proceeds.*

A number of words appear to represent clusters of related meanings and functions: *breeches, pants, tights, trousers, slacks, knickers, shorts, pajamas, trunks;* also *pliers, tweezers, pincers, tongs, forceps, scissors,*

---

5 An asterisk (*) preceding a word or expression or other linguistic form indicates a word or spelling that, so far as anyone knows, does not exist in a written form that can be checked or verified. It may be a conjectured reconstruction of a form that probably did exist before there were written records of the language; it may also be something that is contrary to the nature of the language.

clippers, shears. These are generally taken as plural unless a "quantifier" like *a pair of* precedes the noun. Some specialized instruments also fit this category: *fetters, gallows, bellows, scales. Balances* formerly belonged to this pattern—"Thou art weighed in the balances"—but *balance* has become standard—"his fate was hanging in the balance." We also speak of *Niagara Falls, Deering's Woods, Bradford Motor Works.*

Amends has a plural form and may be used as a plural; it may also be used as a singular as "to make a cowardly amends" (T. S. Eliot). To say "an amend" would be substandard usage. *Odds* is thought of as plural, yet "What's the odds?" is standard. *An odd* does not occur in standard English and seldom if ever in substandard. It is the kind of thing, however, that could turn up in hyperstandard English. *Dregs* and *lees* would be regarded as amusing if used in the singular, although "down to the last dreg" occurs now and then, usually from people who have no idea what a dreg looks like. There is an often-repeated story about James Gordon Bennett, editor of the *New York Herald,* who used to insist that *news* was plural. On a certain occasion he wired a correspondent: "Are there any news?" To which the reply came back, "Not a new."

This process of forming a word from an inflected form or derivational form by deleting a suffix is called "back formation" and the word thus formed may have difficulty establishing its credentials. *New* as a singular of *news* has never been accepted. *Lens* is a singular noun and the plural is *lenses,* but by back formation we encounter a substandard singular *len,* as in:

> Flossie lost a contact *len* in the swimming pool.

The spelling *lense,* used for the singular, seems to be a compromise. More commonly *lens* is employed as though it were a plural:

> The *lens* in my headlights aren't lined up.

This use is also substandard. *Appendix* ordinarily has one of two plurals, *appendices,* a scholarly form relating to matter of secondary relevance inserted at the back of books, and *appendixes,* the latter being reserved for the plural of the vermiform appendix, a part of the intestinal system:

> Removing *appendixes* used to be my uncle's "bread-and-butter" operation.

A substandard usage results from the assumption that *appendix* itself is a plural like bowels or brains:

My cousin had her *appendix* out; *they'd* been bothering her ever since she was in seventh grade.

The standard plural of *license* is *licenses.* In substandard usage, however, *license* is often taken to be the plural, especially in nonurban establishments where hunting and fishing license—as they put it—are sold. Or, a typical expression:

Golly, I better get my *license* renewed. *They* expired last week.

The principle of analogy is hard at work here: *hens* is to *hen* as *lens* is to *len.* We may chuckle at the bumpkin who goes searching for his len or whose license have expired and whose appendix are acting up, but this very process has been in operation in English for many centuries and a goodly number of now perfectly acceptable English words have come about through it: *Cherry* from Old Norman French *cherise; gentry* from French *gentrise; riddle* from Old English *rædels; skate* from Dutch *schaats; marquee* from French *marquise; burial* from Old English *byrgels; pea* from an older *pease.* And on the nonstandard level we have *shay* as in the "Wonderful One Hoss Shay" from French *chaise,* and *Chinee* from *Chinese.* There can be little doubt that *Yankee* also came into English by this route. *Jan Kees* /yàn kéys/ was the equivalent of *John Cornelius,*[6] a familiar combination of names among the early Dutch settlers of New York. It later became a nickname for any Dutchman, and presently, as *Yankee,* for a New Englander.

Foreign Language Plurals

Foreign plurals, or perhaps more accurately, learned borrowings, are the province of the educated, and therefore it is not surprising that the plurals of these words are hazardous.

Dealing with French, German, or Italian plurals is not in itself difficult. We commonly borrow them as complete phrases or otherwise we English them quite unabashedly. The trick is knowing which to do when. The plural of *faux pas* is either /fóh pàh/ or /fóh pàhz/; that of *Weltanschauung* is either *Weltanschauungs* or *Weltanschauungen;* that of *graffito* is *graffiti; spaghetti* is itself the plural of Italian *spaghetto,* a detail we carefully ignore and add /z/.

---

6 The origin of this name has been explained in more than fifty ways, a common explanation being that *Jan Kees* meant 'John Cheese.' But the Dutch word for cheese is *kaas* /kahs/ and has never been *kees* at all.

The most common borrowings, however, are those of Latin origin. Words like *area, arena, senator, action* have been part of the vocabulary of English for so many years that Latinizing them goes beyond even pedantry: *areae, arenae, senatores, actiones.* Others preserve a Roman accent. In all but a small group of words the only case form that matters is the nominative. *Res,* meaning 'thing, matter,' has identical nominative singular and plural forms, but the inflected forms *rem, re, rerum, rebus* all appear in English.

Formula, nebula, larva, alumna, ameba, vertebra may have the Latin plural, written *-ae* or *-æ* and pronounced /iy/, not /ay/. *Nebulæ* and *alumnæ* are confined almost exclusively to academic institutions. The other words have a more democratic distribution, including the *ameba.* For many decades it served in the modest office of illustrating cell division in textbooks in elementary natural science. In 1933 it caught the public interest, however, as the result of an outbreak of amebic dysentery at the Chicago World's Fair—then known as "A Century of Progress." The form *amebæ* is not uncommon but is restricted to written English; after all, it takes some courage to pronounce a word like /əmíybìy/. *Antenna* has the plural *antennæ* as the 'feelers' of an insect, *antennas* as part of the receptive equipment of radio or television. This latter use is becoming replaced by *aerial.*

Latin words ending in *-us* frequently have the plural *-i,* pronounced /ay/. Among them are *locus* and *focus* /lówsày/ and /fówsày/, *cumulus, alumnus, nucleus, stimulus, radius, bacillus, syllabus,* all scholarly words. *Crocus, cactus,* and *fungus* have both *-i* and *-es* plurals, since they appear in day-to-day situations. A man in the military service in the tropics, for instance, may discover fungus between his toes, and we can scarcely expect him to mind the decorous Latin plural in describing his discovery. A member of a garden club in Indiana or Ohio will probably use the plural *cacti,* but a rancher in New Mexico who lives with them all the time may say *cactuses.* *Gladiolus* is a Latin diminutive of *gladius* 'sword,' hence "little sword." It has a variety of plurals. *Gladioli* /glǽdɨyówlày/ or /glǽdáyəlày/ is still standard; *gladioluses* is a regular plural, though seldom used. Just as *lens* has developed *len* by back formation, *gladiolus* appears in the singular as *gladiola,* with some analogical help from all the *-ola* words, and this has in turn given birth to another plural, *gladiolas.* Gardeners as a rule call them *glads.*

Latin has other declensions in *-us,* setting a cruel trap for the unwary: *genus, genera; corpus, corpora.* The plural of *apparatus* is *apparatus,* but people who use the word are seldom strict Latinists. It may be thought of as a collection—a "mass noun"—which cannot be pluralized, but otherwise it is ordinarily *apparatuses.* In the same manner the plural of *sinus* is *sinus,* but it has long since become *sinuses* in the huckster lexicon of speedy relief. *Opus* is the Latin word for 'work,' as in *operation,* the plural being *opera.* But *opera* developed a specialized meaning and went on to its own plural, *operas.*

Words of Latin origin ending in *-um* often have a plural with *-a,* pronounced /ə/. Thus *stratum, erratum, bacterium, addendum, ovum. Curriculum, stadium, symposium, gymnasium* have it both ways. *Agendum* and *datum* belong to this class of words also and have the Latin plurals *agenda* and *data.* For many years the words were confined to academic institutions and meant respectively 'that which is to be done' and 'that which is given (as information)' but presently they were recognized as useful in secular surroundings. No secretary could appear at a meeting with one puny agendum, and no researcher would admit that he had unearthed but one meager datum. *Agenda* and *data* within a reasonable time developed their own plurals as *agendas* and *datas,* both now accepted as standard. *Candelabrum* has a Latin plural *candelabra* but because it involves a cluster of candles *candelabra* commonly passes as a singular. From its nature, *rostrum* appears almost exclusively in the singular. *Rostra* is historically the plural, but only a pedant would think to use it.

Words like *chrysanthemum, geranium, premium, pendulum, petroleum, linoleum, asylum, museum,* and *decorum* have become completely naturalized and never have *-a* in the plural. *Medium* has a plural *mediums* in referring to the statistical quantity and also to a spiritualist practitioner. *Media* covers a wide variety of matters, including cultures for propagating microorganisms, materials used in the visual and plastic arts, and various kinds of devices by which information is transmitted. The latter include what are known as news media, but in an even broader sense, advertising media. The plural *medias* is quite common in referring to these. The pronoun *nostrum* is in a sense already a plural; it refers to a quack medicine and literally means 'our (very) own.' *Quorum* is also a pronoun, again a plural, and is in the genitive case, literally 'of whom' or 'of what.' *Hoodlum* is a homegrown Americanism of uncertain parentage. There is the story, undoubtedly apocryphal, that it referred to a small-time hood named Muldoon, that a newspaper reporter reversed the spelling of his name, making it Noodlum, but the printer misread the first letter. At all events, anyone who makes a Latin plural of this is trying far, far too hard.

In a small list of words we have a linguistic form either of direct Greek origin or derived from Greek by way of Latin, and in these a final *-is* in the singular alternates with a final *-es* /iyz/ in the plural. Thus *axis* side by side with *axes*. Other words in this class are: *analysis, ellipsis, crisis, thesis, classis, parenthesis, synthesis, oasis, neurosis, basis*. Adding a regular *-es* to any of these words would produce an awkward string of sibilants. Save for specialists, few persons have occasion to use these words in the plural. Words with final *-ex* or *-ix* have the regular *-es* plural, along with a change of suffix to *-ices*. *Appendix* has *appendices* only in a restricted scholarly sense. *Index* ordinarily has the plural *indexes,* but in specialized mathematical uses it preserves the historical *indices*. *Matrix* often appears in the plural as *matrices,* even in its applications in industries like mining and typography. *Vortex* and *cortex* come usually one at a time, but *vortices* and *cortices* are the regular plurals. *Vertex* should logically follow the same pattern, but since the word is a familiar one in plane geometry, legions of high school pupils have taken care of the original plural. *Crux* also belongs to this group of words but the plural *cruces* is rare. Graduate students in English have mulled over the crux passages in Beowulf and Chaucer and Shakespeare and have completely naturalized *cruxes*.

There are a few Greek plurals: *criterion, criteria; phenomenon, phenomena*. They seem to have weathered all attempts to regularize them, although both *criteria* and *phenomena* are construed in the singular, usually by persons who are endeavoring to sound more educated than their years in school would warrant. Words like *theme* or *dogma* have Greek plurals *themata* and *dogmata* but it would occur only to a pedant to flaunt them. The regular plurals are acceptable everywhere. On the other hand, if one has the opportunity to pluralize *stigma,* which may be rare, it is wise to remember that the preferred plural is *stigmata*.

Octopus is an anomaly. Nonspecialists do not willingly cultivate the opportunity of becoming intimately acquainted with more than one, if that, at a time, and consequently the plural is for all general purposes redundant. But should the occasion arise, *octopuses* is an acceptable plural. So is *octopi*. But so are *octopods* and *octopodes,* and if someone should insist, so is *octopoda*. It seems unlikely that anyone except an ichthyologist would give it much thought.

Cherub and *seraph* are Biblical words of Hebrew origin. The *-s* plurals are often used, so far as any plural is used in these situations. The historical plurals, however, are *-im,* pronounced /im/ and also /iym/ as in the hymn:

> Cherubim *and* seraphim
> *Falling down before Thee.*

Teraphim 'household gods' occurs only in the plural, although few of us would have much occasion to use the word (Judges 18:5 RSV). We should probably use the Latin *lares et penates,* if we were really stuck for a foreign phrase. With the revival of Hebrew as the national language of Israel, we will encounter more Hebrew plurals from time to time. *Kibbutzim* 'collective farms' is the only fairly common one, and now and then *goyim* 'gentiles' occurs.

It is of utmost importance to know when to use a foreign plural, but it is even more important to know when not to do so. There are people who say *croci* /krówsày/ for *crocuses* and they have their reasons. But to use *-i* as the plural inflection of words like *campus, circus, virus, isthmus,* or *census* would be grotesque, even though such plurals were once accepted usage. The extreme would be to use it on *omnibus,* itself a Latin dative plural[7] or *ignoramus,* actually a verb form, or on *bogus, rumpus, dingus,* and *walrus,* which have never been Latin at all.

Compound Plurals

Plurals of compounds like *spoonful* and *mother-in-law* can prove to be unnerving. The reason is that two conflicting tendencies are at work. Logic suggests that we are talking about spoons and mothers and are secondarily noting that the spoons are full and that the mothers have achieved their status by law rather than biology. Then obviously we ought to have *spoonsful* and *mothers-in-law.* But experience tells us that the tendency in English is to attach a noun or verb inflection at the very last possible point, and that this applies also to groups of words. This we commonly do, for instance, with genitives. Ridiculous as it looks on paper, we have no difficulty understanding a phrase like "The check-out clerk who just waited on me's brother," while "The check-out clerk's who just waited on me brother" leaves us completely confused. It follows then that we should have *spoonfuls* and *mother-in-laws.* Accepted practice, as we might expect, is something of a compromise between these extremes. But each has its own excuse for being.

The basic rule governing such matters is that the plural inflection will

---

7 Some generations ago, when educated people were assumed to know Latin, the plural *omnibi* was sometimes used humorously since it was assumed also that everyone would know it was bad Latin. Then as a further complication, its contraction *bus* was correspondingly rendered *bi* in the plural. The humor of it would be lost on a present-day audience. There is the possibility that it had hard going even in its own time.

come at the end of a phrase or compound, unless there is a valid reason for putting it elsewhere. Compounds like *birdcage, ratrace, toothbrush* have in common that the first element may carry a strong plural idea. There may be several birds in the cage, the race clearly involves more than one rat, and the brush cleans a set of teeth. These facts we ignore and say *birdcages, ratraces, toothbrushes.* The first part of a compound does not need to be a noun, as appears in the following plurals: *write-offs, camp-outs, sit-ins, layovers. Teaspoonful* and *cupful* do not emphasize the idea of fullness, in spite of appearances. There is a difference in meaning between "A cup of vanilla" and "A cup full of vanilla," although it is a subtle distinction. *Cupful, spoonful,* and the rest are built on the same pattern as the adjectives *wonderful, cheerful, beautiful* and are construed as single words rather than as two words or even compounds. Despite the objections of those who find *handsful* more logical and more grammatical than *handfuls,* the latter has been with us for more than 600 years and is regarded as standard.

When we pluralize the first element of a compound like *lady wrestler* the result is ambiguous; it might be *lady's wrestler* or *ladies wrestler* or even *ladies' wrestler.* Neither does pluralizing the second element make things any more clear. Except for this, we might find this kind of appositive compound fairly common in English. Where no ambiguity is possible, as in the case of a few umlaut plurals, a plural appositive is not at all rare: *women drivers, men teachers, gentlemen farmers.* In attributive constructions like *birdcage,* the first element is often plural when it is a mutated plural, as in: *feet tracks, geese feathers, mice traps, teeth marks.* They are regarded as nonstandard but would undoubtedly pass without comment in conversation. With Latin plurals this phrase pattern is extremely common and is accepted as standard: *bacteria counts, alumni receptions, media surveys, theses revisions, data sheets, memoranda pads.* But there are limitations: * *cacti plants,* * *cumuli clouds* would be rejected as nonstandard, if not non-English, in most situations.

There are two patterns in which the plural inflection is not attached to the final element, and both of them are clearly identifiable. Both of them are constructed with a noun as headword, in the one instance modified by a prepositional phrase, and in the other by a function word, usually an adverb. The first group consists of combinations like *attorney-at-law, man-of-war, editor-in-chief.* The combinations are fairly loose, though less loose than *doctor of chiropractic, poet in residence, representative at large.* In all of these it is the headword, of course, that becomes pluralized. And so a combination like the *-in-law* expressions resembles the above group with one major difference. In *attorney-at-law* the primary stress falls on the modifying element, while in *mother-in-law* the primary stress is on the headword, as it does in *brother-in-law, sister-in-law,* and the rest. While *attorneys-at-law* scarcely offers any trouble, the difference in stress pattern accounts for the occasional *mother-in-laws* instead of the standard *mothers-in-law*. The second group of words consists of a noun plus a function word modifier, like *runner-up*. The noun rather than the phrase receives the plural inflection: *runners-up*. The pattern includes expressions like *passer-by, setter-forth, looker-on*. Except for a few set phrases it is not often used, and it has an archaic or literary quality. *Goings-on* occurs only in the plural.

A few compounds were inherited from French in which the adjective follows the noun: *attorney general, notary public, poet laureate*. In formal usage these have the plurals *attorneys general, notaries public, poets laureate,* but *attorney generals* and the rest are also accepted and will ultimately supersede the older pattern. *Jack o'lantern, dime-a-dozen, good-for-nothing* have no headword as such and are pluralized as unit words.

GENITIVES

The English noun system also has an inflection which is popularly called the "possessive," actually a somewhat inaccurate indication of its function. Historically and more accurately it has gone by the name "genitive." It is the last remnant of a fairly complex set of inflections corresponding to the noun cases which operated in English until roughly a thousand years ago. During the Old English period, not only nouns and pronouns, but adjectives and definite articles had forms for five "cases": nominative, accusative, genitive, dative, and instrumental. The nominative case served as the subject of the verb and the accusative primarily as the object. By the time of our very earliest writings in Old English the forms of the two cases had largely coalesced into a single form, and it is only from evidence of related languages that we assume that a distinction must once have existed. This was true both in singular and plural. Formal case distinctions were expressed largely by the forms of the definite article, some of which were preserved for several centuries after the Old English period. The original dative was used with prepositions, and it also indicated the indirect object of the verb. The instrumental simply designated the person or thing by which some action was performed. The genitive had a variety of uses, which are discussed in a later chapter.

A few nouns will serve to illustrate the Old English case system, among them *stān* 'stone,' *engel* 'angel,' *secg* 'warrior,' *fugol* 'fowl':

	singular			
nominative/accusative	stān	engel	secg	fugol
genitive	stānes	engles	secges	fugles
dative/instrumental	stāne	engle	secge	fugle
	plural			
nominative/accusative	stānas	englas	secgas	fuglas
genitive	stāna	engla	secga	fugla
dative/instrumental	stānum	englum	secgum	fuglum

This was actually just one of about half a dozen quite distinct inflectional systems which flourished in Old English, but even at that date as many as three out of five nouns followed this pattern, and between the Old English period and the present time nearly all the rest of them conformed to it. The singular and plural instrumental and dative merged with the nominative-accusative about the time that their distinctive functions were taken over by the prepositions which came increasingly into use: *to, of, by, for, with, from, in,* to mention only a few. This change was pretty well accomplished within a century or two following the close of the Old English period and is one of the features of what we call Middle English. The genitive plural in Old English had the inflection *-a,* which during the Middle English period was reduced to *-e,* pronounced /ə/, and then the inflection was lost altogether, although the construction was preserved in an expression like *six-month-old baby,* which we can also express as *baby of six months.* In effect all that remains of the old declensional system is the following:

	singular	*plural*
nominative	stone	stones
genitive	stone's	stones'

The form which we write as *stone's* is pronounced exactly like *stones.* The inflection is symbolized as $\{S_2\}$. The rule governing the pronunciation is identical to that for $\{S_1\}$ in its regular forms. Phonetically the $\{S_2\}$ morpheme is completely regular.

We may describe the morphology of the English noun as: *base* + ({S_1}) + ({S_2}). In other words, either or both of the inflectional morphemes are optional. But the order is not optional. In a word like *boy* or *girl* the genitive plural is pronounced /bɔyz/ or /gərlz/, being phonetically identical with either the genitive singular or nominative plural. But with nouns having irregular plurals typical phrases are: *old wives' tales, children's diseases, men's agonies, calves' liver.*

Even though the apostrophe (') does not correspond to any speech sound in English, one does not lightly omit it from English writing. Inexperienced writers in fact betray their nervousness by putting apostrophes where they cannot possibly be justified. Some of this may be because the apostrophe of the genitive resulted first of all from a misunderstanding. In Old English, as we have just observed, the genitive inflection was commonly *-es*; thus the genitive of a name like Harold would be *Haroldes*. The vowel was presently syncopated and early in the Middle English period the name began to be spelled as it is at present, *Harolds*. But in some regional dialects of England the *-es* was retained as a full syllable, and in some places, particularly in the East of England, it was often written as *-is*: *Haroldis sword*. We give the name "folk etymology" to the business of explaining matters like this in complete ignorance of the way language operates; the folk etymologists had observed that an earlier pronoun form *hit* became *it* and they supposed that the element *-is* must represent a corruption of *his*, and consequently as early as the thirteenth century there were sporadic constructions like *Harold his sword*. It had a great vogue during the eighteenth century until Bishop Robert Lowth showed how ridiculous it actually was, pointing to its use by writers like Addison and Pope and Prior. The *his* genitive has not completely vanished; it still crops up now and then, chiefly in imitations of archaic style. Early in the sixteenth century the apostrophe, then called "apostrophus," began to achieve some popularity as an indication that a letter had been omitted from the more usual spelling: *bless'd, giv'st*. Shakespeare (or his printer) appears to have been one of the earliest to use it with any consistency.[8] Assuming that *Harolds sword* must be a

---

8 The following passage indicates quite typically how apostrophes were used in Shakespeare's time. Their function was simply to indicate that a letter had been omitted from the spelling:

The King ha's cur'd me,
I humbly thanke his Grace: and from these shoulders
These ruin'd Pillers, out of pitty, taken

corruption of *Harold his sword* and that they ought to acknowledge this information, trivial as it was, writers began to insert an apostrophe: *Harold's sword.* In no time at all the apostrophe became regarded as the "sign of possession." By the middle of the eighteenth century it had been extended to the plural, and the apostrophe was placed after the final *-s,* even though nothing had been or could have been omitted, as in *dogs', rabbits'.* For most of a century some grammarians faulted the practice as stupid. A few writers, George Bernard Shaw among them, have been courageous enough to sack the apostrophe in *don't, isn't,* and *you'll,* but the tenure of the "possessive apostrophe" is unchallenged. Shaw, for instance, writes: "for heaven's sake" or "the rabble raving to its heart's content."

A loade, would sinke a Nauy, (too much Honor.)
O 'tis a burden Cromwel, 'tis a burden
Too heauy for a man, that hopes for Heauen.
—*Henry the Eighth,* III.ii.381–386

Shakespeare regularly spelled *has* as *ha's,* evidently assuming that medial *v* had been lost, as in *o'er, e'er, e'en* and so on. *Had,* on the other hand, was not spelled with an apostrophe. *Note:* In the above passage the spelling is that of the First Folio. Wherever reference is made to Shakespeare or the King James Bible, the spelling and punctuation will be that of the First Folio (1623) and of the Authorized version (1611).

8

pronouns

Our handbooks conventionally define a pronoun as a "word that will take the place of a noun." A pronoun will do that, to be sure, but merely taking the place of a noun is a secondary function. After all, one noun can take the place of another noun without becoming a pronoun. In a sentence like "Malthus had an idea," the word *idea* can be replaced by *opportunity,* as in "Malthus had an opportunity," but that scarcely makes a pronoun out of *opportunity* in spite of the definition. We find that we are usually left groping when we rely on the traditional definitions to give us light and direction. That is true here. As before, we need to assume that most of those who can speak their language with competence also have enough inborn language sense to enable them to sort out the pronouns whenever necessary.

Traditionally the pronoun category has been sort of an *omnium-gatherum,* a pretty miscellaneous catchall. The books use terms like "demonstrative," "relative," "interrogative," and then classify them more broadly as pronouns also. A word like *where* or *that* or *what* may belong to several such classes, each of which has a function quite different from that of the others. It may be wise not to think of them as pronouns at all.

PERSONAL PRONOUNS

What we call "personal pronouns" consists of a small closed list of words containing between two and three dozen items. The precise number depends on several things: how archaic we permit ourselves to be, how tolerant of compounds, how lax about nonstandard usages. Like that of many languages, the pronoun system of English is one of its most stable features; it has been about four hundred years since any new pronoun was added to the standing inventory. We have written records of English covering some twelve hundred or more years, and during this time a few pronouns have fallen out of use. They lingered on for a short while in poetry or in religious language and then vanished beyond recall. But who of us today finds himself hobbled by the loss of the first and second dual pronouns, which we should translate as 'the two of us' or 'the two of you'? In the pitch-dark outlaw-ridden forests of Anglo-Saxon England they may have served a useful function since people commonly traveled in pairs. These pronouns have been lost and so have several others whose sense could be expressed by an existing pronoun. There have been sound changes and spelling changes during these twelve centuries, and yet many of our pronouns have survived with only minor remodelings.

English pronouns have several grammatical characteristics, the chief ones being distinctive forms for person, number, case, and to a limited extent gender. The stability which the pronoun system has enjoyed over the course of its long history is balanced by the fact that it is now largely a linguistic fossil. Indeed, as we shall see, most of our usage problems with pronouns result directly from our concern, whether for better or for worse, with keeping archaic forms alive and active.

Person

One feature of the English pronoun system that has not changed appreciably over the course of time is person. "Person" is a distinction in the form of the pronoun that indicates which person is speaking or writing, which one is spoken to or written to, and who or what is spoken or written about; in other words, the source, goal, and subject of an utterance. The characteristic pronouns are familiar enough. *I* is first person, *you* is second person, and *he, she,* or *it* is third person. Most of the languages we encounter make these distinctions. A few—the Athapaskan languages, and Eskimo, for instance—add a fourth which in some instances corresponds to our third person except that it may signify a greater distance or more immediate personal relationship. We can make such distinctions by adding words: "she over there" in contrast to "she here" or "his house" in contrast to "his own house."

Person distinction does not occur in nouns, although there are some constructions, especially involving proper names and titles, in which nouns assume first person function:

Now children, *Mother* wants you to be quiet.

Your President wishes you every success and happiness.

We find this as a device from time to time in autobiographical writings: Julius Cæsar and Henry Adams, to mention two of the better known autobiographers. In the Gospels there is a phrase "Son of Man" which Bible scholars have discussed at great length, but which obviously had first person significance.

A similar construction also identifies the second person, often indicating unusual politeness or respect:

Would *Mother* care for another glass of lemonade?

It may also be servile or obsequious:

May I inquire regarding *His Excellency's* health?

Could I interest *Madam* in trying on another size shoe?

At one time English verbs had inflectional forms corresponding to the person of the subject, usually a pronoun, and this is still true of many languages that we encounter in school and elsewhere. Indeed, as late as the beginning of the seventeenth century the present tense of an English verb had the following forms:

	singular	*plural*
first person	I find	we find
second person	thou findest	ye find
third person	he findeth *or* finds	they find

As the result of certain social changes, the *thou* pronoun all but disappeared and consequently the need for a corresponding verb inflection. About the same time, though for entirely different reasons, the *-eth* inflection was replaced by *-s* in the third person singular. As a result, except for this *-s* of the third person, all verbal indication of person has been lost. In some nonstandard varieties of English even the *-s* is often lacking, or it may be used indiscriminately for all three persons in both singular and plural. On the other hand, in the copula *be* the person forms show no sign of deterioration. In Present-day English we have:

	singular	*plural*
first person	I am	we are
second person	you are	you are
third person	he is	they are

Other than this there are no person-corresponding forms in English verbs.

Number

A unique characteristic of the English noun is its system of number, that is, the contrast it makes between its singular and its plural forms. Typically a noun plural consists of *base* + $\{S_1\}$. Pronouns are also spoken of as having number, but number in pronouns differs essentially from that in nouns. *Base* in our stock of nouns can include any one of tens, if not hundreds, of thousands of words. The selection of items in the pronoun system is extremely small. A word like *fish*, for instance, indicates a single member of an extensive class; *fishes* has to do with a larger number of items of the class, and certainly more than one. *I* on the other hand refers to one person, and the entire class consists of that single item. In our grammar books *we* is usually called the "plural of *I*" for no other reason than that it fits a particular slot in the "paradigm"; any plurality of *I*'s is either meaningless or recognition of a split personality. As a rule *we* means "I and somebody else" or "I and a number of other people." Some languages distinguish between a *we* that includes the person addressed and another *we* that excludes him, and not unexpectedly these are called "inclusive" and "exclusive" pronouns. We do not need to make the distinction very often, but if the occasion arises we can depend on context or we can point with the hand or say so specifically.

You is the second person pronoun, singular as well as plural. This situation sometimes causes awkward problems, but most of us have learned to anticipate them. In Old English *thou* referred to just one person, and *ye* (later *you*) referred to more than one, comparable to the distinction between French *tu* and *vous*, German *du* and *Sie*, Spanish *tu* and *usted*. Actually in the plural German *Sie* (literally 'they') has replaced *ihr*, and Spanish *usted*, a contraction of *vuestra merced* 'your grace' has replaced *vos*. A simple distinction between singular and plural is easy to employ but difficult to maintain because it gets complicated by various kinds of social considerations. This happened also in English. With the growth of tiny principalities into continually larger and larger kingdoms, the estate of the royal person also grew more exalted, a fact never completely lost on the king himself. Within a moderately short time the kings began speaking of themselves as *we*, speaking on behalf of their realms, of course. This has been regarded an immemorial prerogative of royalty; Mark Twain once commented that the only individuals who could legitimately use *we* were editors, kings, and people with a tapeworm. The speeches of King Claudius in *Hamlet* are egregious examples of this royal *we*. Once the king has spoken of himself as *we*, that is, in the plural, how does a subject address him? Obviously not as *thou,* in the singular, but as *you,* also in the plural. Now that the king is irreversibly *you,* what does a subject do about the queen and other members of the royal household? Within a relatively short while the number distinction has become obscured or lost and *you* has become an emblem of respect while *thou* has come to indicate familiarity or informality. Indeed, as early as the fifteenth century *thou* has come to designate an intimate friend, a social inferior, a person with whom one is vexed or angry, a child, a small animal, a patron saint, or God. The King James Bible, though presumably written in the English of Shakespeare, uses *thou* exclusively for the singular[1] and *you* exclusively for the plural.

The loss of a number-distinctive pronoun contrast has come about as the result of the disappearance of *thou,* so that *you* refers either to the person addressed, or to that person and one or more beside. Our attempts to restore a distinction have not been altogether successful. *You'all* /yɔ́hl/ is the most familiar and is socially acceptable, but it is consistently associated with the Deep South and parts of the Midland and only with those. Whether, as a matter of fact, the distinction between *you* and *you'all* is as scrupulously maintained as the Southerners claim it to be is a topic for frequent and inconclusive debate. *You's* and *you'se* /yúws/, /yúwz/, and /yɨz/ have some currency, almost entirely substandard. *You-uns* represents a tendency to attach *you* as a modifier to another word, *ones*—actually *you*

---

1 In neither the Old Testament nor the New Testament are prayers and petitions ever addressed to more than one person of the Divine Trinity at any occasion; consequently the King James Version of the Bible never addresses God as *you*. In Sonnet XIV of the Holy Sonnets John Donne was careful to observe the proper number: "Batter my heart, three person'd God, for *you*. . . ."

ones—an extension of a class which includes *everyone, anyone, someone*. *You-uns* and a related *we-uns* are substandard. *You guys,* constructed on the same basic pattern as *you-uns,* has been a nonstandard form for many years; it has several equally informal variants: *you's guys* and *you'se guys*. *You men, you fellows, you girls,* and similar expressions are really part of the same pattern. They are acceptable English, but as plurals they are clearly makeshifts. Like *all of you,* a "periphrastic" plural, they clearly indicate plurality, but they do not manage at the same time to set off *you* as being unambiguously singular, which is what should happen if any of them should succeed as the plural counterpart of a singular *you*.

Third person relates to anyone or anything written or spoken about. The singular forms of the pronouns in English are *he, she* and *it*, and the plural of each of them or any combination of them is *they*.

Gender

In the third person singular forms of the personal pronoun we have a special relationship between the individual pronouns themselves and three extremely large classes of English nouns. To this relationship grammarians have given the name "gender," a word that basically means nothing more than 'sort' or 'class' or 'kind,' but we have attached far more specific meanings to it.

The number of genders that an individual language may have varies far more widely than we are likely to imagine. Some languages have twenty or more, but it should be emphasized that the basis of classification in such languages is completely different from our own. Greek, Latin, and German have three such genders, known respectively as "masculine," "feminine," and "neuter." Spanish and French have only masculine and feminine. Whatever its nature, gender consists simply of a system of classifying nouns and linking them morphologically with the articles and adjectives which modify them. Usually it also links these nouns with particular personal pronouns. Speakers of such languages take the gender system of their language for granted; it does not occur to them that speakers of English think it odd for a feminine hand to be linked to a masculine arm by a neuter wrist, as happens in German, or that a German spoon, fork, and knife should be respectively masculine, feminine, and neuter. In Old English a system closely related to this and very similar to it prevailed, but during the tenth and eleventh centuries the fully inflected definite article was reduced to the simple *the*, and at about the same time the inflectional endings of nouns and adjectives largely disappeared. The pronouns remained in the language, as might be expected, but they assumed a different set of relationships. Names of men had regularly corresponded to *he*, of women and girls to *she*. As in Present-day German, words like *wife, child, maiden* were grammatically neuter, which means only that they were qualified by adjectives and articles with neuter gender inflections. Lacking the reinforcement of the definite article and the adjective inflections, these words and others presently drifted into other classifications. *Wife* and *maiden* now corresponded specifically with *she,* and *child* with whatever pronoun the situation seemed to favor. Words like *stone, path, wedge, hill* had been masculine, but once the definite article and adjective distinctions deteriorated, this classification fell apart. The pronoun *it* was generalized to include all of them and thousands of other words besides. Sometimes the resulting arrangement is called "natural gender" in contrast to "grammatical gender," for no other reason than that we regard it as natural. The Frenchman or the German regards his own system as logical; he sees nothing strange in the notion that words like *summer* or *south* should be masculine.

What we now have is a purely arbitrary linking between the pronoun *he* and a great list of words like *Ned, Titus, Admiral Schley, brother, ox, bull, lion;* between *she* and words like *Lois, Eugenia, Madame Curie, sister, cow, lioness;* between *it* and words like *sloth, zipper, coke, fixation, Chinese elm.* So we say it is sex-linked. But *mouse, canary, snake,* and *giraffe* have sex. We explain that by saying that we refer to each one as *it* because the sex characteristics are obscure. But this is not true of *rooster, hen, he-ape, she-elephant,* and particularly *torso,* which we regularly speak of as *it.* Such distribution, even though the list of borderline words is short, must nevertheless be considered arbitrary. In Old English the words *world* and *church* were grammatically feminine and were referred to as *she* simply as a matter of course. In current religious literature the word *church* continues to be designated as *she* by certain writers, and it is often difficult to decide whether such usage is a self-conscious archaism or a wistful preciousness. Great and venerable institutions are occasionally referred to by a feminine pronoun:

God bless America
Land that I love
  Stand beside her
  And guide her. . . .

Universities bearing the names of John Harvard, Eli Yale, or Ezra Cornell would be excluded, and so would Congress and various branches of federal and state government. A battleship, often spoken of as a man-of-war, is sometimes incongruously called *she* with a kind of sentimental personification also bestowed on other engines having axial motion, whether driven by steam, electricity, or internal combustion.

Gender causes few serious usage or grammatical problems in English. The danger lies in trying too hard.

Case

Grammarians have a great deal to say about "case," but they seldom go to the trouble of defining it. The word *case* itself is related to the Latin word *cāsus* 'fall,' and its application to the present situation came about in an utterly absurd manner. During the fourth century B.C., we must believe, a Greek grammarian was explaining to his students the characteristics of the Greek noun. In order to illustrate his point, he extended the four fingers of his left hand and explained that each finger could be associated with an inflectional form of the noun. The names for the different forms have come down to us by way of Latin as "nominative," "genitive," "dative," and "accusative." It takes little imagination to visualize the consequences. A literal-minded member of the class copied the extended fingers as a diagram,

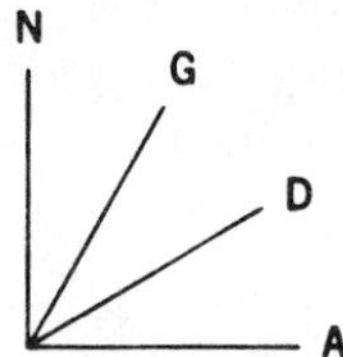

and as soon as he had won his credentials to teach, he began to teach the diagram itself. So in order to name the case forms of a noun or adjective the student ran them through the stages of their decline, and literally "declined" them. They were "cases" because on the diagram they appeared to fall from the upright position. Furthermore we continue to speak of genitive, dative, and accusative as "oblique" cases since they appear as slanting marks on the diagram. In fact, at one time the Greek grammarians carried on a vigorous debate over whether the nominative could legitimately be called a case; after all, its line was vertical.

In a language like Greek or Latin, and for that matter German or Russian, inflected case is a familiar concept. In Old English, as we have observed, there were five cases in the definite article and remnants of five in the noun and adjective systems, although the particular forms had begun to fall together. Presumably there ought to be a grammatical case form corresponding to every grammatical function, but there are dozens of functions, and even in the very earliest forms of the language from which English is ultimately descended there seem to have been no more than eight case forms. This means that every case form has been assigned several grammatical functions. Although the number of recognizable case forms may decrease, the number of functions remains nevertheless the same. The functions are still there, but we no longer depend on the case forms to indicate them. Instead we can tell by its position in a sentence whether a particular noun signifies the actor or the beneficiary or the receiver of an action; and we can tell by the choice of a preposition whether a noun serves a descriptive function or refers to something like time or place or agency. In other words, the case system of Old English has been generally superseded by a variety of other grammatical devices, primarily word order and connectives.

Over against the English noun system, which has become almost completely noninflectional, or "analytic," to use the more precise term, we have a pronoun system which has remained almost wholly inflected, or "synthetic." Pronoun case forms have undergone no significant change in more than a thousand years, and even today they show only sporadic signs of weakening. Long ago the English sentence accommodated itself to the disappearance of distinctive case forms in nouns, and since this is the situation there is no reason why case forms should have remained in the pronoun system. Most of the problems we encounter in connection with English pronoun usage result directly from the conflict between a new sentence structure based on the analytic noun system and the old pronoun system which clings to its historic inflections.

The extremely high frequency of occurrence of English pronouns has been responsible for preserving the forms they have kept almost intact since the English language was first recorded.[2] There is a nominative, or "subjec-

---

2 Two changes should be mentioned. The genitive singular neuter *its* is first cited late in the sixteenth century. Previously writers used *his* (Genesis 1:11 KJV; Shakespeare's Sonnet XVIII, 6) or *thereof* (Matthew 2:16 KJV; *Richard the Third,* I. iii. 154) or *it* (Leviticus 25:5 KJV [*its* in current printings]; *Hamlet,* I. ii. 216). *They, their,* and *them* were Scandinavian borrowings (see page 171).

tive" case, an accusative or "objective" case, and a genitive or "possessive" case. In most of these we have distinctive forms. In a few instances, however, a single form suffices for two cases:

	singular				
	first person	*second person*	*third person*		
nominative	I	[thou]	he	she	it
genitive	my	[thy]	his	her	its
accusative	me	[thee]	him	her	it
		plural			
nominative	we	[ye]		they	
genitive	our	your		their	
accusative	us	you		them	

The second person singular forms have disappeared except in the archaic forms of poetry and in a style still frequently heard in religious worship. *Thee* is used by some Quakers for both nominative and accusative. In the plural of the second person the accusative form has replaced the original nominative as a result of a development exactly parallel to the one by which *It's me* came about. The distinction between subject *ye* and object *you* is carefully maintained in the King James Bible, but *ye* does not occur often in Shakespeare. Except in phrases like "O ye gods!" *you* is regularly used for both subject and object.

When the case endings of English nouns were lost, the variations in word order which had been possible in Old English[3] now became greatly reduced. There was a time when a sentence like

The dragon hath Saint George slain.

would not have been ambiguous at all. Even after nouns had been excluded

3 Cf. C. C. Fries *American English Grammar* (New York: Appleton-Century-Crofts, 1940), chap. 10, especially p. 252. Fries' findings indicated that in English of the period including the eleventh through the thirteenth centuries, the object preceded the verb just about as often as it followed the verb; in other words, position was optional. During the fourteenth century a slight shift occurred; the object appeared after the verb about 60 percent of the time. But in writings of the fifteenth century, the object appeared before the verb only about 14 percent of the time, and by the next century it had dropped to something under 2 percent.

from such constructions, considerable freedom was possible with respect to pronouns: indeed, as long as the subject had the nominative case form and the object had the accusative case form, it did not greatly matter in what order they appeared:

> Him *the Almighty Power*
> *Hurled headlong flaming from the ethereal sky*
> *With hideous ruin and combustion, down*
> *To bottomless perdition, there to dwell*
> *In adamantine chains and penal fire,*
> *Who durst defy the Omnipotent to arms.*
> —Milton, *Paradise Lost*

Word order did not become established in its present-day patterns overnight or even over the period of a decade or two, but within a few generations a definite change had taken place. The part of the sentence occurring before the main verb was felt to be "subject territory" and that following the main verb was "object territory." Consequently if a noun was to function as the subject of a sentence the need for a distinctive subject form decreased, but subject position became vital. Even in Old English the nominative and accusative forms of many nouns had merged into a common form, and yet a few had contrasting forms which were further strengthened by distinctive article and adjective forms. Long before the time of Chaucer the number of distinctions had dwindled to a mere handful—seven or eight sets of words, all of them pronouns: *I, me; thou, thee; he, him; she, her; we, us; ye, you; they, them; who, whom.* Case distinctions in the second person singular and plural have since gone by the board, reducing the number to six.

We can say that in effect for the past ten or twelve centuries two grammatical systems—word order and word inflections—have been in competition within the English language and that in every issue word order has quite generally prevailed. On the grounds of grammatical consistency we should have expected the pronoun system to be "leveled" long ago to a single case or at most two cases, following the pattern established by the English nouns. The only actual leveling that has taken place appears in the second person plural; the pronoun *it* does not represent a leveling since in the neuter nouns and pronouns, subject and object forms are identical even in the earliest English writings, following a pattern that also appears in the other Germanic languages and in Latin and Greek.

The high frequency of occurrence of the pronoun case forms has preserved them as items, much as the irregular plurals of *man, woman, tooth, child* and so on remain as items rather than parts of a systematic pattern. As a result the speaker of English remains sensitive to the contrast between subject and object form over against subject and object function in the English pronouns, but he may find it hard to describe in so many words how he reacts. As a matter of course we put subject forms into "subject territory" and we put object forms into "object territory," as long as there is little need to wonder which is which. With subject pronouns there has never been serious difficulty, even in the language of the less educated:

He is my best friend.

I suppose you are right

There *she* is.

I hope *he* remembers his vitamins.

Object pronouns we also handle with great consistency. There are two constructions which are regarded as object territory: (1) Immediately following the principal verb of a clause or a sentence, as direct or indirect object:

Girls always interested *him*.

Stupid remarks like those worry *me*.

Perhaps you shouldn't have told *her*.

Just tell *me* your troubles.

and (2) Immediately following a preposition, that is, after *at, by, of, in, with,* etc.:

Well, that's the way it was told to *me*.

With *him* we've got all the help we need.

You've done far too many kind things for *us*.

Of *whom* could I have been thinking?

Since word order takes priority over case forms in any situation, it is possible for object forms of pronouns to occur in subject position. The meaning is perfectly clear even though we regard the usage as substandard:

Me and *him* trapped the weasel.

Every speaker of English senses that the weasel is in danger, not the boys. To argue otherwise would be ridiculous and pedantic.

Whenever the object forms of pronouns turn up in subject territory as a result of sentence inversion or other such, there is an overwhelming tendency to change the pronouns to subject form. The history of *whom* illustrates this:

For *whom* are you looking?

In spoken English and increasingly in written English the preposition is placed in final position:

Whom are you looking for?

But in general usage *whom* in initial position has come to be regarded as stuffy and even hypercorrect, mainly because it is so conspicuous in subject territory. And so in spoken English and often in written English the form is:

Who are you looking for?

Although this is often deplored by guardians of the mother tongue, parallel constructions are firmly entrenched in English:

The Good Conduct medal was awarded *him* last February.

Rearranging the elements, we have the following:

* *Him* was awarded the Good Conduct medal last February.

While consistency dictates some obligation to defend this construction, anyone with a sense of English usage immediately rejects it as non-English. It has become so common that we explain it as a "passive" construction. Again, from the King James Bible we have this:

Hee *that is without sinne among you, let* him *first cast a stone at her*
John 8:7

Consistency would now indicate that in place of *hee* 'he' we should have *him,* since consistency demands that it should agree with the *him* of the *let him* construction. But in this instance as well as in the others the force of subject position has dictated the choice of subject form. Any other form would, as we usually express it, "feel awkward," which is commonly a reliable test in such matters.

While subject form has an almost completely unchallenged claim to subject territory, object form has not yet become firmly established in object territory. Usage is still divided, although the long-time drift of English is clearly in the direction of regularization. Even as early as the fourteenth century, object pronoun forms appeared in object position regardless of whether they were objects of the verb or not:

> It's *Bruce.*
>
> It's *him.*
>
> It's *me.*

Carrying on a usage established in translations of a century or more earlier, the King James Bible retained "It is *I*" (Matthew 14:27) and "I am not *he*" (Acts 13:25). Shakespeare was in keeping with the more usual practice of his time:

> *Oh the dogge is* me, *and I am my selfe.*
> —*Two Gentlemen of Verona,* II.iii.25

In formal writing there is no occasion to use a construction of this nature, and consequently it usually appears only in letters, diaries, and representations of spoken English in fiction and plays. In these, however, we have scores of eminent users of English employing the object form of not only the first person singular, but the other pronouns as well.

The only situation in which the subject form may be justified in object territory is following the copula *be* and on rare occasions *become.* To keep this exception consistently in sight calls for more grammatical sensitivity than speakers of English can normally muster, and as a result for all practical purposes the object form regularly follows *be.* On the analogy of Latin—in which not only pronouns had accusative forms, but also adjectives and nouns and even participles and gerunds—the grammarians of the eighteenth and nineteenth centuries strove mightily to restore the English nominative—such as it was—to this position. But even among the grammarians there were some articulate foot-draggers, among them Noah Webster and Joseph

Priestley. The result was not what the grammarians hoped for. In the mind of the ordinary user of English the exact nature of the construction remained as obscure as ever and he was now also burdened with the fear that he might be doing it wrong. He had a vague impression, however, that he could play it safe by putting *I* somewhere following the verb. This may have been responsible even as early as Shakespeare's time for the peculiar construction we find in Sonnet LXXII:

> *And hang more praise upon deceased* I.

The other possibility, and a more likely one, is that Shakespeare needed an emphatic pronoun in this position and felt that *I* was more emphatic than *me*. Not until two or three generations later would people really begin worrying about the correctness of such a construction. In some English sentences, especially those that are introduced by *there* or by an adverbial phrase, the subject and verb are often inverted:

> There was *I*, tired and cross and hungry.
>
> On the bridge stood *Ronald and I*.

Both of these have a literary flavor about them and they might seem a little unusual in ordinary conversation. Yet someone trying to speak "correct" English would not only try to produce a sentence like these, but might go a step further:

> There on the bridge he met *Ronald and I*.

Users of English who can deal effortlessly and unerringly with all of the possibilities represented here merit a special status, though most of them will already have achieved it through other dexterous wielding of the language. The problem will ultimately resolve itself. Meanwhile those who are unsure of themselves will take refuge in constructions which enable them to avoid the issue, or otherwise they simply expose themselves willy-nilly to the judgment of the linguistic elect.

Related to this is another construction in which a verb is followed by a pronoun which in turn operates as a subject of a clause that follows. The danger does not lie in forgetting what is the subject and what is the object, but in trying too hard to do the correct thing:

I wonder *who* (*whom*) is kissing her now.

To make an error like this seems difficult, yet many speakers of English have managed to do so. The reverse is perhaps even more common:

It transforms *he* who uses it into a creature of great power.

Evidently the difficulty is one of long standing. The translators of the King James Bible did this:

Let the same be she *that thou hast appointed for thy servant Isaac.*

—Genesis 24:14

And Shakespeare:

Lay on, Macduffe,
And damn'd be him *that first cries hold, enough.*
—*Macbeth,* V.viii.33

Among the difficulties involving pronouns in object position, the most persistent has to do with words like *and* and *or*, commonly called "conjunctions." In many languages a clear line separates conjunctions from prepositions, but in English the line is often imprecise. In fact, both connect words or groups of words, and one of the few fundamental differences is that in standard English the object form follows the preposition, and the subject form follows the conjunction, unless the word preceding the conjunction is in turn preceded by a preposition. This sounds like a difficult rule to remember. It is. And as a guide for deciding whether to use the subject or the object form of a pronoun, it may be dismissed as valueless. A typical sentence with a preposition and a pronoun is:

Phoebe took a liking *to him.*

A typical sentence involving also a conjunction is:

Phoebe took a liking *to* Knut *and he* (or *him?*).

All of us have encountered the standard explanation, invariably phrased as a rhetorical question: "You wouldn't say 'to he' would you?" Now that is hardly the problem. Even very stupid people have no difficulty deciding which pronoun to use immediately following a preposition. They know that after a word like *at, by, for, from,* or *with,* the pronoun forms are *me, him, her, us, them,* and sometimes *whom.* But what does a person do after *and* or *or?* Most speakers of English have noticed that it varies; usually the object form occurs, but now and then the subject form does. To remember that the pronoun must take the same case as the word following the preposition is beside the point for most speakers of English, including many who are well educated and who occupy positions of social eminence.[4]

Several important considerations govern the usual solutions to this problem:

1. Those who leave the whole thing to blind chance, simply hoping somehow to be able to hit it right, actually do so at least half the time. The linguistically sensitive have the impression that such people make innumerable errors, yet anyone who takes the trouble to listen will notice that they also use the "correct" forms. This is a typical situation in which the listener ignores what he considers "normal" and notices only what to him is "abnormal."

2. In most instances the word which immediately precedes the conjunction offers no clue to the case called for. That is the situation, for instance, when the conjunction is preceded by a proper noun or by some larger grammatical construction:

After a long wait in walked *Mrs. Gonzales and he.*
Please be more considerate of *your brother's children and us.*
The only ones left in the room were *that tattooed trapeze performer and I.*

3. In day-to-day practice we employ many expressions like *Jane and I* or *him and me* which operate as linguistic subunits and which do not come apart even though they are written as separate words. They are what we could call "holomorphs." In "in Just-," a poem by e. e. cummings, the poet mentions *eddieandbill* and *bettyandisbel,* and the reader senses at once that these are inseparable friends. Whether we approve or not, the language often operates with such unanalyzed units, moving them intact to either subject or object position, especially if the first member of the unit happens to be a proper name or other nonpronoun.

4. Thanks in considerable measure to the untiring labors of the Proprietors of the Language in cultivating the *It is I* construction in both written and spoken English, we are now burdened with the impression that the subject form at the end of an utterance is more "genteel" or more "elegant." The grammarians had no intention of encouraging the things that have come about, we may be sure, but such are the results when people go against the inherent nature of the language. A sentence "wants to go" in a certain direction and when through wilfulness or ignorance it is driven in another direction, it bears strange fruit.

---

4 Several interesting examples appear in Thomas Pyles *The Origin and Development of the English Language* (New York: Harcourt Brace Jovanovich, 1971), p. 246.

We have at present an unresolved situation. There is ample reason to suppose that so few persons are any longer sure of themselves in the use of this construction that it has become unimportant as a linguistic status determiner. And so, if one is in doubt, the safest procedure is to use the object form following any verb since that is the one that most commonly occurs in this position.

Pronoun case forms offer problems in positions following certain other words also classified as conjunctions, in this case "subordinators": *as, than, but* (in the sense of "excluding"), *except, save,* and in some situations *like:*

The boy stood on the burning deck
Whence all but *he had fled.*[5]

In Old English *but* was clearly a preposition and was regularly followed by the object form of the noun or pronoun; later it was just as clearly a conjunction. In the intervening five centuries the question has never been clearly resolved. It does not often come up, and few people have cultivated firm habits; instead the speaker of English depends on something he regards as analogical, usually a safe solution. H. W. Fowler suggested that many consider *All but I* (*me*) closely parallel to *It is I* (*me*). If they say *It is I* they will say *All but I;* if they say *It is me* they will say *All but me.* It is doubtful that any except the ultracorrect would say *All except I,* although that is a much closer parallel, and it suggests that if we want to be consistent we should approve of *All but me.*

The difficulty is that another approach to the problem gives another answer. There is, for example, a sentence like:

All my brothers are Detroit Tiger fans but *him* (*he*).

A grammarian identifies this as a shortening, or "ellipsis," of a fuller sentence:

All my brothers are Detroit Tiger fans, but *he* is not a Detroit Tiger fan.

---

5 Bartlett's *Familiar Quotations,* 11th ed., (Boston: Little, Brown, 1937), has this note: "The first American edition of Mrs. Hemans' *Poems* [1826] gave this line 'whence all but *him* had fled.' English editions and subsequent American editions seem evenly divided between 'but *him*' and 'but *he*.' The last edition published while Mrs. Hemans was still living and presumably approved the contents [1829] gives 'but *he*.'"

In written modes a person has the time to reflect about such matters, and consequently the subject form remains firmly established in written English. But in speaking few of us trouble our heads about elliptical constructions. We take the closest analogy:

They all had lunch *with* me.

They all had lunch *before* me.

They all had lunch *but* me.

The connective *as* often makes a comparison:

Is she as tall as me?
—*Antony and Cleopatra,* III.iii.14

Once again we can assume that this should be taken as an elliptical sentence and that Shakespeare really intended to say:

Is she as tall *as I* am tall?

The situation closely resembles that of *but,* since the subject form is the one usually found in written English, and the object form in all but the most formal spoken English.

Comparatives. The connective *than* regularly follows the comparative form of an adjective, and also some words not considered comparatives as such: *rather, other, else.* Ellipsis determines which pronoun form one will use:

No one can possibly be stupider than *him.*

No one can possibly be stupider than *he* (is stupid).

Among reputable writers of English the object form of the pronoun following *than* has long enjoyed favor—more indeed than following the other connectives of this group—evidently because it is used more frequently and is therefore further along the way toward its ultimate development than the others. In spoken English the object form may be regarded as completely established.

One has to be careful with "transitive verbs"—verbs followed by an object. The choice of pronoun case may be critical:

Ruth gave the dog more attention than *I* (gave the dog).

Ruth gave the dog more attention than (she gave) *me*.

Long and intimate acquaintance with the literary modes of English has given some persons considerable adroitness in dealing with matters like these at the same time that they are engaging in all of the sundry brainwork that a social conversation requires. For such competence they deserve extra credit, and consequently we are likely to regard the subject form as preferable. We are led to consider as more correct and in better taste sentences and phrases like:

Is she as tall as *I*?

Whence all but he *had fled.*

To insist on the same virtuosity from those less accomplished in the use of English is to invite disasters worse than any of those we have mentioned.

Accusatives. We noted earlier that in the second person pronoun the nominative *ye* was completely replaced at an early date by the accusative *you,* and that in Quaker speech the nominative *thou* has pretty largely given way to the accusative *thee.* This represents a general trend in English. We may in fact say that the nominative forms occur only as the subjects of verbs and the accusative forms occur everywhere else.

Her? I wouldn't marry her if she was the last woman on earth.

He started the fight, not *me.*

Who, *me?*

Dear *me!*

Me Tarzan. You Jane.

This tendency accounts for a usage like:

Us boys were giving the guinea pig a bath.

Boys is plainly the subject of *were giving,* and the first person plural pronoun simply needs to identify the subject. Grammatically the specific case does not matter, and therefore in the speech of many users of English it is the object form. The usage is still regarded as nonstandard in writing and in cultured conversation, although it is beginning to achieve a borderline respectability.

I, we, us. It has been observed that the pronoun *we* is not the plural of ***I*** in the same sense that *cats* is the plural of *cat,* but that it has the general significance of 'I and someone else.' In some situations *we* is substituted for *you,* most notably in the language of nurses, sometimes in that of veterinarians, and occasionally in that of schoolteachers. This usage seems to be increasing:

> How did *we* sleep last night?
>
> Are *we* ready for an enema?
>
> Did a mean old dog bite *us?*

The first person can also be involved in requests and commands of various kinds. The usual style of request or command is addressed to one or more persons, none of them the speaker:

> *Read* the next three chapters.
>
> Please *get* me a clean spoon.
>
> While you're up *bring* me a glass of milk, if you will.

Including the speaker, however:

> *Let's read* the next three chapters.

The full form is *let us,* but we rarely encounter it outside of certain formulaic constructions, or in formal situations like:

> Let *us* pray.

Let us *therefore brace ourselves to our duties, and so bear ourselves that, if the British Empire and its Commonwealth last for a thousand years, men will say, "This was their finest hour."*

—Winston Churchill

Ordinarily the expression is *let's,* a single syllable. In this respect it is unique. None of the other pronouns are as completely syncopated, and it is only after the verb *let* that the pronoun *us* is so reduced. We should not regard as English and should have difficulty understanding sentences like:

* *Get's* another cup of coffee, Julie.

* *Make's* a ham salad sandwich.

The *'s* for *us* occurs occasionally in Shakespeare's writings as well as in early English writers with verbs other than *let*. It is still to be found in Scottish:

And here's a hand, my trusty frien'
And gie's *a hand o' thine.*
—Robert Burns

Since the /əs/ is reduced to /s/ in this construction, and only here, it is often misunderstood altogether:

Let's us girls go water skiing.

Let's you and him fight.

Let's don't have no trouble.

The object case significance of *us* has long been incidental in this construction. Apparently users of English feel the need to supply another pronoun, not so much in apposition with *us* as to identify the subject of the main verb.

Let us *make a covenant,* I and thou. —Genesis 31:44

Let us *go then,* you and I.

—T. S. Eliot, *The Love Song of J. Alfred Prufrock*

Them. The pronoun *them* offers two minor but sometimes annoying considerations. The first is the use of *them* as a "demonstrative" or pointing pronoun:

You can't never trust *them* cheap nylons.

Move *them* plank over about a foot this way.

The word is spelled the same way as the personal pronoun *them,* but it comes from a completely different source. Originally it was an inflected form of the Old English definite article *the,* in the dative case, and was used only in object functions. It could be either singular or plural but it has been used mainly as a plural demonstrative since Old English times. On the other hand, its use in the nominative is well attested for more than four centuries. It is no longer used by educated writers of English except in identifying the language of the unlettered. Here it continues to be common; and in fact it is looked on as one of the trademarks of substandard English.

The second consideration is that the personal pronoun *them* is one of several significant contributions made to English by the Viking invaders of the ninth and tenth centuries. In Old English the third person plural pronouns were (making some allowance for spelling differences) *hey, her,* and *hem* while in the Scandinavian dialects they were approximately (with some allowance here also) *they, their,* and *them. Hey* and *her* had been substantially replaced by the end of the Middle English period, but it has taken far longer to replace the original pronoun *hem.* It is still very common, especially in spoken English:

That's telling *'em.*

Milo ran *'em* ragged.

The *'em* is a carry-over from *hem*—just as *it* is a carry-over from the earlier *hit*—not a beheading of *them.* If it were, we should expect an analogous *'ey* and *'eir* side by side with *they* and *their,* neither of which we encounter in standard English.

Who, whom. *Who* is not a personal pronoun, but like the personal pronouns it has distinctive forms for three cases: *who, whose, whom.* It functions, however, chiefly as the opening of a question or as a connective, known in traditional grammatical language as "interrogative" and "relative." Functionally it is a member of the class of words that includes *where, when, what, why, which, how,* none of which are inflected for case except *which* with an occasional genitive *whose. Who,* in addition to the genitive *whose,* has an object form *who,* the source of many of our problems.

In certain constructions the object forms of pronouns typically occur:

I saw *him* (*her, them*).

It is *I* (*me*).

Give it to *him* (*her, them*).

But we do not have:

> *I saw *whom.*
>
> *It is *whom.*
>
> *Give it to *whom.*

The single possible exception is an interrogative with strong emphasis on the final word to indicate surprise or disbelief:

> "On the bus this morning I sat with Prof. Quinbus Flestrin." "You sat with *whom?*"

But when it operates as an interrogative it is regularly in subject position and therefore takes the subject form:

> "Who *has been sleeping in my bed?*"

However, when *who*(*m*) operates as the direct object of a verb or as object of a preposition in a question construction, the demands of English word order assign it to the beginning of the sentence, and this is of course normally subject position:

> *Whom* shall we ask to be best man?
>
> *Whom* are you voting for?

In speech and even in much informal writing *whom* is being replaced with increasing frequency by *who.* *Whom* begins to smack of pedantry, perhaps because of the constant danger of using it hypercorrectly:

> *Whom* shall I say this is?

The peril is by no means new. Even such sticklers for correctness as the translators of the King James Bible pitched headlong into the trap, not once but three times (Matthew 16:13; Mark 8:27; Luke 9:18):

> Whom *doe men say that I am?*

When *who* and *whom* are used as connectives, the function of the pronoun within the particular clause determines which form is to be used:

I visited my brother, *who* lives in Duluth.

I visited my brother, *whom* I had not seen since 1945.

The transformational grammarian would explain that these sentences are generated respectively by the following:

I visited my brother. *He* lives in Duluth.

I visited my brother. I had not seen *him* since 1945.

The connective use also occurs following prepositions, the form *whom* being preferred, although the construction is regarded as stilted:

I visited my brother, from *whom* I had heard nothing.

I visited my brother, than *whom* no one is more talkative.

Again the transformational grammarian would offer:

I visited my brother. I had heard nothing from *him*.

I visited my brother. No one is more talkative than *him*.

Such constructions with *whom* were in common use until a few centuries ago, but a present-day writer would almost certainly recast them, probably making two sentences of them.

Because *whom* still flourishes when it immediately follows a preposition, the situation has given rise to a hypercorrection. The preposition may in some instances refer to an entire clause of which the pronoun happens to be the subject. When public speakers or radio announcers have neglected to read their prepared scripts carefully before delivering them, they are tempted to "correct" such a sentence as:

There was a question of *who* was to be chairman.

and to present it as:

There was a question of *whom* was to be chairman.

It is simply a matter of time till the *whom* form of the pronoun disappears altogether, so that *who* remains as an all-purpose relative, like *which* or *that.* Many users of cultivated English deliberately avoid using *whom,* considering it an affectation. Already *who* occurs in spoken English, following both verbs and prepositions, and it is not uncommon in informal writing.

Genitive. Genitive case forms of nouns, as we have observed, are restricted chiefly to nouns relating to animate beings or objects. In other situations we use either the uninflected genitive, or, more commonly, the "periphrastic genitive" with *of.* By their very nature English pronouns are personal; the genitives of pronouns for that reason are inflected rather than periphrastic. Some periphrasis with *of* happens on a limited scale. Thus *a picture of him* would be a "genitive of character," but *a picture of his* would be a "genitive of possession." In most cases *his picture* would be "object genitive."

Genitives of nouns may be either "attributive" or "absolute" as descriptive elements. Thus:

> *John's* book. (attributive)
>
> The book is *John's*. (absolute)

Genitives of pronouns can also occupy both constructions; however the syntactic construction dictates the form to be used. Thus:

> That is *my* book. (attributive)
>
> That book is *mine*. (absolute)

The attributive form regularly precedes the noun; the absolute form follows a "copulative" or "linking" verb, like *be* or *become.* Used with *of* it commonly indicates personal possession:

> An heirloom of *mine*

But

> An old sweetheart of *mine*

The characteristic forms are these:

	singular				
	first person	*second person*		*third person*	
attributive	my	[thy]	his	her	its
absolute	mine	[thine]	his	hers	its
		plural			
attributive	our	your		their	
absolute	ours	yours		theirs	

Originally the first and second person singular genitive pronoun forms were *mine* and *thine* in the nominative and had a complete set of inflectional endings, like an Old English adjective. By the end of the Old English period the inflectional endings had begun to disappear, and before the end of the Middle English period *mine* and *thine* had become restricted in attributive position to words with an initial vowel, paralleling the present-day distribution of *a* and *an:*

> *"Sire Knyght," quod he,* "my *mayster and* my *lord,*
> *Now draweth cut, for that is* myn *accord."*
> —Chaucer, *The Canterbury Tales,* "The General Prologue," 837–838

Mine and *thine* are still used occasionally in poetry, but the effect is intended to be solemn or archaic:

> Mine *eyes have seen the glory of the coming of the Lord.*
> —Julia Ward Howe

Because the pattern of the absolute genitive is quite irregular, we have occasional usage problems. There are three distinct models. The largest group has final *-s*:

your, yours her, hers our, ours their, theirs

Two pronouns have final *-n*:

my, mine thy, thine

And in a third group there is no distinction:

his, his   its, its

In earlier times, especially while *thy* was still prevalent, final *-n* was looked on as characteristic of the absolute form, and these forms developed: *hisn, hern, ourn, yourn, theirn,* as in:

Them there dogs is *hisn* and these here is *ourn.*

Today such forms are looked on as completely substandard, although they formerly enjoyed good standing and even had literary acceptance.[6] Speakers of substandard English tend not only to cling to archaic expressions, but also to assume that the language is more regular than it actually is.

The* -self *pronoun. English has a small group of pronouns with a distinctive *-self* "suffix," the function of which is to strengthen or to intensify the base pronoun. Originally the word *self* was an emphatic adjective which meant 'in fact' or 'even,' so that the phrase *the king self* could be translated into Present-day English as 'even the king.' Such an intensifying function is still evident in:

Larry *himself* baked those biscuits.

His wife decided to water the lawn *herself.*

Once the *-self* forms had become identified with the intensifying function, it was a short step to a "reflexive," that is, a construction in which the subject and object of the verb are the same person or thing:

Robinson Crusoe found *himself* on an island.

The snake rolled *itself* into a hoop.

Where it is possible, the *-self* pronoun may indicate that subject and indirect object are the same:

---

6 In Old English there was an oblique inflection of the genitive pronouns, the *-ne* of the masculine accusative singular. Thus *ūr* 'our' had the form *ūrne,* and *ēower* 'your' had the form *ēowerne.* There is no evidence that the *-n* forms stemmed from these, but the archaic forms may have reinforced the present-day substandard forms when they did appear.

The cowboy rolled *himself* a cigarette.

The dentist found *himself* a secretary.

The *-self* pronoun may also be used with prepositions:

Agatha used to talk to *herself.*

In standard English the *-self* forms rarely if ever take the place occupied by the regular personal pronouns; however we may encounter what has been called the "noncommital" use:

Now here's a picture of the wife and myself.

This would probably pass in spoken English, but is unacceptable in standard written English. The speaker is either excessively modest in avoiding the pronoun *I*, or, as seems likely, he uses this device to sidestep a choice between *I* or *me*. Or:

This girl and myself were looking at Mount Rushmore.

The models for constructing the *-self* forms are also irregular and commonly give rise to nonstandard expressions. In some cases it is the genitive form of the pronoun which is combined with the *-self:*

myself   ourselves   yourself   yourselves

But in others the object form is the base:

himself   herself   itself   themselves

A consistent pattern here yields the forms *hisself* and *theirselves* and also occasionally *meself.* At one time such forms were acceptable as good English; now they are considered substandard.

INDEFINITE PRONOUNS

Speakers of Old English used an indefinite pronoun *man* which remained in the language until the fourteenth century, according to the *Oxford English*

Dictionary. Sometime before 1300 the indefinite *one* had made its debut, although its use as we now know it was not well established until nearly 1500. How well established it is even at this late date raises a question, for with many users of English it continues to be a literary form and they never acquire the everyday ease in handling it that the German has with *man sagt*, or the Frenchman with *on dit*, or the speaker of Spanish with *se dice*. Few speakers of American English are comfortable with several *ones* strung out in the same sentence:

> If *one* falls off *one's* horse and *one* lands on *one's*
> head *one* takes *one's* chances on breaking *one's* neck.

Such a sentence might fare more easily among speakers of British English. The American faced with a *one* he cannot possibly avoid usually works out a compromise:

> If *one* falls off *his* horse and *he* lands on *his*
> head *he* takes *his* chances on breaking *his* neck.

In popular usage, and even in writing, several of the personal pronouns assume the function of an indefinite:

> *You* can't take it with *you*.
>
> *We* certainly take a lot for granted when *we*'re young and simple.
>
> *They* tell me it's going to rain.

Nervous language purists object to this last one on the grounds that *they* has no "antecedent." Such an objection starts from the shaky assumption that all pronouns need to have antecedents.

Sometimes full words assume the function, though not the title, of indefinite pronouns:

> *People* say that there are werewolves in the next county.
>
> A *person* can't have his cake and eat it too.
>
> A *girl* needs to use her head if she wants to succeed as a model.

There are those who send off letters to editors of newspapers and magazines expressing a need for an indefinite pronoun in English and sometimes proposing such a pronoun. But pronouns—indefinite or otherwise—do not enter the language in response to a letter to the editor, or even as the result of a resolution by a commission of distinguished language scholars. They appear as the result of real and immediate needs. *You, we, they, people,* and the rest of the improvisations do not require a word of apology, and as long as no one feels obliged to excuse the pronoun he uses we may picture the present situation as going on indefinitely. But if some expression should unexpectedly become the mark of preferred status, we could anticipate an "approved" indefinite pronoun within a very short while and every user of it would behave as though it had been in the language since the time of Beowulf. On the other hand, we can avoid the issue by using a passive construction, especially where the subject is not only vague but quite unimportant:

> He was called Ragnar Shaggybreeches.

Until now we speakers of English have failed to develop a really satisfactory way of dealing with the problem. *One . . . one . . .* sounds British; *one . . . he . . .* is American; neither sounds idiomatically English. *You* is dismissed as colloquial; *we* is often coy. The passive is also a refuge for those who have reservations about being specific. Possibly the very absence of an approved expression lends the indeterminate subject some value as a status-relevant form. It seems more likely that we do not really need an indefinite pronoun as such in English, seeing that we have been able to operate successfully with makeshifts all these years. Evidently common adoption of the indefinite would conflict with the basic specificity of the English sentence. The Germans and French and Spanish have this feature, it is true, but that does not mean that we users of English are under obligation to copy. All this time we have sidestepped the impulse, perhaps for better reason than we know.

9

verbs

Important as verbs are in our language, identifying them for their own sake ranks with the less useful things we can do with them, in spite of the hours of time schoolroom instruction has assigned to this enterprise. Furthermore, to identify them by means of the definitions offered in the handbooks is hazardous, since the definitions are scarcely more than makeshifts.

Grammarians have ventured a variety of definitions, some of them based on the morphology of the verb itself. For instance, a youngster in elementary school need not have any difficulty understanding: "A verb is a word that can indicate past time," which can be restated more technically, "A verb is a member of a class of words that can take a morpheme indicating past tense or time." After all, if the definition is to make any sense at all, the user of English must already be well up on his variant verb inflections. Again we find ourselves depending on our inherent "language sense" to identify words that fall into the verb category.

INFLECTIONAL FORMS

Second only to the pronoun, the verb ranks as the most highly inflected of the English form classes, or parts of speech. If we exclude from the class of verbs the copula *be*—as many grammarians do—the English verb has at most five distinct inflectional forms, and of these three are morphologically regular. Anyone who has been exposed to the complicated inflections of the verb in a language like French or Spanish or Latin or Greek realizes that the morphology of the English verb practically borders on destitution. Yet for all this poverty of distinctive forms, English easily copes with all the ideas that come by way of languages like Latin or Greek. It employs other means than inflections. For that reason no literate user of English has ever been hard put to it to express his ideas—certainly not on the grounds that his language was impoverished. Much of the humble toil is carried on instead by means of a considerable stock of verb auxiliaries, enabling us to produce without noticeable strain such sentences as:

Toni should have been able to try to keep on writing.

Might Wilcox have begun to need oxygen?

For the time being we are unconcerned with the auxiliaries. Usage problems that have to do with verbs center almost exclusively on morphological features, on irregularities of one kind or another. The actual number of such irregularities is small, but no user of English can afford to take them lightly since they are among the most important of linguistic status indicators in English.

The following paradigm will illustrate the organization of some typical English verbs:

function	*morpheme*	*typical verb forms*			
present	*base*	cut	walk	sing	go
preterite	*base* + {D_1}	cut	walked	sang	went
past participle	*base* + {D_2}	cut	walked	sung	gone
third person singular present	*base* + {S_3}	cuts	walks	sings	goes
present participle	*base* + {iŋ}	cutting	walking	singing	going

Two tendencies are evident here. On the one hand tense distinctions in a verb like *cut* have been completely obliterated so that there is a single form for all three "principal parts." On the other hand, verbs like *sing* and *go* differentiate all three, a fact that one ignores or violates at great peril to his reputation.

The five distinctive forms, where they appear, have their characteristic functions, as follows:

Present. In referring to a verb as a language item, or in looking for it in a dictionary, we cite the present tense form. The base form of the verb indicates general present tense in English, correlating with all subject forms except third person singular. Preceded by a verb auxiliary—a word like *shall, can, might,* etc.—or by the preposition *to,* the verb base is part of a construction called "infinitive." In Old English the infinitive consisted of the verb base with an *-an* inflectional suffix, as in *singan* 'to sing,' *helpan* 'to help,' *bringan* 'to bring,' *hliehhan* 'to laugh.' In Old English as now this form or construction called to mind no specific time, which is the reason it has been called "infinitive." In this respect it is sometimes interchangeable with the present participle which is also "nonfinite."

As early as the Old English period the infinitive had acquired a preposition—usually *to*—in certain constructions, and since it operated very much like a noun it acquired an oblique form. Some grammarians have called this a "gerund." The infinitive of Old English had a number of uses, all of which have carried over into Present-day English:

1. Expressing purpose: "Janousek was sent *to repair* the TV."
2. Expressing obligation (with *be*): "You are *to come* home by midnight."
3. Completing a noun: "Mrs. Minty had a tendency *to put* on weight."
4. Completing a verb: "Betty forgot *to set* her alarm."
5. Acting as subject or complement: "*To watch* Farnham skate was something *to remember.*"

At a later date verbs like *cause, order, request* also came to be followed by the infinitive construction:

The memory of her caused him *to sigh* deeply.

We make little distinction, if any, in Present-day English between later developments of the Old English infinitive and the Old English gerund. Both of them we now call infinitive, and a gerund is something completely different. The gerund originally followed the preposition *to,* and the infinitive did not, as is still true in some constructions, for example, most of the "modals"—*may, can, shall, might, could, must, will, should, would:*

I *shall* return.

You *would* have trouble if you *should* try getting a refund.

The jam *may* taste better than you *might* expect.

The infinitive without *to* is also used to complete the sense of certain verbs like *make* or *see:*

> Not all your pretty talk will make me *change* my mind.
>
> I saw your husband *drive* away with the blue Chevy.

That this is a relatively modern development is evident from a construction less than four centuries old:

> *He maketh me* to lie down *in green pastures.*
> —*Psalm* 23:3

The infinitive without *to* is spoken of as a "flat infinitive" in order to distinguish it from the other.

There are numberless instances of infinitives which do not have *to,* all of them in excellent standing, yet it is generally assumed that *to* is the "sign of the infinitive." Perhaps one reason is that we recognize it easily, as in:

> To be *or not* to be, *that is the question.*
> —*Hamlet,* III.i.56
>
> *To open,* tear along dotted line.

To is not especially sacred or exclusive, but it happens to be the word we use. Long ago there were several other prepositions, chiefly in the northern counties of England—*till* and *at,* for instance. A relic use of *at* survives in *at* + *do,* meaning 'to do,' now commonly spelled *ado* as in *Much Ado about Nothing*. The notion that *to* constituted an integral part of the infinitive is a grammarian's fiction invented during the nineteenth century as a product of the practice then current of "parsing" sentences, that is, breaking them down into their respective parts of speech and identifying each part by name. As a result, *to* became regarded as the equivalent of the infinitive inflection in Latin and Greek.

In recent times the infinitive with *to* as either the subject or "complement" of a verb has become increasingly common and has to a large extent replaced the "verbal noun," that is, the *-ing* form of the verb operating as a noun. As a result of this expanded use there has been a great deal of uneasiness regarding the "split" or "discontinuous" infinitive, a construction which would occur infrequently even if no one had ever raised voice or pen against it. The split infinitive consists of nothing more than a word or phrase, usually expressing manner or time or place, appearing between the *to* and the verb itself:

> *To eventually get* an A in Spanish
>
> *To then and there stop* smoking
>
> *To never again as long as I live eat* in that restaurant

One might with consistency suggest that modals ought not to be separated from their respective verbs, and neither ought the auxiliaries *be* or *have.* Pedantry being what it is, such a "rule" was promulgated with some conviction, and around the turn of the present century it was regarded by some teachers of English as an item to actually enforce.

The mere separation of *to* from its main verb is unimportant, and so is the occasional awkwardness that results. Most of us have made our peace with constructions far more awkward. At times a writer has no other means by which to bring a modifier into an unambiguous position in relation to its verb. Neither style nor clarity depends on whether the infinitive is continuous or split; what really matters is that someone has called attention to it, and that is the only reason that those who have become sensitized react as they do.[1]

Our problem usages commonly have social overtones of some sort; they identify the person who fails to qualify for the linguistic Establishment or who is too eager to show his credentials. In this regard the split infinitive is unique. It is used by both educated and uneducated people, although it is far more common in the usage of the educated. Only those with a well-developed sensitivity to language are likely to want their modifiers so exactly placed that they may need to fracture the infinitive in order to achieve greater clarity. For example:

> Mr. Bixby wanted *to completely paper* the walls and ceiling of his den.

Side by side with the *to* infinitive is a parallel construction with *and*

---

1 Most of our attitudes toward specific items of usage are actually manifestations of the classic "Grandpa's beard effect." Grandpa had a long white beard and one evening just before he went to bed one of his grandsons asked him, "Grandpa, when you sleep, do you put your beard under the blankets or outside of them?" He had never given it any thought till that moment, but from then on he used to lie awake wondering where the beard ought to go.

which is never referred to as an infinitive, but which functions in much the same fashion. It is common in colloquial English, but occurs in all styles of writing:

The maestro wants you to *come and see* that harpsichord.

Harry *ran and caught* the Stockton bus.

With words like *go* and *try* the constructions are sometimes considered to be tautological and are objected to on those grounds:

Floris *went and did* as his father had ordered.

Please *try and clean* the parakeet's cage before your mother comes.

Perhaps the worst that can be said about such constructions is that they sound more colloquial than literary, if that is indeed a fault. Many speakers of English would take them to signify a continued action over a period of time. There is indication that such constructions are making some headway in gaining status.

Third Person Singular. The third person singular of the present tense consists of base + $\{S_3\}$. The pronunciation follows the same general rules as apply to the regular noun plural and the genitive inflections. There are three exceptions to complete phonological regularity. For *say* the more acceptable form is /sez/ rather than /seyz/; the latter a spelling pronunciation and quite rare. Related to it is the *I says . . . and he says* of rapid narrative conversation, especially in relating gossip. It occurs only in these situations and serves as an illustration of systematic leveling. For *do* the form is *does* /dəz/, the vowel having been downgraded to /ə/ as the result of frequent unstressing; for *have* it is *has* /hæz/ rather than /hævz/, a form which may never have existed at all.

In older styles of English as used by Shakespeare and his contemporaries, and as it appears in the King James Bible, the present tense inflections were:

I think	we think
thou think'st *or* thinkest	ye think
he thinketh *or* thinks	they think

The *-eth* inflection stood in a direct line historically with Old English, through Chaucer, and in London literary English well into the sixteenth century, at which time it began to be replaced by *-s*. The *-s* inflection came into the dialects of the northern counties of England as a Scandinavian influence through the Viking invasions of the ninth and tenth centuries. By the beginning of the seventeenth century it had practically displaced the *-eth* in spoken English, although in written English both forms were current:

> It bless*eth* him that giv*es* and him that tak*es*.
> —*Merchant of Venice,* IV.i.184

In poetic and religious language the *-eth* ending maintained a hold much longer, thanks in no small measure to the King James Bible which employed the older style exclusively. By 1700, however, the inflection had largely disappeared from ordinary writing and likewise from scholarly writing. The only exceptions were *hath* and *doth,* and occasionally *saith* /seθ/, which remained in formal use as late as a hundred years ago.

Present Participle. The English present participle consists of *verb base* + {iŋ}. It has no irregularities.

What we call the "progressive tenses" of a verb are constructed by using any form of the copula *be* plus the present participle. The grammar books call the construction "progressive," though as a description the term is inaccurate. The construction actually carries the idea of limited duration:

> Elizabeth is drinking, but she doesn't drink.

At first sight this sentence looks like a contradiction, but it is perfectly idiomatic English. It says that Elizabeth is drinking at this particular moment but for the rest of the time she may as well be written off as a teetotaler.

The historical development of the English present participle can only be conjectured. In earliest times English had a number of nouns, often conveying a verbal idea, and marked by the suffix *-ung* or *-ing*. Among these were *weddung* 'wedding,' *leornung* 'learning,' *rædung* 'reading,' *spilling* 'waste,' *flowing* 'flowing.' The present participle in Old English had an inflectional suffix *-ende* which by the beginning of the Middle English period began to appear spelled as *-end*. Spelling evidence is of no help, but it seems likely that this was further weakened to *-en* or *-in,* an inflection we still have in words like *runnin'*, *playin'*, *workin'*, as they are rendered in the popular spelling.[2] From here it needed to be only a short jump—a hypercorrection, actually—to /iŋ/, at which point it would fall together with the group of nouns having the *-ing* suffix.

Since the *-ing* suffix is now characteristic of both the present participle and the verbal noun, often called a "gerund," occasional problems result. In the position of modifier, either is possible. Thus the phrase *dancing teacher* may refer to a person who teaches people to dance or to a teacher who is dancing. The ambiguity is readily resolved in spoken English by means of stress. *Dáncing teacher,* we realize at once, does not mean the same thing at all as *dancing téacher.* Context ordinarily makes it clear, even in writing, which one is intended in cases like *burning desire, loving cup, speaking engagement, hearing aid.*

There is a distinction in Latin between the gerund and the participle, and some grammarians have supposed that the same kind of thing deserved encouragement in English. Not many speakers of English have strong feelings on the matter, although some have a sense of uneasiness as the result of an ephemeral comment by a teacher in an eighth-grade grammar class. Presumably there is a difference between these two phrases:

> Like a *mother calling* through her door to a frightened child in the night
>
> Like a *mother's calling* through her door to a frightened child in the night

In the one instance the focus is on the mother, in the other on the calling. It is not often that one needs to exercise so minute a distinction, but the device is at hand for those who wish to use it. For the rest it is scarcely worth worry.

The most serious difficulties result from trying too hard. In the case, for instance, of inanimate things the noun is commonly uninflected:

> We received no notice of the *store closing.*

In a situation like this, it is also possible to use a periphrastic construction:

> We received no notice of the *closing of the store.*

---

2 In a number of places, as Mencken reminds us, the *-in* inflection is preferred to the *-iŋ* inflection by the socially elect. H. L. Mencken, *The American Language* (one-volume abridgment by Raven I. McDavid, Jr.) (New York, Knopf, 1963), p. 443.

It would be a stickler for nicety who felt compelled to write:

> We received no notice of the *store's closing*.

Indeed it might offend some users of English because of its contrived preciousness. In the hands of a pedant an insistence on the inflected form, particularly in relating to inanimate objects, can yield interesting results. From a Chicago newspaper:

> One should be careful to keep the toilet bowl closed to prevent *things' falling* into it.

Preterite. The English past tense, or "preterite" /prétərət/, indicates an event or situation that has occurred or that has been in effect at some past time. The exceptions consist chiefly of events or situations that are not likely to come about:

> Oh, if I had the wings of an angel.
>
> Felix wishes he owned a motel.

The morphology of the English preterite is complicated, and like that of the noun plural it abounds in unpredictable features. There is a pattern usually spoken of as regular which applies to most of the verbs in English, but there are also a number of patterns which differ in various respects and which are consequently classified as irregular. These we shall examine in somewhat greater detail since the irregularities themselves have significance in matters of usage.

The regular preterite is constructed by adding the *-ed* inflection to the verb base. In the spoken language the inflection has a variety of allomorphs, as appears when we compare several sets of verbs: *ask, beg, request; patch, sew, mend; caress, fondle, pet.*

/æsk/	+ /t/	/pæč/	+ /t/	/kərés/	+ /t/
/beg/	+ /d/	/sow/	+ /d/	/fándəl/	+ /d/
/rɨkwést/	+ /əd/	/mend/	+ /əd/	/pet/	+ /əd/

There is a parallel here with the inflection for the regular noun plural, the form of the allomorph being governed by the nature of the final sound of the verb base. If it is a voiceless nondental the allomorph is /t/; if it is a voiced nondental the allomorph is /d/. If it is a dental, that is /t/ or /d/, the allomorph is /əd/, allophonically [ɨd].

Past Participle. In all but a small number of verbs in standard English—fifty-two, to be exact—the form of the preterite is identical with what we call the "past participle." This means that except for these few forms the distinction between preterite and past participle is merely one of function and that, for all the grammatical difference it makes, the two could very well have the same form throughout. Regular verbs in English make no distinction between the form of the preterite and that of the past participle, and neither do most of the irregular verbs. The long-term tendency of the language has been toward eliminating the difference, but this development has been extremely slow.

The English past participle has three principal grammatical functions:

1. In connection with the auxiliary *have* the past participle forms the so-called "perfect tense" constructions. The idea is not so much that the action or situation has been completed, which it usually is not, but that the action or situation has current relevance:

Frank has finally found his place.

That means he is still occupying it, in contrast to the idea expressed by the simple preterite, as:

Frank finally found his place.

This says nothing about where he is now.

2. With the auxiliary *be* the past participle constructs what is called the "passive voice," a grammatical construction by which the subject of a sentence can be given object function:

Active: M. J. Brutus, G. C. Cassius, and several other senators assassinated G. J. Cæsar.

Passive: G. J. Cæsar was assassinated by M. J. Brutus, G. C. Cassius, and several other senators.

3. As modifier of a noun:

Gomez had a disgusted look.

They still have covered bridges in New England.

Whether these may consistently be regarded as past participles has been questioned. Some of them, as we shall note by and by, have both the form and the function of adjectives.

"STRONG" AND "WEAK" VERBS

During the early decades of the nineteenth century, one of the major figures in philology, the name then given to language study, was a German scholar named Jacob Grimm. He and his brother Wilhelm are remembered in the popular mind because of "Grimm's Fairy Tales," a collection of folk tales that German grandmothers used to tell to their grandchildren. In the course of his studies in the Germanic languages, Grimm had observed that in these languages—German, Dutch, English, Swedish, Danish, Icelandic—there are two fundamentally different patterns of verb inflection. One verb type constructs both the preterite and the past participle by adding *-ed,* or a modification of it, to the verb base. The other type involves a systematic contrast between the nuclei of the verb itself, as in *drink-drank-drunk.* Grimm was a true Romantic and this latter pattern seemed to him to embody superior virtue; consequently he called it "strong," as though the vowel contrast was something the verbs had worked up on their own account. The other he called "weak" since he thought of the *-ed* inflection as a kind of crutch. In spite of the fanciful nature of the names that Grimm bestowed and the inexactness of the idea behind them, the designations "strong" and "weak" continue to be used in speaking of Germanic—including English—verbs, and grammarians make no apology. Certainly "consonantal preterite" would be more accurate for the weak verb and "vocalic preterite" for the strong,[3] but this has little bearing on our choice of nomenclature.

In Old English the strong verb conjugation was actually the "regular" one. We now consider the weak verb types as regular and the others as irregular—in fact, almost chaotic.

---

3 These terms as applied to Old English verbs appear in Randolph Quirk and C. L. Wrenn, *An Old English Grammar* (New York, Holt, 1957), p. 40. Henry Sweet seems to have been the first to use them.

WEAK VERBS

If we count simply the gross number of verbs in the stock of English words entirely apart from frequency of use, by far the greater portion of them will consist of weak, or what we call regular, verbs.

Long before English had even become recognizable as a separate Germanic dialect, the weak verb pattern operated side by side with the strong verb and contained thousands of verbs. The strong verb classification during the Old English period included no fewer than 320 verbs of which we have record, exclusive of compounds. Many of them occur rarely, some only once or twice in the entire body of Old English literature that we have available. About 140 of this total had become obsolete before the Middle English period was well under way. It would be more accurate to say that in the social and cultural upheaval of the time, the occasional scribes who continued to write in English had become unfamiliar with the fine distinctions in style and meaning that many of the words represented. Consequently the words fell into disuse and shortly were forgotten. Of the remaining ones, nearly a hundred crossed over sooner or later into the regular conjugation, a change that is still in progress as we may realize when a neighbor tells us that he has *mowed* rather than *mown* his lawn, or when a swimmer has *treaded* and not *trodden* water. Within the limitations of the scanty materials available for the period, the *Oxford English Dictionary* indicates that twenty-nine strong verbs had been regularized by the end of the thirteenth century and still another forty-one by the end of the fourteenth.

New verbs added to the English vocabulary or remodeled into it regularly acquire the *-ed* inflection. For instance, in *Webster's Second New International* the word *orbit* appears only as a noun; in *Webster's Third* it is still a noun, but in addition it has acquired three separate meanings as a verb. From the moment various individuals and agencies so much as proposed sending up missiles and capsules to circle the earth in outer space, it was perfectly obvious what the past tense would be for the verb to describe all this: *orbited.* It is difficult, in fact, to think of a suitable alternative. And then there is a verb like *cast,* a member of a small list of verbs in which the present and preterite forms are alike. Nevertheless, when such a verb is given a radically new meaning, or especially when it is incorporated into a compound, it normally moves into the regular conjugation. This happened, for instance, with the verb *broadcast* and its now standard preterite *broadcasted.* A word from another language, as long as it can somehow be made into a verb in English, can also expect to acquire the *-ed* inflection in the preterite. The words *alibi* and *vamoose* will serve as examples. There is this old legal term of Latin origin, *alibi,* properly an adverb, meaning 'in another place,' and after this had served for some time as a noun it became a verb, as:

> Nathan *alibied* himself out of a drunk driving charge.

Vamos is a form of a Spanish verb which may mean either 'we are going,' or 'let's go.' English-speaking settlers in the Southwest—chiefly cowboys, miners, and Indian fighters—were no great sticklers for fine points of Spanish syntax. They assumed it meant 'go' or 'depart' and remodeled it to *vamoose,* so that we have:

> Curley *vamoosed* into that box canyon.

In addition to the hundreds of completely regular weak verbs which construct their preterites and past participles with *-ed,* there are some seven smaller classes which represent different "remodelings" of the "dental suffix." Historically the verbs of each of these classes belong to the weak conjugation even though some of them seem highly irregular.

1. The verbs of this class—about a dozen in all—have a vowel change in the preterite, ordinarily /e/, in contrast to the /iy/ vowel nucleus of the base. The inflectional ending is always /t/, regardless of whether the final consonant of the base is voiced or voiceless. Thus: *keep* and *kept; sweep, swept; sleep, slept; weep, wept; creep, crept; leap, leapt* /lept/, although this last pronunciation is more characteristically British than American where *leaped* is usual. In many varieties of educated spoken English, and much of the uneducated as well, there may occur simply the vowel change and no inflectional element, so that the verbs are pronounced /kep/, /swep/, /slep/, /wep/, /crep/, /lep/. The preterite of *weep* is the only one with etymological justification since it was originally a strong verb; the others appear to have been drawn in by analogy. Authors seeking to reproduce archaic or rustic conversation use the spellings *kep*', *swep*' and so on, ignoring the times these forms pass in the speech of the socially acceptable. Other verbs in this group are *feel, felt; deal, dealt; kneel, knelt* (also *kneeled*); *dream, dreamt* (although usually spelled *dreamed* and often pronounced /driymd/); *mean, meant* (the preterite of *demean* is always *demeaned*); those with devoicing of the final fricative of the verb base: *leave, left; bereave, bereft* (though also often *bereaved*); and those with a different vowel: *lose, lost.*

2. In another brief list of verbs all but the initial consonant or consonant cluster is replaced by /ɔt/ to form the preterite. *Teach* /tiyč/ side by side with its preterite *taught* /tɔt/ is typical. In the eighth and ninth centuries the present tense forms still had an apparent regularity, but several sound changes that took place afterward have resulted in the present state of affairs. The preterites meanwhile have been drawn by analogy into a common pattern, including *catch, caught* which came in from French, and *fight, fought,* a strong verb.

beseech	besought (*now usually* beseeched)
bring	brought
buy	bought
catch	caught
fight	fought
seek	sought
teach	taught
think	thought
work	wrought (*in another sense,* worked)

Verbs like *think, teach, bring, buy, catch, fight* are of such familiar day-to-day occurrence that they have been able to preserve their irregular preterite forms. *Seek* has begun to have an archaic flavor, losing ground little by little to *search* and *look for;* its preterite is also dying out. *Beseech* was originally related to *seek,* and its preterite was *besought,* but *besought* is now rare outside of deliberately archaic or highly stylized writing and speaking. As a result the preterite is being regularized to *beseeched. Buy* has a preterite *bought;* it also has a nonliterary past participle *boughten,* most commonly used in an attributive sense, in situations where it contrasts with *homemade:*

> Jennie wore her *boughten* dress to the dance.

Bring has preserved its preterite *brought* as standard, even though for many years there has been much analogical *brang* (or *brung*). *Brang* (or *brung*) is so readily and so regularly associated with the language of small children that older youngsters automatically shun it and carry their dislike into adult speaking practices. The standard preterite of *work* is *worked,* which came into common use around the sixteenth century; the *wrought* preterite, which is the original, has been preserved in the King James Bible and in semiarchaic usages. The first public telegram sent from Washington to Baltimore on May 24, 1844, by Samuel F. B. Morse read, "What hath God wrought." The phrase was not original with Morse; he had lifted it from Numbers 23:23. *Well-wrought* appears in various set phrases and has acquired a different meaning from *well-worked. Wrought iron* no longer conveys the idea of *work* and as the result of spelling confusion and folk etymology the expression *rod iron* appears occasionally. *Worked up* and *wrought up* in the sense of 'excited, angry' are completely interchangeable in the speech of many users of English. On the analogy of *sought* and *seek,* the present tense of *wrought* is frequently assumed to be *wreak* in phrases like *wreak havoc* and *wreak destruction. Wreak,* with its preterite *wreaked,* originally meant 'avenge' but the more recent developments reflect an understandable confusion with *wrought.* This sense of *wreak* is well established, having appeared around the beginning of the nineteenth century.

Catch is the only nonnative word in this group and is a very early borrowing from Norman-French. The standard preterite is *caught,* and the alternate *catched* is ordinarily regarded as illiterate and nonstandard. From the way such changes take place in English, we should imagine that *catched* ought to be a regularization, if not a corruption, which will overtake and perhaps ultimately replace *caught.* Quite the opposite seems to be happening. *Catched* rather than *caught* is accepted in spoken English in many parts of England and was regarded along with *caught* as standard in American speech and writing a little more than a century ago, since when it has been schoolmastered into oblivion, or at least out of the textbooks and periodicals. *Caught* is the form that appears in Shakespeare and the King James Bible, but *catched* is regular with such writers as Milton, Bunyan, Pope, Steele, DeFoe, Isaac Watts, Samuel Johnson. That *caught* represents a reversal of the normal trend makes it valuable as a linguistic status marker. Here and there the language arbitrarily bends back on its own rules, enabling us to distinguish the "haves" from the "have-nots."

3. In approximately a score of English verbs, all of them monosyllabic, the preterite is identical in form with the present. In morphological terms, the allomorph of the preterite consists of zero or null. It does not call for much imagination to visualize the development. All these verbs have a base which ends in /d/ or /t/, and in Present-day English these would have had the /əd/ inflection. At an early date, however, the vowel of the inflection was syncopated and the final /d/ was assimilated to the final consonant of the verb base. This group consists of the following verbs: *beat, bet, burst, cast, cost, cut, fit, hurt, let, put, rid, set, shed, shit, shut, spit, split, spread, thrust.* Half of them are completely regular in the sense that they have the zero preterite and no alternate preterites or past participles: *cost, cut, hit, put, set, shed, shit, shut, spread, thrust.* The others have alternate forms in considerable variety. *Beat* was formerly a strong verb, and it exactly paralleled the older forms of the verb *eat* (q.v.): *beat, bet, beaten. Bet* survives in occasional regional speech. On the other hand, *beat* and *beaten* as past participles have different meanings in the speech of many people, as "I was beat" and "I was beaten," or "I got beat" and "I got beaten." The phrase *beatup* is highly informal and generally describes decrepitude; *beaten up* is a hyperform which suggests that the speaker is trying too hard. *Bet* has been a puzzle to the etymologists; the first literary citation is from Shakespeare and he gave the preterite as *betted.* Since then the preterite has been either *bet* or *betted* although the past participle is more commonly given as *bet. Burst* is ordinarily regular with *burst* as preterite and past participle, but *bursted* also occurs, chiefly in American usage, and probably represents an attempt to pronounce the closely related *busted* in a respectable manner. *Bust* for *burst* is a phonetic modification which appears to have had associations with the American frontier—as in *bust a bronco*—and the financial dealings of the less prosperous in this country. It was labeled "dialect or vulgar" in the usage manuals of the early part of this century. It has since made its way to greatly improved status, appearing in informal usages and increasingly in literary usages:

> There I was with a *busted* TV and no newspapers.
> The actress claimed to be bankrupt; flat *busted,* in fact.

In these uses and also in the narcotics vocabulary *bust* regularly has the *-ed* inflection:

> Three of my best friends got *busted* last week.

Hurt has the variant *hurted* but this occurs only in children's speech or imitations of it.

The verb *put* is completely regular as a member of this class except for an occasional past participle *putten,* constructed on the analogy of the strong verb past participles:

> I've *putten* on my mittens and galoshes.

Where it occurs, the speaker is usually uneducated. *Rid* has an occasional inflected *ridden,* evidently to obviate any confusion with another nonstandard form *rid,* a preterite of *ride:*

> Eben *rid* his mule to the mill.
>
> Eben *rid* his mule of ticks.

In the latter construction *ridded* would be the likely verb, or possibly the phrase *get rid of* might be used.

The verb *fit* has as preterite and past participle either *fit* or *fitted.* It is a comparative newcomer, as such words go, for the first citations in its present senses are only a few decades earlier than the time of Shakespeare. Useful as we find the word, it occurs as a verb only four times in the King James Bible. The principal senses of the word are 'to be suitable' and 'to make someone or something suitable,' the elements of a contrast between a number of pairs of verbs in English (cf. *hang*) which consist of a verb expressing a simple state or action side by side with a similar and closely related verb expressing such a state or action being caused or brought about. In such pairs the original verb commonly follows an older and now irregular conjugation while the "causative" verb follows a fully inflected weak verb pattern. There seem to be traces of this tendency in the various forms of the verb *fit;* in other words, we should expect the "simple state or action" sense to have the irregular principal parts *fit, fit, fit,* and the causative to have *fit, fitted, fitted.* Thus we have:

> These boots *fit* me perfectly.
>
> Heddy *fitted* the wig to Mrs. Brewster's satisfaction.

Speakers and writers of English apparently feel no compulsion to follow this pattern with any degree of consistency. Where there is a possibility of confusion with the adjective *fit,* we use *fitted:*

> The room is *fit* for a king.
>
> The room is *fitted* for a king.

Spit has the archaic form *spat* in the preterite and past participle. It was first used in the sixteenth century, appears in the King James Bible, but has again gone out of use. *Spitted* has some currency as a nonliterary expression in connection with voiding saliva, but *spitted* more generally carries the idea of impaling something (or somebody) on a stick or skewer like a shish kebab. *Split* has an archaic variant *splitted,* and that is all.

Verbs like *knit, quit, shred, sweat, wed, wet* have alternate forms in *-ed* which predominate in the past participle when it is used attributively: *knitted sweater, shredded wheat, wedded wife.* More recent applications of these verbs are also likely to employ the *-ed* inflection:

I *sweated* out that R and R furlough for three months.

4. A few verbs—only about half a dozen—have /iy/ as the vowel nucleus of the verb base, followed by either /t/ or /d/. In some respects they resemble the verbs of the preceding class, particularly as regards the development of the inflection. The preterite and past participle are distinguished by /e/ in the vowel nucleus. With one exception, *beat,* the verbs in the preceding class had a simple vowel nucleus in both present and preterite; those of this class have a complex nucleus in the present and a simple nucleus in the preterite. The verbs in the group are: *bleed, bled; breed, bred; feed, fed; lead, led; meet, met; read, read* /riyd/, /red/; *speed, sped. Plead, pled* are confined largely to legal language; in other applications the preterite is usually *pleaded.* In standard English *heat* has the inflected form *heated,* but *het* is an old-fashioned form which was acceptable in written English until the seventeenth century.[4] *Het* continues to be common in folk speech:

What are you all *het* up about, Bessie?

Flee, fled generally conform to this pattern, except for the lack of a final stop in the present tense form. The verb has dropped out of day-to-day use but is preserved in journalese as a synonym for escape.

5. A few weak verbs, nearly all of which are characterized by a simple vowel nucleus followed by a consonant cluster, construct the preterite and past participle by devoicing the final /d/ of the base. Typical verbs of this class are: *lend, lent; send, sent; spend, spent; build, built.*

Of the several classes of variant weak verbs, this one appears to have the least analogical attraction; a number of verbs constructed in this manner or in a closely related one form their preterite with either final *-t* or final *-ed.* Thus: *rend, rent, rended; built, built, builded; bend, bent, bended; gild, gilt, gilded; gird, girt, girded. Bended, builded,* and *rended* have limited use; *bended* seems to occur only in the phrase *bended knee.* An elbow would be bent. Few things are any longer *rended* or *rent* except the air and the welkin, usually by shouts or cries. *Gird* and *gild* apply chiefly to the contexts of loins and lilies, occasional pursuits at best.

---

4 This archaic form, spelled *heat* but evidently pronounced /het/, occurs in Daniel 3:19 (KJV): ". . . that they should heat the furnace one seuen times more then it was wont to be heat." Later printings "correct" this to *heated.*

The inflected form of *burn* is *burned* or *burnt,* the shade of distinction being more a matter of style than of usage. The bride's toast may be burnt, and we speak of burnt almonds, burnt umber, and burnt offerings. But a person lying in the sun too long becomes sunburned, and the burned child dreads the fire. Other verbs related by etymology or analogy are: *smell, smelt, smelled; spill, spilt, spilled; bless, blest, blessèd; curse, curst, cursèd. Bereave* has the nucleus /iy/, and like the other verbs in this last group it ends in a single consonant rather than a cluster. The preterite is either *bereft* or *bereaved.* In standard usage the preterite of *scare* is *scared. Scairt* is regarded as nonstandard, but is widespread in informal spoken English.

Wend really has two preterites. *Wended* is closely related to the verb *wind* and is used principally in the semiarchaic phrase *wended* (his) *way,* presumably along a winding path. *Went,* constructed on the older pattern, fell into the conjugation of an entirely different verb, becoming the preterite but not the past participle of *go,* replacing an older preterite *yode.*

6. There is also a small class with two surviving verbs: *sell, sold,* and *tell, told.* In Old English it was a little larger; seven verbs appear in the writings of the period. Besides *sell* and *tell* there were *quell, dwell, stell* (now supplanted by *put* or *place*), *lay,* and *set. Quell* originally meant 'kill, slay' and was spelled *cwell,* but French scribal influence after the Norman invasion was responsible for the change. *Dwell* originally meant 'mislead, stray.' Both verbs were regularized as early as the fourteenth century. *Set* became regularized on the pattern of *beat* and *bet.* Except for a small irregularity in the spelling, *lay* has a regular preterite *laid.*

Sell and *tell* at one time meant 'give' and 'count,' respectively, the latter reflected in *bank teller.* Except for a further development or two brought about by later sound changes, the vowel of the preterites *sold* and *told* is the original one; the /e/ of *sell* and *tell* is the result of umlaut. Because they are in such frequent day-to-day use, there has been no apparent tendency toward regularization.

In some regional speech we have an analogical transfer of another verb: *swell, swoled.*

7. In all the languages we are likely to encounter a few verbs do not appear to belong to any systematic pattern at all. They are irregular in their unique fashion and grammarians call them "anomalous." Such verbs are usually those that we have employed since earliest childhood, having acquired the inflected forms as individual language items rather than as parts of a system. Because they are used in both speaking and writing hundreds of times a day they continue to resist the powerful leveling forces of analogy. There are three weak verbs in this group: *have, say,* and *make.*

Have and *say* belonged to the same small class of weak verbs in Old English. *Have* has a derivative *behave* which presently acquired the inflected form *behaved,* and we might have expected a similar development in *have.* The *had* form appeared as early as the thirteenth century, and it may have had some benefit by analogy from words like *over, ever, even,* in which medial /v/ was lost, resulting in the "poetic" forms *o'er, e'er, e'en.* The full forms were never seriously threatened by these reductions and consequently remained standard. Since *have* and its inflected forms commonly appear in unstressed positions, /hæd/ was less likely to be subjected to "restoration"—puristic or otherwise—of the medial consonant. The idea was there, we should not forget. Shakespeare spelled *had* as we do, but *has* he spelled *ha's,* suggesting that he knew what was "correct," even though he wrote and spoke otherwise. Actually the medial fricative had not occurred in speech or spelling for several centuries. The preterite and past participle of *have* is *had.*

Have, has, and *had* are frequently contracted and attached to the word preceding as *-'ve, -'s,* and *-'d.* This is most common when *have* functions as an auxiliary, but is also used when it has the full verb meaning 'possess, own.'

Joe's been offered a commission in the Navy.

We've decided to sell that beagle.

I'd rather be right than be President.

I've an idea.

The development of *get* as an auxiliary may depend on the weakness of an expression like this last. Most users of English would say instead:

I've got an idea.

The verb *say* has the inflected form *said,* an orthographic remodeling of *sayed.* The pronunciation of /sed/ rather than /seyd/ goes back as far as the twelfth century and possibly even earlier.

Following the analogy of the inflected forms of *bake, rake, quake,* and *stake,* we should expect the preterite and past participle of *make* to have been *maked.* In the northern dialect of Middle English, however, the verbs *make* and *take* were frequently reduced to *ma* and *ta,* and so written, especially before words beginning with consonants. The older past participle of *take, ta'en,* is preserved in Scottish. The inflected form of *ma* was *ma'ed,* respelled *made,* and presently became the standard form throughout the English-speaking community.

STRONG VERBS

In spite of the erosion that has been going on in the verb system of English for more than a thousand years, many of the strong verbs continue to maintain a formal distinction between the present, the preterite, and the past participle. This is a fundamental characteristic; weak verbs never distinguish the latter two.

In dealing with verbs, our school grammars ordinarily speak of the principal parts of verbs, which refer to and identify the specific forms which the individual verb inflections may take. For regular verbs it is quite beside the point to identify principal parts since they are completely predictable.

The irregularities among the weak verbs themselves follow certain regular patterns, and almost without exception the problems concern the degree to which these verbs may or may not be regularized.

In the case of the strong verbs, however, we can take little for granted. There are classes of patterns, it is true, but even the most extensive ones have fewer than a dozen items. This means that we learn them virtually one by one.

The three principal parts of the English strong verbs stem directly from Old English, where just as today they were functioning features of the verb system. But in addition to these, the verb in Old English incorporated a fourth principal part, relics of which continue to cause us trouble, especially in nonliterate speech. These four principal parts and their "distribution" or specific functions are as follows:

1. The first principal part, as in Present-day English, was the base form. In a verb like *singan* 'to sing,' the *-an* was the inflection and *sing-* the base. The inflections for the present indicative, present subjunctive, and present participle were also constructed on this base. All these have been lost except the *-eth* of the third person singular and the *-end* of the present participle, and these have been replaced by *-s* and *-ing*, respectively.

2. The second principal part corresponded to the preterite *sang* in Present-day English, but it occurred in only the first and third person forms of the preterite indicative. In other words, only "I sang" and "he sang." Because it was used far more frequently than the other it ultimately became the general base form in the preterite with a few minor exceptions.

3. The third principal part *sungon* had the base *sung-*, and on this were constructed the preterite indicative plural, the second person singular preterite indicative, and the preterite subjunctive. This seems needlessly complex, but a distinction between singular and plural forms continued until fairly recently, although sporadically:

And they sung *as it were a new song.* —Revelation 14:3 (KJV)

And on the old subjunctive base, also sporadically:

Would you leave if Felicia *sung* 'O Promise Me'?

4. The fourth principal part was the past participle *sungen.* In most instances the preterite plural and the past participle had the same vowel in the base. In the case of the verb *sing* the past participle has come down to the present as *sung,* the *-en* ending having been lost in the sixteenth century. In some strong verbs the *-en* inflection has been preserved: *written, taken, spoken, given.*

There were seven "classes" of these strong verbs in Old English, each with its distinctive arrangement of vowels of the verb base, still to be seen in *drive, drove, driven,* where the nuclei are /ay/, /ow/, /i/, or *fall, fell, fallen,* where they are /ɔ/, /e/, /ɔ/. This kind of vowel pattern—called "ablaut" by Jacob Grimm, but commonly known as "gradation" by present-day language scholars—has sustained a variety of changes, and yet the framework continues to be generally recognizable. And so the child who says *brang* or *brung* in place of the socially preferred *brought* is in effect adopting the more common pattern.[5]

The strong verbs of Old English were affected in several ways. Most of them dropped out of use and into linguistic oblivion, or we should still have had words like *shude* 'to run,' *slithe* 'to injure,' or *slup* 'to glide.' A number of others "crossed over" into the weak verb pattern. *Shave* and *scathe,* for instance, were once conjugated like *take* and *shake.* In general we may observe three principal developments.

Of the various changes, the most far-reaching and important was the consequence of analogy with the weak verb conjugation. As it operates today, the typical strong verb has three parts: *take, took, taken.* The preterite and past participle are clearly differentiated. In the weak verb the present and preterite are distinguished, but not the preterite and past participle, so that the principal parts are simply *talk, talked.* Loss of the past participial inflection or analogy with the weak verb has brought a number of strong verbs into the two-part pattern: *bind, bound; strike, struck; sting, stung*—about twenty in all. This means that the fifty-odd past participles that remain must be learned not as features of a pattern but as separate linguistic items. Indeed, it is quite obvious that the distinctive past participle is completely redundant so far as clarity is concerned. We experience no difficulty, as a matter of fact, in understanding sentences like:

Helen *has drove* all the way to Memphis.

Is that all you *have wrote*?

The pressure toward regularity is relentless and strong, backed by the entire weak verb system and much of the strong. But, as we shall observe again and again, a failure to observe the accepted practice with regard to the strong verb past participles is outrageously conspicuous to all those who "know better." If the distinction between the preterite and the past participle contributed anything to making English more understandable, the weak conjugation, in which it does not occur, would be one grand confusion.

---

5 The analogical pattern is still strong, especially in informal speech. Thus, *snuck* for *sneaked, drug* for *dragged, skun* for *skinned, squoze* for *squeezed,* and so on.

The three-part system is basically anomalous. It is a sturdy remnant of an older and far more extensive pattern which has been preserved—and even to a degree restored by zealous grammarians—as being socially preferred at the same time that remnants of other older patterns, like *ain't, it don't,* and the double negative, have become socially disapproved.

A second important consideration has been the effect of various sound changes. Long before the earliest forms of English or of the dialects we distinguish as Germanic were written down, the vowel distribution of the strong verb system manifested a striking symmetry and order.[6] Much of the early symmetry was still apparent in Old English, but in some instances it had become difficult to follow. *Fight,* for instance, belonged to the same class as *sing* in Old English; thanks to sound changes it has fallen in with *buy* and *catch* instead. *Freeze* once shared a pattern with *lose,* which has now become a weak verb. *Freeze* on the other hand has the same gradation pattern as *speak,* originally a member of an entirely different class.

A third characteristic development consists of a reduction from an older four-part to a later three-part verb. This has not come about with complete consistency, as appears from a look at the verbs *write* and *bite.* The handbooks we use in our schools give the following principal parts:

write	wrote	written
bite	bit	bitten

Both *write* and *bite*, as well as *written* and *bitten*, must have stemmed directly from the original forms, having sustained minor changes of spelling and pronunciation during the transmission. But why should one preterite be *wrote* and the other *bit?* Why not *wrote* and *bote,* or *writ* and *bit?* A study of the Old English verb system indicates that *wrote* is a direct-line development from the preterite singular and *bit* from the preterite plural. Early in the Middle English period the singular-plural contrast in the preterite began to collapse, and presently the remaining preterites were generalized on one base or another—usually on the one most commonly employed. At one time the usual forms would have been *I wrote* and *he wrote* side by side with *we writ* and *they writ.* But writing is rarely the product of team or group activity, and since on the basis of frequency *I wrote* and *he wrote* predominated, the older *we writ* and *they writ* gave way to the analogical *we wrote*

---

6 This is described in Eduard Prokosch, *A Comparative Germanic Grammar* (Philadelphia, Linguistic Society of America, 1939) pp. 164–182. A somewhat simpler statement appears in Morton W. Bloomfield and Leonard Newmark, *A Linguistic Introduction to the History of English* (New York, Knopf, 1963), pp. 367–8.

and *they wrote*. About the same time *he bote* would be coming into competition with *they bit* and continued until the fifteenth century. From early records it appears that the verb *bite* was used not only in connection with teeth and fangs but quite as often in connection with swords, knives, and other medieval instruments of bloodletting. Thus in describing a battle, the writer would note that "the swords bit" as part of a successful engagement. Concern for developments like these seems at first glance to be the dusty and trivial occupation of pedants, yet the final result has great importance. To say, "We writ you about this last week," would imperil an executive's position, even though *writ* is what he used to say as a country boy and even though he could explain it by English etymology. To say, "He bote his tongue to keep from talking" would be silly, for no one would know what he meant.

Two words current in the lexicon of baseball will further illustrate this: *strike* and *slide*. The principal parts of these verbs are, of course:

strike	struck	struck
slide	slid	slid

Strike belonged to the same class of verbs that *write* belonged and if regularity had prevailed we should have had:

strike	stroke	stricken

Stroke was indeed a preterite of *strike,* side by side with *strake,* until the seventeenth century when *struck* came into literary and popular fashion. The change in vowel nucleus from /ow/ to /ə/ represents a "shortening" of the vowel which was carried into the prestige dialect of London from one of the regional dialects of England. *Stricken* does not occur at all in baseball. We can say, "Mr. Greatheart was stricken with remorse," but not, "Major Syrtis was stricken out on the third pitch." In other words, *struck* is used for both preterite and past participle. *Slide* was a verb of the same class and should have had the forms:

slide	slode	slidden

Slided was current several centuries ago but has become archaic, indicating that the weak pattern sometimes loses out to the strong. In standard speech both the preterite and past participle have been leveled to a common form based on the preterite plural, and the principal parts are: *slide, slid.* Nevertheless, *slode* is not completely dead; it remains in a number of British and American dialects. During the 1950s a retired baseball player named Jerome Herman ("Dizzy") Dean was engaged as a sports announcer. In his utterance the same thing had happened to *slode* that has happened in standard English to *stroke,* but when he announced that a runner had "*slud* /sləd/ into third," a considerable cry of outrage arose. It was reported that the teachers of English in Missouri petitioned the Federal Communications Commission to have him banned as an announcer. Such are the pitfalls of analogy. It seems unlikely that *slud* will make much headway in standard English, even as a humorous variant, despite its impressive etymological credentials.

Strong Verb Classes

The peculiar developments of the English strong verb system show up most clearly in a schematic presentation based on the seven original classes of Old English and the other Germanic languages.

Class I. Write. The class as a whole has been preserved as a regular pattern because a number of the verbs that comprise it remain in everyday use. There are several subclasses as it now operates in English:

infinitive	*preterite singular*	*preterite plural*	*past participle*
drive	drove	driv (*nonstandard*)	driven
ride	rode	rid (*nonstandard*)	ridden
rise	rose	riz (*nonstandard*)	risen
smite	smote	smit (*nonstandard*)	smitten
write	wrote	writ (*nonstandard*)	written

Expressions like *driv, rid,* and *riz* used as preterites do occur in the speech of the uneducated in some parts of the country, and they appear in writing only where the writer is trying to reproduce or mock the speech of the illiterate. In nonstandard use the past participle has undergone several developments. An important one is the leveling of the past participle to the preterite, making this a two-part conjugation. During the seventeenth century there was a great deal of this kind of leveling, not only in verbs of Class I but in the others as well, so that writers like John Milton could say "I have *chose*" or "In triumph had *rode*." Past participles like *drove, rose, rode, smote,* and *wrote* are now generally regarded as either archaic or nonstandard. Despite the censure leveled by early prescriptivists like Samuel Johnson and Robert Lowth, these forms appear to have enjoyed some measure of respectability until about the middle of the nineteenth century, after which time they were vigorously schoolmastered into limbo. Past participles like *rid, smit,* and *riz* represent a loss of *-en*, which has occurred in many of the past participles, but also some leveling to the nonstandard preterite. While they are unlikely to appear in formal English, they are often used colloquially, sometimes with humorous intent:

That's the first time that hoss has been *rid* on this ranch.

Cyrus was *love-smit* from the minute he seen Tammy.

In a few verbs of this class the preterite has been generalized on the base of the older preterite plural:

infinitive	*preterite singular*	*preterite plural*	*past participle*
bite		bit	bitten
hid		hid	hidden
light		lit	lit(ten)
slide	slode (*nonstandard*)	slid	slid

Both *hide* and *light* were originally weak verbs. The development of the preterites was no doubt parallel to that of the *meet, met* weak verb type with some further assistance, especially in the formation of the past participles. *Hid* is often used as past participle, although perhaps less today than formerly. The weak inflection of *light* is fully as common as the other and more so in the past participle. *Litten* is possible, but rare.

In several verbs of this class the leveling of preterites and past participles to a single form is well advanced:

infinitive	*preterite singular*	*preterite plural*	*past participle*
strike	struck		struck
chide	chode (*archaic*)	chid	chided *or* chid
shrive	shrove *or* shrived		shrived *or* shriven
stride	strode *or* strided		stridden
strive	strove		striven
thrive	throve		thriven

Strike has a preterite and past participle *struck* which occurs in all segments of American society because of its currency in baseball, so that the weak variant *striked* has made no headway whatever. *Stricken* as a past participle has a distinctly archaic flavor, being used chiefly in set phrases: *grief-stricken, conscience-stricken, stricken with a heart ailment, stricken from the record.* *Chide* and *shrive* are confined to literary contexts. The preterite of *chide* is *chided* or *chid; chode,* historically the singular preterite, is archaic but it may conceivably be lingering on as a folk-etymologized form in the phrase *chewed* (somebody) *out.* The past participle offers an option of *chid, chidden,* or *chided,* a variety of choices of which most speakers of English are completely unaware and which they pass their lives ignoring with little loss to either themselves or the language. The weak preterite of *shrive* is *shrived,* having begun to elbow *shrove* and *shriven* from their places. *Stride* and its preterite *strode* are still in use, but *stridden* would almost certainly arouse comment. *Strided* was in good repute during the late eighteenth and early nineteenth centuries; it survives in the speech of trackmen. Here is a verb that seems to be going over to the noun form: one no longer strides, but takes or makes strides. *Strive* is the only verb of the strong conjugation which came in from a French background. The original *estrivir* entered the language practically hand in hand with the Norman Invasion of 1066 and was presently supplied with a complete strong verb conjugation on the English model. The verb is seldom heard except in commencement addresses, Boy Scout rallies, and on other occasions when the young in years constitute a captive audience. The strong verb preterite *strove* and past participle *striven* often betray a liking for this kind of expression; *strived,* however, is well attested as a variant and has maintained itself side by side with the strong verb conjugation ever since the verb first came into English. In the present tense the verb *thrive* occurs in sentences like:

> Our baby has been drinking buttermilk and *thrives* on it.

Many users of English self-consciously avoid the use of the preterite and past participle *strove* or *striven;* if they are required to use an inflected form they prefer *thrived.*

A few verbs of this class have a strong verb preterite, but the past participle is either leveled to the preterite or belongs to the weak verb conjugation:

infinitive	*preterite singular*	*preterite plural*	*past participle*
shine	shone		shined *or* shone
abide	abode *or* abided		abided *or* abode
dive	dove *or* dived		dived

There is seldom any call for the use of the past participle of these verbs with *have* in order to construct a perfect tense, and this explains why the past participle is unimportant. Rather than "The sun *has shined,*" or "The sun *has shone,*" the nature of the situation leads to "The sun *has been shining.*" *Abide* also has a historic past participle *abidden* which is now archaic, if not obsolete. As a verb *abide* is dropping out of general usage, being replaced in literary English by *remain* and colloquially by *stay*. It retains some currency in phrases like *abide by* (a decision or a promise). *Dive* was a weak verb in Old English and has generally continued as such, but a preterite *dove,* on the analogy of *drove,* has become standard throughout the entire Northern speech area of the United States. It is currently expanding into a wider speech area, rather than receding, thus countering the tendency of strong verbs to cross over into the weak verb pattern.[7] Till relatively recently those who naturally said *dove* could be made to feel uneasy, and where it was possible to make the change, editors altered it to *dived.* In the earlier editions of Longfellow's *Hiawatha* occurs the line:

> Dove *as if he were a beaver.*

This was later revised to *dived.* We should also anticipate the analogical development of a strong verb past participle **diven,* for example; but when *dived* is not used, *dove* occasionally serves also as past participle. Some grammarians of a century ago cited *diven,* probably more in obedience to analogy than because of anything they had encountered in writing or speech.

Class II. Choose. In Old English this was a relatively large and important class of strong verbs. It included about fifty verbs, some of which, like *lose,*

7 The reasons for this are probably sociological rather than linguistic. Some words tend to drop out of the language: *coal* and *scorch* simply do not occur in the speech of many young people born after World War II. On the other hand, the enormous increase in the number of family swimming pools has vastly increased also the number of occasions one needs to choose between the form *dived* or *dove.*

float, shove, have gone into the weak verb pattern. Others, like *brete* 'hew down' or *brethe* 'waste away,' dropped out of the vocabulary at an early date. *Fly* originally belonged to this class but now has the principal parts of verbs from an entirely different class. The following comprise what is left of the original pattern:

infinitive	*preterite singular*	*preterite plural*	*past participle*
choose		chose	chosen
cleave		clove	cloven
freeze		froze	frozen

Cleave has the preterite *clove* and past participle *cloven* but their use is limited to distinctly formal literary situations. *Split* has quite generally replaced it. The weak verb variant *cleaved* describes the function of a meat cleaver, although *cleft,* on the analogy of *leave, left,* is sometimes used, particularly in an expression like *cleft palate.* A derivative noun *cleavage* remains in general use. *Froze* and *chose* with loss of *-en* are sometimes encountered in informal speech but are regarded as substandard as past participles in written English.

Class III. Sing. A distinguishing characteristic of the verbs of this class in Old English was the consonant cluster rather than a single consonant following the vowel. Even in Old English times it was a large class—the largest of all, in fact, with more than eighty strong verbs—and an extraordinary number of verbs which belonged to it have survived to the present with only minor modifications. A few verbs like *ring, string,* and *fling,* in fact, originally belonging to the weak verb conjugation, have been drawn in, wholly or in part.

The verbs of Class III went through a number of sound changes which broke the class up into several subclasses. Some of these subclasses were small, and since the verbs had no analogical backing they presently shifted to other conjugations. *Fight* was at one time a Class III verb, and so was *braid.* Because of a similarity of the preterite to verbs of the *teach, taught* group of weak verbs, *fight* quite early drifted into that conjugation. The Old English past participle of *braid* was *broiden,* related to the word *embroider,* the only remaining indication that it was ever a strong verb.

Had the principal parts of the verb *bind* remained in use into Present-day English, we should have the following forms:

infinitive	*preterite singular*	*preterite plural*	*past participle*
bind	band	bound	bounden

Four verbs now make up the entire subclass and in all of them the preterite and the past participle have fallen together. The preterite is constructed on the plural base, and in common with virtually all the Class III verbs the past participle has lost its *-en* inflection. This was perhaps a kind of assimilation since the base usually has a nasal in its final consonant cluster:

infinitive	*preterite singular*	*preterite plural*	*past participle*
bind		bound	bound
find		found	found
grind		ground	ground
wind		wound	wound

Bounden duty still occurs as a set expression; otherwise this class has no variants. Weak forms may appear in informal situations; a popular columnist describing the woes of domestic life writes: "The [vacuum] sweeper sucked up the penny and grinded to a halt."

An equally durable subclass would have carried over into Present-day English with the following forms:

infinitive	*preterite singular*	*preterite plural*	*past participle*
sing	sang	sung	sung(en)

Usually the preterite of the verbs of this subclass has been generalized on the singular form but in most instances the one based on the preterite plural is also in reasonably good social standing.

infinitive	*preterite singular*	*preterite plural*	*past participle*
begin	began	begun	begun
ring	rang	rung	rung
shrink	shrank	shrunk	shrunk *or* shrunken
sing	sang	sung	sung
sink	sank	sunk	sunk *or* sunken
spring	sprang	sprung	sprung
stink	stank	stunk	stunk
swim	swam	swum	swum

Present-day usage favors the forms derived from the preterite singular, although in most instances the others are not regarded as objectionable. At best they seem old-fashioned or rustic. This is particularly true of *begun* and *swum.* In some parts of the country there is a limited nonstandard use of *begin* and *swim* as preterites. *Shrank* and *shrunk* are about equally favored. In attributive position *shrunken* and *sunken* are quite common, as in *shrunken head* and *sunken patio.*

Over the years the users of standard English have manifested striking changes in attitude toward the preterite forms of the verbs on this list. In contrast to what would today be called the "permissiveness" of Shakespeare, Milton and other distinguished writers of the seventeenth and early eighteenth centuries, the grammarians of the later eighteenth century, eminently Dr. Johnson and Bishop Lowth, have been credited with setting matters right once more. But judged by current standards, they were little less lax than their predecessors. In his *Short Introduction to English Grammar* Lowth remarked: "We should be immediately shocked at *I have knew, I have gave, I have saw,* etc.: but our ears have grown familiar with *I have wrote, I have drank, I have bore,* etc., which are altogether as barbarous." The fact is that Lowth commented on only a few of these verbs—*bear, hide, write, forget, run, choose, begin, drink*—eight in all, and his comments were anything but specific. In editing his *Dictionary,* published in 1755, Samuel Johnson assumed the obligation of deciding which forms were acceptable and which should be rejected. His judgments therefore on the above verbs may be instructive. The list of them is as follows (*or* indicates that Johnson accorded this form second preference):

infinitive	*preterite singular*	*preterite plural*	*past participle*
begin	began	*or* begun	begun
ring		rung	rung
sing	*or* sang	sung	sung
sink	sank (*ancient*)	sunk	sunk
shrink	*or* shrank	shrunk	shrunk
spring	*or* sprang	sprung	sprung
stink	*or* stank	stunk	stunk
swim	swam	swum	swum

Where present-day usage consistently prefers the preterite modeled on the older preterite singular, Johnson almost consistently preferred the preterite modeled on the older preterite plural, in other words accepting a general leveling of the preterite and past participle in this group of strong verbs. In his *Grammar of English Grammars* (1851) Goold Brown preferred the plural forms of all these verbs except for the verb *begin*. Merriam-Webster's *American Dictionary* (1864) approved of only *began* and *swam* as preterites representing the older preterite singular. It gave equal preference to *stank* and *stunk, rang* and *rung*. In other verbs it favored the older preterite plural. *Sang* and *sprang* it labeled "obsolescent," *sank* "nearly obsolete," and *shrank* "old preterite." The *Century Dictionary* was published in 1889 and Funk & Wagnalls *Standard Dictionary* in 1893–1894. Merriam-Webster's *First New International* appeared in 1909. A comparison of the preterites as indicated by these three dictionaries indicates that with minor exceptions the current preferences had come to the fore:

	Century	*F & W Standard*	*Webster*
begin	began, *sometimes* begun	began *or* begun	began
ring	rang, *sometimes* rung	rang, *sometimes* rung	rang *or* rung
shrink	shrank *and* shrunk	shrank *or* shrunk	shrank *or* shrunk
sing	sang *or* sung	sang *or* sung	sang *or* sung
sink	sank *or* sunk	sank *or* sunk	sank *or* sunk
spring	sprang *or* sprung	sprang *or* sprung	sprang *or* sprung
stink	stunk, *formerly* stank	stank *or* stunk	stank *or* stunk
swim	swam *or* swum	swam *or* swum	swam *or* swum

Rather than assume that the eighteenth-century grammarians were responsible for the present shape of these verb inflections, or even that grammarians throughout most of the nineteenth century were especially concerned, we ought instead lay the credit (or blame) where it rightfully belongs, namely, upon the prescriptive purists of the late nineteenth century—a sturdy breed whose tradition and outlook remain firmly rooted in the American educational establishment. As a result we have become acutely sensitized to "correctness" in dealing with the English strong verb. It is possible to say *It don't* or to use a double negative and to chuckle, but in the present state of affairs no person who values his standing as a literate member of a respectable society will casually use a preterite where a past participle ought to be, or a past participle where a preterite ought to be. There is no chuckle by which a person can excuse himself for such an affront to "good" English.

The verb *drink* is something of an anomaly. Its principal parts are:

infinitive	*preterite singular*	*preterite plural*	*past participle*
drink	drank	drunk	drunk *or* drank

Samuel Johnson preferred *drunk* to *drank* as the preterite, in effect leveling it to a two-part verb. The return to favor of *drank* as the standard preterite is not in itself surprising, for it follows the pattern of the preceding verbs. Following Johnson, however, there is a remarkable agreement among the usage authorities in accepting *drank* as the preterite and in labeling *drunk* as "formerly." *Drunk* is still encountered from time to time, but is regarded as old-fashioned. As early as the seventeenth century, however, *drank* was accepted as a past participle, side by side with the more usual *drunk*. Apparently there is a vague taboo on the form *drunk,* and some substandard occurrence of *drinked* may be accounted for by the same reasoning. Webster's *American Dictionary* (1864) gave *drunk* a narrow preference over *drank,* Funk & Wagnalls *Standard* (1893–4) did not cite *drank* at all as a past participle, but the *Century* (1889) stated "sometimes *drank.*" There is still no complete agreement on the subject, as lexicographers and dialect geographers will readily admit. *Drunken* as a past participle is now archaic, and is principally used in an attributive sense: *drunken brawl.*

Some ten Class III strong verbs make up a subclass in which preterite and past participle are identical. This is probably a simple leveling to a two-part conjugation since there seems little reason to suppose that the preterite was constructed on the Old English preterite plural. The form which represents a carry-over of the earlier preterite singular is in a few instances completely lacking, and otherwise either archaic or of limited regional currency:

infinitive	*preterite singular*	*preterite plural*	*past participle*
cling	(clang)	clung	clung
fling	(flang)	flung	flung
sling	(slang)	slung	slung
slink	(slank)	slunk	slunk
spin	(span)	spun	spun
sting	(stang)	stung	stung
string	(strang)	strung	strung
swing	(swang)	swung	swung
win		won	won
wring		wrung	wrung

Goold Brown (1851) admitted *slank* and *swang* as alternate preterites for *slink* and *swing.* Webster's (1864) labeled *slank* "obsolete or rare," and *stang* and *swang* as "obsolete." *Swang,* although not a literary form, appears in the speech of many educated Americans and Britishers. *Slang* is now regarded as archaic but occurs in the account of David and Goliath (I Samuel 17:49, KJV). And the preterite *span* of *spin* was acceptable not many generations ago as appears from the verse:

When Adam dolve and Eve span
Who was then the gentleman?

Irregular as it may seem in Present-day English, *run* was at one time a verb of this class and it had the following principal parts:

infinitive	*preterite singular*	*preterite plural*	*past participle*
rin	ran	run	run(nen)

Run replaced *rin* in the sixteenth century in the present tense, although *rin* continues to be used in folk speech in Scotland and Ireland. On the other hand, in the speech of many persons the verb has been leveled to a single form, like *cut:*

Pete *run* the mile in the track meet last week.

Run as a preterite form of *ran* is regarded as nonliterate.

A few verbs like *climb, help, swell, melt, fight* also belonged to the Class III conjugation in Old English. In each instance enough relics of a pattern remain to occasion usage problems. In literate English *climb* has been completely regularized and *climbed* is both preterite and past participle. But in nonstandard usage the forms *clomb* /klowm/ and *clumb* /kləm/ are quite commonplace. Of some fourscore words that once made up the Class III pattern, *climb* is the only one that had the final *-mb* cluster, and unlike verbs with *-nk, -ng,* and *-nd,* it had no analogical support. In parts of New York and Pennsylvania the preterite *clim* /klim/ occurs, evidently a "shortening" of the /ay/ diphthong to /i/ before the consonant cluster. *Help* had the support of only one other verb, *yelp,* and not surprisingly both verbs became regularized early. An older form *holp,* pronounced /howp/, is to be found in the Southern states, including Maryland and Delaware, mainly in folk speech. *Holpen* is found in Luke 1:54 (KJV) but is considered archaic. In standard spoken and written English *swell* is a weak verb with *swelled* as preterite and past participle. *Swoll* is still current here and there, although it is usually regarded as old-fashioned; *swoled* also occurs occasionally, probably formed on the model of *sell, sold.* *Swollen* remains in good standing as a past participle; while *swelled* implies a general expansion, *swollen* describes more specifically the physiological consequences of contusions, concussions, and contact with stinging creatures. There is a significant difference between:

> Harry has a *swelled* head.
>
> Harry has a *swollen* head.

Melt has likewise become regularized, but like *swell* it has preserved a strong verb past participle for some specialized uses, especially attributive. Thus: "A dish of melted butter," but "A mass of molten metal." *Fight,* as we have noted, has been a weak verb for a long time, but in some regional speech it has fallen into the same conjugation as *bite:*

infinitive	*preterite singular*	*preterite plural*	*past participle*
bite		bit	bit(ten)
fight		fit	fit(ten)

Fit and a preterite *fout* /fawt/ occur in some varieties of rustic speech.

In its preterite and past participle *hang* has forms parallel to the verbs *sting* and *swing.* Historically it belonged to Class VII, but several centuries ago it became confused with a closely related weak verb so that in the language of some parts of England it began to be treated like a Class III strong verb:

infinitive	*preterite singular*	*preterite plural*	*past participle*
hing	hang	hung	hung

It had an intransitive meaning: 'To be suspended from some point or device with no support underneath.' The related weak verb had the meaning 'To cause to be suspended from some point or device with no support underneath.' The weak verb had the following principal parts:

infinitive	*preterite*	*past participle*
hang	hanged	hanged

Words which manifest the greatest resistance to analogical leveling are words in constant use, especially household words. It is difficult to picture a situation, especially a household, where the word *hang*—especially referring to a mode of capital execution—would be in common use. Presently both verbs collapsed into one, the transitive for the present tense serving for both transitive ("causative") and intransitive uses, and the strong verb plural preterite serving as the model for the general preterite and past participle. The result:

infinitive	*preterite singular*	*preterite plural*	*past participle*
hang		hung	hung

Seven states of the Union presently maintain hanging as the maximum penalty for first-degree murder. The number continues to decrease. Legal language, so far as hanging is still honored, continues to employ the transitive distinction, but only when applied to human beings, living or defunct: ". . . *hanged* by the neck until dead." The verb is also employed in exclamations: "Well, I'll be *hanged!*" *Hung* is not infrequently used in both these situations. The distinction adds nothing whatever to the clarity of the situation, but there are those who feel that it should be preserved. Consistency has nothing to do with it. To be consistent a person should also say that a coat or hat is hanged on a hook or rack. But no one does.

Class IV. Bear. English strong verbs of this class, along with the other three remaining classes, tended to be less clearly defined, even at a relatively early stage of the language. Verbs that originally belonged to the Class IV pattern and which now survive as strong verbs are: *bear, shear, tear, steal, break,* and *come*. The conjugation as it operates at present is as follows:

infinitive	*preterite*		*past participle*
bear	bare (*archaic*)	bore	born, borne
shear	(sheared)	(shore)	shorn *or* sheared
steal		stole	stolen
swear	sware (*archaic*)	swore	sworn
tear	tare (*archaic*)	tore	torn
wear		wore	worn

Break and *come* are still strong verbs, although they have not been typical of verbs of Class IV for a long time. *Swear* previously belonged to Class VI, along with *take* and *wake; wear* was originally a weak verb. *Born* and *borne* are not distinguished as a rule in the speech of persons who live in the North Central or Southwestern parts of the United States or in much of New York and New England; the spelling distinction is maintained, however, by all educated speakers of English, and indicates the two meanings of the verb *bear:* 'produce offspring' and 'carry.' *Shear* has all but moved into the weak verb class. *Shore* is found in some nonstandard speech, and *shorn,* the past participle, has some metaphorical uses and occurs also in various compounds. For the rest this is a small but regular class.

Class V. Break. This was also one of the smaller classes of strong verbs in Old English, and even there it differed from the verbs of Class IV in respect to minor details, chiefly the vowel of the past participle which has now become leveled with that of Class IV. Originally Class V contained these verbs: *tread, speak, weave, give, get, eat, see, sit, lie.* Most of them have become anomalous; a number of others have merged with the weak verb conjugation. As they remain in Present-day English, the verbs of Class V have little more than token regularity:

infinitive	*preterite*		*past participle*
break	brake (*archaic*)	broke	broken
heave	(heaved)	*or* hove	heaved *or* hove
speak	spake (*archaic*)	spoke	spoken
weave	(weaved)	*or* wove	woven *or* weaved

Tread, eat, see, and *lie* have gone over to other conjugations; *give* and *get* have done the same and have the further complication of being strongly influenced by Scandinavian. *Heave,* originally a strong verb of Class VI, is generally a verb of the weak conjugation, but on the analogy of *weave* it has a variant preterite and past participle. *Weave,* on the other hand, is becoming regularized; we usually say that a driver *weaved* through traffic rather than that he *wove. Break* and *speak* have the archaic preterites which were standard in the seventeenth century. We assume that *break* and *brake* are pronounced /breyk/ in Present-day English, but it is probable that *break* and *speak* would have rimed in the seventeenth century. To be consistent *break* should be pronounced /briyk/ but words with *ea* spellings show some striking irregularities. The past participle *broke* is regarded as nonstandard except to indicate that one is short of ready cash.

Class VI. Take. In Old English times, as now, this was a small class of strong verbs. Many of the verbs that originally belonged to it have remained in current use, though regularized, like *bake, ache, wade, wax,* or have enrolled in other classes like *heave, slay,* and *draw.* The following verbs have generally retained the historic forms:

infinitive	*preterite singular*	*preterite plural*	*past participle*
take		took	taken
forsake		forsook	forsaken
shake		shook	shaken
wake	(waked)	woke	waked *or* woke

Take was a Scandinavian strong verb which belonged to Class VI in Old Norse and was adopted into English as though it were a native word. In the verbs of this class we have long had some leveling of the preterite and past participle.

> *For you* have *but* mistooke *me all this while.*
> —*Richard the Second,* III.ii.174

In the colloquial style we may encounter: "He was *took* for every cent he had," or "I was all *shook up.*" *Shook up* has been in the language for a long time; it occurs in a sixteenth-century play, *Ralph Roister Doister.*

Wake as we use it represents the blending of the senses of two different verbs, one meaning 'to become awake' and the other 'to cause (someone) to become awake.' The first verb was a strong verb with the following principal parts:

infinitive	*preterite singular*	*preterite plural*	*past participle*
wake		woke	woken

The other was a weak verb:

infinitive	*preterite*	*past participle*
wake	waked	waked

To add to the problem, we have still another verb *waken* which expresses either of these senses, but has the inflections of a weak verb:

infinitive	*preterite*	*past participle*
waken	wakened	wakened

Furthermore, there is also the option of an intensifying prefix *a-*: *awake* and *awaken,* with generally the same meaning and these principal parts:

infinitive	*preterite* ("*weak*")	*preterite* ("*strong*")	*past participle*
awake		awoke	awoke, awoken
awake	awaked		awaked
awaken	awakened		awakened

When the particle *up* is added, the number of possibilities is astounding.

Class VII. Blow. In Old English this class had the appearance of a catchall, and the situation has improved but little in the ten centuries that have followed, except that the total number of verbs involved has decreased. The significant distinction between preterite singular and preterite plural which appeared in the other classes was not characteristic of the verbs of either Class VI or this one. The past participle furthermore had the same vowel nucleus as the present tense, but quite regularly preserved or added the *-en* inflection. A number of verbs of this class closely resemble verbs of the weak conjugation, the result being that some of the verbs of the Class VII pattern crossed into the weak conjugation while several weak verbs by analogy acquired variant strong verb forms, some of which have literary status.

The verbs that have preserved or that have acquired one or more of the distinctive characteristics of this class are:

infinitive	*preterite* ("*strong*")	*preterite* ("*weak*")	*past participle*
blow	blew	(blowed)	blown (blowed)
grow	grew	(growed)	grown (growed)
know	knew	(knowed)	known (knowed)
throw	threw	(throwed)	thrown (throwed)
crow	crew (*British*)	crowed	crowed
show		showed	shown, *sometimes* showed
mow		mowed	mowed *or* mown
sow		sowed	sowed *or* sown
flow		flowed	flowed flown (*archaic*)
fly	flew		flown
slay	slew		slain
draw	drew	(drawed)	drawn
sew		sewed	sewn *or* sewed
hew		hewed	hewn *or* hewed
hold	held		held holden (*archaic*)
fall	fell		fallen
saw		sawed	sawed *or* sawn

The usage problem with many of these verbs centers on whether one ought to use a strong or weak preterite or a strong or weak past participle. The principle of analogy is less dependable here than in any of the strong verb classes. Actually only two verbs, *fall* and *hold,* have no weak verb variant inflectional forms; *blow, grow, know,* and *throw* are completely regular in standard speech and especially in literary styles, but in nonstandard English the weak verb inflected forms are extremely common. To many persons the difference in usage is one of the clearer status markers in Present-day English. In American speech *crow* has moved completely into the weak verb class. *Crew* as a preterite is British, although American readers may encounter it in reading: "The cock *crew*" (Mark 14:68, 72 KJV); "The morning cocke *crew* lowd" (*Hamlet,* I.ii.218). *Blow, grow, know, throw, draw, slay,* and *fall* remain three-part verbs; the preterite is distinguished from the present by vowel contrast, and the past participle by the addition of *-n* to the present tense base, or in the case of *fall* usually *-en.* Milton and his contemporaries often wrote it as *faln.* Like *blow* and the others, *draw* has a nonstandard inflected form *drawed; slay* sometimes has a weak form *slayed,* usually a nonce invention.

Sew and *show* were originally verbs of the weak conjugation; *saw* in Old English was a noun which later became a weak verb by "functional shift." The preterite remains in the weak verb conjugation and as a rule so does the past participle. Most verbs of Class VII have a base ending in *-ow, -aw;* and the formation of a strong verb past participle in verbs like *sew, show,* and *saw* is clearly analogical. *Sow, mow,* and *hew,* on the other hand, were strong verbs in Old English, and the only connection they maintain with this conjugation is a variant past participle. There is a touch of the archaic about words like *sewn, shown, sawn, sown, mown,* and *hewn* and they are becoming relegated to poetical use or to descriptions of handcrafted articles. *Hand-sewn* and *hand-hewn* are manifestly more costly than *machine-stitched* or *machine-chopped.* A staple implement of the gangster era was called a sawed-off shotgun; *sawn-off* would have been otiose. The past participle of *hold* has been leveled to the preterite *held;* the older *holden* is now archaic.

Fly, flee, and *flow* all have to do with motion, possibly away from a place, and quite understandably they have been subject to confusion as far back as our records of English go. *Flee* was originally a strong verb, along with *choose* and *freeze,* of Class II, but it became a weak verb with vowel modification: *flee, fled. Flow* is ordinarily a weak verb. The archaic past participle would be puzzling in a sentence like: "A lot of water *has flown* under the bridge." In Old English *flow*—like *blow, grow, know,* and *throw* —was a strong verb of Class VII, and its principal parts if continued to the present day would have been *flow, flew, flown.* Instead these principal parts belong to another verb, originally in Class II: *fly, flew, flown.* This development came about as a result of a sound change, not analogy. It is not usual to have two verbs competing for the use of the same set of principal parts, but where this happens the verb in most common currency is likely to be favored. *Fly* has a weak verb variant in sports: "Silberstein *flied* out to center field" rather than "Silberstein *flew* out to center field."

ANOMALOUS VERBS

About a dozen verbs follow no discernible pattern, and consequently they cause difficulty, chiefly among speakers of nonstandard English, who suppose that a pattern exists and that one may follow it in constructing a preterite and past participle. In the case of a verb that has been newly adopted into English this is a safe assumption to make since new verbs follow the weak or regular pattern. Yet at a certain point the language learner comes to sense that the regular pattern is an untrustworthy guide, not for linguistic reasons but for social reasons. The socially acceptable form is *knew* or *known,* and not *knowed.*

A verb must be learned at a tender age, or in any case mastered into a habit that is perfectly learned as the result of repeated use. Otherwise the force of analogy will presently drive it into one of the more common patterns. For instance, the verbs *speak* and *tread:*

infinitive	*preterite singular*	*preterite plural*	*past participle*
speak	spoke		spoken
tread	trode (*archaic*)	trod	trodden

As the spelling shows, both of these verbs originally belonged to Class V. *Speak* has retained the characteristics typical of verbs of this class; most of us use it every day. By contrast the verb *tread,* which has dropped out of daily use, has been considerably remodeled. *Trode* as a preterite was in use until a few hundred years ago: "They *trode* upon one another" (Luke 12:1 KJV). To the extent that it is used at all, the preterite is now *trod,* constructed on the past participle *trodden,* which was earlier *troden.* More recently *trod* has become confused with the verb *trot,* which came out of French and follows the weak conjugation. Both verbs have to do with getting places on foot, and as a result *trot* has affected *trod* so that this has acquired a set of weak inflections: *trod, trodded.* The older inflections of *tread* are preserved in phrases like *downtrodden,* or in a line of verse: "Tread where Thy feet have *trod.*" In newer uses *tread* is commonly a weak verb:

> I just *treaded* water till someone threw me a life belt.

There is also some development of *tread* on the analogy of *shed* and *spread* with a zero preterite and past participle inflection.

A similar but even further development has occurred in the verb *seethe,* originally a strong verb of Class II, which meant 'cook, boil,' but which now means this only metaphorically, as in "*seethe* with anger" or "*seethe* with passion." In this sense it has long been a weak verb: *seethe, seethed.* As a strong verb its principal parts were:

infinitive	*preterite singular*	*preterite plural*	*past participle*
seethe	sod		sodden

The occurrence of *d* in place of *th* follows a complex development in the Germanic languages known as "Verner's Law." *Sod,* however, remained in common use for a long time and as late as the seventeenth century we encounter "And Jacob *sod* pottage" (Genesis 25:29 KJV) where a modern rendering would probably have *boiled* or *cooked.* Since then the verb form *sod* has dropped out of use and *sodden* has all but lost contact with the original verb. A person described as "sodden" is plain drunk—the language abounds in euphemisms having to do with alcoholic saturation: *stewed, soaked, oiled, soused,* and so on. By extension into another direction it refers to a water-soaked condition of the turf in springtime after the frost and during the spring rains. The lawns are said to be sodden. On the analogy of *sadden* 'make heavy hearted,' *sodden* has been reconstructed as a present tense form and has acquired inflected forms in the weak conjugation: *soddened* 'made very wet.'

Among the anomalous verbs are the following:

infinitive	*preterite*	*past participle*
lie	lay	lain
sit	sat	sat
bid	bade /bæd/	bidden
give	gave	given
come	came	come
eat	ate	eaten
get	got	gotten
stand	stood	stood
see	saw	seen
go	went	gone
do	did	done

The problem of the verb *lie* is a difficult one, since, as every speaker of English knows or soon discovers, it has long been confused with the verb *lay* and largely replaced by it. Such confusion is commonly ascribed to carelessness, permissive teaching, or the consequences of whatever political administration one habitually blames for the state of the world. It consists of a composite of several problems. Careful writers continue to distinguish between *lay* and *lie,* although the past participle of *lie*—that is, *lain*—is becoming increasingly uncommon. It is beginning to reflect a self-conscious correctness. In spoken English, certainly, the inflected forms of *lie* are recessive, and many persons regard a conspicuous use of them as pedantry. So far as clarity of meaning is concerned, *lay* has stood in for *lie* since the end of the thirteenth century, according to our written records, and did so regularly during the seventeenth and eighteenth centuries. No one is ever confused. The distinction is a social one.

In the case of the distinction between the strong verb *hing, hang, hung* and the weak verb *hang, hanged,* the contrast was between an intransitive verb and a transitive; more specifically between an intransitive verb and a causative. *Hing,* when it was still a live English word, meant, as we have already noted, 'occupy a suspended position' and *hang* meant 'cause (someone or something) to occupy a suspended position.' An analogous situation obtains in *sit* 'occupy a seated position' while *set* means 'cause (someone or something) to occupy a seated position.' There is an old distinction between *fall* and *fell* (a tree, for instance), between *rise* and *raise,* between *drink* and *drench,* and it may have had something to do with the difference between *drip* and *drop.* Whatever causative alternates there were for words like *work* and *stand* have disappeared long ago. In fact, except for *lie* and *lay, sit* and *set,* and a few other pairs in which the causative function is virtually forgotten, a genuine causative in English has been successively expressed in several ways. There was a construction with *do:* "The king *did* him go," which was current even in Old English and which lasted till the seventeenth century. The verb *do* was then assigned to other uses and now we have essentially the same construction with *make:* "The king *made* him go." This means that we really don't have much use for a special causative distinction between verbs. *Lay* is understandable in the sense of 'occupy a horizontal position,' though it may not appear very often on the literary level and has appeared there only now and then during the past century and a half. Yet if necessary one can express a causative idea with:

> Make that idiot dog *lay* down in his box!

In other words, the verb *make* is far more frequently used to express causation than is verb contrast, regardless of the verbs. Furthermore, both *lay* and *lie* are normally phrased with the intensifying adverb *down*. The preterite forms are *lay down* and *laid down*, both ordinarily pronounced /lèy dáwn/. Anyone trying to decide from this what the present tense form ought to be when he has both *lay down* and *laid down* in mind will automatically settle on *lay down*, unless he has been scrupulously schooled in the "rules." Much has been said and written about the importance of keeping *lie* and *lay* clearly distinguished, and by extension *sit* and *set* also, but there is no confusion in meaning. And if one really needs a causative, there is always *make*. The danger lies in trying too hard, that is, using *lie* for *lay:*

> The faithful dog *lay* its head in its mistress' lap.

Here again we have a distinction which has social relevance and only that. Those who have mastered the situation often regard such an ability as a measuring stick by which to gauge the linguistic competence of their fellows. In their zeal, some persons have taught dogs to drop to the carpet when told "*Lie* down!" but to assume and maintain a posture of studied nonchalance at the command "*Lay* down!" Such demonstrations say something about dogs, even more about their masters, but nothing about *lie* and *lay*.

Bid is sparingly used outside of card games, auctions, and contracts with commercial firms or government agencies. In these situations the word has a usage hallowed by tradition, but in other situations the user of English finds himself left to his own devices. Commonly he selects a synonym with a less erratic morphology. In the verb *bid* two Old English strong verbs have fallen together and there are distant influences from still a third. There was *biddan*, a Class V verb, which could be taken to mean such things as 'ask, pray, command, order, require,' and also *beodan*, a Class II strong verb meaning 'command, announce, offer.' The most usual development is:

infinitive	*preterite*	*past participle*
bid	bid	bid

This puts it in the class of weak verbs like *fit* and *rid:*

> How much am I *bid* for this stuffed loon?
>
> McAdam & Co. have *bid* low on the bridge across Grand Canyon.

There is also this development:

infinitive	*preterite singular*	*preterite plural*	*past participle*
bid	bade		bidden *or* bade

The preterite singular should have developed into a form *bad,* and the preterite is so pronounced, although spelled *bade:*

> Ruprecht *bade* his supervisor a Happy New Year.

The spelling pronunciation /beyd/ is fairly widespread, and this has status connotations to those who know that the standard form is /bæd/. Some tendency exists to level this to a two-part verb with *bade* as past participle. *Bidden* remains preferred in writing and standard speech. All of the usages that apply to *bid* also pertain to the closely related *forbid.*

The verb *give* has shown little if any tendency to develop a weak verb preterite like **gived,* even among speakers of substandard English. In rustic or illiterate speech the one-part conjugation of the verb is most common, as clearly a mark of this style as *ain't* or *knowed* or the multiple negative:

> I've *give* you ever' blasted cent you got comin'

Leveling of the preterite and past participle generally to *gave* or *given* is not uncommon but is regarded as nonstandard.

Leveling of verbs to a one-part conjugation demonstrates that a systematic indication of tense by a contrast in verb forms is not necessary for comprehension or clarity. Verbs like *beat* and *cut* are good illustrations. Here the development was originally phonological as an assimilation of a final *-d* or *-t.* In the language of the users of nonstandard English, however, such a leveling tends to go much further, and it could conceivably comprehend all the monosyllabic verbs in the language. *Give,* as we have just indicated, often appears as a one-part verb. So do *run, come, see.*

> Tobias was just fifteen when he first *run* away from home.
>
> It just *come* to me now what Lizzie put in that salad.
>
> He *see* all his relatives at the family reunion.

Occurrence of forms like these offers no threat to the language of those who use standard English. However, they illustrate the principle of analogy, that words have a tendency to follow patterns. In standard English the verbs *give, run,* and *come* have no analogs. The nonliterate user of English, groping momentarily for a pattern, solves the difficulty in the most direct way he knows, by reducing the entire conjugation to a single form.

Stand was originally a strong verb of Class VI, and until about the sixteenth century it had these principal parts:

infinitive	*preterite singular*	*preterite plural*	*past participle*
stand	stood		standen

Since *standen* had little if any analogical support, the verb presently became reduced to two parts. The unusual characteristic of this verb is the *-n-* of the verb base, which does not occur in the preterite. It is known to language specialists as a "nasal infix" or sometimes simply "*n* infix," found in modified form in the verb *bring* but not in the preterite *brought.* During the sixteenth and seventeenth centuries there was some use of the weak form *standed,* including the form *understanded,* but this does not seem to have been preserved, even in nonstandard speech.

Eat has a preterite *ate* and a past participle *eaten,* both of which have generally withstood remodeling because they are in such common use. As may be gathered from the *ea* spelling of the base form, *eat* at one time belonged to the same class of verbs as *speak* and *weave.* The preterite *ate* follows the pattern of *meet-met,* a weak verb, and it is commonly pronounced /et/ in Great Britain, although in the United States /eyt/ is favored by nearly all cultured users of English. The standard pronunciation /eyt/ is actually a spelling pronunciation, dictated and enforced by schoolteachers during the nineteenth century, though as late as the second half of that century /et/ was recognized as an allowable pronunciation.[8] It is now regarded as rustic or old-fashioned. *Eaten* is regarded as standard. In some speech communities the verb has been reduced to a two-part conjugation: *eat, et;* in others it has become a one-part verb, simply *eat.* Geograph-

---

8 Noah Webster, *American Spelling Book* (Middletown, Conn., William H. Niles, 1831) (reprinted by Teachers College, Columbia University, New York, 1962). Webster's rimes are instructive here. He rimes *date, hate, fate, grate,* but not *ate.*

ically the two are difficult to isolate, one from the other. Only the *eat, ate, eaten* forms appear in standard writing.

Get has a preterite *got* and a past participle either *gotten* or *got,* and consequently it is pretty much in a class by itself unless one counts *tread, trod, trodden,* or the nonstandard *set, sot, sot.* Like the verbs *bet* and *let* it should in all consistency have moved into the pattern of the zero preterite verbs of the weak conjugation, but there is little tendency in that direction, even in nonstandard speech.

In day-to-day usage the verb *get* has several distinct meanings. The most common one, 'obtain, acquire, gain possession of,' retains the historic principal parts:

infinitive	*preterite singular*	*preterite plural*	*past participle*
get		got	gotten

The past participle *gotten* has been leveled to *got* in England, a situation which makes some Americans uneasy since they suppose that they and their countrymen need to keep the language "pure," in other words, to sound like Englishmen. Some of the uneasiness undoubtedly results from the Englishman's own inability to figure out how the Americans do it, and the assumption that Americans automatically say *gotten* wherever the British say *got.* It is only partly true. Since the verb *get* can also mean 'possess, own,' especially in preterite uses, it reflects the end point of 'obtain, acquire.' Such a shift in meaning is not at all uncommon; it appears in the word *win*[9] and in *chase* and *catch,* derived from the same French word. Nevertheless we still encounter those who object to this use of *get* on the grounds that it really has to do with obtaining. In the sense of possessing we have a newer use of the word, reflecting a more recent development, and in that sense the

---

9 Win originally meant 'labor, strive,' a sense still employed in John Keats' "Ode on a Grecian Urn":

> *Bold Lover, never, never canst thou kiss,*
> *Though* winning *near the goal—*

In the speech of elementary school students in several places a still further development is being observed: 'defeat':

> "We *won* the Tigers in the last inning."

preterite and past participle are regularly leveled to a common form, *got.* As a result in American English these two sentences do not mean the same at all:

I've *got* two tickets for the game.

I've *gotten* two tickets for the game.

The phrase *have got* has been the target for a good deal of criticism by those who feel nervous about their language. In fact, they manage to make others feel guilty about using *got* at all. The argument runs simply that *have got* is redundant and therefore bad English. But what we actually have here is a completely normal development.

I *have* a present for you.

will pass as acceptable and idiomatic English. There is no emphasis on ownership. On the other hand:

That's all the money I'*ve got.*

As an auxiliary, *have* has for many decades been contracted to *-'ve, -'s,* and *-'d,* and in unstressed positions it tends to disappear altogether. This contraction has also been extended to *have* in the sense of ownership, and that is the reason why users of English commonly find themselves adding the verb *get,* not so much to reinforce the idea of possession as to express it at all:

I'*ve got* news for you, Phil.

Patsy'*s got* a sore throat.

As an expression of obligation *have got* followed by an infinitive is completely established in English:

Rumford *has got* to be at the airport at two.

This phrase, along with the others, has aroused the objections of those who imagine that all the work can be done with *have.* In much spoken English, especially nonstandard, the *have* auxiliary is lost:

When you *gotta go,* you *gotta go.*

The verb *get* in the sense of 'obtain' has a secondary meaning 'become.' Here the *gotten* participle is usually preserved:

> It's *gotten* so you don't even want to answer your phone.

Get is often used in situations where *become* seems too formal and where *be* suggests a static condition:

> Burt *got* cold sitting in a draft.
>
> I almost *got* eaten by flies in that filthy kitchen of Mabel's.

A nonstandard development in the language of school children makes *got* the verb base, replacing entirely the *have got* construction. As the *-'ve* and *-'s* are ordinarily pronounced, the youngsters have failed to hear them. Where we should normally expect: *I've got, he's got,* such usage instead renders it: *I got, he gots.* Regardless of whether we approve or not, the expression follows a pattern more regular than the standard one. Chances for its survival are extremely promising, in spite of all elementary teachers do to stamp it out. It will doubtless be regarded for some time as a feature of substandard English. There does not seem to be any reasonable alternative into which the children's language can be directed.

The only way to explain why the verb *see* has maintained its integrity over the centuries is that it is in such common and constant use, not that it follows the pattern of any other verb. The forms are:

infinitive	*preterite singular*	*preterite plural*	*past participle*
see		saw	seen

In nonstandard English the preterite is expressed as *seen, seed,* or *see. Seen* represents a leveling to the participle form, a rather infrequent type of leveling. Usually the past participle is leveled to the preterite, but *seen* bears little resemblance to any other past participle of the strong verb conjugations. *Seen* is characteristic of less cultivated speech of the Midland area. *See,* a complete leveling, occurs mainly in the Northern dialect area. *Seed,* simply a shift into the weak verb conjugation, is chiefly a Southern form. Few verbs have such clearly marked geographical distribution. Leveling of the past participle to *saw* is less common.

Go had the principal parts *go, went, gone*. The forms *go* and *gone* are very much like *do* and *done* in spelling, but the vowels are of course pronounced differently. There were differences in the vowels even in Old English, but later developments in English spelling concealed them. Our very earliest records show the past participle to be anomalous; it follows the general strong verb pattern, however, with the final *-n*. In Old English the preterite was written *ēode,* becoming *yode* in Middle English, related to the Latin verb *īre* 'go.' During the fifteenth century the preterite of *wend* began to supplant *yode* and soon replaced it completely. There is some tendency, especially among speakers of nonstandard English, to level the preterite and past participle to a single form, *went:*

Connie has *went* to the supermarket.

Despite its high frequency of use, *go* does occasionally shift to the weak verb pattern with the form *goed.* It is usually considered hypocoristic or rustic.

Do as an auxiliary verb or as a verb with full meaning has been anomalous from early Old English times. In fact, the preterite *did* has remained unchanged for a thousand years. In nonstandard speech the past participle *done* regularly replaces *did* as a preterite, and "He *done* it" is consequently regarded as one of the typical illiteracies. Taken by itself as a language development, the simplification of *do* to a two-part verb with *done* as its all-purpose inflected form is no more of a corruption than the same thing where it has occurred in scores of verbs and in which it is now accepted as an accomplished fact. But *do* is used again and again in daily conversation and anyone who fails to notice that *did* and *done* occur in situations that are not only different but mutually exclusive obviously does not come from a select social background. All he may have had opportunity to hear is a type of speech where the two forms are run into one. The other possibility is that he is unbelievably dull in reacting to what goes on all about him in language. In either case, as a result of this and related usages, many doors will be closed to him.

SUMMARY

In comparison with many languages, including languages that are genetically closely related, English has a rudimentary system of verb inflections. In general the pattern of inflections is strikingly regular.

Two conflicting tendencies in the development of English have been responsible for much of the irregularity. Many of the irregularities can be identified as relics of a verb system which manifested a striking orderliness somewhat more than a thousand years ago. But in contrast to this system we have another which has in Present-day English largely replaced it. We should expect the older system to have remained essentially intact as an operating system, or otherwise to have gone over wholly to the new. But neither one has happened in quite this way. While old forms do remain, the system itself is badly shattered.

A basic feature of the English verb system is a contrast between the present tense form and the preterite form. This is consistent; only about a score of verbs are excepted from this condition, all of them highly identifiable. For social well-being it is, of course, essential that one should not only distinguish between the present tense and the preterite forms, but equally essential that he should make the correct distinction. To say *catched* in place of *caught* is to most educated speakers of American English a clear error; it involves using the regular verb inflection instead of one of the variants. To say *brang* instead of *brought* is an error of another kind. In other words, a user of English can fall into pitfalls in every direction, and the fact that he presently trips into one or another marks him indelibly as a person of less favored social or educational background.

But there is evidently no area of English usage where one finds so little tolerance as in dealing with the differences, where they exist, between preterite and past participial forms. There have been relentless pressures toward simplification, and yet regardless of these, some fifty-two verbs continue to distinguish between a preterite and a past participle.

By the end of the Old English period, as we have suggested, the English language had largely disposed of this distinction as a result of the vast spreading of the weak verb, the crossing over of numerous strong verbs into the weak verb pattern, and the reduction of many of the remaining strong verbs to a two-part conjugation. At the beginning of the eighteenth century it seemed only a short while before the past participle as a distinctive verb form would disappear altogether. Bishop Lowth and Dr. Johnson have been credited with pumping air into the strong verb system and bringing it back to life, but Lowth's comments applied to only a few verbs, and Johnson's preferences fell some distance short of our own. In spite of this we know that to use a preterite form when the verb conjugation makes available a socially acceptable past participle is a grave sin against the canons of English usage.

The first consideration is the high frequency with which these words occur. The history of language shows repeatedly that constant use does not wear out a word or accelerate change, but instead tends strongly to preserve it. How would a person get through an ordinary day without words like *go, come, take, be, eat, drink, know, speak, write?* There are other words like *strive, smite, slay, forsake* that we readily recognize, and yet we might go a thousand days without needing to use any one of them. Oddly, *slay* and *forsake* have developed no variant forms. *Strive* has had alternate weak forms since the time it came into English, but the strong forms continue to prevail.

The second consideration is that despite a good deal of reshuffling, the several present-day patterns of strong verbs conform generally to old strong verb patterns. There is enough force of analogy to keep them from collapsing. The largest single remnant of any class is from Class III: *begin, drink, ring, sing, sink, shrink, spring, stink, swim.*

But neither explanation accounts for the extraordinary vitality of the contrast, now functionally redundant, between the forms of the preterite and past participle in this relatively small set of words. In Class III, for instance, there were several developments, only two of which concern us at the moment. In the first the distinction between the preterite and past participle has been preserved: like *begin-began-begun* are *drink, ring, run, shrink, sing, sink, spring, stink, swim.* In the second the distinction has been leveled out: like *cling, clung* are *fling, hang, sling, slink, sting, string, swing, wring.* No rule or generalization about form or meaning or frequency of use will enable a person to assign a verb to one category or the other. It must be done by memory and nothing else. And the memory must be infallible. Furthermore, usage changes gradually over a period of time. As we have indicated, Dr. Johnson preferred *drunk* to *drank* as the preterite of *drink,* and *shrunk* to *shrank, stunk* to *stank.* He gave only *sunk* as the preterite of *sink,* and noted that it was "anciently *sank.*" For *ring* the only preterite he cited was *rung.* That was in 1755. Lindley Murray, author of the famous *English Grammar,* which in the early days of the Republic was *the* grammar, followed practically the same formula forty years later. He preferred *shrunk, swum, sunk,* and so on. *Began* and *drank* were the only exceptions. Goold Brown (1851) advocated the leveled forms of all these verbs, except for *began.* Only with Merriam-Webster's *American Dictionary* (1864) did any reversal of this general trend appear. *Began* and *swam* had preference, with no variants; *stank* and *rang* were preferred to *stunk* and *rung.* But *sank* was labeled as nearly obsolete and *sang* and *sprang* as obsolescent.

Judging from the preferences expressed by the editors of the *Century*

Dictionary (1889), Funk & Wagnalls *Standard Dictionary* (1893–1894), and Merriam-Webster's *First New International* (1909), there must have been a considerable restoration of past participles between the close of the Civil War and the first decade of the twentieth century. Culturally, of course, it coincided with an unprecedented expansion in education and the extension of a sense of "belonging" to hundreds of thousands of persons from socially undistinguished backgrounds. It was their anxiety among other things that evoked much of the schoolmastering of the language—a trend found especially in the strong verb system. The grammarians of the previous century were responsible for setting the tendency in motion, but many writers continued to ignore the "rules," as the writing of the period indicates. When they first appeared, these distinctive past participles were hypercorrections, and little more. The fact that they were adopted practically overnight—within a single generation, at any rate—indicated the presence of a ready-made need. They became linguistic status markers that were unquestioned, as they still are today.

The total number of irregular verbs in Present-day English—strong verbs and variants of the weak verb conjugation—is actually small, so limited as a matter of fact that thousands of users of English ignore a feature like the distinction between a preterite and a past participle. They serenely explain how "we *done* it," or that "John *come* home stoned last night," or that "Penny *seen* that movie." There are others who realize that there is a distinction and they conduct a hesitant walk between doing too well and not well enough. The person who *swang* his arms or *slank* into a dark corner is trying too hard where many speakers of American English are concerned; the one who *begun* to make excuses because he *run* his auto into a culvert isn't trying hard enough.

It is a mistake, however, to suppose that the system has now achieved stability. A generation ago the judges consulted in S. A. Leonard's *Current English Usage* accorded the expression "She *sung* very well" a grudging rating of "disputable." Only four or five decades previously, "She *sang* very well" would have been considered obsolescent. Such instability and arbitrariness may easily shake anyone who is looking for consistency and order in the English verb system. But if orderliness in language had been a matter of considerable consequence, we should by all means have waved farewell long ago to the distinction between preterite and past participle, carrying to its conclusion a remodeling that has been going on for more than a thousand years. Yet we preserve the distinction with great care and tenderness. Efficiency in language is vastly overestimated. Efficiency should have dictated a common form, or some more obvious pattern of distinctions. But instead we have permitted and even encouraged some language forms to lag behind the others in becoming regularized, for a variety of reasons, all of them social and none of them linguistic.

AUXILIARIES

According to a tradition followed by grammarians for about two thousand years, there are eight parts of speech. If the tradition could be a little more elastic we might have an easier time of it. Not all the words slip easily into the categories so arbitrary prepared for them. Words like *must, can, shall, might* need to be berthed somewhere, and for want of a better place grammarians have assigned them to the verb category, specifying them as "auxiliary verbs." We find the term Englished to "helping verbs," especially for elementary instruction, since this supposedly simplifies matters.

If we need to give them a name, however, "auxiliary" will do, and "verb auxiliary" will do even better, as an indication of their grammatical function. Auxiliaries in English are not limited to simply one type. *Be, do,* and *have* are auxiliaries with precise functions. They are among other things fully inflected. Auxiliaries like *must, can, shall, might* actually have little in common with words of the verb class, either semantically or morphologically. To borrow traditional terminology, they do not "show action or state of being," and in general they are completely uninflected. There is no infinitive **to must,* or third person singular **George shalls;* or present participle **mighting;* or past participle **we have would.* It is said that *should, would, could,* and *might* are preterite forms and therefore express the past time of *shall, will, can,* and *may.* If this kind of reasoning held water, we ought to have a time contrast between: "I will take my vitamins now," and "I would take my vitamins this morning." The two sentences mean different things, but the contrast is not a contrast in time.

These auxiliaries are not only defective with respect to inflections; as a rule they are followed by a verb: "I *must* leave," "You *might* do the same." The verb is omitted only where the context makes it clear which verb is intended:

> Mr. Loomis can sing tenor, *can't* he?
>
> If Prissy can go to camp this summer, so *can* I.

When an auxiliary is used in making up a verb phrase the auxiliary is used with the "flat infinitive" form of the verb: *must rest, can find, shall expect.* In standard English only one verb auxiliary precedes the verb, although in spoken English of the South an expression like *might could* is possible where other speakers say or write *might be able to:*

> It was just something I thought *might could* be done.
> —Senator John J. Williams (Delaware)[10]

Unlike the auxiliaries *be, do,* and *have,* these auxiliaries generally ignore time-bound events or circumstances and express instead relationships in which time does not materially figure, like obligation, necessity, contingency, permission, ability, desire. In Latin these ideas were largely expressed by verb inflections, all of which were identified as "subjunctive." The "subjunctive" is still expressed by inflectional forms in the Romance languages. In the Germanic languages, including English, most of this work is carried out by a number of auxiliaries which are called "modal" because they express grammatical "mode"—sometimes called "mood."

Again we are confronted with a problem resulting from a historical development. At a stage in the history of the language preceding the emergence of English as an individual language, a fully inflected subjunctive mode operated in the Germanic languages. But even in the earliest records—in Wulfila's translation of the Bible into Gothic of the fourth century—there was already some use of words in an auxiliary function. Four or five centuries later, in Old English itself, the number of auxiliaries had considerably increased and writers had the option of using a subjunctive inflectional form or a modal auxiliary. By the end of the Old English period the remnants of the inflected subjunctive virtually disappeared and the system of auxiliaries assumed the modal function. Our school textbooks, taking their cue from Latin, still indicate that English maintains a subjunctive inflection, and writers periodically mourn its decline, as though it happened recently. A few relic phrases mark the place where it used to be: "If I *were* you," "God *save* the Queen!" "If it *be* he," and just about there it ends. As late as the time of Shakespeare the idea of possibility could be expressed by an uninflected third person singular form of the present tense:

> *If it* assume *my noble Father's person.*
> —*Hamlet*, I.ii.244

10 *Time,* October 13, 1952, p. 27.

It is still used from time to time in exhortations, resolutions, and the like:

> Resolved, that this House *stand* adjourned.

But in present-day spoken usage and in much of the written style such constructions are obsolete or deliberately archaic, except for occasional phrases with forms of *be*. Even here the pressure toward regularity has largely dismissed "if I *were* you" in favor of "if I *was* you," especially in speech. Expressions like "if I *could be*" or "if I *should be*" are admittedly longer and somewhat clumsier than the simple "if I *were*" but they are more in keeping with the style of Present-day English and it is reasonable to suppose that they will be used more and more. In fact, we may assume that the subjunctive expressed by the inflectional system of the verb is for all normal purposes dead. Except for a few set expressions, it has been replaced by the system of auxiliaries.

The shade of difference between the ideas of obligation and of necessity is a narrow one, as it is between most of the ideas conveyed by these verb auxiliaries. As a result the meanings have shifted from time to time in all the Germanic languages, including English. At one time, if we include the preterites as separate items, there were a score or more of these modal auxiliaries. Some of them, like *will* and *would,* in spite of minor modifications in spelling and pronunciation, are still clearly recognizable in form even though in Old English *will* meant 'wish' and *would* meant 'wished.' But others of them have long since vanished from the standard speech. For instance, who recognizes *unne* 'grant, allow,' with its preterite *uthe?* The last citation the *Oxford English Dictionary* gives for this word is 1275. Or *thar,* sometimes also spelled *tharf,* 'need' with a preterite *thurt.* Except for occasional appearance in Scottish, this auxiliary became obsolete around 1400.

A few of them have done better. *Maun* 'must' came into the language by way of Scandinavian rather than Anglo-Saxon and remained in literary usage until the sixteenth century. It continues in Scottish, as in this line from Robert Burns:

> *For I* maun *crush amang the stoure*
> *Thy slender stem.*
> —"To a Mountain Daisy"

Of a preterite, however, there is no trace. *Dow* 'be valid, avail,' related to our word *doughty,* is entered in our dictionaries with the label "chiefly Scottish." The general significance today is 'to have strength or ability,' but it has long ceased to be used regularly as a modal auxiliary. Sir Walter Scott was a great one for reviving archaic and obsolete words in his novels; the preterite of *dow* as he used it came out in two ways: *dowed* and *dought. Mote* is archaic and it refers in a general way to possibility. Lord Byron used it deliberately to lend an old-fashioned effect, for after the sixteenth century it had fallen out of literary use. But the preterite of *mote* is *must* and that shows no signs whatever of aging or of obsolescence. From Old English times to around 1400 *must* conveyed the idea of permission or ability, much the same sense that *may* expresses in Present-day English. Not till 1300 did *must* first come to be used in the current sense of general necessity. *To wit* is one of the few modals of which an infinitive form has survived, thanks to its preservation in legal language. The present tense form is *wot,* as in the phrase *God wot* 'God [only] knows.' The preterite form is *wist,* now archaic, as in "Moses wist not that the skin of his face shone" (Exodus 34:29 KJV).

The verb *dare* is both a regular verb and a verb auxiliary, and as such it has a double set of inflections. It was originally a modal and typically has the "enclitic negative" *-nt,* as in *daren't.* Combining the inflected form with this negative results in *dassn't,* a substandard form used with all the personal pronouns: "I dassn't, you dassn't, etc." Like the other modal auxiliaries, *dare* has the uninflected third person singular of the present tense, as in "He dare not mention it," although "dares not" is preferred and "doesn't dare" is the usual form. *Dare* has the usual weak verb preterite, *dared,* but also an archaic one, *durst. Owe* belongs to this class of verb auxiliaries historically, though it no longer figures in any of the characteristic constructions and inflections, except for its older preterite, *ought.* In the earliest records we have, it had begun to operate as a regular verb in the sense of 'have, possess,' now expressed more or less by the verb *to own,* derived as a matter of fact from the same Old English source. The earlier meaning of *owe* remained in use till around the beginning of the eighteenth century. It occurs in its older use in this line from Shakespeare:

> *Nor lose possession of that faire thou* ow'st.
> —Sonnet XVIII

Verbs that indicate possession, like *have* and *get* in Present-day English, quickly slip into expressing the idea of obligation. Originally it would have been:

> Philip *has* an errand to run.

But it has now become:

> Philip *has* to run an errand.

Owe acquired this meaning early in the Old English period, and that has remained its primary meaning since. The preterite *owed* dates from the fifteenth century. Before that the regular preterite was *ought,* originally 'possessed,' but taking on its present sense of 'be obliged' around 1200. As a verb auxiliary, *ought* has its peculiarities. In common with some borderline verb auxiliaries it takes not the flat infinitive, but the infinitive with *to.* We say:

> You *should get* a haircut.

But with *ought* it becomes:

> You *ought to get* a haircut.

The negative follows the regular pattern with the enclitic negative: *oughtn't.* A holdover from an older usage occurs in a compound construction with *had,* to indicate obligation—this would not appear in writing, and is preserved in local dialects:

> You *had ought* to be in England, now that April's there.

The negative of this is found quite commonly in the Northern states and is limited generally to spoken English:

> Bluestein *hadn't ought* to drive a Volvo like that.

Necessity is an idea expressed in some languages by the subjunctive inflected forms, in English and related languages by modal auxiliaries. As a result the verb *need* has taken on several formal characteristics of an auxiliary. It has the negative enclitic:

> You *needn't* bother getting up.

As a regular verb, *need* has the regular inflection for the third person singular of the present:

> Do you realize that your dog *needs* a bath?

But the uninflected form appears when *need* is employed as an auxiliary. This began during the sixteenth century and continues to be followed in Present-day English, especially in formal literary style.

> One *need* only look at the results to be appalled.

Related to this is a construction in which both *need* and *want* occur. These are not yet acceptable in standard English but are becoming increasingly common in spoken English. They appear to be Midland in origin:

> Open the door. The dog *wants* in.
>
> Stop the bus. Grace *needs* out at the next corner.

Such a use of adverbs—chiefly *out* and *in*—may follow either *need* or *want* and is characterized by the deletion of an infinitive which would be present in standard English:

> Open the door. The dog wants *to come* in.
>
> Stop the bus. Grace needs *to get* out at the next corner.

About a dozen words or expressions, all of them mastered at an extremely early age, perform the yeoman service of the English modal system. We learn them so perfectly that each one fits its proper place in our speech—such a precise place, in fact, that the possibility of a synonym is eliminated. Indeed we employ them altogether spontaneously because our habits regarding them have long been buried deep in the subconscious. For that reason discussions of the English modal system are traditionally superficial or philosophical.

In spite of the shifts in meaning that have occurred during their history, the English modal auxiliaries figure in relatively few usage problems. The more notorious ones have come not from deficiencies in the language itself but as the result of authoritarian tinkering with the language. The amount of counsel the handbooks bestow on the auxiliaries *need, dare, must,* and *ought to* is trifling. We have, on the other hand, no end of instruction in the use of *may* and *can, will* and *shall,* and by extension *might* and *could, would* and *should.*

The *may-can* problem offers a vivid illustration of a popular and widely prevalent misunderstanding about language, namely, that things can go on changing century after century, but that at some specific point in history the grammarians through their great influence are able to pull a word up short and lock it into place so that it no longer changes. Consider then this conversation:

> "Mother, *can* Fungo and I go to the woods and kill snakes?"
> "You *can,* Bathurst, but you *may* not."

Mother has been a schoolteacher, and Bathurst is being reminded once again of something every educated person has been told: *can* is supposed to be used to express ability, and *may* to express permission. Most educated persons, in addition to those with flimsy credentials like Bathurst's, typically lack such a distinction in speech and especially in writing. But schoolmastering has left its mark. Many writers—and a substantial number of self-conscious speakers of English as well—find themselves lacking any clear conception of how *can* and *may* actually operate. As a result they simply select at random. In practice the only thing that guides them is a generalized sense of uneasiness about using *can* at all. Characteristically the result is a hypercorrection, another instance of shooting beyond the target as they employ *may* for not only permission but for ability as well, at the same time that they carefully avoid using *can* in either situation.

The first citations of the verb auxiliary *may* in Old English indicate that it could still be used as an independent verb expressing the general notion of being strong or having power. In a medical handbook of the period there occurs, for instance, a reference to some characteristically noisome infusion of herbs with the notation: "It may against many infirmities." We should say, "It is effective," or "It works." At the same time, however, *may* was more commonly used as a verb auxiliary in the sense "be able" and it was etymologically related to the words for being strong. Presumably a strong person is more likely to get things done, a sense reflected in the old word *main* which lingers on in the phrase "might and main." By the fifteenth century this sense of *may* had dropped out of general use. Even before the end of the Old English period *may* had begun to express permission, that is to say, the idea that an event could happen under certain conditions over which the speaker had some control. But along with this there was the notion that it is possible for something to happen so long as nothing interferes. Thus the remark "It may rain" does not indicate that the Weather Bureau has extended its official permission but that the speaker considers rain a strong possibility, barring a strong east wind, hail, or other such condition. This is the principal meaning at present in spoken and written English. The line between permission and possibility is not always easy to draw precisely:

> The housemother says I *may* get mono from kissing boys.

In its earlier uses *can* signified knowing how to do something rather than having the physical capacity to carry it out. The word is etymologically related to *cunning* 'having special knowledge.' In written English of the present, especially in affirmative statements, *can* regularly expresses physical or mental ability:

> Gerhard *can* speak Japanese like a native.

The general idea of *can* is that something happens because there is nothing to prevent it, in contrast to *may* where the speaker always reserves the option of offering an obstacle or of being aware of one. The small boy who asks his mother whether he "can" go to the woods understands this; his instincts tell him that if he asks her if he "may," he runs the chance of reminding her of an objection.

The negative of *can* has quite widely displaced the negative of *may;* in the vocabulary of many users of English *mayn't* does not exist, although the full form *may not* occurs occasionally. It applies to possibilities, often vaguely specified:

> This *may* not be the best time to talk to your father.

We find an archaic use of this in a line from Whittier:

> *We* may *not climb the heavenly steeps*
> *To bring the Lord Christ down.*
>
> —Our Master

The speaker of Present-day English who sees these lines by themselves supplies his own meaning of *may* and is likely to read them as: "We may—by God's grace and favor—climb the heavenly steeps, but then again we may not succeed." If the reader is familiar with what Whittier had in mind, he will interpret it as "We are barred from climbing . ." *Can't* expresses inability or incapacity:

> You *can't* get there from here.

It may even be understood as denial of permission because of an obstacle:

> You *can't* take twenty-three hours this semester. As your faculty advisor I still can't go that far against the college rules.

Whenever there is a critical need for a distinction between permission and ability the speaker or writer of English usually resorts to a phrase like *be allowed to* or *be permitted to* over against *be able to*. We may think that a useful distinction has been lost, but neither we nor our linguistic ancestors have depended on the distinction for several generations. The meanings are clear; the danger lies not in using *can* for *may* but in insisting on using *may* where *can* has had a rightful place.

The "school-book rules" pertaining to *will* and *shall* are more explicitly stated than those for *may* and *can*. They have at one time engaged the attention, though not necessarily the convictions, of virtually every teacher of English in our elementary schools and often in the more advanced years as well. It is assumed that the basic distinction between the two auxiliaries is one of meaning, between a simple prediction of future events, called "simple futurity," and a firm resolve to bring about these events, called "strong determination or purpose." In other words, it depends on whether one regards the future passively or actively, as something to be endured or as something to be manipulated. Now these "rules" declare that with a subject in the first person, either singular or plural, *shall* expresses futurity and *will* expresses determination; with a subject in the second or third person, on the other hand, *will* expresses futurity, and *shall* expresses determination. Why there should be this reversal is never explained.

Mere mention of *will* and *shall* in the same breath arouses in many persons a feeling of deep uneasiness, bordering on guilt or embarrassment. It seems strange that anyone should need to feel that way about his own language. Many of our "rules," as we have noted, are Johnny-come-latelies. We did not become sensitive to split infinitives till fairly late in the nineteenth century, and carelessness about distinguishing preterites and past participles was only a minor fault till about a hundred years ago. Even clergymen were sometimes decidedly lax in these matters as recently as the time of the Civil War. By comparison, therefore, our instruction regarding the proper use of *will* and *shall* is ancient, representing one of the earliest deposits of prescriptive purism of which we have record. As early as the first quarter of the seventeenth century some of the language scholars were already puzzling their brains about the matter, and in 1653 John Wallis in effect settled everything by formulating the "rules" in substantially the form our handbooks have continued to follow. Grammarians occasionally invent new rules and write them into the school books. Rarely do they recognize that an older rule is false and delete it. *Will* and *shall* have been around for so long that few grammar textbook compilers dare to pass over them in silence.

In matters of usage we assume that standard English and social acceptability go hand in hand. Sometimes there is divided usage among the socially privileged and then members of the speech community accept both without noticing which one the speaker used. In any event it is usage that really determines correctness. There have been and still are people who try to do it the other way. Ambrose Bierce, to mention one of them, insisted that it was a grave error to speak of a criminal being executed since it was the sentence that had to be executed and the criminal that had to be hanged. For all his earnest concern, he never changed English usage. Anyone who works with language, and especially with varieties of language that reflect distinctions in educational and social background, is tempted again and again to assume the mantle of a lawgiver. Those unfamiliar with the science of usage suppose that lawgiving—or "prescriptivism," as it is called—is entirely proper, for in the popular mind the grammarian by virtue of his high calling as grammarian has an obligation to dictate rather than to merely record. It is instructive in this connection to read Henry Bradley's remarks on *shall* in the *Oxford English Dictionary,* or those of H. W. Fowler in his *Modern English Usage,* since in such matters both men were faithfully on the side of good usage. But with respect to *shall* and *will* they fell into the assumption that any departure from the cast-iron rules must be, according to Fowler, who was quoting from Bradley, "a mark of Scottish, Irish, or provincial, or extra-British idiom."[11] Fowler thereupon cited a number of usages by reputable Britishers "contrary to British idiom," in effect poking a hole in the statement he had just made. For if all Britishers follow the rule,

---

11 *Modern English Usage* (London, Oxford Univ. Press, 1926), p. 526.

but many of them don't, where are we? The most recent revision of Fowler (1965), made by Sir Ernest Gowers, reluctantly but realistically admits: "The 'Scottish, Irish, etc. idiom,' especially as followed on the American continent, has made formidable inroads; and insistence on the rules . . . may before long have to be classed as insular pedantry." And so, in view of all of the exceptions that have been mentioned, one wonders whether these "rules" may not have been an illusion.

Shall and *will* and their respective preterites, *should* and *would,* were among the Old English modals. *Shall,* closely related to German *schulden,* meant "to owe [money]" and this sense of the word was prevalent till the time of Chaucer. The notion of obligation, being closely related, also appeared very early. In one of the opening incidents of *Beowulf,* for instance, we find Beowulf himself at the head of a troop of fully armed combat soldiers debarked on foreign soil. They approach a sentry who immediately gives a challenge. A word by word translation of the sentry's words is: 'I shall know your origin,' but translated into Present-day English it means: 'I am required to know your origin.' This use of *shall* carried over well into the sixteenth century and is to some degree reflected in our handbook "rules."

Will, as the related noun clearly indicates, originally had to do with desire or resolve, a meaning which was carried well into the eighteenth century. We now usually say *wish* or *want to,* but in the writings of Shakespeare and the King James Bible the earlier meaning was very common:

> *Thou com'st in such a questionable shape*
> *That I* will *speake to thee.*
> —*Hamlet,* I.iv.42–43

> *I* will *haue mercy and not sacrifice.*
> —Matthew 9:13

In English and in the Germanic languages generally, the notion of present time is indicated by the present tense of the verb, and past time by the preterite. In Old English there was no specific expression of future time (which has given rise to the old joke that Anglo-Saxon had no future). In a number of languages—particularly French, Spanish, Italian, and Latin, to mention a few—indication of future time is clearly marked. It is signified by inflectional endings of the verb.

When the user of Old English needed to refer to an event that had not yet happened, he did exactly what his linguistic descendants have been doing ever since, that is, use a present tense form along with an adverb or noun to specify the time:

> Judy *sits* Mrs. Harrison's baby *Friday evening.*

Actually we have a number of grammatical devices to convey the notion of future time:

> I'*m* getting married *in the morning.*
>
> Richard *is to see* the dentist *at 11:15 Tuesday.*
>
> The neighbors *are going* to put in a swimming pool.

The *going to* future, as it is often called, is certainly the most common one in everyday speech where it is heard as *gonna.* Our school-books maintain the fiction that *going to* (*gonna*) does not exist except among the underprivileged. Much of the material designed for teaching English to speakers of other languages, however, makes use of *going to* to indicate future time because it offers relatively few teaching problems and because it is the form they will encounter in actual contact with speakers of English.

The early grammarians had good reason for assuming that whatever appeared in one language could be found in another. It might not come out the same way. "Case" in an English noun is a world away from "case" in Latin. Since they needed to find something in English that would correspond to the inflections in other languages for future tense, they assumed that *will* and *shall* fit the specifications. A really careful look would have showed them that all the modals deal with something that has not yet happened, and in a sense that is what future tense is all about. But to include *can, may, must, ought,* and all the others would have made things complicated beyond belief. Even the need to account for both *will* and *shall* was more than they were prepared for. If one found it difficult to tailor the facts to the language, there was an easier way, namely, to set up a "rule" and trust the language to follow. That is why we have this curious but false "reversal" rule.

English verb constructions generally refer to factual events and circumstances. English modals on the other hand emphasize not the event or circumstance but the relation between what is supposed to exist or to take place and the objective world as the speaker knows it. In the case of *may* and *can* he suggests that the event will probably happen since in his opinion the circumstances seem favorable. *Will* and *shall* do not first of all predict an event. Instead they say that the speaker has confidence that the event will happen sooner or later:

> I *will* be there at noon.
>
> You *will* enjoy their shrimp salad.
>
> It *will* take all the nerve George has got to speak to the dean.

Shall further suggests that certain conditions need to be met:

> I *shall* be there at noon [if I can get a ride].

There is even the further suggestion that the speaker or writer expects to assume charge of the conditions:

> You *shall* have our finest service [even if we have to engage additional employees].
>
> All examinations *shall* be of the comprehensive type [or there will be an explanation].

In this respect usage has changed since Elizabethan times. The earlier style appears in the Ten Commandments:

> *Thou* shalt *not kill.*
>
> *Thou* shalt *not commit adultery.*
>
> *Thou* shalt *not steal.*

The translators of the Revised Standard Version assumed that a word-for-word modernization would be adequate:

> *You* shall *not kill.*
>
> *You* shall *not commit adultery.*
>
> *You* shall *not steal.*

To the speaker of Present-day English statements like this are simply assurances that something is going to happen. His response is: "Well, that's very interesting. How can you be so sure?"

Again, in spite of what the handbooks tell us, *will* is commonly used to note events or situations which the speaker knows to be true:

You *will* need an umbrella and a raincoat.

There *will* be someone at the boxoffice with tickets for you.

If these things do not turn out that way, the speaker's reliability rather than his intelligence will be called into question. There is little evidence in actual usage to suggest that we need to be greatly concerned about whether the subject is in the first person or the second or the third:

I'm getting my books; I *will* be there in a minute.

You *will* find us in the Minneapolis phone book.

Our tree expert *will* be happy to inspect your elm tree.

That is the way the language works, though it is not the rule that a seventeenth-century mathematician dreamed up.[12]

Few of us are aware of making the choice of *shall* or *will* in daily conversation since the distinction is obscured under the *-'ll* contractions: *I'll, you'll, he'll, she'll, we'll, they'll, Roger'll, Mrs. DeVries'll, the librarian'll.* If and when these are expanded into full forms, chances are heavily in favor of *will* in all of them.

The morphology of the English verb, as we have noted in some detail, makes a distinction in form between the present tense and the preterite, and this corresponds with some consistency to a current event or situation and an event or situation some distance away in the past. Historically the preterites of the modal auxiliaries also had time significance. However, since the typical modal does not express the action or relationship itself, the preterite conveys a more remote or weaker manifestation of that attitude. Corresponding to *may* and *can* are the preterite forms *might* and *could:*

The front wheels *may* need to be aligned.

The front wheels *might* need to be aligned.

---

12 John Wallis (1616–1703) was known chiefly for his contributions to mathematics. He invented the term *interpolation,* and the symbol for infinity: ∞. To put himself to sleep he worked problems in mental arithmetic and one night worked out the square root of a number fifty-three digits long; next morning he dictated the result to twenty-seven places. It was correct. He was one of the first to make a science of cryptanalysis. His contribution to language study—he was fluent in Latin and knew Greek, Hebrew, and French—consisted of an English grammar: *Grammatica Linguæ Anglicanæ* (Oxford, Leon. Lichfield, 1653, Repr. Scolar Press Ltd., Menston, England, 1969).

A similar remoteness is indicated when *would* and *should* occur in contrast to *will* and *shall:*

> This *will* be a good time to clean the attic.
>
> This *would* be a good time to clean the attic.

The same applies in questions:

> *Shall* we have the plumber come and look at it?
>
> *Should* we have the plumber come and look at it?
>
> *Will* I make a good Lady Macbeth?
>
> *Would* I make a good Lady Macbeth?

Again the spoken forms are quite commonly contracted, sometimes written as *-'ld* but more usually *-'d: I'd, you'd, he'd, they'd, Mr. Bettys'd.* The contraction for *had* is, of course, formed in the identical manner. As a rule this causes no confusion since the context indicates which auxiliary is called for. We do have some uncertainty regarding the full forms of a few expressions: *I'd better, I'd rather, I'd as soon.* Historically these have been *had,* as:

> *I* had *rather be a doorkeeper in the house of my God. . . .*
> —Psalm 84:10 (KJV)

Since a certain degree of choice is involved, it is easy to assume that *I'd* is a contraction of *I would* instead of *I had,* especially since the latter is idiomatic; consequently the phrase becomes *I would rather* or *I would as soon:*

> *I* would *rather be a doorkeeper in the house of my God. . . .*
> —Psalm 84:10 (RSV)

There is divided usage here. Some users of English regard *had rather* and the rest as archaic; others regard *would rather* as hypercorrect and somewhat precious.

The early grammarians were perceptive in sensing a distinction between *will* and *shall.* Unfortunately they took as their starting point the Latin language where matters like these are completely stable. That is true of any dead language. In Latin there had been a clearly identifiable set of inflections to indicate future time, and the grammarians could see no plausible reason why English should not have a future tense system as well. It did not occur to them that English might perhaps be organized on a different structure. There is no evidence that Wallis or his contemporaries in general ever actually looked closely at the language practices of some of its more distinguished users—Shakespeare, for instance, or the translators of the King James Bible.

The early grammarians, we must remember, had not the faintest notion that the study of language should be, or even could be, conducted in a scientific manner. Wallis was himself a mathematician, many of the others were clergymen—Bishop Lowth and Isaac Watts, for instance—or authors, like Samuel Johnson. They supposed that the English language would presently begin to follow their rules, whether or not the rules conformed to actual practice. As a result we have had generations of parents and teachers and other guardians of the language striving with the purest of motives to make the rules operate. But unless the user of English has been rigidly schooled in these matters, he goes his own way and uses *will* and *shall* and the other verb auxiliaries as he has learned them, from the people all around him. And unless the listener has been equally well schooled to be able to distinguish "correct" from "incorrect," it will never occur to him to notice whether these modals have been improperly used. Since the entire operation is quite unrealistic, the handbook employment of *will* and *shall* ranks fairly low on the scale of language status forms that one ought to observe. The reward hardly matches the effort. The only risk a person runs is that he may try too hard to do the right thing.

Nevertheless we should not gather that anarchy is rampant. *May* and *can, will* and *shall,* and likewise *might* and *could, would* and *should,* are useful in indicating shades of meaning which the discriminating user of English senses and appreciates. That anyone measurably improves his status, however, by conspicuously demonstrating his control of the "rules," or that he suffers reproach and ignominy because he ignores them—this seems quite unlikely.

10 modifiers

"Modify" is a word from a small list of words with both a distinctive grammatical use and an everyday one. Many things can be modified: automobiles, military aircraft, household appliances, academic programs, and so on. Modification may be regarded as a change of some sort which involves the external aspects of anything but which leaves the basic pattern or structure unaffected. Grammatical modification typically operates this way. We can begin with a general expression—a noun like *bird,* for instance. By adding the modifier *black* we limit the notion to birds that are black, but meanwhile we have also eliminated all blue, red, gray, and speckled ones. In such a situation *bird* is known as the "headword," and *black* the "modifier." Crows and grackles happen to be among several varieties of birds that are black, but the words *crow* or *grackle* are not for that reason modifications since they do not combine a headword with a modifier.

Much of what we have been taught in schools about modifiers has been tightly bound to the concepts of modification as it operated in Latin. Such modification as there was depended on two parts of speech: adjectives, which modified nouns, and adverbs, which modified verbs. With a few minor qualifications, that was all there was to it. As a result of this grammatical inheritance we continue to assume that adjectives and adverbs do all the modification that gets done in English, and conversely, that any word which modifies another must be either an adjective or an adverb. This could lead to problems, and it does. In a sentence like "It's his fault," a grammarian might argue that *his* must be an adjective on the grounds that it modifies *fault*. Obviously *his* is a pronoun, if we feel seriously obliged to give it a name, but these grammarians take care of that difficulty by saying that it is a pronoun used as an adjective. Applying this kind of analysis to a different situation, one might argue that a truck is an automobile used as a wagon. The difficulty begins with the definition: "An adjective is a word that describes a noun." While an adjective may, and frequently does, describe a noun, other words can also describe nouns, and adjectives can do other things than describe.

The matter becomes clearer when we think of modification in English as a function which a number of words representing a number of parts of speech can assume. We have been told that modification is a quality or characteristic of adjectives and adverbs, but that is where we have been misled. It happens to be a function that is frequently assumed by adjectives and adverbs. But the identity of a part of speech and what it can do grammatically are quite different matters in English. A noun, for example, may be a subject of a verb since that is frequently a function of nouns. Also a noun may function as a direct object, indirect object, object complement, or object of a preposition. But there is no reason why a word of another part of speech cannot assume, say, the function of the subject of a verb. In English we find that nouns commonly function as subjects, but not because they are nouns; similarly adjectives most commonly function as modifiers, but not because they are adjectives. An adjective may typically modify a noun, but there is no reason why it should not function now and then as a subject or object:

> *Black* is the color of my true love's hair.
>
> Gertrude usually wears *pink*.

The notion that only an adjective may modify a noun and only an adverb may modify an adjective is again an inheritance from Latin. In English a noun does either one:

> Our *paper* boy is named Morton.
>
> There stood Jarvis, *waist* deep in fourth graders.

To put it simply, modification is a function which any part of speech may on occasion assume. It happens, of course, that adjectives and adverbs do most of the modification, and by meaning they are best suited for this function. A noun has limitations as a modifier, for it serves to identify and that is about all. With *book* as the headword we have a choice of modifiers; we can choose, for instance, *chemistry,* which is obviously a noun—and get the phrase *chemistry book;* or we can attach a verb form like *borrowed* and have *borrowed book.* In such cases there is a yes-or-no choice: the book is either a chemistry book or not, it is a borrowed book or not. But when the modifier is an adjective, the choice is broader. We may say *dull book,* but as experience will tell us, it does not stop there. Compared with another book, it may be more dull, and we should say *duller book.* And it may actually be the *dullest book* that we have come across.

It was relatively easy to distinguish adjectives from adverbs in Latin, and for that reason the grammarians have supposed that it must also be easy in English. The borderline, however, is less clear than we should imagine. In some words, like *hard* or *fast,* there is no difference in form, and in some varieties of spoken English—chiefly among the less educated—adjectives and adverbs are exactly alike. Whether the difference we so carefully cultivate contributes importantly to the meaning or whether it is essentially a matter of style and therefore of usage may be questioned.

No part of speech in English has undergone so overwhelming a remodeling as the adjective has between Old English times and the present. The only inflection that remains is that for comparison, the *-er* and *-est* of the comparative and superlative degree. It is distinguishable by its position with respect to the headword, and little more. In Old English times the adjective had what a grammarian would call a "full" inflectional system. Like other languages of the Germanic family, it had two types of declension, commonly known as "weak" and "strong," thanks once more to Jacob Grimm, but more precisely "definite" and "indefinite," corresponding quite closely to the difference between the article *the* and the articles *a* and *an.* Each declension furthermore had singular and plural inflections, and these in turn had gender-related forms corresponding to masculine, feminine, and neuter nouns, and all of this in addition to a declension in five cases. In theory any adjective therefore could have as many as sixty different inflectional endings in the positive degree alone. By the time of our first written records of English, however, many of these individual forms had fallen together into a single form so that the actual number was nearer ten or a dozen. Except for a few special forms, the endings merely indicated that it was an adjective, and information about case, number, and so on depended on the definite article and word order. But it was still complex. The inflectional system had its advantages, especially in poetry—of which the Anglo-Saxons produced vast quantities, much of it extremely good—since an adjective could occur at some distance from its headword. Once the inflections began to disappear, they fell away rapidly and by 1500 it was virtually impossible to find any trace of them. The position before the noun had been commonly but optionally occupied by the adjective. After inflections had given way to word order, the position itself distinguished the adjective.

COMPARISON

A distinctive feature of modifiers in English—both adjectives and adverbs—is something we call "comparison," that is, an indication of various degrees of intensity. Comparison is accomplished by the *-er* and *-est* inflections, or the *more* and *most* "degree words"; but not both at once. The simple form of the adjective, like *big,* is known as "positive"; the "comparative," as the name suggests, indicates that two and sometimes more matters are related in regard to the degree of some quality or attribute, as *bigger.* "Superlative" indicates the ultimate degree of a quality or attribute, as *biggest.* A hundred years ago grammarians managed to argue many things without looking foolish. Some grammarians of the time suggested that comparison was, after all, entirely a matter of degree, and therefore *biggish* should also have a place in the system.

English has irregular nouns and irregular verbs which prove to be among the chronic hot spots in usage; it may also be expected to have some irregular modifiers—words that do not conform to the typical *big-bigger-biggest* pattern for comparison:

positive	*comparative*	*superlative*
good, well	better	best
bad, ill	worse	worst
old	older	oldest
	elder	eldest

positive	*comparative*	*superlative*
far	farther	farthest
	further	furthest
many, much	more	most
little	less	least
	littler	littlest
	lesser	

A form like *gooder,* which represents a regularization of *better,* has no currency outside the talk of small children. *Badder* and *baddest,* however, are becoming increasingly common in a specialized sense relating to personal conduct or behavior. A person may have been "badder" as an adolescent than he is now; one would scarcely dismiss a play as the "baddest of the season" on esthetic grounds, although the expression would make sense if the play outstripped its competition in prurience. There is no indication that these words have literary standing at this time, though they may conceivably gain acceptance in the future.

The distinction between *older* and *elder* or between *farther* and *further* depends more on style than on meaning. Historically *elder* and *eldest* were the standard forms, having developed by umlaut from the original adjective. The comparative and superlative of the counterpart adjective *young* were *yinger* and *yingest,* but these have now been lost except as personal names. On the whole *elder* and *eldest* have given way to the regularized *older* and *oldest,* constructed by the regular pattern on the base *old. Elder* is preserved in a few phrases like *elder statesman* or *elder educator,* reminding us of dignity rather than age. It has become fashionable to avoid reference to age as such, so that instead of *elder citizen* we have the expression *senior citizen.*

Farther and *farthest* have long competed with *further* and *furthest.* Strictly speaking, they are all bastard forms since a regular comparison of *far* gives **farrer* and **farrest.* In spoken English many people manage to be noncommittal with pronunciations like /fə́ðər/ and /fə́ðəst/. The form *furtherest,* a hodgepodge of both comparative and superlative, is substandard for all its pretentiousness. Stylistically there seems to be some preference for *farther, farthest* in speaking of literal spatial distances and for *further, furthest* in metaphorical senses:

Isn't Saturn *farther* from the sun than Jupiter?

Having another baby is the *furthest* thing from my mind right now.

More and *most* are the comparative and superlative of *many* and *much.* In English we commonly make a distinction between the use of the positive *many* and *much.* Things that can be counted—known as "count nouns"—we describe with *many,* and those that from their nature cannot be—known as "mass nouns"—with *much*:

Griswold has *many* potatoes but not *much* gravy.

Many speakers of nonstandard English use *much* to cover both senses, often as a carry-over from a foreign language background where there is no such distinction. With the comparative and superlative this distinction disappears:

Griswold has *more* potatoes and still *more* gravy.

Little may refer to physical size or dimension, but it may also indicate degree or amount; as a result it has developed, or inherited, an elaborate set of forms. *Less* and *least* refer to degree in inverse ratio to *more* and *most,* and some grammarians have contended that they ought to be regarded as comparative and superlative markers for ideas or things that are negative. Thus *less neat* would have to be a comparative just as *more messy* is. Nothing is to be gained from arguing points like these. *Less* does, however, indicate quantities or amounts: *less water* or *less pudding.* But it has also spread to phrases like *less people* or *less highways.* While this usage is widespread and is to be found among well-educated speakers and writers, there are many who prefer *fewer* and *fewest* for things that can be counted and *less* and *least* for those that cannot:

Griswold has *fewer* potatoes and *less* gravy than I have.

Lesser does not involve quantity but relative standing or importance. It sounds faintly archaic, yet it is difficult to think of an equally fitting word in a phrase like *lesser of two evils.* There are those, of course, who simply say *less of two evils.* Naturalists apply the word to various relatively obscure plants and animals: *lesser emerald bird of paradise.*

As a result chiefly of phonetic developments, some comparisons which were common in older phases of English have changed to such a degree that the original relationships are no longer evident:

positive	*comparative*	*superlative*
out	outer	outmost
	utter	utmost
(be)neath	nether	nethermost
(be)fore	former	foremost
		first
aft	after	
(be)hind	hinder	hindmost

Utter has moved almost exclusively into metaphorical uses. The phrase *utter darkness* gives a picture of total darkness without regard for location; *outer darkness* on the other hand is the situation one may encounter after leaving a well-lighted place. In the same way we speak of *utter despair, utter confusion, utter abandon.* But in the course of time the word has gone far beyond a mere comparative sense. It is difficult to imagine anything transcending, for example, *utter idiocy,* or *utter delight.* Within living memory *nether* has become archaic, and even in its heyday it never applied to many situations. *Nether regions* has sometimes been employed as a euphemism for hell, and *nether garments* a hundred years ago was a catchall term for trousers and especially for underwear. That was a time when no decent person so much as mentioned these items by name under any circumstances. Today there is no reluctance whatever, and anyone who speaks of *nether garments* renders himself mildly suspect. As is the case with *utter, nether* has taken over the functions of the superlative. One doesn't wear anything more nether than nether garments.

Rathe is an archaic modifier which means 'soon,' but it survives only in the comparative *rather.* Expressions of time have a tendency to become expressions of preference:

Helen'd *sooner* take the bus to Chicago.

I'd *quicker* enlist in the Navy than do that kind of work.

Aft is used in the positive degree as an adverb of place. In nautical circles *fore and aft* is a common expression and the more salty recruits even use the words in speaking of their homes or automobiles. In fact they tend to become apoplectic when someone refers to "the back of the boat."

Hinder /háyndər/ has a homograph /híndər/ 'prevent,' which may be one reason it is dropping out of use. It appears several times in the King James Bible. *Hindmost* is rare except in "The devil take the hindmost!" for which most of us would say "the last."

In *Alice in Wonderland,* after nibbling at a prepsychedelic mushroom, Alice discovers herself looking out over the treetops, and her comment is "Curiouser and curiouser." Lewis Carroll explains: "She was so much surprised that for the moment she quite forgot how to speak good English."

Curiouser would surely have difficulty passing as conventional English. But comparatives like *smaller, richer, larger, poorer* are accepted without demur. Or, to express it in another way, *small, rich, large, poor* may be inflected for degree of comparison while *curious* may not. The handbooks seldom offer explicit instruction at this point to let one know which modifiers are inflected and which are compared by *more* and *most.*

The problem centers about a situation related to the one encountered with nouns, pronouns, and verbs—a competition between two systems, one old and the other new. In this case the older system is inflectional or synthetic, with the endings *-er* and *-est;* the newer is periphrastic, or analytic, making use of the function words *more* and *most.* In many situations the two are interchangeable, or practically so:

> That was the *abruptest* ending I've ever seen.
>
> That was the *most abrupt* ending I've ever seen.

The "rule" commonly invoked here is that shorter words are inflected and longer words are compared periphrastically. Length of the adjective happens to be an incidental consideration; the rule sometimes breaks down:

> Galena is the *chicest* girl in her sorority.
>
> Of all the U and non-U people we know, Asaph is the *U-est.*

Constructions like these may occur but they border on the ridiculous. Actually the movement from inflected to periphrastic comparison has been slow and erratic. Some words that have been in the language for a long time possess the inflection by right of inheritance and maintain it through frequent and widespread use. Not all of them are monosyllabic, although that is the impression we get; some are disyllabic and trisyllabic: *prettiest, mightiest, heaviest, pleasantest, uncommonest, unluckiest.* In fact, some very short words, like *chic* or *non-U,* have come into the language since *-er* and *-est* stopped being "productive inflections," that is, since the time when they could be added to any and all modifiers. Many of the longer modifiers have been transferred to the periphrastic pattern, chiefly because they are less commonly used, but in his day Milton appears to have had no compunctions about using superlatives like *secretest, famousest, virtuousest,* or *powerfulest.* We look on them as quite unconventional. Over the years the tendency has moved in the direction of using *more* and *most* rather than the inflectional comparison in new situations. That is the reason *chic,* even though it is monosyllabic, appears strange when it is inflected. A word like *groovy*—which fits into the pattern of *-y* modifiers, like *heavy, pretty, tiny, bloody, ready*—is immediately naturalized to *groovier* and *grooviest.* It may be analogy or a carry-over of an Old English pattern, but many words with the *-y* ending, regardless of length, can take the inflectional endings: *bloodthirstiest, wishy-washiest, hoity-toitiest.* Most of them are colloquial rather than literary. Where there is doubt or hesitation, one is safest with the *more* and *most* constructions, even where the inflected forms would be acceptable: *most mighty, more heavy, more handsome.*

Past and present participles of verbs often modify nouns, and in some cases they have so completely shaded into adjectives that it is difficult to assign them finally to one class or the other. To borrow a device from the transformational grammarians; the construction "It is an accepted practice" is derived from "Someone accepts the practice." This approach will not work on a phrase like *aged servant;* "He is an aged servant" is not derived from "Someone aged the servant." In such cases it is more satisfactory to assign the modifiers to the adjective class: *devoted companion, wrinkled complexion, worried look, cracked voice, failing health.* In constructions like these either the inflected or the periphrastic comparison is possible, although the inflected comparison is limited generally to spoken English and the intended effect is humorous if not mildly grotesque:

> Senator Bassoon is the *longwindedest* member of the legislature.
>
> Sven said that Futilia was the *dancingest* girl he had ever met.

It is difficult to imagine how many English teachers in their presentation of Shakespeare's *Julius Cæsar* have been confronted with Mark

Antony's "This was the most unkindest cut of all." Obviously this is "bad" English and just as obviously Shakespeare was a "great writer." How to reconcile these two? The teacher may try to pass over it in haste, or may take refuge in the old "poetic license" dodge.

Originally the degree words *more* and *most* had to do with relative size rather than with degree or intensity. In the Old English poem *Beowulf* the wicked Grendel is described as being "more than any other man." Little by little, however, the words came to be used as "intensifiers," in much the same sense as our *very*. In fact, the inflected comparison has long been used in this sense:

> The kids next door have the *wildest* parties in their apartment.
>
> My brother-in-law plays the *stupidest* jokes on people.

The same idea can also be expressed by the periphrastic comparison:

> Melvin is a *most thorough* scholar.
>
> That's the *most imbecilic* question I've heard all week.

As late as the time of Shakespeare *more* and *most* were still looked on as intensifiers, and the expressions *most unkindest, most noblest,* or *more longer* would have been the equivalent of our own "very unkindest," "very noblest," or "somewhat longer." All of these and many others occur in the writing of the Elizabethans. Indeed, St Paul is quoted:

> *After the* most straitest *sect of our religion, I liued a Pharisee.*
> —Acts 26:5 (KJV)

Such double comparatives are no longer tolerated in the language, written or spoken, of the educated, primarily because like *this here, my father he,* and double negatives, they are regarded as tautology. They do linger on, however, in folk speech as *most nicest* or *more quieter,* but especially *more better* or *less worse. Worser* is now regarded as nonstandard. It was used by distinguished writers from the fifteenth century till practically the beginning of the present century. It is the only comparative—unless we include *less*—that does not end in *-er* and for that reason it seems to require reinforcement of the comparative sense. *Worser* is becoming archaic, but still passes unnoticed in much of our conversation.

ABSOLUTE ADJECTIVES

It is a common failing of those who do not know any better to suppose that the language has an obligation to itself and the people who use it to be logical. And so on a logical basis we discover a number of modifiers that are impossible to compare for degree: *unique, perfect, round, full, square, complete, final, empty, impossible, dead, black, fatal, chief, extreme, right, wrong, honest, just, ceaseless, infinite, supreme.* But this assumes that each of these words has simply one meaning. Not only is there a literal meaning, but another which is either literal or figurative:

> Charles I has been *dead* for more than three hundred years.
>
> Bisbee is *dead* after 9 P.M.

Now no one can be deader than Charles I. On the other hand, Charles I is just as dead as Oliver Cromwell and for that matter William of Normandy or Ivar the Boneless. So in that sense *dead* cannot be compared. But whether Tombstone or Bisbee is more lively after 9 P.M. can be decided by anyone who has the necessary curiosity and enterprise.

Many arguments center about usage points just like these. There are those who are convinced that such headlong extensions of meaning ought to be prohibited, preferably by a dictionary. To say:

> I'm perfectly *dead.* I studied till three this morning.

This is, one must admit, something other than the literal sense of the word. The meaning is clear; what distresses some listeners, however, is the gratuitous hyperbole it represents. Innumerable words that we use every day have gone along some such route to their present use, and we should scarcely think of returning them to their earlier places: *walk, starve, sell, glad, noon, nice*—to mention only very few. Whether *unique,* for instance, ought to mean only 'one of its kind,' or whether it should be permitted to indicate 'rare' or 'remarkable' does not depend ultimately on etymology or on a college of grammarians, but on the law of supply and demand. Many things strike us as being rare or remarkable, but very few are literally unique. *Perfect* means 'without fault or error' and consequently nothing can be *more perfect,* so the argument goes (even though the framers of the United States Constitution spoke of a *more perfect union*). A thing has to be *round* or not, as simple as that. And so it goes. If one insists on being precise, a compromise is possible: *more nearly unique, more nearly perfect, more nearly round.* Such advice is not widely followed. Absolute adjectives like these are often compared, even by careful speakers and writers of English. Failure to observe the "rule" seldom results in vague or imprecise language; conspicuous observance of it, on the other hand, may give one the reputation of being pedantic.

DANGLING COMPARISON

James Russell Lowell in "The Vision of Sir Launfal" concludes the prolog with this couplet:

> *He sings to the wide world, she to her nest;*
> *In the nice ear of Nature which song is the* best?

Two and only two items are being compared here. May a speaker of English use the superlative degree of an adjective in comparing only two items? The question has engaged the attention of usage specialists for many years. Because no confusion is possible, consistency does not demand one or the other. The best that can be said for the comparative in such situations is that it is available and deserves to be used. About so feeble a rallying point, however, one cannot expect to generate much excitement, and in popular usage the superlative is common in such constructions. In fact, there are situations in which the comparative would be ridiculous:

> They debated who should be the *former* to enter the room.

The English comparative shows little sign of decay and less indication of ultimately disappearing. This is particularly true of comparisons involving *than* where only the comparative is possible:

> Ralph always looks *busier* than Ivy.
>
> *The pen is* mightier *than the sword.*
> —Logan Pearsall Smith.

What we sometimes call the "dangling comparative" has become extremely familiar in phrases like: *higher education, greater opportunities, lighter teaching loads, longer-lasting, faster pickup, fewer cavities.* The basis for the comparison is never mentioned but may readily be supplied by the reader or listener. The construction seems to serve its purpose and we may look forward with some confidence to having it with us for a long time.

ADJECTIVES AND ADVERBS

Adjectives and adverbs are often mentioned in the same breath since they share a common function as modifiers. Like adjectives, words of the class we call adverbs have some rather general qualifications by means of which we seek to identify them. The handbooks, for instance, refer to adverbs as words that will modify verbs, adjectives, or other adverbs—a functional definition. On the other hand, adverbs are words that tell "how," "when," and "where"—a notional definition. A test for a good definition is whether one can reverse it and not be left with any residue; by such a test the above definitions are full of holes. Adverbs do modify adjectives, it is true, but so will other classes of words. In *blood red* or *beet red* a noun modifies an adjective, in *light red* another adjective does, and in *flaming red* a verb does. And furthermore, not all words that tell "how, when, and where" are necessarily adverbs:

> The bus driver looked *sick.*
>
> Let's talk about that *tomorrow.*
>
> Juanita decided to stay *home.*

There are those who feel compelled for the sake of consistency to argue that *sick, tomorrow,* and *home* should be classified as adverbs. The how-when-where qualification moreover opens the door to several additional classes of words, among them "connectives," like *namely, as, however, nevertheless;* or the degree words like *very, rather, somewhat, quite;* or "negators" like *not, never, nowhere.* One suspects that the adverb class of words, as it is ordinarily conceived, is actually a catchall into which grammarians toss any words they cannot clearly pigeonhole by precise definition. A look at what dictionaries do with adverbs will bear out this suspicion.

Our language sense tells us that we do in practice distinguish from other classes of words a relatively large and important class of words which do in fact "modify verbs, adjectives, and other adverbs," and which do indeed "tell how, when, and where." But the words in this class do not match up on a one-for-one basis with the adverbs of the handbooks.

Perhaps we are dealing with several smaller classes which frequently overlap.

There is a difference in meaning between these two sentences:

Ernst fell *silent* (stopped talking).

Ernst fell *silently* (made no noise coming down).

The contrast is the *-ly* ending. It suggests that the presence or absence of the ending merely shows which sense of the verb *fell* the speaker or writer had in mind, since otherwise *silent* and *silently* are pretty much the same.

To define an adverb as "a word that ends in *-ly*" is misleading, however, since there are scores of adjectives that end in *-ly: kingly, manly, scholarly, lively, cowardly, beastly, heavenly, bodily*. These adjectives consist of a noun plus the suffix *-ly*. The suffix itself is etymologically related to a noun *like,* meaning 'shape, appearance, form.' Some words like *early, only, timely, deadly* belong to this group also, although the connection is less immediately clear. Since they are adjectives, all these words can be compared for degree, but because of their nature they seldom are.

What may be considered the "real adverbs"—the hard core about which all the other adverb-type words and expressions are gathered—consist of an adjective in good standing and the *-ly* ending: *bad + ly, badly; nasty + ly, nastily; gentle + ly, gently*. A simple rule regarding modification in English is: adjectives precede nouns; adverbs follow verbs. This is not always true, but serves as a rule-of-thumb index. To illustrate the first: *gray mare, happy birthday, gastric ulcer, sweet seventeen;* the second: *slept soundly, responded feebly, talked tirelessly, smiled mechanically*.

In addition to appearing in attributive position, an adjective in English may also appear in "predicative" position, that is, following a typical linking word like *is, become, seem, appear:*

The mare is *gray*.

Mark's birthday seemed *happy*.

We realize that a noun can serve as the modifier of another noun, as *workhorse, heart condition, Ash Wednesday;* there is this limitation, however, which distinguishes it from an adjective in the same construction: it cannot serve as a modifier in predicative position. That is to say, we should find sentences like these to be un-English:

*The *horse* is *work.*

*My uncle's *condition* is *heart.*

On the other hand, a noun can appear in predicative position, but not as a modifier; instead it is what we call a "predicate noun" or "predicate nominative." Then it is in effect the equivalent of the noun in subject position, not its modifier:

Phil is all *work,* and no *play.*

My uncle is wonderfully kind; he is all *heart.*

Several verbs besides *is, become, seem, appear* operate as linking verbs or copulative verbs. Many of them also serve a more general function. *Appear* is typical:

Nancy *appeared* competent (seemed to know what she was doing).

Nancy *appeared* unexpectedly (came into view as a surprise).

The list of words in this class is rather long, about sixty in all, among them: *come, fall, feel, get, go, grow, keep, look, prove, remain, run, sit, smell, stand, stay, turn,* as in "come clean," "fall sick," "feel rotten," "get fat," "go batty," "grow old," and so on. As a result a certain ambiguity is possible unless one distinguishes between adjectives and adverbs, because after a copulative verb either an adjective or an adverb is possible:

Herbert turned *cold* from the suggestion.

Herbert turned *coldly* from the suggestion.

But, as usual, the number of situations in which such a contrast proves critical is limited. Language has a built-in avoidance of ambiguity.

One of the marks of nonstandard English, usually in speech, is the use of a form without *-ly* in an adverbial function, particularly as a verb modifier:

Ruthie sings real *nice,* don't she?

Warren handled the baby just as *careful* as he could.

While we should ordinarily be inclined to write these off as carelessness, it was not so long ago that such forms appeared in the best places, indicating that they are more archaic than corrupt.

> *I am my selfe* indifferent *honest.*
> —*Hamlet,* III.i.123

> *For the house which I am about to build shall be* wonderful *great.*
> —II Chronicles 2:9

On the other hand, because the adverb without *-ly* often characterizes nonstandard English, the *-ly* may be supplied where it does not belong, and the result is a hypercorrection. Following a copulative verb an adverb then takes the place of the adjective:

> That dog kennel next door smells *horribly.*
>
> Otis' jokes fell *flatly.*

Most of the discussion of this practice, however, centers on the choice between:

> I feel *bad.*
>
> I feel *badly.*

Taken literally, *I feel badly* indicates that the speaker is wearing thick gloves, or has impaired circulation, or has suffered nerve damage. But since the expression has been so widely current for such a long time, it has taken on respectability and has moved from hyperstandard usage to standard usage. Meanwhile it has attracted several related expressions: *look badly, taste badly, sound badly.* Many discriminating users of English still dislike these latter combinations, but there seems to be little doubt that time is on the side of *badly* in such situations. In a style of writing now usually dismissed as old-fashioned, *poorly* serves an analogous function:

> Mrs. Phoebell has been feeling *poorly* all spring.

Bad and *poor* call up distasteful associations, and *badly* and *poorly* are evidently intended to soften any harsh effect.

Feel well or *look well* or *taste well* can be subjected to the same criticism on the same grounds, since we consider *well* an adverb rather than an adjective. But the construction has held a long and respected place in our utterance and any attempt to dislodge or modify it would itself be an over-correction.

In the early records of the English language the words which modified verbs and which could accordingly be considered by our classification as adverbs were often really nothing more than inflected forms of nouns or adjectives, usually the dative case, but sometimes the genitive. The latter lingers on in phrases like *of a morning* or *of a weekend,* and in an even older inflected form, *mornings* or *weekends.* This looks like a plural, but is really a genitive. It also appears in early forms like *agains, whiles,* and *amongs,* all of which presently developed an excrescent final *-t,* as we have already noted. Ordinarily the dative inflection consisted of a final *-e,* and very early in the Middle English period this disappeared, leaving an adverb that did not differ in any way except in function from the corresponding adjective. There are numerous survivals of this development, sometimes called "flat adverbs": *hard, fast, slow, soon, scarce, fine, soft, loud, quick, late, high, low, even, rough, wrong, right, much, tight, loose,* to mention some of the more familiar ones. A few adverbs have only the flat form; we do not say, "Don't drive so fastly," or "Come back soonly." Others have had a double development, as in the case of *hard,* where "He works *hard*" means something other than "He *hardly* works." In point of style, the flat adverbs have an advantage of directness:

> Judy's parents looked *high* and *low* for her.
>
> They've been playing *fast* and *loose* with our account.
>
> Gary talked down to those people something *fierce.*

As has been indicated, *-ly* is a reduction of an earlier *-like,* literally 'form' or 'body,' and thus *manlike* would have been interpreted as 'having the form or shape of a man.' Presently this spread to other nouns and from there to adjectives. The *-like* suffix is still used, though chiefly in rustic speech:

> Rufus got up and talked real *slowlike.*

Because they represent the prevailing adverbial pattern, the *-ly* adverbs are often considered more elegant, especially by people who have developed an aversion to the nonstandard use of adjectives in adverb constructions. Such people fall into the danger of assuming that flat adverbs are also "wrong." From time to time well-meaning but overzealous purists have hewed down road markers under the misguided impression that *Go Slow* is a corruption of the English language. In some cases the *-ly* adverb may be stylistically preferable; in others the *-ly* adverb is the only one permitted. In *Go Slow* it makes no difference. But the linguistically fearful feel impelled to attach *-ly* wherever there is any shadow of doubt. From some such impulses we have:

> Thank you *muchly*.
>
> You tighten the bolt *thusly*.
>
> Be sure to come back *soonly*.

Many users of the language regard these as inexcusable hypercorrections.

DEGREE WORDS

Modification of the modifiers themselves is largely accomplished by a variety of expressions sometimes called degree words. By tradition they are usually, though unrealistically, lumped together with adverbs. At one time *more* and *most* were principally used as degree words in connection with adjectives and adverbs, as we observed in a phrase like "the most unkindest cut." Degree words serve to augment or diminish the force of the modifier. Grammarians have been at a loss to supply really appropriate names for them; they have been called "intensifiers" and "down-toners." In a drug-oriented subculture they might be referred to as "uppers" and "downers."

A common characteristic of degree words is their lack of specificity. It is difficult, for example, to rank for relative degree of intensity such expressions as: *pretty good, quite good, somewhat good, rather good, fairly good.* In Old English there were a number of intensifiers, among them the word *swithe,* related to the word for 'strong' and a *swithe hand* was what we more matter-of-factly call a *right hand. Swithe blithe* we can translate as 'very happy.'

The development of such degree words is often the result of historical accident. With the decay of inflectional markers early in the Middle English period, word order became the most important grammatical marker. As corollary to this, any word that occupied the position of a modifier presently became a modifier. Some words have seemed naturally to fall into such positions and in the course of time they have lost their earlier meanings and have gone on full-time status as degree words. *Very* is typical. It came into English from French where it originally meant 'true,' a meaning evident in Chaucer's description of the Knight:

> *He was a* verray, *parfit gentil knight.*
> —*The Canterbury Tales,*
> "The General Prologue," 72

This meant, of course, 'a true and perfect and gentle knight.' But the idea of 'true' still is not lost, though it has become archaic, as in the Nicene Creed:

> Very *God of* very *God.*

In a diluted sense it remains in phrases like:

> Martha ran like the *very* wind.
>
> I'm taking the *very* first bus to Memphis.

We may suppose that originally *very* received as much stress as the other modifiers in such series as these, but as soon as the stress was lowered by so much as a degree, *very* would be regarded as the modifier not of the headword but of the adjective or adverb immediately following. In this respect *very* is far from unique; *sore* appears in archaic expressions like *sore afraid* and *sore afflicted; full* remains current in *full well,* and only there. *All* has been an intensifier from Old English times and shows no signs of obsolescence. It has, in fact, become an element in compounds like *already, altogether, almost, alright,*[1] *always, also.* *Clean* is less commonly used—*clean gone* and a few other expressions are chiefly set phrases. Some other

---

1 Despite the relentless pressure of analogy, the decision whether to spell this word as *all right* or *alright* continues to be far more important than the situation suggests. The other words in this group were written as single words well before the time of Chaucer. But *all right* is a newcomer. The first citation given in the *Oxford English Dictionary* is from Charles Dickens' *Pickwick Papers* in 1837. The *Oxford Supplement* lists several spellings of *alright,* the earliest in 1893, with the comment, "A frequent spelling of *all right.*" Other dictionaries, past and current, tend to be less kindly in this respect. The phrase *all right* usually characterizes an informal written or spoken style, which means that the cautious user of English regards it as a borderline expression. Regardless of how it is written, it seems destined to stand in the shadow of its synonym *okay* which appeared at almost the same time but which has since become completely international.

words are used in such structures and may be construed at once as intensifiers: *flat out*. *Brand* is restricted generally to the phrase *brand new* but this may be rephrased as *brand spanking new,* in which case *brand* itself is a potential degree word. *Stark* also has to do with being strong; it is used in a few phrases like *stark naked, stark staring mad.*

Right has been used as an intensifier from earliest Old English times. Consequently it occurs in some archaic expressions like *right early, right nice,* but it is still current in speech and writing: *right away, right on. Mighty* is becoming old-fashioned and seldom appears in writing unless it is to represent or burlesque folksy speech.

> Them oats is sure lookin' *mighty* peart, Mr. Silo.

While *awful, powerful, dreadful, terrible* and the like are commonly employed as intensifiers, they have long been the target of puristic disapproval, principally on the grounds that in a phrase *awful silly* there really is nothing especially awful about being silly. In spoken English all of these expressions are likely to occur. The forms with *-ly* fare a little better, but not much:

> They're *awfully* strict at that school.
>
> We felt *dreadfully* sorry for Grandma when her parakeet died.

Plenty is used informally in spoken English, as in *plenty cold* or *plenty large,* and it has no counterpart with *-ly*; that is to say, **plentily cold* and **plentily large* makes matters worse instead of better. *Real* as an intensifier has a secure place in spoken English, although purists frequently disapprove of it on the grounds that it represents an unauthorized shortening of *really.* The fact of the matter is that *real* has made its own way with no support from *really.*

By a process of development which closely parallels that of *very* and the other intensifiers, a few phrases like *good and* and *nice and* have also become degree expressions. They are common in spoken English and could pass unchallenged in much informal written English as well. Perhaps one might argue that the phrase *nice and warm* is simply another way of saying *nicely warm* and that this is about the closest thing we have in Present-day English to the classical figure of speech known as "hendiadys."

The English temperament has traditionally favored understatement above exaggeration, which may be part of the reason whv intensifiers have often been cast in a bad light. Another reason is that by their nature they tend to outshout each other—the "crescendo effect" one observes again and again when people come together at potentially noisy social gatherings—and end up saying really very little. As such things go, down-toners have had a much easier time of it than intensifiers, for the reason probably that meiosis offends us less than hyperbole. *Rather, somewhat, quite,* and *more or less* find a warm welcome in written as well as spoken English. *Pretty* has achieved respectability in recent years, though it continues to suggest an informal style. *Something* is used colloquially with modifiers in an adverbial sense and may convey a dyslogistic meaning:

Annie has been drinking *something awful.*

Kind of and *sort of* began as qualifiers of nouns in expressions like:

Fritz is the *kind of* person you can always count on.

By transfer, however, this has become a modifier of nouns when they serve as modifiers:

Daddy Warbucks has been *a kind of* father figure.

And presently, less acceptably:

Daddy Warbucks has been *kind of a* father figure.

Extended to adjectives, these phrases are often presented in a grotesque spelling, *kinda* and *sorta,* to represent marginal literacy. They pass without comment in informal speech. It is possible to find *kind of a* and *sort of a* in acceptable writing, even by competent authors, and at the very worst we need to conclude that there is little stigma attached to their use.

Past Participles. Past participles of verbs commonly serve as modifiers, and as we have observed, they often border so closely on adjectives that they are all but indistinguishable from them, especially where no agent or agency is stated or implied:

Linda always looks *relaxed.*

That's the third time that dog's got *wet* today.

Generally modifiers like these can be qualified by any of the intensifiers or down-toners—*awfully relaxed, quite relaxed, somewhat relaxed.* While *very* can be used with a word like *wet* and also with a few others—*very wet, very drunk, very tired*—with other past participles some careful writers and speakers insist that the intensifiers should be *very much,* as in: *very much lost, very much disappointed, very much intoxicated.* The expression *very much drunk* would not be regarded as a comment on a person's crapulence, simply because there is no subject, real or implied, for the word *drunk.* But we do say *very much afraid* and *very much asleep,* and these ought to follow the same "rule." For some users of English our bewilderingly complex behavior in choosing between *very* and *very much* is a delicate linguistic status indicator.

Dangling Adverbs. Some adverbs modify constructions instead of individual words, and noteworthy among these are the "dangling adverbs," so called because they seem to have no specific connection with what they presumably modify. Within recent years the dangling modifier has gained enormously in popularity, and new forms make their appearance with some regularity. The most conspicuous one is *hopefully:*

> *Hopefully,* Ronald won't run out of barbecue sauce.
>
> *Hopefully,* your air conditioner will be repaired next week.

Translated, these mean, "I hope Ronald won't . . ." or "You may begin to hope that. . . ." But an entire phrase has been collapsed into a single word and the person responsible for hoping, or whatever such, has remained in concealment.

The dangling adverb presumably had its beginning in adverbs like *evidently, supposedly,* and the like. More recently it has spread to a great variety of situations:

> *Regrettably,* all the programs have already been sent out.
>
> *Thankfully,* that problem still hasn't come up.
>
> *Unforgivably,* I had left my camera in the tent.

The dangling adverb has received some unfriendly comment from those who regard it as illogical, which it surely is. Whether it serves any useful purpose in communicating, and especially in identifying who are the "right" people and who are the "wrong" ones, will determine whether it remains in use, not whether or not it satisfies the demands of any system of logic.

Typical of the adverbial types that appear now and then has been a great expansion of *-wise* forms. The suffix itself is extremely old; there are examples of it in Old English and in related languages like Old Saxon and Old High German. It has kept alive these hundreds of years mainly because of a few words like *sidewise, crosswise, lengthwise, edgewise.* Not long ago *-wise* was propelled into vogue in the construction of hundreds of adverbs, many of them grotesque and many invented to apply to a single situation:

> *Mars-fly-by-wise* we're in better shape than when we were working *Atlantic-splashdown-wise.*

This kind of modifier has been a darling of the people in business, government, and the military—especially those who communicate in what they call "directives." They are less than the ultimate in graceful diction. We have evidence that the vogue has passed, but there is no guarantee that something else like it will not develop by and by.

11

connectives

Many of the formulations that appear in the system of grammar usually presented in our schools were worked out by various Greek philosophers who flourished twenty or more centuries ago. In those days a philosopher could comfortably wear a grammarian's hat, and vice versa; in fact, it was often quite impossible to distinguish the philosopher from the grammarian. They were both busy looking at language.

As they examined their language with some care, the Greeks recognized certain large classes of words, and these correspond rather broadly to the classes of nouns, verbs, pronouns, and modifiers that we find in our own language. No respectable grammarian, whatever his other convictions, quarrels with this basic classification, and we find that these categories—however we may choose to identify them—make sense even to small children.

Some other words, however, especially the short little ones that we spell with two or three letters, have proved more difficult to classify. Ultimately the Greeks worked up a system that they applied to the Greek language, and then passed it on to the Romans who with only minor modifications adapted it to Latin. Through a series of historical accidents it has become part of our own cultural heritage. Our commercial and scholarly dictionaries pay respect to these ancient classifications through the part-of-speech labels which they assign to various items in the lexicon. But we have been provided with other explanations. The Greeks themselves used the collective term "particle," as though these little words were the twigs and leaves that got mixed into a basket of oranges. Some English grammarians—Henry Sweet among them—spoke of "declinable" and "indeclinable" words. More recently it has been the practice of linguists to divide parts of speech into "content words," like nouns, verbs, and modifiers on the one hand, and function words or structure words on the other. These structure words are what we depend on to accomplish a host of grammatical services, such as introducing questions, or expressing negation, or linking the elements of an utterance. They have little or no intrinsic meaning, as many of us have discovered when we tried to define them outside of their contexts. The *Oxford English Dictionary,* for example, takes some 216 column inches of small type to deal with a word like *to*, but all it actually does is indicate the various functions of the word as part of a sentence or phrase.

Among the structural elements of English are several sets of words and phrases sometimes called "connectives." They relate various words or phrases or sentences to each other. In the conventional school grammars they are classified under different headings, most familiarly as prepositions and conjunctions, but also as some of the adverbs and a few of the pronouns.

To distinguish nouns from verbs has never been exceptionally difficult for users of English. Given the proper clues, even elementary school children can quickly master the art. Verbs and nouns have distinctive inflectional systems, for example, and distinctive grammatical functions, and they fit into different positions or "slots" in a typical sentence. Because of this we are likely to assume also that all except the dullest school pupils can keep prepositions and conjunctions apart, an attitude we have inherited from the traditional grammarians. The Latin grammarians found it more difficult to tell nouns from adjectives than to tell prepositions from conjunctions, and that ought to say more than we realize about using Latin as a measuring stick for our own language. In languages like Latin and Greek there were clearly differing functions for prepositions and conjunctions; we on the other hand find it next to impossible to formulate a description of a preposition that will include all prepositions and no conjunctions, or a description of a conjunction that will include all conjunctions and no prepositions. For all practical purposes, in the speech of many users of English the two classes of words have fallen into one.

In spite of this, an important consideration in English usage hinges on one's ability to make an instant and infallible distinction in order to determine the form of a following pronoun. This we have already considered in dealing with pronouns. In standard English we have certain rules: for example, following a preposition—disregarding for the time being that it is all but impossible to define a preposition—a pronoun appears in the object case form, if it has an object case form. Further, following a conjunction—disregarding also the same problem in identifying a conjunction—the pronoun appears in the case, whether overtly indicated or not, of the word linked to it by the conjunction.

> We gave some "his and hers" towels to *him* and *her*.

Such a sentence offers no problems. On the other hand:

> We gave some towels to *Bill* and *her*.

The speaker needs to remember that *Bill* has no distinctive object case form but that it is nevertheless theoretically an object, and that consequently the pronoun that follows must be in the object case form.

To exercise these rules properly calls for an acute "language sense." Those who possess such a language sense, whether by inheritance or training, not infrequently prove intolerant of others who fall into ways of error in manipulating pronoun cases following prepositions and conjunctions. How the blessed ones keep the classes distinct in the absence of any clear guidelines to direct them is a question that has long puzzled grammarians. With great reluctance they find themselves having to conclude that each of us consults some kind of "list" that has worked its way into our mental pores at a very tender age, and that we have learned infallibly just which ones are prepositions and which are conjunctions and exactly where each goes. Such a conclusion seems to shut the door on any systematic ordering of the data, and if that kind of thing happens too often it may eventually put the grammarians out of business. On the other hand, there is also a possibility which Noam Chomsky and his colleagues have broached, namely, that all of us are actually a good deal smarter in respect to language than we think we are, or we should never have been able to learn language at all.

PREPOSITIONS

English makes day-to-day use of about sixty prepositions and four or five times as many prepositional phrases. The real work gets accomplished by about nine old wheelhorses: *at, by, for, from, in, of, on, to, with.* Speakers of Old English employed just a few less than forty prepositions, and we should have been troubled by what seems to us the impreciseness of Old English in that respect. But they managed, for in a number of prepositions it made a difference whether the noun used was in the accusative or the dative case. The list of prepositions even today is not a closed one, making it in that respect unique among the structure word classes. Whether on the other hand we have a crying need for prepositions like *via* and *per* depends on one's individual taste. Some of us regard *By Air Mail* as fully as clear and expressive as *Via Air Mail,* and there are those who find *ten miles an hour* just as good English as *ten miles per hour.*

In certain instances one has difficulty deciding whether style or usage ultimately determines the choice of preposition. We can, for example, make a useful distinction between *in, inside of, into,* and *within,* and we can describe the distinctions with precision, yet not many speakers of English find that they need to be so specific. To employ them regularly calls for an acutely developed sense of style. On the other hand, there are those who reject *in back of* as inelegant not because of style but because of usage. It is a linguistic newcomer, and many people distrust innovations, useful or otherwise. That English has pairs of expressions like *before* and *in front of, upon* and *on top of, within* and *inside of* would lead us to suspect that the distinction may be in some manner significant. The first expression in each instance is the earlier one, by hundreds of years. Consequently the first is more general in meaning and the other more precise, but whether the distinction relates to position or contact evidently depends on the context. At any rate, *in back of* has developed by analogy. It has been suggested, on dubious grounds, however, that *in back of* was created by Americans so they could avoid using the indelicate word *behind.*

A few prepositions have given the more nervous members of the English-speaking community some bad moments. *Between* and *among* are typical. In his *Dictionary* Samuel Johnson remarked: "*Between* is properly used of two and more; but perhaps this accuracy is not always preserved." Where Johnson lighted on this notion is easy to discover; it takes no more than an elementary exposure to English etymology to find that *between* is etymologically next of kin to *by twain.* Other usage authorities have faithfully parroted what the master decreed and as a result some stupid and awkward sentences have come into being because a writer feared to violate the "rule." English does distinguish between one and more than one in its system of singulars and plurals; it does not, however, distinguish between two and more than two. *Between* in that respect goes back to a very early period in the history of the English language when there was still something of a viable dual number. The only other words in English that refer to duality as such are *both, either, other,* and the *-er* inflection of the comparative degree. It has been largely forgotten in *either* and *other* and is occasionally overlooked in *both.* With a loss of a strict sense of duality by the users of English, *between* came instead to refer to a more general relationship as in the old phrase:

> That's *between* you and me and the bedpost (or gatepost).

In an Old English manuscript of about A.D. 970, we have an account of the Twelve Apostles and the writer informs us that "They cast [the] lot between them" (*Ond hie sendon hlot him betweonum*). *Among* has on the whole a broader sense of distribution than *between. Between* deals with a one-to-one relationship, or even several closely related ones.

> *Between* sobs he kept calling her name.

This is more typically English than:

> *Among* sobs he kept calling her name.

Whenever the subject of prepositions is mentioned, someone may be counted on to wonder whether it is proper "to end a sentence with a preposition." In the Germanic languages, prepositions have always been sanctioned at the ends of sentences, and examples of this construction occur in writings of the Old English period. In Shakespeare and the King James Bible they are fairly common. One of the first persons to voice his scruples on the subject was the poet John Dryden. Thoroughly familiar with Latin and Greek, it was often his practice when he was unsure about his writing in English to compose a passage in Latin and then translate it into English. He discovered that in Latin prepositions did not occur at the ends of sentences and since he trusted his Latin better than his English, he decided that the preposition in final position must be an error. In fact, he revised a number of things he had written earlier in order to eliminate all terminal prepositions. It was some time later that Robert Lowth in his *Short Introduction to*

English Grammar suggested that one could overdo this matter of ending sentences with prepositions, even though he had no strong feelings on the matter and used them himself when he felt so inclined. But if the construction is not properly handled, the result can be an awkward sentence. Lowth's successors saw no grays; only blacks and whites; they simply branded all such prepositions as unwholesome English.

Much of the argument leveled against the final preposition centers on the name *preposition* which is derived from a Latin word that means 'placed before,' a characteristic of these words in Latin. There was no reason why this characteristic had to apply to English as well, although there were grammarians who supposed it should. To give something a name and then to argue from the name itself is one of the classic circular arguments. But it is this sort of argument that has made thousands of thoroughly decent users of English timid about putting prepositions at the end of utterances. The result is a sentence like:

> *Of* what could I have been thinking?

It puts the speaker at the other end of the dilemma. This kind of construction is bookish and clumsy.

More often than we realize, the language moves—or is pushed by language reformers of one kind or another—into a direction from which it eventually backs away. Presently it resumes its normal course. The taboo, such as it was, against the terminal preposition has always had its share of skeptics and dim-viewers, that is, of persons who put prepositions where they "felt good" and not where some purist thought they ought to go. The danger lies not in getting the preposition at the end of the utterance, but in working too hard to get it elsewhere.

CONJUNCTIONS

Compared to the list of prepositions in English, the stock of conjunctions is remarkably small. In fact, where conjunctions leave off and other connectives take up may be difficult to determine. Much of the time it seems immaterial. All of us have heard a youngster tell a story: "And . . . and . . . and . . ." or "Then . . . then . . . then. . . ." It makes very little difference—not a grammatical difference at least. Yet we call *and* a conjunction and *then* an adverb.

The faults committed against *and* and *but* are seldom errors of usage, although a stylistic error known as "faulty parallelism" occurs occasionally, especially in the writing of learners. In Present-day English *and* has become simply an all-purpose connective; originally, however, it contrasted things or ideas, as reflected in Greek *anti* 'against,' or Latin *ante* 'before,' or the English word *answer,* compounded from *and* 'toward, against,' and *swear* 'affirm.' In present-day usage *and* has dwindled down to little more than a plus sign; in fact, the conventional symbol *&*, called an "ampersand," may be written in a number of ways, one of them the simple + 'plus' in elementary arithmetic. Nevertheless, in spite of all the latitude we sometimes permit ourselves with respect to *and,* it must still connect grammatically like terms.

> Mr. Traherne encouraged his students to study *and* getting involved in some sport *and* that they should live decently.

The worst that can be said about a sentence like this is that it is clumsy and difficult to follow. When one tries to use the same verb in both the copulative and transitive senses, and links the complements with *and* the results are likely to be puzzling:

> The tree grew taller *and* a fine crop of apples.

The same strictures are in order with respect to parallelism in the case of the conjunction *or.* Its primary function is to indicate that there is a choice, sometimes strengthened by the addition of *either:*

> Charles wants to be *either* constable *or* alderman.

With *neither,* the conjunction *nor* is preferred by careful writers and speakers, although in a relaxed style *or* is quite common. There are those who maintain that *either . . . or . . .* and *neither . . . nor . . .* are permissible only when there are two alternatives, and that they are improper when used with three or more:

> Charles wants to be *either* constable *or* alderman *or* justice of the peace.

As indicated earlier, *either* is a relic left over from an old dual number which operated in English till about a thousand years ago. Rather than emphasize duality, *either* now serves chiefly to indicate that there is a choice.

A few years ago the double conjunction *and/or* enjoyed considerable vogue. It was borrowed from legalese and federalese, two genres of written communication in which grace of utterance is likely to be roundly suspect. Where one needs to be terse, the expression can sometimes be justified:

> Weapons *and/or* ammunition may be procured locally.

On the other hand nothing is gained in:

> Philemon plays the guitar *and/or* sings songs of social protest.

If it came to an issue, it might be more fitting to say:

> Philemon plays the guitar or sings songs of social protest, or both.

In few places does the often trivial distinction between prepositions ignite such fires of indignation or arouse such a sense of uneasiness as it does in the case of *like* and *as*. Any language historian worth his salt knows that this development would have been well on the way to running its course if everyone had kept quiet about it, but the issue is not what might have happened. The fact is that many people regard the distinction as critical and even inviolable.

Tobacco companies are not noted for the subtlety of their advertising approach, and some years ago there appeared this slogan:

> "Winston tastes good, like a cigarette should."

The fat, if we may call it that, was on the fire. At the signal innumerable teachers of English leaped to the barricades in defense of their beleaguered tongue. It was a windfall of publicity for the cigarette manufacturers, and only the most artless would suppose that they had not hoped it would turn out pretty much this way. Since then a number of advertisers have experimented with similar expressions, all aimed at doing mischief to the language and arousing the teachers once again, but they seem to have failed. The slogan in question is completely unambiguous; even a somewhat dull elementary school pupil can understand it.[1] But should the connective be *like*

---

1 An apocryphal story—but considering the state of the profession not hard to believe—concerns the teacher who gave the students this "Winston tastes good" jingle to correct. The answers came back—a number of them: "Winston tastes well like a cigarette should."

or *as?* We realize that *as* can be either a conjunction or a preposition:

> Alvin is as tall *as* I am. (conjunction)
>
> Alvin is as tall *as* me. (preposition)

In ordinary conversation a person can use one or the other construction without arousing criticism. Both have been around for a long time. *Like* has a venerable history as a preposition:

> Mr. Scoby thinks *like* me.
>
> It's just *like* him to go off to Sioux Falls without a coat.

A pedantic and now old-fashioned rephrasing of the first sentence results in something like:

> Mr. Scoby thinks *as* I think.

To many users of English such a construction sounds awkward and overworked, but *as* must fill its role as a conjunction. Over the course of time *like* has slipped into the same position and this has brought with it some objections. Those who dislike the usage cannot say that it is clumsy or unclear, for it is neither one, but it does have a touch of novelty and unexpectedness about it. Those who defend it argue that *like* has been used as a conjunction by many of the great writers for the past three or four hundred years. Such considerations scarcely mollify the objectors. Once again we have something that is perfectly understandable, that follows faithfully the patterns of English structure. But those who do not like it simply do not like it. They think of it as a linguistic arriviste, the kind of coinage we should associate with anyone whose control of the connectives borders on the uncertain. They should know better, however, than to try to combat the expression on grammatical grounds. Advertisers find *like* useful as a conjunction because it has a touch of the "plain but honest folks" about it, and consequently it has been pressed into service to market a wide variety of products, including a President of the United States. Eventually this kind of utility will have worn itself out because people will have become accustomed to the usage.

But there is a distinction between *as* and *like* that is occasionally overlooked by those who suppose that they should use *as* whenever the issue is the least cloudy. In a familiar figure of speech we sometimes say:

Perkins worked *like* a beaver.

Our folklore honors beavers as industrious little fellows who get things done without the help of government subsidy or trade union membership. The sentence simply means that Perkins worked hard. On the other hand:

Perkins worked *as* a beaver.

Few alert writers of English would let themselves get caught in so obvious a trap. The sentence means that Perkins has been gnawing down saplings with his incisors and building dams and mud shelters with his little brown paws. But in more elaborate constructions, writers sometimes lose their way. And there are times when the very niceties can get in the way of clarity. George Bernard Shaw (*Time,* November 20, 1970) said, "I work as my father drank." At first glance this appears to be a muddle of tenses, as though he meant to say, "I worked while my father drank." "I work like my father drank" would have been understandable, but it would not have been Shaw. The error is not uncommon; it results when one tries too hard to avoid the "incorrect" use of *like:*

Ah! Autumn! The sight of it!
The smell of it! The feel of it!
The sound of it! Underfoot the red
and golden brown leaves crinkle and
crunch as *corn flakes.*
—*Arizona Highways,* October, 1966

There is little doubt that *like* will presently achieve full acceptance. It appears regularly as a conjunction in writing from which it would have been edited with the greatest severity twenty and even ten years ago. The phrase "Tell it like it is," originally a Southernism, is now used everywhere in America. Those who happen to dislike *like* as a conjunction explain the development as a relaxation of standards, a neglect of "grammar fundamentals," or a malign conspiracy by the linguistically disenfranchised. The canonization of *like* as a respectable expression just happens to be a normal development. At this moment no one need feel himself obliged to follow such a development, and many of us do not. The reason, however, probably rests less on purely esthetic grounds than on the time one begins to collect his Social Security.

TAUTOLOGIES

In the preface to Robert Lowth's *Short Introduction to English Grammar,* which is often regarded as the fountainhead from which have come all our authoritarian ideas on correctness—chiefly by those who have never read Lowth carefully—we find this sentence:

> *The reason, which he* [*Dr. Johnson*] *assigns for being so very concise in this part, is, "because our language has so little inflection, that its Construction neither requires nor admits many rules."*

Certainly Lowth could scarcely have been aware that the "reason is . . . because" construction would one day be listed among the grave errors in writing and speaking. How grave an error it is, indeed, may be questioned since it occurs regularly in the speech and writing of countless people, most of them well educated.

Obviously we have two constructions that have been telescoped into one: "The reason is that . . ." and ". . . is because. . . . " As a rule, the first part of this expression is removed by some distance from the other which means that the speaker or writer has started to lose the sense of causation and feels he ought to express it again, with *because.* It is one of a number of varieties of tautology, as we call the repetition of a grammatical figure. Certain forms of it are frowned on in speech and writing:

> *This here* hoss looks sick again.
>
> *George Washington he* was the first president.
>
> You always say the *most nicest* things.
>
> John Keats *wasn't never* very healthy.

"The reason is . . . because . . ." scarcely fits this classification. Despite tautology, it is sometimes the only way a speaker or writer has of extricating himself from a problem sentence. For example:

> The *reason* Diane and her cousins have decided to go to Yugoslavia next summer instead of Switzerland and the Italian Riviera as they originally planned *is that*. . . .

Many writers and speakers of English instinctively feel that the conjunction *that* in a construction like this makes a feeble and even a confusing transition. But one takes his choice. In spite of objections raised against it, the expression promises to be with us for a long time.

A less conspicuous instance of tautology, perhaps because it does not turn up in writing as often as it does in speaking, is the expression:

> I *can't help but* think. . . .

There is the notion of contrast here between what is and what should be, often noted by the conjunction *but,* and expressed in:

> I *cannot but* think. . . .

Outside of self-conscious speech or deliberately literary contexts, this construction is not common. Standard English usage generally prefers:

> I *cannot help* thinking. . . .
> I *cannot help* think. . . .

Tautological or not, many speakers of English seem to feel that *but* makes their meaning more clear.

PAIRED CONNECTIVES

When we compare things we ordinarily use the paired connectives: *as . . . as.* . . . They are indispensible in our family clichés: "*as* cool *as* a cucumber," "*as* dull *as* dishwater," "*as* happy *as* a clam," "*as* thick *as* hops." Till about a hundred years ago the first of these connectives in a negative comparison was quite regularly *so:* "*not so* cool *as* a cucumber," for instance. It still occurs, almost exclusively in writing, but few writers or editors any longer pay attention to it. In fact, to many users of English it sounds distinctly pedantic. Why a distinctive negative form should have disappeared in this manner is not altogether clear. We do know that English negatives seem to be having a difficult time of it, perhaps because negation in English has been so completely overhauled during the past four or five centuries. The distinction between *aught* and *naught* is now archaic, and *nor* following *neither* comes increasingly into competition with *or.* In fact, in some parts of the country the phrase *any more,* once characteristic only of negative and interrogative constructions, appears regularly as an affirmative statement, supplanting the adverb *nowadays.* Typically the negative would be:

> They never tell you that *any more.*

The affirmative has become:

> That's all they tell you *any more.*

And in some localities, though only in spoken English, it is:

> *Any more,* that's all they tell you.

There is reason to suppose that the *not so . . . as* construction has dropped out of use for reasons related to this phenomenon. In absolute constructions *so* continues as the only possibility with negations, but here it operates as a degree word rather than as a connective:

> "How's your husband's gout?" "*Not so* good."

This tendency to telescope two kinds of comparisons into a single construction results in a peculiar form of unclarity:

> Aileen is *as bright as* Floreen.
>
> Aileen is *brighter than* Floreen.

Running the two together produces a sentence like:

> Aileen is *as bright or brighter than Floreen.*

The problem is more grammatical than one of usage; the modifier *bright* has been left dangling without any connective to bring it to a conclusion.

> Scrimshaw is *equally strong as* his brother.

Two sentences have been collapsed into one:

> Scrimshaw is *as strong as* his brother.
>
> Scrimshaw and his brother are *equally strong.*

One or the other is possible, but the constraints of taste in language should keep speakers and writers from trying to say both at once.

CONCLUSION

Some of these differences may appear trivial, yet to many speakers of English, and especially to careful writers, they are meaningful. We do judge people by the way they handle the English language, just as we judge them by the way they play the piano or operate an automobile on a freeway or handle a sailboat. In the end all of them depend on a skill born of long practice. Practice does not necessarily make perfect, if one practices the wrong thing; then it merely makes permanent.

12

derivation

In common with words like *linguist,*[1] *inflection,* and *grammar,* the term *derivation* has two distinct meanings when it is used in connection with the study of language. The familiar one, and for that reason the one that comes immediately to mind, has to do with the origin of words. *Cent,* we are told, is derived from the Latin word *centum* 'one hundred,' being the one-hundredth part of something, usually a dollar. *Nickel* comes from the name of a metal which in turn takes its name from a subterranean goblin, Old Nick, who supposedly cheats miners by substituting nickel for the more valuable copper. *Dime* comes from a French word *disme,* which in itself comes from Latin *decima* 'ten,' therefore one-tenth. *Dollar* is a sixteenth-century respelling of a German word *thaler* /táhler/, a shortening of *Joachimsthaler,* as something that came from Joachimsthal, 'valley (or dale) of Joachim (or Yokum),' a locality where a particular coin was first minted. Such derivations we call "etymologies," and ultimately there are as many of them as there are words in the language. Many people find them entertaining, but they serve little useful purpose except perhaps to show how things happened—a small aspect of history without any moral attached.

1 *Linguist* has both a popular and a technical meaning. In popular usage a linguist is one who knows several languages, usually to the extent of being able to read or speak them. In its technical sense the word *linguist* refers to a person who makes a systematic study of a language or a number of them. Whether he can actually speak or write the language is often immaterial.

As we use the term *derivation* in a more technical sense we have in mind a branch of morphology which stands in contrast to inflection. Both inflection and derivation have to do with certain alterations that are made on the base of an English word. The inflections of a noun or a verb, for example, fit it to a specific grammatical situation; whether it is singular or plural, a noun is still very much a noun. By derivation we construct a new word out of previously existing materials, and quite commonly we jump from one part of speech to another. The distinction between derivation and inflection is a narrow one but a vital one.

We have already observed the extraordinary simplicity, at least in its broader outlines, of the English inflectional system. The noun has a base and two inflectional morphemes, the modifier has a base and two inflectional morphemes, and the verb has a base and four inflectional morphemes. Aside from the copula *be* and the pronoun system, there it ends. There are many irregularities, but they contribute nothing to clarity, and so far as the essential grammar of English goes, they are altogether superfluous. Attempting to regularize the various parts of speech, however, has dire social consequences. Imagine a person maintaining a reputation for being intelligent, let alone educated, if he should express himself with expressions like *gooder* or *catched* or *oxes*.

The derivational system of English, like that of the inflectional system, has a fundamental orderliness. In fact, the basic pattern is something over which a person acquires control early in life—not much later on the whole than he masters the inflectional system—though few people, if any, master all of its complex irregularities.

As a rule each of our day-to-day words consists of a single root morpheme—words like *girl, take, find, green.* Further analytical procedures will not succeed in breaking them into smaller components.[2] Some words have for all practical purposes fallen into this classification also because no one except an etymologist ever thinks of them as consisting of more than one morpheme: *window, nostril, manure, chair, count, surgeon.* They have been accepted as unit morphemes for hundreds of years.

In spite of being written as single words, many others, however, betray

---

2 Otto Jespersen suggested long ago, in *Language* (London: George Allen & Unwin, 1922, p. 400) that initial *fl-* indicates "movements . . . not . . . characterized by loud sounds" in words like *flow, flag, flake, flicker, flutter, fling, flit, flurry, flirt.* There are several such groups of words, another being those with initial *wr-*, all having the idea of twisting: *wring, wrest, wrong, writhe, wrinkle, wrap, wrist.* The problem is not so much with *fl-* and *wr-* as with the rest of the word. What, for instance is the "meaning" of *-ing* in *fling* and *wring?*

their beginnings as two or more free morphemes: *gentleman, wonderful, nosedrop, earthworm, toothache.* The list is extremely long and it keeps on growing. In still other words, an independent element appears side by side with a dependent one: *stupidity, fractional, accomplishment, gangster, supremacy.* In addition to all of these there are words made up of two or more morphemes, both or all of them dependent: *congregation, instantaneous, benevolence.* An important distinction in this connection is that between free and bound morphemes.

How does a language typically go about supplying itself with new words to fit the needs that arise? In this respect languages differ enormously. Navajo, for example, transfers scarcely any words at all, and the few it has transferred are virtually unrecognizable: *American*—or Spanish *Americano*—is Navajo *beligano;* Spanish *toro* 'bull' becomes *dola.* Generally the Navajo depends on native linguistic materials, although this may lead to unexpected consequences. The word *nuclear* had to be translated into Navajo, but the interpreter comprehended it as a compound of *new* and *clear,* and as a result these two English words have been translated literally as the Navajo equivalent of English *nuclear.* Pidgin English, in almost complete contrast to Navajo, accepts words from any source whatever and many persons look on it as a kind of linguistic kitchen midden even though linguists have discovered that it has a unique and thoroughly respectable grammar. Until a couple of generations ago German sought to be completely self-sufficient as a language. It even translated words like *hydrogen* and *oxygen* literally and somewhat unimaginatively as *Wasserstoffe* and *Sauerstoffe.* Recently German has been taking over words wholesale from everyday English. The French were at it as early as anyone; the French words for *north, east, south,* and *west* were transferred from Anglo-Saxon. In spite of the celebrated French Academy, whose function it is to keep the French language pure, the French vocabulary is constantly being augmented by English words.

During relatively placid cultural and political periods, in which few changes take place, there is little need for new words. We find that during the early Anglo-Saxon period the English language was largely on its own, borrowing virtually no words from other languages. The only exception was the Scandinavian dialects from which a number of words were acquired during the ninth and tenth centuries. But many of them were already so much like those of English that it scarcely mattered which was which. The others were without exception words for which English already had an expression, but which nevertheless replaced an English word: *window* for *eyethirl, husband* for *make; take* for *nim, sky* for *lift,* to mention a few. Even following the Norman Invasion of 1066 several generations passed before Norman French words began coming into English in appreciable numbers. Many of the ones transferred were overwhelmed by the patterns of English. The verb *estrivir* 'strive,' as we have noted, came out of the encounter with a new preterite and a new past participle: *strive, strove, striven;* French *gentilhomme* was remodeled to *gentleman; finir* became reconstructed on the base of the present plural—*finissons, finissez, finissent*—and was standardized as *finish.* Words adopted during the first phase of this contact often bear only a superficial resemblance to their Norman originals, but once the process of adoption started, thousands of new words poured into English, not only from French, but also from Latin and Greek. Where necessary the nouns were given an English nominative plural; verbs went into the English mold and acquired a weak verb conjugation. Side by side with the native English suffixes like *-ness, -dom, -hood,* there appeared numerous words with suffixes like *-ity, -itude, -ance,* from French and before that from Latin.

This phase of word formation generally came to an end long ago. Words continue to enter the English language as there is a need for them, but the tendency is for English to make new combinations of elements already in the language rather than to go abroad for entirely new linguistic items. In that respect the language has swung full circle and the situation is remarkably like the situation a thousand years ago, except that the working stock of morphemes is different from what it was then.

If we had a "pure" English to deal with—that is, an English which had never been subjected to outside influences of any kind—we should unquestionably find the derivational system a good deal easier to handle. Yet even here we might encounter problems, among them the conflict between an older dying construction and a newer one in process of becoming generalized. In the history of the English adverb, for example, there have been several developments. One of these consisted of an ancient dative case inflection *-e* which became lost very early, leaving a number of flat adverbs. Another was the equally ancient genitive, usually with the inflectional *-s*, as in *nowadays, evenings, sometimes.* Still another was an occasional suffix *-ward,* meaning 'direction to a place': *homeward, upward, leeward, toward.* Relatively late to arrive on the scene was *-like* which after becoming established was reduced to *-ly*, the usual form in Present-day English. This problem was pretty well settled four or five centuries ago, but remnants of the older pattern continue to compete with the most recent one, especially where the *-ly* suffix makes unauthorized appearances. English uses a wide variety of word-building materials, brought in from many places far and near. That is why we sometimes have difficulties.

As we looked at the English inflectional system we noticed that in the major parts of speech we regularly begin with a base to which several kinds of inflectional morphemes may be added. A word like *man* may have the genitive inflection $\{S_2\}$, spelled *man's* /mǽnz/:

> A *man's* house is his castle.
> —Sir Edward Coke.

Or we may add the plural morpheme $\{S_1\}$ and in this case the result is written *men* /mén/:

> All *men* are created equal.
> —Thomas Jefferson.

Furthermore, we may add the genitive inflection to the plural and here the word is *men's* /ménz/:

> The work of *men's* hands

But an English word which typically belongs to one form class, or part of speech, often assumes the grammatical functions of another form class by means of functional shift, which is to say, it takes the characteristic word-order positions or inflections of another form class. The noun *man* can thus become a verb in good standing by adding various inflectional morphemes of the verb class:

> How many sailors does it take to *man* this life-boat?
>
> The sentry post was *manned* by a near-sighted corporal.

The derivational system of English resembles the inflectional system, but only superficially. We start with a base and add one or more morphemes, with the important difference that we meet not grammatical needs, but vocabulary needs. In making the noun *man* over into a verb we in effect created a new set of meanings. The noun *man* relates to a male human being, or at least to an individual member of the human race. But it does not require a human being to *man* something; a pigeon or a cat or even a computer can do that. There are limitations to functional shift, to be sure. In this case we cannot make a modifier of the word *man* by adding the inflections for degree: *-er, -est.*

It is possible to add several derivational elements to the base *man,* thereby making a modifier of it: *-ly, -like, -ish,* resulting in the forms *manly, manlike, mannish.* And so we may say:

> They were large *manly* creatures.
>
> They were large *manlike* creatures.
>
> They were large *mannish* creatures.

Anyone who knows English recognizes at once that the reference in each case is quite different: in the first case probably to athletes, in the second chimpanzees or baboons or visitors from outer space, in the third to adult human females. These examples simply indicate the vocabulary-building possibilities offered by derivational morphemes. They afford an economical means for augmenting the vocabulary of English, at the same time making possible extremely narrow shades of meaning.

Contrasted with the relative meagerness of the number of English inflections, the supply of derivations is little short of lavish. Inflections come down in a direct line of descent from the Old English inflectional system,[3] while derivations can come from any source at all. Many of them are still of native stock, having been carried down from Old English; others come from Greek or Latin, or from Latin by way of French; from Dutch, as the *-kin* originally of *mannikin* 'little man' and *bumpkin* 'little barrel,' later extended as a dimunitive to names like *Billikin, Peterkin, Hodgkin;* or from Russian *-nik* as in *nudnik* 'a bore,' extended to Yiddish expressions *nogoodnik, allrightnik,* then reinforced by *sputnik* to produce *beatnik, Vietnik.*

AFFIXES

English content words—normally nouns, verbs, and modifiers—may be regarded as consisting of a simple word base with the option of one or more

---

3 Strictly speaking, the *-s* inflection of the verb in the third person singular present tense is Scandinavian and not Anglo-Saxon.

"affixes." An affix is a morpheme which may be attached at the beginning or end of a base or to one or more morphemes ultimately attached to such a base.

First of all, we have independent words like *right, sin, lead, slime*. Affixes may be attached to these in several ways: *upright, sinful, mislead, slimy*. All these words have been in the language for a long time. There are other language forms, however, which are never used as independent units and which in nearly every case came into the language in combinations that were already established. A base like *-fect-* occurs in *perfect, ineffectual, refectory,* and by extension *feckless:* similarly *-turb* is a component of *disturbance, turbulent, turbine.* Sometimes they happen by chance to resemble English morphemes: *-bell-*, for instance, in *rebellion* and *bellicose,* but from a different source in *belladonna* and *embellishment.* At this point a person needs to rely on his common sense and his experience with English to tell him that neither set of words has anything to do with the kind of bell that speakers of his language associate with cows, doors, or weddings.

An affix that is attached at the head of another element is called a prefix, and one that is attached after is called a suffix. In English several suffixes may come in a string: *in + dis + crim + in + at + or + y, indiscriminatory; mis + under + stand + ing, misunderstanding; un + for + get + ful + ness, unforgetfulness.* This sort of word building can go on and on, the prize example for many years being *antidisestablishmentarianism.* It strikes many people as being a highly unlikely combination of morphemes and yet it happens to be a word with a precise meaning. It has no direct application, however, outside of discussions about doing away with the Establishment. If such discussions occur frequently, the word may prove useful beyond the usual expectancy for such things, but if not it is simply another linguistic curiosity. The "longest word" contender at the moment appears to be a disease: *pneumonoultramicroscopicsilicovolcanoconiosis,* for what it is worth, something that affects the lungs of miners. It has forty-five letters.

PREFIXES

Many of our more readily recognizable prefixes come from Latin: *ab-, ad-, ante-, con-, de-, ex-, in-, ob-, per-, post-, pre-, pro-, re-, sub-, super-,* among others. Some have kept their original spellings even after being adapted to French phonology; others have been so radically modified that they are in effect new prefixes altogether. Quite a number of scholarly prefixes come from Greek: *a-, ambi-, amphi-, arch-, auto-, cata-,* and so on, a few of them having additionally come through Latin and even through French. In fact, Arabic has made its contribution, mostly the prefix *al-*, originally a definite article, but now part of words like *alcohol, apricot, artichoke, elixir.*

Native English words seem on the whole so commonplace that we scarcely recognize the prefixes they often incorporate. The phenomenon is old. Even in Anglo-Saxon times the prefix *a-*, now completely disappeared in its earlier form, represented as many as six or seven senses which had been carried over from still earlier prefixes. Few of us would suspect that the first syllable of *enough, alike,* and *aware,* which Chaucer would have spelled with *i-* or *y-*, was a remnant of Old English *ge-*, still in common use in German and Dutch. And other prefixes have drifted far from their earlier significations. At one time the prefix *be-* carried the general sense 'about,' as in *bedeck* and *bedizen.* It is still used, however, with a much altered meaning, in words like *behead* 'remove the head,' and *bequeath* 'give as a (verbal) promise,' *becalm* 'cause to become calm,' *bereave* 'take away or steal (by death),' and the very common words *behave, believe, become, begin.* The prefix is still actively productive. Apparently there are no limits to its applications; the *Oxford English Dictionary* (sv *be-*) quotes the following: "The *bestarred, beribboned, be-Legion-of-Honoured* . . . pensioned throng." Another prefix, *for-,* occurs in words like *forbid, forbear, forgive, forsake, forlorn, forget.* At one time it meant 'completely' but that could be extended to 'destructively.' From such examples one would gather that the prefixes themselves have undergone radical changes of meaning; actually the entire word has changed its meaning and the prefix is no longer recognizable as a prefix. This is especially true in the situations where dropping it leaves curious residues like *queathe, reave, lieve,* and *lorn.* Sometimes, however, the prefixes themselves shift meaning. *With-* is a prefix, and it is also an independent preposition having the idea of close association. Yet in its earlier meanings it signified almost the opposite, namely, 'against,' as appears from several of the older combinations: *withhold, withdraw, withstand.* The older sense is preserved in one of the meanings of the ambiguous expression, "to fight with him." The idea now conveyed by *with* was expressed earlier by *mid-,* but this has meaning only in *midwife* (literally, 'accompanying a woman'). *Mid-* now has a completely different significance, of course, generally that of occurring halfway in some extent of space or time: *midland, midriff, midnight, midterm, midshipman.*

The prefix *and-*, as we have noted, originally meant 'against,' as in the verb *answer* 'to swear or affirm against,' With a slight change in the form of the prefix it has often been extended to mean 'reversal of an action,' as *uncoil, unfasten, unpack, undo, unwrap, untie, unhorse, unloose.* It appears at first sight of being identical with the negative prefix *un-*, but it has in this case retained its distinctive meanings. It is no longer employed to create new combinations, although some decades ago Amos and Andy coined the term *unlax* 'relax' which is still part of the general vocabulary.

The system of prefixes gives the English vocabulary an astounding richness and flexibility. English *over* is related etymologically and semantically to Greek *hyper,* Latin *super,* French *sur,* and German *über.* But such a situation brings problems of its own. We might argue that *oversee* and *supervise* need to mean exactly the same thing since in Latin and English the components match one for one. Furthermore, *survey* and *supervise* are etymologically related. We realize that a supervisor ordinarily commands more status than an overseer. A supervisor may be an elective county official or director of an academic program, or may serve in a management function in a corporation; an overseer looks after the indigent, directs workers in a mill, or does pastoral work in certain religious groups. A surveyor has a specialized occupation which distinguishes him from both the supervisor and the overseer. It is in this manner that English can employ closely related words to express a wide variety of meanings.

In dealing with prefixes, we realize that some are productive, that they attach freely in numberless places without appearing to subject the language to undue strain. Indeed the construction is immediately meaningful, even though it is brand new. Over against these are the "sterile" or nonproductive prefixes. The *a-* of *alike* and *aware* we sense at once is dead beyond resurrection; *a-* of *abed, asleep,* with the general meaning 'in' or 'on' would arouse surprise if it were used with a noun: **atable,* **abath,* **abicycle;* but with a verbal it still has some vitality, although somewhat archaic: *ariding, afighting, awhooping, ahollering.* The latter forms were once in good literary style, but are now quite out of date. Even a prefix like *be-* can within limits be put to work, meaning 'equip or adorn with,' as *beclothe* or *betinsel,* and yet we realize how narrow such limits are when we try to introduce **berug,* or **befurnish.* Prefixes run by fashions; *anti-* attaches easily and naturally: *antiwar, antigun, antibomb, anti-inflation, antipollution;* and as may be expected, *pro-: prowar, progun,* and the rest. During the early thirties *super-* was a great favorite, and we had *super-six* autos (they were sixes, not twelves), *Supersuds* soap, and *super-suction* denture adhesive. More recently *mini-, micro-, maxi-,* and *midi-* have been in vogue.

On the analogy of *telescope, telegraph,* and *telephone,* the word *television* came into being and although it was readily understandable, it soon aroused harsh comment, the reason being that *tele-* was Greek and *vision* was Latin. Such linguistic miscegenation has ample precedent; exactly the same combination occurs in *post-Christian.* Or: *ultraright, pseudo-foot-and-mouth-disease, retake, belabor, debug.* Some time ago it was reported that astronomers had to decide whether to adopt the Greek *pericynthion* or the Latin-Greek hybrid *perilune* in referring to space travel to the moon: *perilune* won.

Creating new words from the existing stock is not always done in the orderly manner that language purists commend. A word like *helicopter* has its origin in two Greek words, *helico* 'spiral'—as in *helix*—and *pter* 'wing.' But this kind of word division is so foreign to anything characteristically English that most of us simply split it as *heli* + *copter.* After that it has been a simple matter to put it together in other compounds: *heliport* and *helimail. University* makes possible *multiversity.* An *amphibian* as a creature that has its existence in two worlds derives its name from *amphi-* 'both' and *bios* 'life,' but to the military an amphibious operation is one carried on by sea and land. Now suppose we add air. *Tribious* would be etymologically sound, but *triphibious* is the word that has come into being. *Para-* is a prefix in good standing from Greek, meaning 'next to' or 'in addition to' as in *paradigm, paradox, paraphernalia,* and more recently *paramilitary* and *paralinguistic,* the last two Greek-Latin hybrids. But we also have *parasol* which might appear to come from the same source. Actually it comes from Late Latin *parare* 'protect from' and *sol* 'the sun.' By analogy the French developed *parachute*—from *para* 'protect from' and *chute* 'fall, descent.' Now *para* has been detached from *parachute* and we have *paratroop, paradoctor, paramedic.* This last word has two quite distinct meanings stemming from the two *para-* prefixes. The older meaning, born during World War II, refers to a medic attached to a paratroop company; the more recent one to a laboratory technician or medical assistant.

Somewhere in all this, as happens often elsewhere, the person who is sensitive to language finds that words and parts of words are being thrown about with abandon. He is likely to raise objections. As remarked above, *television* has not passed unchallenged; neither has *multiversity* or *heliport* or *triphibian.* But those who raise objections commonly do so on the basis of their familiarity with languages like Latin and Greek, reminding us of John Dryden's distress at discovering prepositions at the ends of sentences. Much of our linguistic snobbery is carried over from other languages. If the objector can come up with a more useful word—one that people can remember and use with some ease—then he has justification; otherwise he is being a busybody. The argument over *pericynthion* versus *perilune* is typical.

Along with this we discover that in the course of time some prefixes are channeled into more specific uses and that ultimately there is a "right" and a "wrong" usage. Many words of Latin origin continue to have the native English negative prefix *un-*, for example, *unrepentant, undeclared, undecided, uncoordinated,* and hundreds more. The general tendency is to employ *un-* with words of native origin or words that have come into English from French. Various allomorphs of the $\{in_1\}$ morpheme, on the other hand, are used for words that are transferred directly from Latin. In earlier times there was much more latitude in these matters, and *un-* occurred in situations where it would now sound un-English:

> *Thine eyes did see my substance, being yet* unperfect.
>
> —Psalm 139:16

> *Are you not mov'd, when all the sway of Earth*
> *Shakes, like a thing* unfirme?
>
> —*Julius Cæsar,* I.iii.4

> *And that they are endowed by their Creator with certain*
> unalienable *rights.*
>
> —Thomas Jefferson

The possibility of making such combinations freely without regard for etymology has become considerably limited. The reason is that the constructions have become pretty largely standardized.

Over against various considerations that have to do with adding prefixes, we also have the possibility of subtracting them, that is, for one reason or another dropping a well-established element, with a good chance of incongruous results. The first is a type of back formation which has been called "lost positive." As a rule we can make a modifier negative by the simple device of adding a negative morpheme: *happy, unhappy; competent, incompetent; obedient, disobedient; verbal, nonverbal; famed, defamed.* Ordinary logic suggests the possibility of reversing this process, taking a negative and making a positive out of it. From time to time people have made a game of this, coming up with descriptives like *ane* or *kempt* or *sheveled* or *gruntled.* The thing is actually not as outrageous as it sounds.

The modifier *couth* was an Old English word which remained in use until after the time of Chaucer; its negative, *uncouth,* was dusted off by Sir Walter Scott and presently gained general acceptance; and *couth* is presently on its way to becoming an acceptable word. *Kempt,* originally a mutated variant of the participle *combed,* has humorous overtones, but young people have begun using it seriously and it stands a reasonable chance of gaining acceptability. *Gruntle* 'to cheer somebody' has some literary standing. The principal danger is that the listener thinks of these expressions as intentionally amusing, since they have all been created by back formation. But the borderline is very narrowly drawn, and unexpected things happen. The language develops the need to express a specific style of sophistication and because *couth* is available, and no one laughs, it becomes socially approved. For the moment such forms as *ept* and *sipid* and *defatigable* appear to be too intricate to be generally useful. *Scrutable* and *trepid* happen to be in acceptable usage, though it is not difficult to see why they are seldom used.[4] In any event the unpracticed user of English experiments with these words at considerable risk.

Side by side with the lost positive we have the phenomenon of "apheresis" /əférəsɨs/, a common enough linguistic practice which labors, however, under an uncommon name because its most diligent practitioners feel themselves a little embarrassed by it. Phonetically it consists of the omission of an unstressed initial element. Often it represents a deliberate attempt to mimic the speech of the very young, and sometimes it is undisguised baby-talk. A typical example is *'cause* or *'cuz* as a reduction of *because:*

I don't eat breakfast *'cause* I like to sleep late.

Woofy is cwyin' *'cuz* him hurt his heddie.

Apheresis appears to lend itself to creating a pleasant and informal atmosphere and is often exploited with that end in view. While it is far from uncommon in running speech, conventional spelling normally covers it except where the user is striving for an effect. Unfortunately he is seldom an accurate judge of the effect.

Some of the spellings have become conventionalized: *'bout* for *about; 'scuse* for *excuse; 'cept* or *'cep* for *except; 'spose* for *suppose.* Words like

---

4 "The Lost Positive," *Time,* 21 Sept. 1953.

'tenshun and *'tatoes* for *attention* and *potatoes* are often seen in print; *'tenshun* is hardly what a typical drill sergeant makes of it. *Specially* for *especially* is sometimes written *'specially* as a bread-and-butter variant, intended to represent the utterance of the young. Actually *specially* has long been in the language by its own right; *especially* bears the clear marks of a separate borrowing from French. While not exactly the result of apheresis, *tummy* from *stomach* has developed by a similar process—an attempt, namely, to simplify the pronunciation. The expression has been around for a long time and is supposedly a delicate way of referring to the stomach itself or the abdomen in general.

Several words have entered the language by this route but they have been so long in use that they have acquired full respectability. *Vantage* is a shortened form of *advantage* and has been in the language for about seven hundred years. *Vanguard* has displaced the original form *avantguard*. *Squire* has been in the language over against the full form *esquire* but has developed an independent meaning. *Cute,* a shortening of *acute,* has had an unusually difficult time of it. The word has been in the language for well over three centuries, but until a relatively short time ago it still bore an apostrophe, *'cute*.

Aeroplane very early became *airplane,* in both England and the United States, and it had become *'plane* as early as 1909, but not till after World War I did the apostrophe generally disappear. The word *telephone* itself was half a century or so older than Alexander Graham Bell's invention and was at the time applied to any one of a variety of musical gimcracks. The form *phone* made its appearance in print within ten years after Bell's instrument was introduced. For many decades the telephone companies waged a valiant campaign to at least keep the apostrophe in sight, *'phone,* but within recent years this has pretty well disappeared.

Names, and especially feminine names, are subject to apheresis. *Alexandra* has become *Sandra; Annette, Nettie; Rebecca, Becky; Elizabeth, Liz* and *Beth* and *Betty; Helena, Lena; Margarita, Rita*. In fact, many of the abbreviated names have long been regarded as acceptable names in their own right.

Around and *round* seem to trouble those prone to distress on such matters. *Round* has been accepted as an adverb and preposition for many years; it has all but completely supplanted *around* in England, though *around* is still acceptable in the United States. With an apostrophe the nervous ones can quell their qualms and have it both ways, *'round*. Almost identical with this is the development of the spelling *'til,* supposedly the shortened form of *until.* Actually it is an affected spelling of *till,* a preposition in good standing in English since well before 800 A.D. The spelling *'most* occurs chiefly in efforts to render *almost* in a condescending fashion. *Most* as an adverb—without an apostrophe—has been in recorded literary usage since the beginning of the seventeenth century, but has been in and out of acceptability as standard English, often gaining a grudging entrance under the *'most* spelling and being tagged a dialect form. It has appeared from time to time in recent years spelled as *most*—without apology.

Words like *good-bye* and *good-night* are frequently used in addressing infants and are consequently subject to a good deal of hypocoristic shortening, the resulting forms being *bye* and *night,* both with an apostrophe in the more fastidious writing. From these have in turn developed *bye-bye* (and *bye-bye now*) and *night-night* or *nightie-night.*

Problems

There are several specific problems that have to do with prefixes. They have received far more attention than they perhaps merit, but they are regarded as crucial usage items:

Inflammable. This word is derived from the verb *inflame,* which means, as the name clearly suggests, 'to burst into flames, or cause something (or someone) to do so.' It came into English from Latin and is comprised of the morphemes $\{in_2\}$ 'into' and {flamma} 'flame' and consequently anything *inflammable* may be regarded as likely to burst into flames. Many English words have the initial $\{in_2\}$ morpheme, among them: *include, incline, incendiary, incandescent, incident, invade, infer, invent, intoxicate.* But it occurred to someone that *in* also means 'not,' as in *insane, indecent, incapable.* It could be argued that some very dull person might suppose therefore that *inflammable* meant 'fireproof' and would deal with inflammable materials accordingly. To obviate that peril, the word *flammable* 'likely to burn' was jacked into its place and a new meaning was pumped into it. There are those who feel that a useful distinction has been thrown away and that nothing has been provided to compensate for it.

Irregardless. The word has a prefix *ir-* which is an allomorph of $\{in_1\}$ 'not' before initial /r/. This is essentially a telescoping of two words, sometimes called a "blend," in this instance of *irrespective* and *regardless.* The principal objection raised against the word is that it is tautological: *in-* and *-less* say the same thing. *Irregardless* has four syllables, rolls off the tongue easily, and sounds literary; for that reason it has attracted many people who employ the language for show rather than for exact sense. There are, as we realize, those who are grieved that such a word should exist at all, standard or otherwise. It is ordinarily recognized as nonliterary and stands little chance of general adoption. Those who recognize the word for what it is are less irritated by its tautology than amused by its phony pretentiousness.

Disinterested. The meaning 'not having a selfish interest or concern' is the principal one and it has been in use for about three centuries. Earlier than that there was the meaning 'not interested; unconcerned,' but this meaning fell from general use several hundred years ago. Much has been said and written about *disinterested,* mainly taking the view that this word is beginning to be employed in place of *uninterested,* and that since the modifier *disinterested* is for some unspecified reason one of the bastions of Western civilization, the barbarian hordes will swoop down on us when the identification has taken place. The peril is vastly overrated. The development is proceeding in another direction. English has several doublets in which *un-* is contrasted with *dis-: un-* meaning 'is not and never was,' and *dis-* meaning 'was once but is no longer.' Thus: *unarmed, disarmed; unengaged, disengaged; unproved, disproved; unable, disable; unaffected, disaffected; unconnected, disconnected.* From here it is only a short jump to *uninterested, disinterested.* Even though many of us do not use it, this is a good word and the new meaning is a useful one: 'no longer interested.' It has more than an even chance of being adopted before long.

SUFFIXES

The English suffix system is presumably as old as its prefix system. Both systems were operating in the very earliest writings from the Old English period, and many of these we can trace to sources that are hundreds of years older.

Among the suffixes of Old English were several that distinguished nouns: *-dom* (also an independent word *doom*) 'authority, judgment' in *wisdom, kingdom, freedom, Christendom, stardom; -hood* 'state of being' in *brotherhood, priesthood, childhood, likelihood, neighborhood; -ness* 'condition, quality' in *goodness, darkness, sickness, weariness, nothingness, foolishness; -ship* 'condition, office, ability' in *friendship, fellowship, judgeship,* *gamesmanship.* Among the suffixes that distinguished modifiers were: *-less* 'without' in *witless, mindless, topless, penniless; -ful* 'abounding in' in *graceful, powerful, merciful, careful, sorrowful; -en* 'made of' in *wooden, golden, brazen, leaden.*

Latin, either directly or by way of French, provided numerous other suffixes: *-ate,* in *locate, placate, nauseate, marinate; -ize,* in *civilize, organize, terrorize, canonize; -ify,* in *notify, qualify, horrify.*

We realize that we can string out affixes in either direction from the base syllable, and the upper limit depends as much on a person's inventiveness as on the limitations of the language. The signal that there will be no more suffixes within a particular construction is the introduction of an inflectional element. To add a plural *-es* to *-ness* or *-hood* or *-ship* closes that word, just as adding *-ed* to *-ate* or *-ize* or *-ify* closes that. This is one of the fundamental distinctions between English derivations and inflections.

Suffixes, like prefixes, can be either productive or sterile. In order to make a noun out of an adjective we most commonly employ the *-ness* suffix: *redness, gladness, greatness, happiness, effectiveness, comprehensiveness.* It is a general suffix with a rather low specificity. *Redness,* for instance, can apply to apples, sunsets, Marxists, and fire-fighting apparatus; words like *crimson* and *scarlet* have no such general application. The longer a word has been in the language, the more general its applications tend to become, and it is conceivable that some words ultimately grow so general that they are virtually useless. The *-ness* suffix, for all its generalness, proves extremely useful and continues enormously productive. In Old English there was a suffix *-th* which is preserved (usually with mutation of the vowel of the base) in roughly a score of nouns derived from still older adjectives and verbs: *warm, warmth; deep, depth; weal* (or *well*), *wealth; strong, strength; long, length; foul, filth; slow, sloth; dear, dearth; broad, breadth; true, truth; dead, death; hale, health; merry, mirth;* also *till, tilth; grow, growth; spill, spilth; bear, birth; gird, girth; steal, stealth; mow,* (after)*math.* To this list also belong *cool, coolth,* sometimes regarded as humorous; and *dry, drouth* (also *drought*). *High, height; sly, sleight; thief, theft* were at one time part of the pattern but went to a further development. Despite the existence side by side of the *-ness* and the *-th* constructions, we seldom have difficulties, though they may prove too subtle sometimes for the uneducated. In general we are careful not to confuse, say, the *deadness* of a small town in Nebraska with the *death* of such a town. With respect to royalty we say, "Your royal *highness,*" and not "Your royal *height.*" Many things are characterized periodically by *dryness,* among them dead bones, milch cattle, wit, and martinis, but *drought* does not apply to any of them. We feel that on the whole we can stand on stable ground here, that we know our way around. It is a very old pattern; whatever discrepancies may have existed in times past are now shaken out of it. But English uses a great assortment of building materials, brought in from places far and near, and that often causes difficulties.

The suffix *-dom,* having to do with judgment or authority and figuratively with domain (etymologically unrelated), is still an active pattern. By now it has begun to express a collective sense, meaning 'of all the . . .' Thus one could reasonably refer to a dog (depending on the dog) as the "finest specimen of Franklin County *dogdom.*" *Kittendom* is also possible, but a user of standard English cannot go far beyond that. *Boredom* appears to be in a class by itself. *Officialdom* is a good newspaper and magazine word; *clerkdom, inspectordom,* and a few others are recognizable as English constructions. It is easy to wander into the grotesque in this area.

We recognize the *-itude* suffix in *altitude, attitude, amplitude, certitude,* and a few others, many of them scientific or semiscientific. It is just this flavor of the suffix that Mark Twain exploits so delicately:

> *"Trouble has done it, Bilgewater, trouble has done it; trouble has brung these gray hairs and this premature* balditude."
>
> —*Huckleberry Finn,* Chap. 19

Along with nouns like *idiocy, clemency, accuracy, tendency* and other expressions with a *-cy* suffix, there is *normalcy,* a relatively old word as such things go, though seldom used. During the 1920 political campaign, the candidate for the Presidency, Warren G. Harding, groping for the word *normality,* happened to say *normalcy* instead, to the delight of the newspaper reporters. It has since acquired a distinct meaning of its own, as contrasted with *normality.*

Many of the suffixes in English seem to signify practically the same thing, so that it often matters little whether a person uses one or the other. But to follow this as a general principle may lead to unforeseen results. The inappropriate past participle is, as we have observed, gauche; the wrong suffix is not so much gauche as incongruous.

Even though English suffixization offers a rich field for humor, few writers have more than superficially exploited it, perhaps because the borderline between the acceptable, the amusing, and the really grotesque is so hard to determine with certainty. We recognize Mark Twain's *balditude* as burlesque hypercorrectness. S. J. Perelman plays with the language in another way when he writes: "Women loved this impetual Irish warrior who would rather fight than eat and vice versa." Shakespeare played at the game occasionally. There is the scene shortly before the death duel in which Hamlet is speaking to the fatuous courtier Osric:

"Sir, his definement suffers no perdition in you, though I know to devide him inventorially, would dosie [*dizzy*] *th'arithmaticke of memory, and yet but yaw neither in respect of his quick saile, but in the veritie of extolment, I take him to be a soule of great article, & his infusion of such dearth and rareness, as to make true dixion of him, his semblable is his mirrour, & who els would trace him, his umbrage, nothing more."*

—*Hamlet,* V.ii.117–125

Mrs. Malaprop's expressions, from Sheridan's *The Rivals,* are clearly between the amusing and the grotesque, and they are for that reason classics. Sheridan, more than the others, puns also on the word base:

Mrs. Malaprop. *Observe me, Sir Anthony.—I would by no means wish a daughter of mine to be a* progeny *of learning; I don't think so much learning becomes a young woman; for instance—I would never let her* meddle *with Greek, or Hebrew, or Algebra, or* Simony, *or* Fluxions, *or* Paradoxes, *or such inflammatory branches of learning—neither would it be necessary for her to handle any of your mathematical, astronomical,* diabolical *instruments;—But, Sir Anthony, I would send her, at nine years old, to a boarding-school, in order to learn a little ingenuity and artifice. Then, Sir, she should have a* supercilious *knowledge in accounts;—and as she grew up, I would have her instructed in* geometry, *that she might know something of the* contagious *countries;—but above all, Sir Anthony, she should be mistress of* orthodoxy, *that she might not misspell, and mis-pronounce words so shamefully as girls usually do; and likewise that she might* reprehend *the true meaning of what she is saying.—This, Sir Anthony, is what I would have a woman know; and I don't think there is a* superstitious *article in it.*

—*The Rivals,* I.ii

Through all this there is visible enough of a pattern to make the English system of suffixization workable, but at the same time there are enough irregularities to take the heart out of any diffident users. We pair up, for example, words like *arrive* and *arrival, survive* and *survival, revive* and *revival;* but there are also *deprive* and *deprivation, connive* and *connivance, contrive* and *contrivance*—but also *contraption.* Similarly we have *deceive* and *deceit* or *deception, receive* and *receipt* or *reception, conceive* and *conceit* or *conception.* Side by side with them we have *perceive* and only *perception, believe* and *belief, relieve* and *relief, achieve* and *achievement, retrieve* and *retrieval.* Analogy works up to a point and then it unexpectedly breaks down. As a device for vocabulary building the derivational system of English appears at an early glance to be a linguistic Land of Beulah; indeed there have been persons who spent much labor on trying to work out a teaching system based on the assumption that all of this is essentially regular rather than the mare's nest it actually is.

A striking illustration of the thing we have to deal with may be found in a set of some sixty word bases, all of them derived directly from Latin. Attached to the base is either an adjective-forming suffix *-id* or a noun-forming suffix *-or*, or both, along with a variety of further derivatives constructed on the noun or the adjective and occasionally on the base itself. As may be expected, some of the words are confined to technical or scholarly use, but many of them are household words that we meet every day.

The basic pattern is unmistakable:

acrid	-ly	-ness	-ity
arid	-ly	-ness	-ity
avid	-ly	-ness	-ity
flaccid	-ly	-ness	-ity
florid	-ly	-ness	-ity
gelid	-ly	-ness	-ity
limpid	-ly	-ness	-ity
livid	-ly	-ness	-ity
placid	-ly	-ness	-ity
rapid	-ly	-ness	-ity
stolid	-ly	-ness	-ity

In a few of them the pattern is defective:

lurid	-ly	-ness	
sipid			-ity
sordid	-ly	-ness	

A number of adjectives of this classification follow a pattern identical to the "regular" one above, but in addition they have one or more derivatives that are outside any special pattern:

acid:	acidify, acidize, acidization, acidic
frigid:	frigorific
gravid:	gravity
lucid:	lucent, lucently, lucency
morbid:	morbific
putrid:	putrefy, putrefaction, putrescent, putrilage
rabid:	rabies
solid:	solidify, solidification, solidarity
timid:	timorous, timorousness, timorously
torrid:	torrefy
vivid:	vivify

On the other hand, there is one adjective which has none of the regular derivations, only a relatively rare irregular one:

trepid: trepidation

Corresponding to these adjectives is a set of nouns characterized by a final *-or*, about a dozen of which do not have an adjective with final *-id*. Many of these nouns are irregular with respect to derivational structure:

dolor	-ous	-ously	-ousness	
vigor	-ous	-ously	-ousness	
clangor	-ous	-ously		
clamor	-ous	-ously	-ousness	*also* clamant
glamor	-ous	-ously	-ousness	*also* -ize *and* -ization
savor	-ous	-ously	-ousness	

Even less regular are:

favor:	-ite, -itism, -able, -ably, -ableness
flavor:	-ful, -some
labor:	-ious, -iously
sopor:	-ific, -ose, -iferous
furor:	(*base* fur-): -y, -ious, -iousness, -iously
ardor:	(*base* ard-): -ent, -ently, -entness
honor:	-able, -ably, -ability, -ableness, -ific, -ary, -arily
terror:	(*base* terr-): -ible, -ibly, -ify, -ific, -ifically, -ism, -ist, -istic, -ize

Glamor is not of Latin derivation but has been drawn into the pattern by analogy. It happens to be a remodeling of *grammar*.

Both *favor* and *flavor* came into the English language at an early date, being Norman-French expressions with Latin reinforcement. We are not even sure what the Latin original for *flavor* actually was; it may well have been a corruption of the word from which we derive *fragrant*. The derivatives of *labor* should have been **laborous,* and so on, but both noun and adjective passed into English by way of French. *Sopor* is the kind of word that might turn up in a pathology clinic, but only there, and that explains the heavy Latinization of its derivatives. We must be careful not to press too hard the relationship between *furor* and *fury,* the latter with all the derivatives, for the words came into English quite independently of each other, a further illustration of the maddening irregularities of this system. *Honor* was high among the chivalric virtues, consequently it won an early place in English and has been accorded the kind of suffixization the language would bestow on a native word. *Terror* is a word that has proved its usefulness, actively and passively, again and again, as is witnessed by the rich store of derivatives.

Where the original pattern remains substantially intact, that is, a noun with *-or* over against an adjective with *-id*, the two may develop in different directions with respect to meaning. The older structure and relationships are still largely evident in the following:

candor	candid	-ly	-ness		
fervor	fervid	-ly	-ness	-ity	fervent
fetor	fetid	-ly	-ness		
pallor	pallid	-ly	-ness		
squalor	squalid	-ly	-ness	-ity	
torpor	torpid	-ly	-ness	-ity	

In still others the suffixes are attached to several bases, all related:

horr-	horror			-ible, -ify, -ific, -endous
	horrid	-ly	-ness	
splend-	splendor	-ous		-iferous, -iferously, -iferousness
	splendid	-ly	-ness	
rig-	rigor	-ous, -ously, -ousness, -ism, -ist, -istic		
	rigid	-ly, -ness, -ity, -ify, -ification		
stup-	stupor	-ous		-efy, -efaction, -endous
	stupid	-ly, -ness, -ity		

Root	Word	Suffixes	Shared endings
tum-	tumor	-ous	-efaction, -escent, -escence
	tumid	-ly	
vap-	vapor	-ous, -ize, -able, -ific, -ish	
	vapid	-ly, -ness, -ity	
flu-	fluor		-ent, -ency
	fluid	-ly, -ness, -ity, -al, -ize	
liqu-	liquor		-efy, -efaction
	liquid	-ly, -ness, -ity, -ize, -ate	
ranc-	rancor	-ous, -ously, -ousness	
	rancid	-ly, -ness, -ity	
hum-	humor	-ous, -ously, -ousness, -ist, -istic	
	humid	-ly, -ness, -ity, -ify, -ifier	
val-	valor	-ous, -ously, -ize	-iant, -iantly, -ue, -uable
	valid	-ly, -ness, -ity, -ate	

In an assortment like this, etymology has a field day. Both *splendor* and *splendid* follow the regular pattern, but the concept they represent is an open challenge to grandiloquence and in times past words like *spendiferous* and *splendacious* have sprouted like weeds. *Rigor* in its derivatives *rigorist* and *rigorism* has strong ecclesiastical overtones. *Tumor* and *tumid,* as representing an object and a condition, have to do with different classes of physiological phenomena. Originally a tumor was simply any kind of swelling. *Vapor* and *vapid* distinguish a concrete and an abstract concept. *Fluor* is actually an unusual linguistic form contrasting with *fluid* since fluor happens to be a mineral. The words are etymologically related in a most roundabout fashion. As contrasted with *liquid, liquor* has been severely specialized, referring only to beverages having an appreciable alcoholic content. The word is thus used attributively in phrases like *liquor trade* and *liquor industry,* where *liquid* would be completely out of place. *Liquid* can refer to substances which are nongaseous and nonsolid, but also to readily available assets. *Rancor* exists only in the mind as an attitude or expression of it; *rancid* refers to something that has physically gone bad. Both *humor* and *humid* presently go back to the notion of moisture, but unless a person understands the "four humors" of classical medicine the point is lost. There were bad humors like phlegm or yellow bile or black bile which made people respectively phlegmatic, choleric, and melancholic; and a good humor like blood which made one sanguine. In the course of time the meaning of the noun transferred from cause to effect while the adjective retained its literal significance. *Valor* and *valid* come from the same source as the verb *avail* and signify the various ways in which a person or thing is available, literally and figuratively.

Beginning with virtually an iron regularity this pattern drifts at its outer edges to something just short of complete confusion. Analogy operates to a point, then drops out of sight altogether, affording the unwary user of the language untold numbers of opportunities to fall into error. Even the practiced speaker or writer of English needs to thread his way with some caution.

BACK FORMATION

Prefixes are sometimes lost, as we have observed, either by intent or by chance. Suffixes are likewise often lost, but sometimes the element that is discarded is not actually a suffix at all. Instead it is merely part of a word that looks like a suffix or inflection. The result is back formation, a process to which we have already made passing reference. Many words have come into the vocabulary of English by back formation, most of them standard, some of them of questionable status, and still others quite unacceptable.

Side by side with *creation* is *create,* the two words having entered English at approximately the same time toward the end of the fourteenth century. *Donate,* an analogical back formation from *donation,* came into American English about the time of the Civil War and has had an uphill struggle all the way. Currently it seems to have been granted all the rights and privileges of citizenship, but both the *Oxford English Dictionary* (1897) and *Webster's First New International* (1909) labeled it "vulgar" in the sense of 'give,' as:

> We'll *donate* your old neckties to the Salvation Army.

From *ruination* we have the verb *ruinate,* but this is considered rustic. On the other hand, *coordinate* and *legislate,* also back formations, seem to have enjoyed good standing from the very first. The English language has something over a thousand nouns that end in *-ation,* every one of which can potentially generate a back-formation verb with *-ate.*

While it is unclear exactly where the word *beggar* came from, some etymologists hold that it came from the name of an early mendicant order, the Beghards. After the word was modified to *beggar* the step to *beg* as a verb was only a short one. Many words of this class have experienced no difficulty. *Helicopter,* composed as we noted, from *helico* 'spiral' and *pter* 'wing,' has nevertheless been subjected to back formation with *helicopt* as its end product. Indeed, *baby-sit, cadge, chain-react, scavenge* are back formations that no one would consider questionable. *Burgle* from *burglar* seems to be making it in England but in the United States it is still regarded as humorous, and *burglarize* is preferred. As a back formation from *usher* the verb *ush* would be considered amusing. A silly game involves plovers that plove, vipers that vipe, beavers that beave, vultures that vulch, and so on.

In order for a back formation to succeed, two things are necessary. First, it has to fill a vocabulary need, and second, it must be linguistically believable. Words like *char, decadent, dishevel, botany, greed* came about by back formation; they fill a useful function and it might be difficult to find a word preferable to any one of them. Although *destruct* is a back formation from *destruction*—on the analogy of *construct* and *construction*—it has survived the competition with *destroy* because it has a specialized meaning in connection with rockets and other military equipment. It has even given birth to a phrase, *self-destruct:*

> This capsule will *self-destruct* in five minutes.

Diagnose has been in the English language for more than a hundred years, coming from *diagnosis,* but it has met with little objection other than the mild hint from the *Century Dictionary* that perhaps *diagnosticate* would not be unsuitable. *Prognosis* still has *prognosticate,* although the *Random House Dictionary* cites *prognose. Grovel* comes from *groveling;* but since it has had sponsors like William Shakespeare and Bishop Joseph Hall its status has never been in doubt. *Enthuse,* from *enthusiastic,* was labeled by the *Oxford English Dictionary* in 1891 as "an ignorant back formation" and all the citations were unmistakably American. The *Century,* without the British bias, but also dated 1891, admitted it as "colloquial." Funk & Wagnalls *Standard* (1894) called it "slang," and *Webster's First New International* (1909), "Colloq.; chiefly U.S." *Webster's Third* has admitted it without comment; the *Random House Dictionary* admits it but suggests that it might perhaps be rephrased. The formation of this word is unsystematic as compared to most other back formations, especially those that have been admitted to good usage. Lopping off 60 percent of a word without analogical precedent has undoubtedly stood in the way of ultimate acceptance of *enthuse,* but if and when it comes into good standing the reason will be that it has filled a linguistic need.

Scores and probably hundreds of words have been worked into the lexicon of English by way of back formation, but it remains a snare for the unwary. How far is a person permitted to go, after all, in this kind of word creation? *Baby-sit* is solidly "in," *burgle* is borderline, *ush* is "out." An awareness of these limits is not something a person acquires from a book of rules, but from a general sensitivity to the larger patterns of language.

CONCLUSION

The considerations that hold for the inflectional system of English are valid also with respect to the derivational system. In both we have older patterns that are in competition with newer ones. The older patterns no longer exist as patterns; they are represented by a few individual items, often bearing little apparent relation to one another. This is true, for example, of the scores of English words in which initial *be-* occurs: *bedraggle, beseech, behave.* And sometimes, as is the situation with initial *a-*, the prefix itself springs from a great variety of sources. Still other patterns are widespread but they have been shattered in so many places that they are no longer reliable as patterns, the situation with the *-or* and *-id* words.

English has the resources for creating innumerable words out of its stock of morphemes—fifty or more prefixes and eighty-some suffixes. These are standard. But in addition English has long had affixes which suddenly appeared, rode the crest of fashion for a short while, and at last vanished with only a word or two to mark the spot. Some decades ago a now forgotten genius detached *-teria* from *cafeteria* with the result that the land was filled with *groceterias* and *washeterias* and *drugeterias,* to mention only a few. The morpheme *-rama* was detached from *panorama; -burger* has come off *hamburger; -matic,* from *automatic,* has given us scores of new words. More recently *-naut,* literally 'sailor,' from *Argonaut,* has been responsible for *astronaut* and *cosmonaut.*

What constitutes a useful new word in contrast to a creation that is no more than conspicuously clever may be difficult to decide, but the possibility of mistakenly falling into the latter is probably the thing that keeps this kind of cleverness from getting altogether out of hand. Being regarded as bright and clever has its drawbacks; other people are likely to mistrust the person so regarded. And that is why even the most flamboyant writers and speakers take refuge in rather matter-of-fact kind of language most of the time.

13
syntax

Phonology deals with the sounds of a language and morphology with the shapes or forms of the individual words. Syntax has to do with the relationship of the elements—usually words—in larger grammatical units, from phrases to complete sentences.

There are a number of ways of indicating such grammatical relationships, but three of the more familiar ones are: matching or correspondence of inflectional forms, linking by means of various connectives, and fixed patterns of word order. Some languages depend chiefly on matching forms and only secondarily on other devices, as for instance classical Greek and Latin. Others rely mainly on word order, among them Mandarin Chinese. English happens to use all three, but the most important one is word order, which means that in this respect the grammar of English is more like that of Chinese than that of, say, Latin. Whether one system actually functions "better" or "more efficiently" than another is really a pointless question, even though a great deal has been said and written on the subject. Apparently it takes about as much effort, or as little, to remember the order in which things need to go as it takes to remember the correspondences between an assortment of endings.

In the earliest written records of English that have come down to us the correspondence of inflectional forms still served as the primary syntactical device. There were some connectives, it is true, but judged by our own exacting standards they seem loosely defined; furthermore, most of the patterns of word order could be ignored without serious loss of meaning. Writings of related languages that go even more distantly into the past afford clear evidence that the ancestral language from which English and its linguistic relatives are derived was essentially an inflected one. Some scholars have supposed that such a slow drift from inflection toward the use of connectives or toward a fixed word order represents a decline and a "loss of grammar," while others have hailed it as an improvement and an increase in efficiency. It is probably neither one. Language change is slow, but inevitable, and over a long period of time it appears to have something of a direction also. But if we attribute such situations to chance rather than to a destiny or other teleological instrument we shall probably be more right than wrong. Once, however, a particular grammatical system has prevailed, the language begins to set its course in the direction of another system, though that cycle may take another three or four thousand years.

The drift of English from an inflected or synthetic language to an uninflected or analytic language has not come about rapidly. Nor has it come about uniformly; there are residues of the older system here and there. Word order has grown more rigid than most of us realize and with the help of a few connectives it is able to accomplish just about all the grammatical chores that users of English need to have done. Nevertheless we cling to a few inflections, more perhaps for social reasons than for clarity.

AGREEMENT

What we call "agreement" or "concord" or "congruence," with slightly different meanings in each instance, involves a correspondence in form of two or more words representing different form classes or parts of speech. In many languages one form of a modifier correlates with the singular of a noun and another correlates with the plural. Where we say *the green tree* and *the green trees,* French, for instance, says *l'arbre vert* but *les arbres verts,* and German says *der grüne Baum* but *die grünen Bäume.* There is a little of this still remaining in English. We can say *this tree,* but not **this trees,* because the form of *this* has to agree in number with the noun; therefore the accepted form is *these trees.* On the other hand, when we use the definite article we do not need to observe number agreement; *the tree* and *the trees* are equally acceptable. In Old English, however, the definite article was required to agree with its noun. The noun was inflected for number and case; the article was inflected not only for number and case, but also for gender, and the gender depended on the noun. Number, case, and gender operated as functional grammatical devices in classical Greek and Latin, and some of this inflectional grammar still operates in German, French, Spanish, and other western European languages. Like the definite article, the adjective was fully inflected and it "agreed" with the noun. Old English, in fact, made use of two adjective declensions or sets of inflections, sometimes known as the definite and indefinite. Present-day English has definite and indefinite articles; Old English had definite and indefinite adjectives as well. When word order began to assume major functional importance toward the end of the Old English period, the agreement of adjective and article forms with noun forms began to disappear, and of course not a trace of it remains.[1] There is still a relationship between adjectives and nouns in Present-day English, but it is expressed by means of patterns of word order.

The more highly inflected a language is, the more items must be in agreement; but conversely, the less inflected it is, the less need or opportunity there will be for agreement. In Present-day English many sentences make no use of agreement whatever:

> My oldest brother used to work at the produce market when the market stood at the corner of Jefferson and Third.

Not a single word in a sentence like this is obligated to a particular inflectional ending because another word or inflected form occurs, yet the meaning is perfectly clear.

We can, to say it another way, construct English sentences with word order as the primary grammatical device, making little or no concession to the earlier inflectional system. To do the opposite, that is, to put together an English sentence with inflection as the principal device and generally ignore word order, is by now probably impossible, even in very brief utterances.

---

1 We are at the mercy, of course, of manuscript evidence, and this is often abundant for one century and scanty for another. If we remember that the Anglo-Saxon scribes carried on a scribal tradition which preserved even as late as A.D. 1000 many of the features of Old English of A.D. 800 and earlier, the picture becomes clearer. After the Norman Invasion, the traditions were forgotten or neglected, and the differences between writings of 1000 and 1100 seem enormous. To take a comparable situation, imagine all our literature to be destroyed except a King James Bible and a set of Shakespeare's plays—both in the seventeenth-century spelling. Imagine the problems of a language scholar of A.D. 2600 who has this Bible and the set of Shakespeare and who is trying to match them up with the New English Bible and a set of T. S. Eliot's writings, if these are all that remain of the twentieth century and he has little or nothing between then and now.

Genitives

The declensional system of Old English made provision, as we have observed, for two numbers and five cases in the inflection of nouns. The problems having to do with number are mainly problems of morphology and not of syntax. With respect to case, however, there is still a certain amount of inflectional debris that needs to be considered, even though word order and the connectives have assumed the essential responsibilities.

Typically the genitive case in Old English was indicated by an inflection, but during the past ten centuries it has become possible to express the genitive relationship in not one but three different ways. In the first place, as may be expected, the inflection remains unchanged, as in: *the dog's house.* Next, the inflection has been replaced by a function word, usually *of: the house of the dog.* Finally, the inflection is lost and its function taken over by a specific pattern of word order: *the doghouse.* Here the old genitive has fallen into the characteristic *modifier* + *noun* pattern.

In the course of time these several genitive constructions have acquired their special territories. Most of us sense that *the doghouse* and *the dog's house* do not fit in the identical environments, and that there are really very few situations at all where anyone would speak of *the house of the dog.* The choice of one or the other is, in other words, a matter of usage.

The inflected genitive, as the recessive form, is being restricted to a constantly narrowing domain. It is now used almost exclusively in connection with names of persons and nouns referring to animate things, and for that reason it still predominates in pronouns: *his picture.* In a special sense we employ the connective *of: a picture of him,* or *that picture of his.* With the neuter pronoun an expression like *the idea of it* is the only one possible; Old English would have permitted something we should translate as *its idea.* With names of persons: *George's wife* rather than *the wife of George.* On the other hand, when authorship or such is ascribed to a person, the periphrastic construction is usual: *the Iliad of Homer* rather than *Homer's Iliad,* and *the Temple of Bacchus* or *the Arch of Titus* rather than *Bacchus's Temple* or *Titus's Arch.* With animals it seems to depend on the size. We say *horse's mouth* rather than *mouth of the horse.* But as the creatures get smaller and more stupid there is an increased tendency to use the *of* genitive:

> *And* the voice of the turtle *is heard in our land.*
>
> —Song of Solomon 2:12

On the other hand, some decades ago praiseworthy objects and situations were described as *cat's pajamas, bee's knees,* etc. And till aerial photography became a commonplace matter, any view from aloft was called a *bird's-eye view*. The *of* genitive usually serves in identifications: *the House of Hapsburg*, or *The Castle of Otranto*. Occasionally the construction has been extended to other institutions, lending an aura of grandeur, for instance, to barbershops and the like: *House of Freddé*. When the inflected genitive refers to inanimate things the construction is usually one hallowed by long use: *stone's throw, harm's way, pity's sake, night's rest, heart's desire, wit's end, day's journey, water's edge*. For inanimate objects the periphrastic genitive with *of* is standard: *pleasure of your company, population of Amsterdam, bag of bones, Legend of Sleepy Hollow*. In fact, when it comes to a choice between a string of inflected genitives and a string of *of* constructions, the latter is far more acceptable: *her father's doctor's wife's college's president*, as against *the president of the college of the wife of the doctor of her father*. As a result of exigencies, real or fancied, of journalists, the inflected genitive is occasionally resuscitated in phrases like *Amsterdam's population, program's completion*, and the like. This construction is easily and quickly overworked.

Language handbooks refer to the genitive as possessive and consequently they have fostered the idea that the genitive form or construction primarily expresses ownership or possession. The term goes back at least as far as the Roman rhetorician Quintilian (first century A.D.). Actually there are a number of relationships which in a broad sense might be considered to be descriptive but which taken one by one are difficult to distinguish clearly from each other. A phrase like *stick of wood* may be a "genitive of material" or a "partitive genitive" or even a "descriptive genitive." It certainly is not a possessive. Among the more typical genitives are:

	inflected	*periphrastic*	*syntactic*
ownership	Guy Fawkes' horse	Garden of Allah	the Smith house
material	hell's half acre	heart of gold	turkey dinner
character	King's English	burden of proof	love feast
description	Bright's disease	robe of white	Easter bonnet
origin	goat's milk	Wizard of Oz	Georgia peach
subject	mother's love	call of duty	horse laugh
object	women's liberation	head of the class	book review
measure	stone's throw	IQ of 86	mile run
apposition	England's Isle	City of Omaha	Pope John XXIII
partitive		pound of cheese	bread loaf
superlative	actor's actor	holy of holies	
instrument		eaten of worms	wind-blown

From very early times the genitives of phrasal constructions have presented difficulties. In Chaucer's *Canterbury Tales* we find the following subtitles: "Heere Bigynneth the Tale of the Wyf of Bathe" and "Heere Endeth the Wyves Tale of Bathe," and, on the other hand, "Heere folweth the Prologe of the Clerkes Tale of Oxenford" and "Heere endeth the Tale of the Clerk of Oxenford." An expression like *the Wife's tale of Bath* undoubtedly strikes most of us as confusing; it is far more clear as *the tale of the Wife of Bath*. If English had remained fully inflected as it was in Old English, the matter would have been settled simply enough: *Bath's Wife's tale*. However, when the periphrastic genitive came into general use for nonanimate nouns, a phrase like *Wife of Bath* would replace the earlier *Bath's Wife*.[2] Now we have side by side two phrases: *Wife of Bath* and *Wife's tale* which have somehow to be fitted into a single expression. Chaucer availed himself of the two possibilities open to him at the time and, in fact, still another: "Heere begynneth the Man of Lawe his tale." The "group genitive" presently came into being and in spite of logic we find early uses of it. In 1536 William Tyndale was burned at the stake and just before he was strangled to death by the executioner he shouted, "Lord, open the King of England's eyes."

There are relics; now and then the expression *somebody's else* shows up where we should expect the more recent and more acceptable *somebody else's*. The inflection is now attached to the last item of the noun phrase, no matter what that item happens to be:

> Snow White stayed at *Happy, Grumpy, Bashful, Sneezy, Sleepy, Doc, and Dopey's* house.

In spoken English such expressions are relatively common. They do not appear in print, of course, since few writers would think of writing them. And if they did, any editor would suggest more conventional constructions.

Objects

The English noun has no inflectional indication of an accusative case, and none either of a dative case; yet a great deal of time is spent in our elementary schools on the difference between the direct and the indirect object.

---

2 The *of* at an early period denoted origin. It seems to have begun with French *de*—Charles de Gaulle, for instance—and corresponds to German *von*, Dutch *van*, Italian *di*, and so on. William I was William *of* Normandy. *Of* appears in English records as part of a surname as early as 1122.

The difference is not in the least confusing in Present-day English, but is likely to give trouble to anyone learning Latin since the direct object is normally expressed by the accusative case and the indirect object by the dative. The accusative and dative in Old English paralleled Latin in this respect; yet even in Old English the distinction was disappearing. In characterizing the function, the accusative is sometimes described as "receiver of an action," and the dative rather loosely as "benefactor of an action." In a sentence like:

Grimbold gave *his cat* a *dried fish.*

the phrase *dried fish* is the direct object and *his cat* is indirect object. The grammatical function is indicated by a set position in the sentence itself. But we can express the same grammatical idea by means of a connective:

Grimbold gave a *dried fish to his cat.*

To his cat Grimbold gave a *dried fish.*

We have, in other words, the option of a word-order pattern or a connective to express the direct object and the indirect object.

The importance of this distinction between a direct object and an indirect object in Present-day English has been much overrated. Our patterns are so simple and foolproof that even our least gifted writers have no problems here. But if one works at it, ambiguity is possible, as witness a couple of lines from popular songs of several decades past:

Beat me, Daddy, eight to the bar

Throw Mama from the train a kiss.

And with verbs like *make, choose, call, give* and others in which the complement may be either a direct or an indirect object, we occasionally encounter situations like:

"Please call me a taxi." "Happy to oblige; you're a taxi."

Demonstratives

During the Old English period, in spite of the importance of inflectional endings indicating case, these endings were becoming blurred in the noun and adjective declensions, but remained in operation in the definite article.

Some of this case-indicating function was also carried on by the demonstrative or pointing word *this*. The definite article presently collapsed to the single form *the* for both singular and plural, a distinction retained, however, in the contrast between *this* and *these*. The functional difference between *the* and *this* seems to have been the difference between specifying and pointing. *The cup* in contrast to *a cup* makes the difference between something named specifically and something named generally. *This cup* in contrast to *the cup* does even more than specify: it points to the particular object. The nominative singular neuter of the definite article was *that* and its plural was *tha,* which by sound change became *tho*. A distinction presently arose between *that* and *this* in grammatical pointing. *This* identified something close at hand in space or time; *that* something relatively more removed. *Tho* as the plural of *that* is what Chaucer used and it remained in use till about the middle of the sixteenth century. But from an Old English dative singular and plural there was also *them,* as in the phrase *them days*. We have observed how the object form of *you* displaced *ye,* and we have observed also the inroads object forms continue to make on subject forms. The development of *them* was characteristic of the same pattern. It was current from Old English times and is still widely used, with either a subject or an object:

> *Them* questions we don't ask around here.

It is now regarded as illiterate or rustic. For some time, however, *them* offered promise of becoming the standard form, and it was simply by accident that it was ultimately shunted aside. *Those* is a relative latecomer, but as the plural of *that* it has been completely established in standard English.

Pointing is now the chief and virtually exclusive function of the demonstratives. At an earlier stage of the language, when this function was less clear, some reinforcement was permitted by means of words like *here* and *there*. These remain in folk speech:

> *Them there* kids is fightin' again.
>
> *This here* book is all you need for to learn yourself real good grammar.

Verb Congruence

Problems of verb congruence have been represented as among the cardinal offenses against the English language. We realize that English has an enormous stock of verbs, and that most of our sentences employ at least one or two of them. On the other hand, the number of inflections is extremely small, and the number of inflections that can figure in a problem of congruence is even smaller. This suggests that the variety of misdemeanors has been grossly overrated and that it must be the same "error" perpetrated again and again, but on different verbs.

Our grammar books have not been altogether blameless. Many of them state uncritically: "The verb agrees with its subject in number and person." The schoolchild does not really know what this means, but he is willing to believe it. It is something like raising an issue in a catechism class about the divine attributes: where would you go to check up on it? The statement has some validity, to be sure, but not as much as we have been led to believe.

In an inflected language a verb form normally corresponds to the form of its subject; in many of the languages that we use, this correspondence prevails in number and often also in person. In Latin, for example, the present tense of the verb *cantō* 'sing' had the following forms:

[*ego*] *cant-ō* 'I sing'
[*tū*] *cant-ās* 'you (sg) sing'
[*is*] *cant-at* 'he sings'
[*nōs*] *cant-āmus* 'we sing'
[*vōs*] *cant-ātis* 'you (pl) sing'
[*ei*] *cant-ant* 'they sing'

It is apparent that the *-ō* ending corresponded with the subject *ego* just as the *-āmus* ending corresponded with the *nōs* subject. With verb endings so clearly distinguished, the pronouns were redundant and were seldom used, especially in the third person where there would be another subject nearly all the time.

Old English preserved some of the distinctions, mainly that between singular and plural, but also in the singular between forms corresponding to the three persons:

ic sing-e 'I sing'
þū sing-est 'thou singest'
hē sing-eþ 'he sings'
wē sing-aþ 'we sing'
gē sing-aþ 'you (plural) sing'
hīe sing-aþ 'they sing'

Occasionally in Old English the pronoun—especially *thou*—could be omitted as redundant, a practice which ended only because the pronoun itself disappeared.

> Com'st with good report?

As is apparent from the plural forms, person-congruent forms of the verb either had become meaningless or were becoming so since the pronoun forms carried the grammatical load. But in earlier English some number congruence occurred, especially with singular and plural subjects in the third person:

> *þæt* mægden sing*eþ* 'the girl sings'
>
> *þā* mægden*u* sing*aþ* 'the girls sing'

This much reinforcement we should regard as redundancy. In standard English of the present, word order unfailingly indicates which one is the subject and which one is the verb, and for that reason the reader or listener can scarcely go astray. But for a long time many writers, and presumably speakers, of English fortified the construction with a pronoun which served to carry on the function of a weakened verb inflection:

> The skies, *they* were ashen and sober.
>
> My little boy, *he* growed about a foot.

Such constructions are no longer accepted as literary English but are quite common in speech of all levels, especially in informal situations.

Actually the possibilities for any kind of noun-verb agreement in Present-day English are comparatively small. No distinction of form exists in the preterite singular or preterite plural of our English verbs. The French say *il prendait* but *ils prendaient;* the Germans *er nahm* and *sie nahmen;* in English the singular and plural verb forms are identical: *he took* and *they took.* Furthermore there are the English modals, and these are uninflected with regard to either person or number forms: *I should* and *they should.*[3] Nor is there a special form in the present tense corresponding to first and

---

3 Modals like *can, may,* and *could* enable a writer to suggest something when he is reluctant or unable to make an out-and-out commitment. For that reason a count of the relative number of constructions using modals is often revealing. When it runs higher than 20 percent, the writer has provided himself with all the exits he needs; a count of 25 percent and even higher is not uncommon.

second person singular and plural subject forms or third person plural subjects. Agreement of a verb with a noun therefore in Present-day English, except for the copula *be,* is limited to the final *-s* of the third person singular present indicative active of the verb.[4]

We should not be surprised therefore to find that the *-s* inflection of the verb, since it is anomalous, has been leveled out of the speech and writing of many users of English, especially those from less cultured backgrounds. Commonly we speak of it as "lack of agreement" and we set about in various ways to remedy the situation, that is, to restore an earlier status quo. In writing the defect is clearly noticeable as a rule, and although it is not commonly listed with the Deadly Sins it is nevertheless a fault. The *s*-less style is appearing more frequently in writing at all levels, particularly that of students. Several explanations are offered: more persons of marginal brains or possessing a marginal command of English are enrolling in advanced English courses; the schools have neglected to make the students aware of the distinction between the base form of the verb and its inflected forms, especially this inflection; or, a change is actually occurring in the language as a result of which the present tense will be reduced to a single form, indicating that these spellings are merely early emblems of the change. All three explanations undoubtedly relate, and the last one is not to be discounted.

Thanks chiefly to high incidence of forms of the copula *be,* a substantial amount of person and number congruence still occurs in English. While the verbs of English have lost all number- and person-congruent forms except the final *-s*, the copula *be* has preserved most of its forms since Old English times. A sampling of material from reputable newspapers and magazines and from works of fiction shows that the number of such uses seldom drops much below 25 percent of the total nor greatly exceeds 35 percent, averaging therefore a little over 30 percent.

The copula *be,* after all, carries on several important functions in Present-day English, three of which already operated in Old English. Specifically, it links the subject with either the "predicate noun" or the "predicate adjective," in one case identifying and in the other describing:

Mr. Troxell *is* an indefatigible bird watcher.

His wife *is* remarkably patient.

---

4 In a sampling of some 18,000 noun-verb constructions (excluding those that employed a form of the copula *be*), the *-s* inflection occurred in 23.1 percent of the total number of constructions.

With the past participle of the verb it forms what we call the passive of the verb, the receiver of an action thus becoming the subject of the sentence:

> The Delaware River *was* crossed by George Washington.

Within comparatively recent times, that is, since about 1600, another construction has gained in frequency of occurrence and therefore in importance. This is the so-called progressive, formed from *be* plus the present participle of the verb. It indicates that an occurrence is temporary rather than something habitual or continued:

> Shawondasee *was* gazing northward.

Much narration and a great deal of our conversational English involves temporary situations or events, and consequently the construction occurs there more commonly than it does in expository styles of writing. Of the *be* forms employed in general writing, those constituting part of the progressive constructions come to something less than one-fifth of the total.

Forms of the copula *be* in Present-day English retain a certain amount of person and number congruence, although it is limited and inconsistent. In the present tense *I* correlates with *am,* and the third person singular subject with *is.* The common form correlating with other subjects is *are:*

I am	we are
you are	you are
he is	they are

In nonliterary English the second person singular sometimes appears as *you is* in contrast to the plural *you are.* But it is far more usual to have *is* serve as the common form for all subjects except *I.* In some varieties of spoken English, even that is ignored as *is* correlates with all subjects in the present tense.

In the preterite we make no distinction for person in standard English, but number congruence is consistent:

I was	we were
(you) was	you were
he was	they were

You was and *you were* at one time distinguished singular and plural *you* respectively, and a number of the older grammarians, including Noah Webster, strongly upheld the distinction, but *you was* has now been schoolmastered into substandard status. In the speech of the uneducated *was* is commonly the preterite form, singular and plural alike, of the copula *be*.

Repeatedly we have observed that the language of the uneducated or of the less educated tends to adhere to older language practices. In this feature, however, the language of the less educated has simply wiped out many if not all of the older person-congruent and number-congruent distinctions, such as they were, and has made do with a simple distinction between the present and preterite. The meaning is clear, of course, since word order carries the grammatical load. What we call "lack of agreement" is not so much a grammatical defect as a usage one, since it is a mark of social differences. It happens to be one of the more visible usage errors. It must be clear that apart from the *-s* inflection of verbs in the third person singular present indicative active—which is already showing signs of becoming archaic in some varieties of Present-day English—the only possible subject-verb agreement that remains in English is to be found in the present and preterite forms of the copula *be*.

Lack of agreement so far as it applies to English is simply a premature collapse of certain form distinctions; the meaning is in no way lost or obscured. In other words, we reward with higher status those who observe the arbitrary pattern of noun-verb congruence and withhold such status from those who ignore it.

REFERENCE

In ordinary spoken and written discourse we depend on a number of grammatical devices to assure the reader or listener that we are still on the same subject. The most elementary way of doing this, of course, is to repeat the name of the person or object:

> Mary *had a little* lamb,
> *Its fleece was white as snow;*
> *And everywhere that* Mary *went,*
> *The* lamb *was sure to go.*

Naturally one can carry this to great length, but it quickly becomes clumsy and repetitious. We use pronouns instead:

Little Bo-peep
Has lost her sheep
And can't tell where to find them;
Leave them *alone,*
And they'*ll come home,*
Wagging their *tails behind* them.

An important function of an English pronoun, specifically in the third person, is to serve as a substitute name for a person or thing, one or more than one, whether it is clearly identified or merely indicated. A noun mentioned as a preliminary to whatever follows is the antecedent of the pronoun. The pronoun and its particular noun stand in a grammatical relation to each other, and this is called "reference." Thus we say that a pronoun must "refer" to a noun. Referring may be accomplished in a number of ways, depending on the language, but very commonly—and this is true also of English—there are specific correspondences which we call agreement.

An English noun must be either singular or plural, and pronoun reference takes advantage of this by distinguishing singular and plural pronouns: *he,* or *she,* or *it* in the singular and *they* in the plural. Agreement between pronouns and nouns makes use of number; it can also make use of gender—in the singular, at any rate. *Mary* and *Little Bo-peep* are members of a large class of words that correspond to the forms of the pronoun *she; lamb* and *sheep* to the pronoun *it.* In formal situations where only one antecedent is possible we sometimes use *the same.* It can refer to any gender and either number. If used in informal situations, however, the result is incongruous:

Little Bo-peep
Has lost her sheep,
And can't tell where to find the same.

Many of the problems that we encounter in the area of pronoun reference are grammatical rather than problems of usage; the most common difficulty is ambiguity, that is, unclarity regarding the antecedent of a pronoun:

Buster kicked Gus and *he* didn't enjoy it at all.

Or, from Jespersen:

If the baby doesn't thrive on raw milk, boil it.
—*Essentials of English Grammar,* p. 153.

There is little opportunity to encounter serious problems in the use of gender in English pronouns. Variations are usually intentional and are often supposed to be humorous because of the incongruity:

> If that's your boyfriend, tell *it* to stop honking the horn.
>
> I tried to milk that cow but *he* wouldn't stand still.

Relatives

So far as morphology is concerned, the problems of reference center largely on *who* and *whom.* Words that relate one construction to another—known as relatives—figure more importantly in the area of syntax.

In Old English, reference was largely accomplished by the definite article. When this became simplified to *the* at the close of the Old English period, several other grammatical devices came to be used. The word *that,* for instance, had been a definite article, but even in late Old English it not uncommonly served as a relative. Words like *who* and *whom* had been interrogatives—interrogative pronouns, actually—from a declension that included also *whose, what,* and *why. Which,* along with *whether,* was a kind of interrogative adjective. From question function to relative function is not a long or complex step and we need not be surprised to discover several of these words presently assuming relative functions. The development, however, has been far from uniform.

In general we employ *which* to refer to nonhuman nouns—specifically those that correspond to the pronoun *it.*

> Mr. Lamprey would like to have you return the book *which* you borrowed from him.

During Elizabethan times, however, it was sometimes used for human beings (and divine):

> *I am the Lord thy God,* which *haue brought thee. . . .*
>
> —Exodus 20:2.

This usage, where it occurs, is regarded as rustic or deliberately archaic. Even as early as the fifteenth century *who* was coming into use in referring to human beings; in Shakespeare and the King James Bible, *who, that,* and *which* are employed somewhat indiscriminately, although Shakespeare appears to prefer *that* while the King James Bible, following an older style, prefers *which*. Our usage now employs *who* for human beings:

> *The brave men, living and dead,* who *struggled here, have consecrated it, far above our poor power to add or detract.*
>
> —Abraham Lincoln, "Address at Gettysburg."

That may refer to either human or nonhuman referents, but one must be careful not to mix antecedents:

> The house *that* belonged to my brother *that* I showed you.

On the other hand, *that* can refer to both human and nonhuman referents at once:

> The little girl and the dog *that* sat on the steps.

What as an older interrogative is employed in a limited sense, as object of a "dependent clause":

> I told you *what* I wanted for Christmas.

In the language of the uneducated the use of *what* is often extended as a general relative:

> That fellow *what* I was talking to. . . .
>
> You remember that car *what* I brought. . . .

Omitted relatives are of two kinds, the first a construction which occurred in Old English. Here the omitted relative would ordinarily serve as the subject of the following clause:

> There's a man stops for me on this corner every morning.

This is relatively rare in writing, but occurs in all except the most formal styles of speech. A construction like the following, however, would be regarded as semiliterate:

> I'm looking for my brother, was here a minute ago.

The other type of omitted relative was borrowed from Scandinavian during the Viking invasions. Here the object of the dependent clause is deleted:

She is the girl I love.

Speakers or writers of English do not see anything ungrammatical or incongruous about this. King Edward VIII, in fact, addressed his nation and empire by radio, speaking of "the woman I love." This is a characteristically English construction which does not, however, translate word for word into other languages, as teachers of modern foreign languages have discovered again and again:

* *Elle est la fille j'aime.*

* *Sie ist das Mädchen ich liebe.*

* *Ella esta la muchacha yo amo.*

As a result we sometimes get the impression that there is something wrong with English, that it is perhaps better to say:

She is the girl *that* I love.

She is the girl *whom* I love.

However, there is nothing about the English expression that needs changing; the rephrasing comes through as a pedantic preciousness that is likely to be more offensive than the other.

Antecedents

Unless the situation makes it obvious what the writer had in mind, the antecedent must be clearly specified. In bad writing the antecedent may at times be difficult to discover. As a result of this possibility we have alarmed ourselves about antecedents when there was no need for alarm. Ordinarily an antecedent should be a person or a thing or a group of them. But it may be a situation, expressed by a clause and referred to by a pronoun:

Aunt Cleo took up sand painting when she was 86. *This* disgusted Uncle Ralph.

> Someone borrowed Kelly's lab manual, *which* made it impossible for him to finish the experiments.

Such a construction, like many others, can be abused, especially when a single word within the clause is in competition with the clause itself as a possible antecedent for the pronoun:

> Xavier had a wisdom tooth extracted. *It* seemed the wise thing to do. *It* was impacted.

Lapses like these are not hard to make, but easy to remedy once the writer notices what he has done. Teachers of composition and others charged with the oversight of the writings of the young and ungifted become distressed at "faulty reference." It seldom results in serious usage errors except when someone reacts by overcorrecting what he wants to say or write.

Collectives

The "collective noun" in English has long been a usage problem. This is a noun which has a singular grammatical form but which expresses some kind of plurality: *family, couple, team, crowd, class, drove, flock, coven, committee, number.* Taken literally, any one of these is a unit and may be so construed:

> The *class of 1942* held its reunion in the VFW Hall.
>
> The *newly-wed couple* is living in the Strongheart Apartments.

Many times, however, the sense of plurality predominates over the singular form. Commonly we deal with such words "notionally," by acknowledging the plural idea and constructing the sentence accordingly. The sentence type we select is determined on the basis of whether the subject is represented as a homogeneous unit or as a collocation of individuals:

> The *crowd was* pushing into the street when the troops arrived.
>
> The *crowd* went in all directions and *they* hid under the trees.

An insistence on a strict singular construction may, in fact, produce bizarre results:

> A *couple of boys visits* my house every Friday evening and I invite *it* in and talk with *it*.
>
> The dog walked into the room where the *family* was seated and *it* shouted with joy.

Our usage practices with respect to collectives are relatively lax. The reference, however, must be consistent, whether it is based on number or gender or person. Jumping capriciously from one to the other within a single sentence leads to confusion:

> Love occurs when *a couple* is attracted to *each other* with affection and in can be found all the traits of *that one person* of whom *they* have dreamed to meet all *your* life.

Sentences like these are common enough in everyday spoken English, and the hearer has an adequately clear idea of what is meant. Many of our public figures use incredibly loose pronoun reference, but when they are quoted, some kindly editor often brings the pronoun reference to a more conventional style.

In standard English the words *anyone* and *anybody* are regularly construed as singular:

> Does *anyone* feel a draft?
>
> *Anyone* has to be insane to enjoy that movie.

But when the speaker or writer assumes that his response may come from several individuals within the group addressed, *anyone* and *anybody* are often, though informally, treated as plural:

> Would *anyone* like to take off *their* jackets?
>
> *Anybody* who can afford that kind of vacation has a lot more money than *they* know how to spend.

These expressions would have difficulty passing in written English, except in letters or other informal writing, but we frequently encounter them in conversation. *Anyone* and *anybody* belong to a small class of words known as indefinites, indicating that the antecedent is unspecified. With the antecedent itself left in the air, the pronoun can scarcely be more specific. Consequently, while the phrase *his or her* or simply *his* is expected in formal writing and speaking, the less definite *they* does not seem illogical otherwise.

Everyone and *everybody* obviously refer to a number of persons, but because they are regarded as individuals the words are construed as though they were singular:

> *Everyone* looks happy.
>
> *Everybody* was holding *his* head in *his* hands.

Immediately following *everyone* and *everybody,* a plural-congruent form of the verb is considered un-English:

> * *Everyone look* happy.
>
> * *Everybody were* holding *their* heads in *their* hands.

Nevertheless, at some distance from either *everyone* or *everybody,* notional plurality rather than strict singular form is likely to dictate the reference:

> *Everyone* in this crowd must have had *their* Wheaties.
>
> Will *everybody* present please hand in *their* papers before *they* leave?

Most commonly, if the singular-congruent form immediately follows the indefinite, number forms will be consistent throughout the sentence:

> *Everyone* has had *his* Wheaties.
>
> *Everybody* hands in *his* papers as *he* leaves the room.

Whether to use *none* with singular or plural agreement in the verb is often a hotly debated point of usage. A hundred years ago it had not occurred to anyone to worry about it. As a general rule, *none* has been regarded as singular: "If none of these absurdities is taught. . . ." But since earliest times, where the reference has been to persons, the word *none* has been considered as plural: "None of their countrymen were. . . ." The standard argument in this issue is: "*None* means the same as *no one,* and you can't say 'No one of their countrymen were. . . .'" On the face of it an argument like that sounds quite convincing; it fails to recognize, however, that we do not have any exact synonyms[5] in English, and that *no one* and

---

5 In a sense there are some "exact synonyms." *Often* and *frequently, seldom* and *rarely* cover the same number of occurrences during a given interval; yet one is the commonplace expression and the other the literary one. Many plants and animals are known by different local names, and to that extent they are synonyms.

none are not interchangeable grammatically. Different "rules" apply. *No one* can be construed only as a singular and it corresponds to *nobody:*

> *No one* seems to notice that Bradley is wearing a respirator.
>
> *No one* has any business sunbathing that way.

None, on the other hand, operates as either singular or plural, depending on the manner in which it is qualified by other words in the sentence.

> *None* of the boys *is* qualified for the debate team.

Here the emphasis is on the not-a-single-one-ness of the list of possibilities. But:

> *None* of the boys *are* qualified for the debate team.

The emphasis in this sentence is on the plurality, on the assumption that all of the candidates are bad.

Usage of individual writers and speakers is divided on this problem. Typically we have two grammatical analyses, both equally valid, by which we can explain the construction of the sentence. The expression "None of the boys *is*. . . ." assumes that *none* is the grammatical subject of the sentence and that *of the boys* is a modifying phrase. Such an analysis is in keeping with the more conventional statements about matters of this kind and will be defended chiefly by those who have enjoyed extended exposure to traditional grammar. Following a notional approach to the same sentence, we can identify *boys* as the subject for a perfectly sound reason, namely, that living beings are of greater importance and concern than any negative pronoun. Carrying this interpretation still further, the phrase *none of the* is analyzed as a modifying expression, filling the same slot as *many of the, all of the, most of the, some of the.*

Whenever two sets of "rules" converge on a single expression, each of them yielding a different answer, we encounter a usage problem. In some instances one expression is preferred by the educated and the socially acceptable and is regarded as "correct." In the above instance no such broad judgment is possible. Most users of English evidently regard the question of correctness at this point irrelevant since they have never realized that *none is* or *none are* can be a question at all. They simply use the form that "feels best" on any occasion. By grammatical criteria one is fully as justifiable as the other, and therefore the ultimate choice is largely a matter of taste. The *Oxford English Dictionary* finds that the plural construction has the weight of preference behind it where persons are involved. Most of the recent handbooks on usage for one reason or another also prefer the plural.

The pronouns *either* and *neither* have only incidental bearing on usage in the area of syntax. They commonly offer a choice or lack of choice between several things, yet they are construed as singular:

Either of them *is* better than nothing at all.

Neither of the men *speaks* Polish.

With *or* or *nor* the subject appears to emphasize the notion of plurality more strongly; at the same time, however, the noun or pronoun directly preceding tends to dictate the form of the verb. There are some three possibilities:

Either he or I *am* lying.

Either he or I *is* lying.

Either he or I *are* lying.

Quite plainly each construction represents a different analysis of the sentence, and although on grammatical grounds each one of them can be explained, on stylistic grounds it is hard to defend any of them because they all sound awkward. The first supposes that the verb ought to be governed by the nearest noun or pronoun, the second that *he* is the subject and *I* some kind of alternative, and the third that both *he* and *I* function as subject. At times prudence suggests starting over. This is such a time. If we add one word we can say:

Either he *is* lying or I *am*.

With the negative this is not possible. The subject is assumed to be plural and the verb correlates accordingly:

Neither he nor I *are* lying.

In recent years a fashionable device for blowing air into a sentence and in this way inflating it to more impressive length has been the *one of those* construction, and it has raised an issue for some of the usage experts to fret about:

Magdanz is *one of those* people who (*is* or *are*) always finding Utopias.

Obviously it would be simpler and would say the same thing to phrase it as:

Magdanz is always finding Utopias.

But if there is good reason to use the full form, the decision rests ultimately on whether the user of English prefers to regard as the subject the grammatical *one* or the notional *people*. Either construction is unambiguous and either way of saying it makes sense. The plural form seems to have the weight of preference behind it.

In several situations a "singular" verb form—either a verb with the *-s* inflection in the present tense, or *is* or *was*—occurs in Present-day English where strict consistency would regard the subject itself as plural:

All work and no play *makes* Jack a dull boy.

Bread and water *is* all you get.

But in these and in similar situations the two items make up a unit. Where a negative connective, *neither . . . nor . . .* , is used the verb is often in the singular-congruent form even though a number of items have been enumerated:

Not snow, nor rain, nor heat, nor gloom of night stays *these couriers from the swift completion of their appointed rounds.*

In inverted sentences a similar casualness about precise congruence has been characteristic of English for a long time:

And now abideth *faith, hope, charity, these three. . . .*
—I Corinthians 13:13

It was *a lover and his lass.*
—*As You Like It* V.iii.14

A set amount or number, when regarded as a unit, may also be construed as singular:

This 50 acres *is* being offered for sale.

Fifteen cents *is* all I used to pay for a hamburger.

WORD ORDER

From time to time we have made reference to English word order as one of the principal devices in English syntax. It is nothing more than what the name indicates: the sequence, namely, in which various elements of a sentence or other construction follow each other. The early grammarians paid only passing attention to it and spent their time on considerations of agreement of form, for the reason that agreement had been important in Latin whereas word order had been unimportant. Word order was not grammar, but style. Latin nouns and their modifiers tended to come in order of importance and the verb often came last of all.

Marcus Juliam amat. 'Mark loves Julia.'

The *-m* ending on *Julia* was all that was required to indicate that this word was the object of the verb. If one wanted to emphasize something else, it was no problem to reverse the word order:

Juliam Marcus amat. 'It is Julia [not Claudia] that Mark loves.'

And occasionally the verb was more important:

Amat Marcus Juliam. 'Mark loves [not just sighs about] Julia.'

The arrangements which were possible in Latin would not work in English, and the grammarians concluded that the fault must lie with the way English was put together—a "thin" kind of language. What they neglected to notice was that the word-order positions in English expressed the grammatical relationships that inflections indicated in Latin. The user of Latin needed to be careful of the word endings and far less of word order; the user of English needs to be careful of word order and far less of the endings.

For hundreds of years English word order has been fixed, which means that by now it is all but foolproof. On the other hand, the speaker of English takes word order so much for granted that he can scarcely conceive of an alternative. The structural grammarians, who reached the peak of their productivity during the 1940s and 1950s, recognized the vital importance of word order as a grammatical device in English. It would be a mistake to suppose that no one had ever noticed it before. A number of grammarians had made comments about word order, just as various explorers had landed in America before 1492, but the structural grammarians, like Columbus, got the thing on the map. The transformational grammarians and their structural predecessors are in agreement on this matter: the nature of English word order.

Word order is the primary grammatical device of English, and as has been indicated, it can supersede structure words where necessary or convenient, and it can also supersede the inflections of English nouns or verbs or pronouns. Early in his career as a speaker of English the youngster catches enough of the significant material to create a sentence like:

Daddy take Dolly ride Grandma house.

Left to the laws of chance or probability, these six words could be arranged in any of 720 different combinations; but well before his third birthday the normal child realizes that he must reject the other 719 in favor of the single one that represents acceptable English word order. To move so much as a single word out of this order destroys the sense, yet from the above combination the speaker of English gathers that it must be something like this:

Daddy is taking Dolly for a ride to Grandma's house.

Tampering with English word order is not something that comes to us readily or easily. Time spent in mimicking foreigners in their attempts to learn English ultimately enables a person to construct a sentence like:

In the rain stood getting wet all night Grover.

It is not a major accomplishment, yet it does not come easily, for intuition tells us that there is a way in which an English sentence naturally falls into place, and the language appears to put up a vigorous fight whenever it is drawn or driven in another direction.

NEGATION

Negation is such a commonplace and immediately useful feature of language that we usually take it completely for granted. Outside of a paragraph or two of cautions against the use of the double negative, our school grammars largely ignore it and devote their time to identifying the various kinds of objects. Negation, however, is not as simple a matter as we should suppose.

Indeed, during the time for which we have written records of English there have been several systematic remodelings of the manner in which negation is indicated, and there are evidences that a further remodeling may presently be under way.

One of the most striking aspects of the overall development has been the transfer of the negative element from the beginning to the end of the negated word. From being a prefix of sorts—more properly a "proclitic"—it has become a suffix of sorts—an "enclitic." And from being a feature which could be assigned to almost any part of a sentence it has become narrowed almost completely to the tense-bearing expression—a verb or auxiliary—or to a time adverb. Shifts like these take a long time to run their course and the ones that are going on now are far from complete.

In Old English the burden of negation was assigned to a negative particle *ne,* used either as a separate word or assimilated to another word. In a sentence like *Hi ne mihton ealle ætgædere wunian* 'They were not able to live all together'—literally, 'they not might'—it is a separate word. Much of the time, however, it was joined to a following word as a proclitic, particularly when the word began with a vowel or with /h/ or /w/. Some of them were verb auxiliaries like *will*—whence our *willy-nilly.* Some were adverbial or pronominal, and several of these are still currently in use, though modified in both pronunciation and spelling: *ne* + *æfre* > *næfre* 'never'; *ne* + *ān* > *nān* 'none'; *ne* + *āwiht* > *nāwiht* 'naught' or 'not.' In fact, in Present-day English there are ten or twelve words or phrases which preserve in some manner this negative *ne* particle.

Verb forms like *nabbe* '(they) have not,' *nis* 'is not,' *nist* 'wist (= knew) not,' *nas* 'was not' were carried over into Middle English, but by the end of the Middle English period they had become obsolete or archaic. *Ne* was also brought into Middle English; however, it no longer operated as the primary negative but as a reinforcement of the principal negator: *The wratthe of God ne wol nat spare no wight ne for preyere ne for yifte.* 'The wrath of God will not spare no person neither for prayer nor for gift.' A significant development is the shift of *nat* 'not' to a position immediately following the verb auxiliary. Occasionally, though not often, *nat* occurred following the verb itself when there was no auxiliary: *And yet his resoun refreyneth nat his foul delit or talent.* 'And yet his reason curbs not his foul delight or talent.' *Ne* did not altogether disappear till the eighteenth century; it continued to be used in archaic constructions, often in the sense of *neither . . . nor . . .* :

With throats unslaked, with black lips baked,
We could ne *laugh* ne *wail.*
—Coleridge, "Rime of the Ancient Mariner."

Current printings of the poem render it as *nor . . . nor . . .*

In Elizabethan English this pattern of negation, but using *not,* had become a general one:

And I am sure, two men there are not *living,*
To whom he more adheres.
—*Hamlet,* II.ii.19–20

I cannot *deeme of.*
—Ibid., 10

And I do thinke, or else this braine of mine
Hunts not *the traile of Policie, so sure*
As I have us'd to do.
—Ibid., 45–47

The negative *not* is common to the three sentences, in the first following the copula *be,* in the second with the auxiliary *can,* and in the third with the verb *hunt.* We still use the first two:

We are *not* alone.

Father, I *cannot* tell a lie.

With regard to the third, where users of English once said:

Stanley went *not* home.

We now say:

Stanley did *not* (or *didn't*) go home.

This can scarcely be considered a simplification. To a person learning English as a second language it often seems needlessly complicated. Yet we may think of it as merely a rearrangement of the items. The main verb has been supplied with an auxiliary *do* which assumes the tense and person inflections while the verb assumes the base form. One would like to suspect that a couple of grammarians were responsible for dreaming up these complexities to amuse themselves on a rainy afternoon, but the development has come about in a completely orderly fashion. The old "rule" assigned the negative element *not* to the position immediately after the tense-bearing word, whether copula, auxiliary, or verb. By the new "rule" the negative *not* (or enclitic *n't*) immediately follows and ordinarily is joined to the auxiliary, and if there is no auxiliary *do* is added.

In Present-day English it is the verb phrase that normally carries the negation; in fact, in more than three out of five negations in English the verb phrase is involved. The time expression *never* follows at some distance but it is more frequent than any of its competitors. Other elements are only occasionally negated:

> *Nothing* succeeds like success. (subject)
>
> He gets *no* help from his father. (direct object)
>
> It's *nothing* at all. (predicate noun)
>
> I told *nobody* your secret. (indirect object)

As was noted earlier, after causative verbs fell out of use as a distinguishable type, English developed a new causative pattern with *do*. A Medieval romance from the middle of the fifteenth century reads:

> *Tho traytouris will I* do *honge.* 'Those traitors will I cause to hang.'

By the sixteenth century *make* had assumed this function and *do* came to be treated as a "tense bearer," in other words, an auxiliary which had the function of carrying person and tense inflections.[6] Such an inflection-bearing *do* was making its appearance in writings in the early seventeenth century:

> *Welcome deere Rosincrance and Guildensterne.*
> *Moreover, that we much* did *long to see you,*
> *The neede we have to use you,* did *provoke*
> *Our hastie sending.*
>
> —*Hamlet,* II.ii.1–4

6 It is not unusual for a language to provide a convenient evasion when a certain set of forms becomes complicated in any way. In German and Dutch local dialects speakers have the option of adding a diminutive, which makes a noun neuter. It seems possible that while the English verb system was undergoing this remodeling, many users of English automatically resorted to using *do* to cover their uncertainty. In Afrikaans *det* 'did' (Dutch *deedt* 'did') is a general past tense bearer, and the same is true for *done* in some types of black speech in this country.

This use of *do* still occurs occasionally, chiefly in bad poetry. In such a case it enables a rimester to eke out a line with an extra syllable:

Once there was a little girl
And her friends loved her dear
Her parents loved their little girl,
And she did *their hearts cheer.*
Ah! They loved their little darling,
As with them she did *roam*
And they called her little Susan
The pride of their home.

—Julia A. Moore, "Little Susan," *The Sentimental Song Book* (C. M. Loomis, Grand Rapids, Mich., 1876), p. 45

The speaker of Elizabethan English had open to him the choice of two forms of negation, one with *do,* and the other without:

Time stands *not* still.

Time *does not* stand still.

The second pattern was the one that presently prevailed. The construction is relatively infrequent in the King James Bible, although it had clearly become established. It is somewhat more common in Shakespeare, suggesting that it was usual in spoken English of the period.

By the second half of the seventeenth century the negative *not* was being written as one word with the auxiliary. The first citation given by the *Oxford English Dictionary* is 1652, of the word *mayn't.* This called for a further remodeling, the results of which still raise problems. The first citation for *don't* with a third person singular subject, as in *it don't,* is given for 1706, and reading of the literature of the period makes it apparent that *don't* was not only the preferred form; it was the only form. In Archbishop Richard Whately's *Miscellaneous Remains from his Commonplace Book 1816–60* we find "'I *don't* think so' . . . is good English. But we should not say 'he *don't* think so', but he *doesn't* think so." A great deal of schoolmastering has been brought to bear on *he don't* and *it don't.* Though both expressions are beginning to sound archaic, many well-educated people continue to prefer them, especially in informal conversation; in England a phrase like *it don't matter* manages to get in print, even in the most distinguished periodicals. Except for *be, have,* and *do,* the verb auxiliaries are uninflected for person; thus we have *I won't* and *he won't,* and analogically we might therefore expect *I don't* and *he don't*. There are many people who regard *it don't* and *he don't* as little short of barbaric, and others of unimpeachable refinement who regard it as perfectly acceptable, who in fact think of *it doesn't* and *he doesn't* as mildly stuffy. At this point one takes his choice, but also his chances. In addition to contractions like *mayn't*, there was *an't*, which appeared in print as early as the beginning of the eighteenth century. It was spelled *an't* as a contraction of *are not* and *am not*. We have evidence that it was regarded as socially acceptable early in its career, but during the nineteenth century it became clearly identified with the language of the unlettered, specifically the Cockney speech of London. Charles Dickens used it as a stock distinguishing mark of the underprivileged. Merriam-Webster's *American Dictionary of the English Language* (1864) ignored *ain't*, but cited *an't* (pronounced /eynt/) with the following definition: "A colloquial contraction of *am not* or *are not*, as in the phrases *I ān't, we ān't, you ān't*, &c. *He ān't* follows either the analogy of the others, or is a corruption of *he is not*." As a colloquialism it was presumably on even footing with *can't* (pronounced /kahnt/), and *won't*. Funk & Wagnalls *Standard Dictionary of the English Language* (1893) included *ain't* (pronounced /eynt/) with the following: "[Colloq.] Am not; are not; also, illiterate for *is not, has not*, and *have not*." There is a cross reference to *an't*, also, in spite of the spelling pronounced /eynt/. The definition: "Are not [idiomatic since 1706]; am not colloquial, [1737]; is not [under ban]; a contracted form. The later *ain't* [1788] is under ban in all the senses." The *Century Dictionary* (1889) offers two entries for *an't*. The first, pronounced /ahnt/ or /eynt/, is defined as: "A colloquial contraction of *are n't, are not*, and of *am not*, and with greater license also of *is not*. In the second pronunciation also written *ain't* or *aint*." The other *an't*, pronounced /eynt/, is defined: "A dialectal reduction of *ha'n't*, a contraction of *have not* and *has not*. Also written *ain't, aint, hain't, haint*." While *an't* comes off with a rather clean bill of health, *ain't* in the same volume does less well. It is cited along with *an't* as a variant spelling, both pronounced /eynt/, but defined: "A vulgar contraction of the negative phrases *am not* and *are not*; often used for *is not*, and also, with a variant *hain't*, for *have not* and *has not*." Just when *ain't* plunged to its present estate at the bottom of the linguistic Tartarus is difficult to say, but it was probably during the first decade of the twentieth century. It is popularly regarded as the mark of total depravity in usage. Whether this opinion is also shared by the well-educated, who sometimes use it among themselves as a kind of reverse snobbery, would be difficult to say with certainty.

By the middle of the seventeenth century, as we have observed, the negative particle *not* was being written as one word with the auxiliary, and with syncopation of the vowel the enclitic negative *-n't* made its appearance. In spoken English the full form is now rare, except in formal public addresses or in emphatic use:

> We *will not* be going to Bermuda, and that's final!

The spelling contraction is regarded as acceptable in informal writing as well as in much that borders on the formal. To cite an example, in "The Talk of the Town" department of the *New Yorker* magazine, the number of contracted forms and full forms is approximately even.

Syncopation of the vowel is simply the first stage in a gradual weakening of the negative element. Currently a second stage is under way as we encounter with increasing frequency an unreleased final /t/, especially in words like *can't* and *aren't*. We may expect confusion to increase as time goes by, unless English develops a variant negative or a construction by which negation may be strengthened.

MULTIPLE NEGATION

In the Old English period and most of the Middle English period it was comparatively easy to strengthen the negative idea: the speaker or writer merely added another negative, or two, or as many as the situation seemed to warrant. We use the expression "double negative," but it would be more accurate to call it a "multiple negative" or "redundant negative." Few of us encounter more than two negatives, but it is possible to put together a believable English sentence with four or five negatives. Even though six and even seven negatives can be jammed into a single sentence, it is hard to avoid the impression that the speaker is straining for effect:

> There *haven't none* of these dogs *never* done *no* harm to *nobody nowhere nohow*.

In Old English a sentence with two negatives was permitted, and even the best writers sometimes used three or four without apology or embarrassment. Alfred the Great, the most scholarly Englishman of his generation, wrote this line—here translated literally:

Therefore shall no *wise man* not *hate* no *man.*

And Chaucer's celebrated Knight "*never* yet *no* abusive words did *not* say to *nobody*":

He nevere yet no vileynye ne sayde
In al his lyf unto no maner wight
—*The Canterbury Tales,* "General Prologue," 70–71

If one goes simply on impressions, it seems that multiple negation was the rule rather than the exception in Old and Middle English writing. The fact is, many sentences and even extended pieces of writing are no more extravagant with negatives than the most fastidious writing of the present. But if a writer wanted to use more of them, he could. It was during the period between Chaucer and Shakespeare that multiple negatives fell out of fashion. Elizabethan writers used them, to be sure, but with less gusto and abandon than writers a few centuries earlier had. Shakespeare's Celia could tell Rosaline, for instance:

I pray you beare with me, I cannot *goe* no *further.*
—*As You Like It,* II.iv.9–10

But this is pretty anemic negation. By the eighteenth century a shadow had fallen across anything stronger than simple negation. Words like *hardly* and *scarcely* convey only the absence of affirmation, yet expressions like *can't hardly* or *aren't scarcely* were written off as bad English. For many users of English even *but* is a borderline item:

I *don't* doubt *but* that he will come.

I *can't* help *but* think things will be better tomorrow.

Anyone who happens to be sensitive to negation will probably want to remove all suggestion of redundance with:

I *don't* doubt that he will come.

I *can't* help thinking things will be better tomorrow.

Prohibition of the multiple negative has always been represented as being completely logical, but the reason hundreds of thousands of speakers of English react as they do has nothing to do with logic. It is a reaction fostered by teachers and parents and other guardians of the language. Strict application of logic would upset the entire thing. The "rule" that is offered in support states that two negatives make a positive on the grounds, one might presume, that this goes on in mathematics. But the student of elementary algebra who writes his equation $-a + -a = +2a$ has obviously been off somewhere woolgathering when he should have been putting his mind to algebra. The proper formulation is $-a + -a = -2a$. Two negatives, therefore, should be stronger than one. Every school pupil already knows that; it is the kind of intelligence that is revealed to babes but hid from the wise and prudent. That is why youngsters are often reluctant to part with a construction which seems so harmonious with the general nature of English.

From the character of negation itself, the verb is most likely to undergo negation, with the time expression next. But that depends on the emphasis, for any part of a sentence may have a negative element attached to it:

> *Nobody didn't never* tell *nothing* to *nobody.*

In a sentence like this everything that can conceivably take a negative has one. Not even the most resolute antipurist would be likely to launch such a massive assault, however, on the true, the good, and the beautiful. It is actually a composite of five separate negations:

> *Nobody* ever told anything to anybody. (subject)
>
> Someone *never* told anything to anybody. (time)
>
> Someone *didn't* ever tell anything to anybody. (verb auxiliary)
>
> Someone told *nothing* to anybody. (direct object)
>
> Someone told something to *nobody.* (indirect object)

It does not matter that several of these expressions are quite unlikely to occur either in written or spoken English; the equivalent construction under other circumstances is not only conceivable, but likely (cf. page 342).

It has always been the mark of good breeding to know how much of anything is permitted under certain conditions. This undoubtedly accounts for a growing preference among users of English for a somewhat restrained negation. Multiple negation was simply too much negation. The worst thing anyone can say about it is that multiple negation is tautological, in a class with *this here, George Washington he,* and other such expressions.

There is little reason to suppose that the single negative will presently go out of style, especially in writing. The status of the multiple in spoken English is less easy to predict with any degree of confidence; there are reasons to suppose that it may shortly make a comeback. In fact, there is some question whether it has been consistently avoided all these years by those who know the language best:

> *"Barney* [*Rosset*] *and I go to the tennis matches,"* [*Samuel*] *Beckett said not long ago. "We play games, and we talk politics. We don't talk literature. I* don't *talk literature much with* nobody. *It's bad enough to have to write these books without talking about them too."*[7]

The lowering of stress on the *-n't* enclitic frequently calls for reinforcement, and those who "know better"—which is the same as saying "those who can get by with it"—throw in another negative:

> You *didn't* get *nothing.*
>
> You *can't hardly* expect much more.

And if there is the possibility of a misunderstanding the speaker grins or offers some other nonlinguistic signal to indicate that the lapse was intended.

The true double negative, in which two negatives actually do cancel out each other, is found in highly proper writing and sometimes in speaking that borders on the prim and precious. It consists of a negative of time or manner and a base with a negative affix, both of which apply to the same word: *not unaccustomed, not entirely useless, hardly unprejudiced, never insensitive.* This is a form of intentional understatement, which may even conceal a touch of guarded libel. The young man who has been recommended as "not incapable" of earning a living will remain solvent, if his luck holds, but he evidently lacks the qualities that distinguish the young man on the go. And the lad who has brought home for his mother's inspection a girl who has caught his fancy and who is told by the mother that the girl is "not unsightly" will thereby be cautioned against entering her in the local beauty contest.

Understatement is a consideration of style, not usage. When someone describes his general condition as "not bad," he is exercising a negative form of exaggeration. It has been part of the style of the English language since

---

7 Martin Mayer, "How to Publish 'Dirty' Books for Fun and Profit," *Saturday Evening Post,* 25 Jan. 1969, p. 34.

its earliest days. We are told in *Beowulf,* for instance, of an incident in which a member of Beowulf's party flings a dart at a sea creature. The author comments, "It was more slow with respect to swimming in the water," a rather charming way of saying that the beast had been killed.

ANACOLUTHON

Aside from the hardships the unpracticed writer experiences in dealing with the eccentricities of English spelling and punctuation, his ultimate undoing usually comes about when he tries to deal with the matter of "complete" and "incomplete" sentences. It is taken for granted that speakers of English automatically produce complete sentences. At any rate there is no record that anyone has ever gone on speaking without eventually running out of breath. But that is a long way from what we call a complete sentence in writing.

Teachers of elementary writing courses have performed their labors with more thoroughness than natural modesty permits them to suppose, but the fact is that many of us feel uneasy when we happen upon an incomplete sentence. It is almost like catching a clothesline thief red-handed or unlatching the bathroom window and coming face to face with a voyeur. The fragmentary sentence seems to reflect a certain untidiness in putting words together, but many readers do not look on it as that; rather they see here the mark of a morally unreliable person.

Of course, we do not have to do much reading to find that our better writers have put together sentences that lacked a front or a back end. Such sentences are not very common in newspaper writing or in magazine articles, but fiction writers use them almost shamelessly, especially writers who have prepared radio or television material. Young people being taught the niceties of proper writing recognize in this a conflict between the law and its observance. They bring the matter to their teachers, and the teachers in turn defend the Establishment with a few time-hallowed answers: "I suppose if you were as famous (or made as much money) as Hemingway, I might let you write incomplete sentences too," or "As long as you're only learning this business, you have to learn to write complete sentences. You've got to learn to walk before you can run."

Now this assumes that the authorities decided long ago what constitutes a complete sentence. The authorities have really had precious little to do with it, for the idea of a sentence as something that needs to be punctuated is more recent than we might suppose. What help the authorities have lent has been mainly after the fact, merely confirming or otherwise trying to regularize what general practice of writers and typographers had established. Punctuation as we know it has developed within the last five hundred years, practically all of it after the invention of printing. Not until the sixteenth century did Aldus Manutius (Aldo Mannucci), a printer and classical scholar, devise a system for dividing a series of words on the printed page; prior to that the writer or copyist wrote on and on, leaving it to the imagination or ingenuity of the reader to determine where sentences left off or took up. How far we have come may be gathered from looking at a sample of the work of William Caxton, the first English printer:

After dyuerse werkes made / translated and achieued / hauying noo werke in hande. I sittyng in my studye where as laye many dyuerse paunflettis and bookys. happened that to my hande cam a lytyl booke in frenshe. which late was translated oute of latyn by some noble clerke of fraunce which booke is named Eneydos / made in latyn by that noble poete & clerke vyrgyle / whiche booke I sawe ouer and redde therin. How after the generall destruccyon of the grete Troye. Eneas departed berynge his olde fader anchises vpon his sholdres / his lityl son yolus on his honde. his wyfe wyth moche other people folowynge / and how he shypped and departed wyth alle thystorye of his aduentures that he had er he cam to the achieuement of his conquest of ytalye as all a longe shall be shewed in this present boke. In whiche booke I had grete playsyr. by cause of the fayr and honest termes & wordes in frenshe / Whyche I neuer sawe to fore lyke. ne none so playsaunt ne so wel ordred . . .

—Prologue to Caxton's translation of "Eneydos."

The date of this was 1490. Where Caxton supposed a sentence ought to end is anything but clear. Indeed, one can go on reading more than three times as much of the above passage before the sense demands a complete stop, and at that point Caxton's punctuation does very little to slow down a present-day reader. Yet if this passage were read aloud, apart from its antique style and old-fashioned words, most listeners would consider it quite a normal discourse. For a basic difficulty, as we shall presently see, stems from the existence side by side of a written language and a spoken language, both of which cover largely the same grammatical territory. At times the two appear to coalesce, as when people write down what has been spoken or read aloud what has been written. The equivalence that we take for granted is really an illusion. No writing can capture with any degree of precision the tones of voice and other features of speech, and all of us have experienced what astonishing differences there can be when two people read the same poem or essay.

The traditional grammarians never thought of their activity as a science, or not, at any rate, as an exact one. Any definition therefore that brought the student within general range of the subject was as much as they hoped for. So they came up with a statement that is familiar to all of us: "A sentence is a group of words expressing a complete thought." As long as a student kept in mind the distinction between a sentence and a phrase on the one hand, and a sentence and a paragraph on the other, the grammarian felt capable of taking it the rest of the way. Their successors mistook such casualness for negligence and felt obligated to add things like "containing a subject and a predicate" and "The verb of the predicate must be in a finite mode," until it got to be a big patchwork, like a state constitution.

There are certain characteristics, however, that every written sentence has in common with every other written sentence. We can generalize, for instance: "A written sentence consists of a string of words beginning with a capital letter and ending with a period, or occasionally with a question mark or exclamation point." Anything less offers doubtful claims to being a sentence at all. But all of us, including the worst writers in the country, operate within somewhat narrower limits; most persons undertaking to write one or more sentences feel that they ought to pay their respects, and sometimes that is all, to the spelling and punctuation conventions of the language. It does not matter as much as we think it does whether the aspiring writer can call the various parts of a sentence by name. Yet to keep matters tidy there ought to be something one writes about—a subject, if you will (which by coincidence is what the grammarian calls it)—and something he writes about it—a predicate (strictly a grammarian's term). Further than that a writer does not have to go, for he can be in business with brevities like: "Speed kills," "Crime doesn't pay," "Love conquers all." A cut above this, including enough talent to manipulate the simpler words, and a person is ready to compose the classic handwritten notes of instruction about operating heating and plumbing facilities that tourists discover in modestly priced motels. There is this note of explanation beside the doorbell of a Pennsylvania Dutch home:

> Bell dont make. Bump.

At the far end of the scale from this we have various kinds of writing that are acknowledged as important literature. Such writing demands special talent, diligent practice, and patient revision.

In spite of our constant dependence on spoken language, we tend to look down on it. Ever since men learned to write, professional scribes and later professional writers were given special deference. The strong silent man or the man of few words, even though he is fundamentally stupid, is likely to impress people more than the brilliant but glib chap with an answer for every situation. Similarly we are likely to regard the written language as having more substance than the spoken, forgetting that the written language depends constantly for its vitality on the spoken. From time to time a spoken language has disappeared or has changed radically over a long period, while the written style derived from it has remained virtually unaltered, true to its traditions. This has happened a number of times; Latin is one of the more striking examples. It has happened from time to time in English and French and German, in which case the written language becomes stylized and sterile. A tradition grows up and we have a literary style, but then a few rebels break out of the pattern to remind their fellow writers that they need to listen to the language as it is, not as it was. The gap between the written and spoken style closes up somewhat, a new style is born, and by and by the cycle is repeated.

There are many respects in which the grammar of written English differs from that of spoken English and vice versa. Traditional grammar concerned itself with writing because the grammarians assumed, and correctly so, that it was scarcely necessary to teach the students how to talk.[8] But it did not take them long to make the next step, supposing that the grammar of written English was the only grammar, that the other did not merit notice since it was at best a nightmare of solecisms. To this the structural grammarians reacted, and sometimes overreacted. They saw language through the eyes of the anthropologist and sociologist as a characteristic form of human behavior. Writing was a pale copy of the real substance, straitened by an archaic spelling and an assortment of ambiguous symbols of punctuation. The sentence, however, was not their immediate concern; it was in their long-range plans as something they wanted to deal with after they had settled the more pressing problems of phonology and morphology. The spoken and written sentences had a number of features in common—linearity, for instance. In the written mode it was presumably clear where

---

8 As early as 1568 Sir Thomas Smith published a book—in Latin—on the reforming of English spelling. This set off a rash of publication of similar works, and presently the authors found themselves casting around for a model of "correct" English on which to base their spelling revisions. This in turn led to the birth of the science of "orthoëpy," the study of pronunciation. Some of the orthoëpists, like Alexander Gil, author of *Logonomia Anglica* (1619), regarded it as their obligation to tell people how the language was to be pronounced.

one started because there was (or should be) a capital letter at the beginning, and there was (or should be) a period at the end, and if they were not there then the teacher or editor or other authority figure "corrected" the sentence by supplying one or the other or both.

Our convictions regarding the nature of the complete sentence in written English have unquestionably developed recently—more recently indeed than we might suppose. Modern journalistic practice, of course, encourages the short sentence, so that a mouth-filling period a couple of hundred words long is unheard of. But here, for example, is a sentence from a speech by John Milton, from the celebrated "Areopagitica":

When a man writes to the world, he summons up all his reason, and deliberation to assist him: he searches, meditates, is industrious, and likely consults and confers with his judicious friends; after all which done he takes himself to be informed in what he writes, as well as any that wrote before him; if in this the most consummate act of his fidelity and ripeness, no years, no industry, no former proof of his abilities can bring him to that state of maturity, as not to be still mistrusted and suspected, unless he carry all his considerate diligence, all his midnight watchings, and expense of Palladian oil, to the hasty view of an unleisured licenser, perhaps much his younger, perhaps far his inferior in judgment, perhaps one who never knew the labor of bookwriting, and if he be not repulsed, or slighted, must appear in print like a puny with his guardian, and his censor's hand on the back of his title to be his bail and surety, that he is no idiot, or seducer, it cannot be but a dishonor and derogation to the author, to the book, to the privilege and dignity of learning.

Apart from its high style, this is like much of ordinary talk, going on and on, without seeming to come to earth anywhere. Editors and professional writers have long since brought the sentence to bay, and they know in a general way[9] where the sentence begins and ends. Many of the things that appear in print could be punctuated in the virtually interminable style of Milton's writing, but we have grown accustomed to chopping them into shorter lengths with commas and periods and the like.

Since the structural grammarians had committed themselves to the oral sentence as a starting point, they were under something of an obligation to

---

9 Rudolf Flesch, *The Art of Plain Talk* (New York: Harper & Bros., 1946) sets up a formula for "readable style" in which sentence brevity is regarded as a virtue. How much effect his advice is having on current writing is difficult to judge. The general tendency toward shorter sentences must be obvious to anyone who does much reading. In the King James Bible, Ephesians 1:3–13 is a single sentence of 215 words; the Revised Standard Version breaks it into five sentences averaging 38.6 words; the New English Bible makes seven sentences of it, averaging 31.4 words

indicate certain features that all spoken sentences had in common. Punctuation, on which the traditional grammarian could always rely, was outside of this dimension since we don't tell our listener that we are thinking a comma or a semicolon or period. We can say that a sentence has a clearly distinguishable beginning, namely, as a person begins to talk. Structural grammarians also recognized phonological phenomena that coincided with the end of conventional sentences—a pause longer in duration than the pauses between words or between phrases, certain pitch contours, and several types of "terminals." Adults have been trained to recognize, or at least to respond, to such things, and they are also aware of the conventions of etiquette which permit them to break into a speaker's discourse at a particular place with set phrases like, "Excuse me, Trellice . . ." or, "I hate to interrupt you, but. . . ." The small child ordinarily learns that these things exist by such admonitions as: "How often do I have to tell you not to interrupt your mother while she's talking!" These are actually only generalizations and there are exceptions to all of them. Even an assumption that seems fairly obvious, namely, that a sentence is spoken by a single person, is violated again and again. Normally just one person takes the responsibility for a written sentence, but an oral one is not uncommonly a team product:

> *"What tremendously easy riddles you ask!" Humpty Dumpty growled out. "Of course I don't think so! Why, if I ever* did *fall off—which there's no chance of—but* if *I did—" Here he pursed up his lips, and looked so solemn and grand that Alice could hardly help laughing.* "If *I did fall," he went on,* "the King has promised me—*ah, you may turn pale, if you like! You didn't think I was going to say that, did you?* The King has promised me—with his very own mouth—*to——to——"*
>
> *"To send all his horses and all his men," Alice interrupted rather unwisely.*
>
> —*Through the Looking Glass,* Chapter VI

The transformational grammarians have had it best of all. They have started from the assumption that if the proper generative procedures are followed, the end product will be an English sentence, spoken or written. In one sense there appears to be an obvious circularity here, if we assume at any rate that the generative grammarians are concerned about English sentences in general. It is clear that they have a reasonable hunch where all this generative procedure is presently going to bring them to land. Their concern, however, is with "complete" sentences, a consideration which cannot fail to endear them to teachers of English. Failure to follow the proper procedures—such as neglecting the step by which the noun phrase or the verb phrase is generated—produces incomplete sentences.

As long as human beings have been using language, we may be reasonably sure that they have also had the option of expressing themselves in "complete" sentences. We all realize that "incomplete" sentences are possible, both in speaking and writing, and in spite of the inflated claims made for it, the complete sentence does not necessarily express an idea more adequately or clearly than the other. Yet there is the suggestion, whether valid or not, that the complete sentence is the product of more care, and for that reason more trustworthy. What this means is that in the written mode, where the complete sentence is virtually unexceptionable, the person creating the sentence has the advantage of time. No matter how hotly he is pressed, he still has some time to reflect on what he is putting to paper. There is even a good chance that he may not be pressed, and that he has taken the time to make the sentence say just about what he wants it to say.

This imperfect distinction between the nature of the written and the spoken mode raises some real bugaboos. For example:

> "Are you going home now, Hector?"
> "No, Miss Phryne, I am not going home now. I am going to the library."

Teachers of English do encounter this kind of response, and some of them undoubtedly rejoice that the good seed has yielded its increase. Others see it as a lot of tautological monkeydoodle.

Actually there are many situations in which a short nonsentence, rather than the conventional sentence, complete with subject and predicate, is demanded. Our language instruction books give little or no attention to such situations. But from long familiarity with talk, we have no difficulty deciding where they are proper. Again:

> "Will you have some more tea?"
> "Yes, I shall have some more tea."

If this occurred at all, it would betray the respondent instantly as someone who had learned English from a copybook. And less than anything does a speaker of English want to sound that way.

The incomplete or fragmentary sentence is more common in spoken English than we ordinarily realize. In fact, the speaker who delivers only complete sentences frequently raises suspicions in the mind of the perceptive listener. Door-to-door salesmen and telephone solicitors frequently have their "pitch" thoroughly memorized, as is obvious when one compares their confidently worded opening gambits with the poor fumbling responses they produce later in the conversation when one reduces them to answering unexpected questions.

Just as there are "rules" for writing, so there are "rules" that govern conversation—never written, but spontaneously followed by the "right" people. Among these is a rule that permits a speaker to break off a sentence that he feels is going amiss and to start again at whatever point he feels he can best pick up the thread of what he was saying. The result when set to paper exactly as it was delivered may be frightening, especially to the speaker himself. This breaking off and starting again is called "anacoluthon." Here is an example:

In our efforts throughout the world, on outpost positions, I mean positions that are exposed to immediate Communist threat, physical threat, if we will help these people hold out and get ourselves back where we belong as reserves to move into any threatened danger point if they carry it to that point, carry it to that level, then what we will be doing it will be taking these 22 million South Koreans, pushing programs for getting them ready to hold their own front line.[10]

This sentence is a direct quotation from President Eisenhower, who was notorious for shapeless sentences like this one. But few public figures have ever been accorded his reputation for "sincerity." There is undoubtedly a connection. It is easy to imagine that a person who talks like that cannot possibly have an ounce of guile in his system.

In an ordinary narrative or description or other stretch of talk which runs several sentences in length, we would like to suppose that the sentences are being created for the situation at hand, not recited like an epic poem at an Anglo-Saxon or Viking victory feast. This means that the speaker has certain limitations placed on him, especially his opportunities for revisions as he goes along. In that respect an author is lucky; he can decide to sleep on it and finish it next morning when his mind is clearer, or he can slap something together and hope that he will be able to put it into proper shape when he revises his manuscript. But the speaker cannot temporize; even in ordinary conversation we do not expect to hear anyone say, "Go on talking, all of you, but in about ten minutes I should be able to think of the word that's bugging me right now." There are solutions: some speakers elect to speak very slowly and deliberately, which often makes them appear thoughtful and precise, though unless their speech is very carefully timed it can give them

10 *U.S. News and World Report,* Aug. 29, 1952, p. 30.

the unwelcome reputation of being stupid. One may also slow down the talk with standard "hesitation signals"—a kind of structured stammer: "ah . . . ah . . . ah . . ." or "er . . . er . . . er . . ." but many listeners have small patience for this. Skilled conversationalists and adroit public speakers ordinarily have command over a repertory of "stalling devices" which in themselves say nothing, which the speaker is able to deliver as if by preprogramming: "I have examined the situation before me with some care and a good deal of thought and in appraising the situation it occurs to me that . . . ," which with all the air let out means "I think." Likewise: "If I may be permitted to use the word . . . ," which means, "Excuse me while I try to think of the word." The speaker has prevented anyone from interrupting him, which is perhaps vitally important, and he has borrowed a few seconds of time—enough to enable him to marshal his thoughts.

But the most common device of this nature is the simple anacoluthon, the interrupted sentence. In face-to-face conversation it goes on more often that we should imagine, for the speaker is supplied with instant feedback from the expressions on the faces of his audience, and the least suggestion of bewilderment or disagreement is his signal to break off and to approach from a different angle. It is also possible to address the beginning of a sentence to one member of an audience, make a switch, and conclude the sentence speaking to another person.

Strange as such sentences look in writing, and especially in print, their seeming formlessness in conversation seldom disturbs the hearer. In immediate conversation he may sense, without being able to phrase it in so many words, that a sentence is being custom-manufactured for him. And so it is. It has the imprint of "sincerity" that the carefully wrought sentence lacks, and this explains why an audience will ordinarily listen with interest to a speaker even when he gropes and fumbles for words but will respond with murky boredom when a prepared speech is read to them.[11] The contrast is

---

11 Some years ago I was invited to give a talk on "The Archaic Language of Shakespeare's *The First Part of Henry the Fourth,*" a subject scarcely calculated to compel wide-eyed and open-mouthed fascination. The audience was the freshman composition class at the University of Minnesota in lots of about fifteen hundred at a time at the huge Northrup Auditorium. Since I was at some distance from the first row, the members of the audience were unable to see whether this was an extemporaneous talk or whether it was being read to them. I took the precaution of chopping the sentences of the first two paragraphs into fragments, and from there on I could read the rest of the talk. Apparently I had convinced many of the students that this was an extemporaneous offering, for a surprising number of them stopped me in the corridor later during the year to thank me for the "interesting" talk.

comparable to that between the young man fumbling awkwardly through a marriage proposal or a job interview or a request for a raise in pay and the "city slicker" who can make every word fall neatly into place, but who, as we all realize, is every inch a scamp.

Among matters that are accorded special reverence is, as we realize, the familiar rule governing the "complete" sentence. The suggestion that a fragmentary or a stop-and-go sentence is at times preferable to a nicely engineered sentence, complete with subject and predicate, offers violence to one of our most precious classroom traditions.

That is why the fragmentary sentence and anacoluthon are important in English usage. The complete-sentence rule is nothing more than a broad generalization; there is no point in trying to find ways to break it on the flimsy grounds that "Rules are meant to be broken," but there are times when exceptions are desirable. Typically the "right" people have the language sensitivity and the social sense to recognize such times; the others as typically fear to break the rule at all.

word index

Page numbers in *italics* indicate specialized treatment of words.

a/an, 91, 175, 253
a-, 296, 313
abdomen, 76
abed, 297
abide/abode/(-ed), 207
about/'bout, 300
acclimate, 76
across/acrosst, 90
actual, 95
acute/'cute, 301
addendum/-a, 140
address, 76
ado, 184
adult, 76
advantage/'vantage, 301
advisor, 82
aerial (*see* antenna)
after, 257
aftermath (*see* mow)
against, 89
aged, 69
agendum/-a, 140
agriculture, 95
ain't, 2, 12, 86, 202, 225, *344*
airplane/(')plane, 301
à la carte, 117
à la mode, 117
alcohol, 99, 115
alike, 296–297
alkaline, 114
all, 269
all right, 100, 269
alma mater, 120
almond, 100
almost/most, 100, 269, 302
alms, 87, 99, 136
already, 100, 269
also, 269
altar, 100
alternate, 113
altogether, 269
alumna/æ, 139
alumnus/-i, 139
always, 100, 269
am, 326
amateur, 95
ameba/-æ, 139
amends, 137
among, *278–279*
amongst, 90
amphibian, 298
an, *83, 91,* 175, 253
analine, 114
analysis/-es, 141
-ance, 292
and, 85, 92, 164–165, 280–281

andante, 118
annihilate, 83
an't (*see* ain't)
antelope, 134
antenna, 139
anti-, 297
any, 124
anybody, 74, 333
anymore, 286–287
anyone, 333
apparatus, 112–113, 139–140
appear, 264–265
appendix, 137, 141
applicable, 76
apron, 115
are, 109
are'nt, 66, 345
arid, 307
around/round, 301
arthritis, 89
as, 166–167, 263, *282–284,* 286–287
asinine, 114
ask, 54, 106, 110, 115,
ask/-ed, 109
asleep, 297
associate, 96
at, 184, 277
-ate, 304
athlete, 89
athletics, 136
attack(t), 90
attention ('tenshun), 301
aught, 286
aunt, 106
aural, 109
automobile, 76
aversion, 97
awake(n), 218
aware, 296–297
awful, 270
awfully, 270, 272
axis/-es, 141
azure, 97

baa, 58–59
babble, 113
baby-sit, *312–313*
bacillus/-i, 139
back (in . . of), *278*
bacterium/-a, 140
bad/worse/worst, 254
bad/-ly, 264
bade, 82
badly (feel), *266*
balances, 137
balcony, 98
balditude, 305
balk, 98
balm, 89
balmy, 100
baloney, 72
barmy (*see* balmy)
barracks, 136
basis/-es, 141
bass, 134
bath, 135
be, 152, 162, 174, 181, 185, 187, 190, 232, *234–236,* 325–326, 341, 343
be-, 296, 313
bear, (n.) 134
bear/bore/born(e), 210, 215–216
bear/birth, 304
beat/-en, 195
beatnik, 294
becalm, 296
because/'cause, 285, 300
become, 162, 174, 264–265, 296
bedeck, 296
bedizen, 296
beef, 135
been, 103
before, 257, 278
beg/beggar, 312
begin, 209–211, 232–233, 296
begonia, 72
behave/-ed, 198, 296
behead, 296
behind, 257, 278
belfry, 86
believe, 75, 296
belladonna, 295
bellicose, 295
bellows, 137
beloved, 69
bend/bent/(-ed), 197
beneath, 257
bequeath, 296
bereave/bereft, 193, 198, 296
beseech/besought/-ed, 194

best (*see* good)
bet, 195
better, 254
(had better), 248
between, *278–279*
betwixt, 90
bid/bade/bidden, 222, 224–225
big/bigger/biggest, 254
bind/bound/bounden, 201, 208–209
bird, 115
birth (*see* bear)
bison, 134
bite/bit/bitten, 202, 205, 214
black, 261
bleed/bled, 197
bless/blest/blessed, 69, 198
blouse, 132
blow/blew/blown, 218–220
blown, 88
boatswain, 83
book, 131
boot, 104
boredom, 305
botany, 312
both, 279
bottle, 98
bra, 58–59
braid, 208
brand, 270
brandy, 115
brang/brung, 194, 201, 231
(*See also* bring)
bravo, 118
brazen, 304
brazier, 97
breadth (*see* broad)
break/broke/broken, 215–217
breakfast, 73
breeches, 102, 136
breed/bred, 197
bride, 115
bring/brought, 194, 226
britches (*see* breeches)
broad/breadth, 304
broadcast (*see* cast)
bronchial, 115
brooch, 103
broom, 104
brother/brethren, 133
brother-in-law, 91–92
brotherhood, 303
buckaroo, 118
buffalo, 134
build/built/(-ed), 197
bulb, 99
bulk, 98
bumpkin, 294
bureau, 104
-burger, 313
burgle, 312–313
burial, 138
burn/-ed/-t, 198
burst/(-ed), 195
bush, 57
business, 86–88
bust/(-ed), 195–196
busy, 41, 101–102
but, 166–167, 281, 286, 346
butte, 104
buy/bought, 194
by, 277

caboose, 132
cactus/-i, 139
cadge, 312
cafeteria, 313
cain't (*see* can't)
calf/-ves, 99, 106, 135
call, 321
calm, 89, 99
calve, 99
can, 49, 125, 183, 234–235, *240–242*, 245, 247, 249, 341
candelabrum/-a, 140
canonize, 304
can't, 19, 49, 86, 241, 345
captain, 85
card, 109
careful, 304
cast, 192, 195
catafalque, 98
catch/caught, 194–195, 231
catercornered, 86
caterpillar, 87
cause, 183
cavalry, 115
cave canem, 120
cayman, 132
ceaseless, 261

cement, 70, 75
cent, 289
centigrade, 118–119
centimeter, 118
centipede, 118–119
century, 95
ceramics, 70
certain, 93
chain-react, 312
chair, 87
chalk, 98
char, 312
character, 26
cherry, 138
cherub/-im, 141
chic, 258–259
chicken, 108
chide/(chid)/chode/chidden, 205–206
chief, 135, 261
child/children, 115, 132–133
childhood, 303
chili, 118
chimbley (*see* chimney)
chimney, 91
choose/chose/chosen, 207–208, 210, 321
church, 155
civilize, 304
clapboard, 73
class, 332
classis/-es, 141
clean, 269
cleave/clove/cloven (cleft, cleavage), 208
clerk, 83, 93
clerkdom, 305
click (*see* clique)
climb, 213
cling/clung, 212, 232
clippers, 137
clique, 102–103
clock, 105
close(t), 90
cloth, 135
  -es, 82
coarse, 109
coffee, 105, 115
coiffure, 117
colonel, 87
combatant, 76
come/came/come, 215–216, 222, 225–226, 232–233, 265
committee, 332
complete, 261
comprehensiveness, 304
comptroller, 82
confusion, 97
controller (*see* comptroller)
conversion, 97
cookie, 115
cool/coolth, 304
coop, 103
coordinate, 311
coot, 104
cord, 109
cordial, 95
corpus/corpora, 139
corrupt, 70
cortex/-ices, 141
cost, 195
cough, 105
could, 70, 100, 183, 234–235, 240, 247, 249
  coulda, 70
coup d'etat, 116
coupe, 116–117
couple, 332
coupon, 105
course, 109
courteous, 95
cousin, 108
couth, 300
coven, 332
cow/kine, 131, 133
crabbed, 69
creature, 97
creek, 102
creep/crept, 193
crick (*see* creek)
crisis/-es, 131
criterion/a, 141
critter (*see* creature)
crocus, 139, 142
crook, 69
crosier, 97
crosswise (*see* -wise)
crow/crew/crowed, 219
crowd, 332
crux, 141
crystalline, 114
culture, 95
cumulus/-i, 139
cupboard, 73

cupful, 143
curious/-er, 258
curriculum/-a, 140
  -vitae, 121
curse/curst/cursed, 69, 198
cut, 182, 195
cute, 104, 301
-cy, 305

dachshund, 118
dais, 82
dare/(dassn't)/durst, 237, 239
darkness, 303
data, 112–113
datum/-a, 140
dead, 261
  dead/death, 304
deal/dealt, 193
dear/dearth, 304
debt, 82
debutante, 117
decadent, 312
decision, 97
deep/depth, 304
deer, 133–134
defatigable, 300
destruct, 312
diagnose, 312
dialog, 3
diamond, 88
diarrhea, 72
didn't, 86
dime, 289
disastrous, 89
dishevel, 312
disinterested, *303*
disturbance, 295
dive/dove/-ed, 19, 207
diversion, 97
dizzy, 41
do/did/done, 184, 222, 223, *230*, 233, 234–235, 341–343
doctoral, 114
does, 53, 186
doesn't, 86, 343–344
  (*See also* don't)
dog, 105
dogdom, 305
dogged, 69
dogma, 141
dollar, 289
-dom, 292, 303, 305
donate, 311
don't, 66
  it don't, 2, 12, 86, 202, 211, *343–344*
doth, 187
doubt, 82
dour, 82
down, 224
  and out, 79
draft, 83
drama, 113
draught (*see* draft)
draw/drew/drawn, 217, 219–220
dreadful, 270
dream/-ed/-t, 193
dregs, 137
drink/drank/drunk, 191, 210–212, 223, 232
drive/drove/driven, 201, 204
drought, 304–305
drouth (*see* dry)
drove, 332
drownded, 91
dry/drouth, 304
duke, 104
dummox, 132
duty, 104

earth, 93
easier, 97
easy, 78
eat/ate/eaten (et), 83, 195, 216, 222, *226–227*, 232
eclair, 117
edgewise (*see* -wise)
educate, 95, 97
effectiveness, 304
either, 279, 281, 336
elder/eldest, 254–255
electoral, 114
eleven, 85
elf, 99, 135
elk, 98–99, 134
ellipsis/-es, 141
elm, 89, 98
else, 167, 320
'em, 171
embalmer, 99

embellishment, 295
embrace, 103
emerald, 88
empty, 261
-en, 304
enchilada, 118
encore, 118
endive, 119
engage, 103
engagement, 118
engine, 103
enjoy, 103
enough, 296
ensemble, 118
entente, 118
enthuse, 312
entourage, 118
entree, 118
entry, 118
envelope, 118–119
envoy, 118–119
epitome, 83
e pluribus unum, 120
ept, 300
-er, 91, 279
erratum/-a, 140
escalate, 105
escape, 114
especially ('specially), 301
esquire/squire, 301
eternal (*see* tarnal)
even, 267
evening, 89
evenings, 292
everybody, 74, 334
everyone, 334
except/('cept), 166, 300
excuse/('scuse), 300
execute/-ive, 84
exposure, 97
extra, 72
extreme, 261
eye/eyen, 133

facetious, 2
failure, 100
fairly, 268
faith, 39
falcon, 98
fall/fell/fallen, 201, 219–220, 223, 265
family, 332
famousest, 259
far/farther/farthest, 93, 255
fashion, 108
fast, 253, 267
fatal, 261
feckless, 295
feed/fed, 197
feel/felt, 193, 265
fellowship, 2, 303
feminine, 114
fetters, 137
few/fewer/fewest, *256*
fiancée, 117
fifths, 109
fight/fought, 194, 202, 208, 213–214
film, 89, 98
filth (*see* foul)
final, 261
find/found, 209
fine, 267
finish, 292
first, 257
fish, 134
fission, 96
fit/(-ed), 195, 196
flammable (*see* inflammable)
flat, 270
flavor, 308–309
flee/fled, 197, 220
fling/flung, 208, 212, 232
flock, 332
flow/flowed, 219–220
fly/flew/flown, 219–220
(flied), 220
focus/-i, 139
fog, 105
folk, 98
food, 104
fool, 104
foolishness, 303
foot/feet, 131
for, 109, 277, 296
forbear, 296
forbid, 225, 296
(*See also* bid)
forceps, 236
forecastle, 83
forehead, 73, 83
foreign, 105
forget, 2l0, 296
(*See also* get)

forgive, 296
forlorn, 296
former/foremost, 257
formidable, 76
formula, 139
forsake/forsook/forsaken, 217, 232, 296
fortune, 94, 97
foul/filth, 304
four, 109
freedom, 302
freeze/froze/frozen, 202, 208
friendship, 303
frog, 105
from, 277
front (in . . of), 278
fuel, 104
-ful, 304
fulfil, 87
full, 261, 269
fungus/-i, 139
furor, 308–309
further/furthest, 255
fury, 309
future, 95

gallows, 137
gamble, 90
gamesmanship, 304
garage, 41, 70
garçon, 116
gas, 115
gaseous, 113
gasoline, 114
gendarme, 41
genre, 41
gentle/-ly, 264
gentleman, 291–292
gentry, 138
genuine, 114
genus/genera, 139
get/got/gotten, 199, 216, 222, 227–229, 237, 265
  gotta, 228
  gots, 229
ghouls, 104
gild/gilt(-ed), 197
gird/girt(-ed), 197
gird/girth, 304
give/gave/given, 216, 222, 225–226, 321
gladiolus, 139
gladness, 304
glamor, 308
gleam, 102
glim (*see* gleam)
go/went/gone, 182, 198, 222, *230*, 265
  (going to), 245
goat, 131
golden, 304
golf, 99
gonna, 70, 85, 104, 245
  (*See also* going to)
good/better/best, 254–255
good and, 270
good-bye, 302
goodness, 303
goodnight, 302
goose/geese, 131
gorgeous, 97
gourmet, 117
governess, 87
government, 87
governor, 87
goy/-im, 142
graceful, 304
graduate, 95
grammar, 289, 308
granary, 112
grandeur, 95
grandpa, 85
grass, 115
gratis, 112
greasy, 77–78
greatness, 304
greed, 312
grievous, 26, 114
grind/ground, 209
groovy/-er, 259
grouse, 134
grovel, 312
grow/grew/grown, 219–220, 265
  grown, 88
grow/growth, 304
gruntle, 299–300
gubernatorial, 114
gules, 104
gulf, 99
gymnasium, 140

habeas corpus, 120
hairdo (*see* coiffure)

hale/health, 304
half, 99, 135
handkerchief (*see* kerchief)
hang/hung/hanged, *214–215,* 223, 232
happiness, 304
harass, 76
hard, 253, 267
hardly, 346
has, 40, 42, 84
 (*See also* have)
has to, 84–85
hasn't, 86
hath, 187
have/had, 42, 70, 185, 186, 190, 198–199, 234–235, 343
 have to, 84–85, 238
 haven't, 66
 haz, 42
he, 150–168, 328
headquarters, 136
health (*see* hale)
hearken, 93
heart, 93
hearth, 93
heat/-ed (het), 197
heave/hove(ed), 216–217
heavy/-iest, 259
heinous, 114
helicopter, 298, 312
help, 99, 213–214
her, 158–159, 165
herb, 83
heretical, 83
hers, 175
herself, 99, 176–177
hew/hewed/hewn, 219–220
hiccough, 83
hide/hid/hidden, 205, 210
high/height, 267, 304
him, 158–170
himself, 99, 176–177
hinder/hindmost, 257–258
his, 158–159, 175–176, 252, 333–334
historian, 83
historical, 83
hog, 105
hold/held (holden), 219–220
holp (*see* help)
homage, 83
homeward (*see* -ward)
homogeneous, 114
honest, 261
honor, 83, 208–209
-hood, 292, 303–304
hood/hoodlum, 104, 142
hoof, 103, 135
hoop, 103
hoosegow, 118
hoot, 104
hopefully, 2, *272*
horrify, 304
horror, 309
hors d'oeuvres, 117
horse, 133
horticulture, 95
hose/hosen, 133
hosiery, 97
hotel, 83
hour, 83
house, 79, 132, 135
however, 263
hue, 104
humane, 83
humor/-id, 310–311
hurt/(-ed), 195–196
husband, 292
hysterical, 83
hysterics, 136

I, 150, 152, 326
idea, 72, 75
 idear, 91–92
-id, 307–309
idiot (ijjit, idget), 96
-ify, 304
ignoramus, 113
ill/worse/worst, 254
illegal, 126
illegitimate, 126
illogical, 126
illuminate, 126
illusion, 126
illustrate, 126
imaginary, 92
imbecile, 126
immediately, 95
immerse, 126
immobile, 126
immoral, 126
immure, 126
imperil, 126

impossible, 126, 261
imprison, 126
in, 277–278
index, 141
indigo, 126
individual, 95
ineffectual, 295
inelegant, 126
inert, 126
infantile, 114
infidel, 126
infinite, 261
infirm, 126
inflame, 126, 302
inflammable, 126, *302*
inflate, 126
influence, 126
inform, 126
infrequent, 126
infuriate, 126
-ing, 108
ingot, 126
-in-law, 143–144
inside of, 278
inspectordom, 305
insurance, 75
interesting, 88
international, 85
interpret, 87
into, 278
iron, 115
irradiate, 126
irregardless, *302–303*
irreligious, 126
irrespective, 126, 302
irreverent, 126
irrigate, 126
irruption, 126
is, 40, 42, 84, 264–265, 326
isn't, 86
issue, 96
it, 150–158, 328–329
its, 157*n.*
itself, 176–177
-itude, 292–305
-ity, 292
-ize, 304

judgeship, 303
just, 261
juvenile, 114
juzgado (*see* hoosegow)

keep/kept, 193, 265
kempt, 299–300
kerchief, 135
kibbutz/-im, 142
-kin, 294
kind of, 271
kindergarten, 118
kine, 133
(*See also* cow)
kingdom, 303
kitty-cornered (*see* catercornered)
kneel/knelt, 193
knickers, 136
knife/-ves, 135
knit/knitted, 197
know/knew/known (knowed), 219–221, 225, 232

laissez faire, 116
lariat, la riata, 118
larva/-æ, 139
larynx, 115
lasagna, 118
late, 267
laugh, 106
law, 58–59
lay/laid, 198, 222–224
lead/led, 197, 295
leaden, 304
leaf/-ves, 135
leap/leapt, 193
learned, 69
learning, book-, 93
least, 235, 257
(*See also* less)
leave/left, 193
lees, 137
leeward (*see* -ward)
legislate, 311
legislature, 95
lend/lent, 197
length (*see* long)
lengthwise (*see* -wise)
lens, 137
-less, 302, 304
less/lesser, *255–256*, 260

let, 162, 169, 195
let's, *169*
library, 87
license, 138
lie/lay/lain, 88, 216, *222–224*
life/-ves, 135
light/lit/(litten), 205
like, 166, *282–284,* 292
-like, 264, 267, 292
likelihood, 303
lingerie, 117
liquor/-id, 310
literature, 95
little/littler/littlest, 98, 255–256
loaf, 135
locate, 304
locus/-i, 139
long/length, 304
look, 265
loose, 267
lose/lost, 193
loud, 267
louse/lice, 131
low, 267
luxury, /-ious, 84
-ly, 264, 268, 292–293

macron, 113
magna cum laude, 120
majestic, 97
make/made, 184, 199, 233, 321, 342
man/men, 131, 178, 293
manlike, 264, 294
manly, 294
mannikin, 294
mannish, 294
many/more/most, 255–256
margarine, 114
marinate, 304
marquee, 138
marry, 109
mathematics, 136
matinee, 117
matrix, 113, 141
maxi-, 297
may, 125, 183, 234, 240–242, 245, 247, 249
mayn't, 241, 343–344
mayonnaise, 117
me, 158–168
  it's me, 17, 158, *162–165,* 166
mean/meant, 193
means, 136
measles, 136
measure, 97
medium, 140
meet/met, 197
melt/-ed/molten, 213–214
menu, 117
mercantile, 114
merciful, 304
merry, 109
merry/mirth, 304
mezzanine, 114
micro-, 297
mid, 296
mid/midst, 89–90
midi-, 297
midwife, 296
might, 183, 234–235, 247, 249
mighty, 270
  -iest, 259
milieu, 118
milk, 98, 99
million, 100
mindless, 304
mine, 175
mini-, 297
mirth (*see* merry)
mischievous, 76, 114
mislead/misled, 26, 69, 295
mohair, 115
molasses, 136
molten (*see* melt)
mongoose, 132
monsieur, 118
moon, 104
moose, 132, 134
moot, 104
more, 254, 255–256, *258–260,* 262, 268
  or less, 271
morning, 109
most, 254, 255, *258–260,* 268
mother-in-law, 142–144
mountain, 62, 108
mourning, 109
mouse/mice, 131
mouthful, 135
mow/(after)math, 304
mow/mowed/mown, 192, 219–220
much/more/most, 255, 267–268
muchly, 268

mugwump, 115
mulberry, 86
multiversity, 298
mumps, 136
muse, 104
museum, 75
must, 125, 183, 234–235, 237, 239, 245
mute, 104
my, 91, 158, 175
myself, *177*

'n', 86
naked, 69
namely, 263
nasty/nastily, 264
nation, 96
nature, 94–95, 97
naught, 286
nauseate, 304
nebula/-æ, 139
need, 238–239
needs, 89
negligee, 117
neighborhood, 303
neither, 281, 286, 336
nephew, 40
-ness, 292, 303–304
nether/nethermost, 297
neuralgia, 72
neurosis/-es, 141
never, 263, 342
nevertheless, 263
news, 26, 104, 137
nice and, 270
nickel, 289
night, 131
-nik, 294
nobody, 74, 335
none, *334–335*
noon, 104–105
nor, 281, 286
normalcy, 305
nostrum, 140
not, 105, 263, 341–345
nother, 66
nothingness, 303
notify, 304
nowadays, 287, 292
nowhere, 263
nuclear, 115, 291
nucleus, 139
nudnik, 294
number, 332
nut, 131

oak, 131
oasis/-es, 141
oats, 136
obligatory, 76
ocean, 96
octopus, 141
odds, 137
of, 40, 53, 277, 318–320
office, 105
officialdom, 305
often, 82
old/older/oldest, 254–255
omnibus (omnibi), 142
on, 105, 277
once(t), 90
one, *178*, 336–337
ones, 153
ongoing, 2
ooze, 104
opus/opera, 140
or, 164–165, 281
-or, 308
oral, 109
orange, 105
order, 183
organize, 304
orphan(t), 90
other, 167, 279
ottoman, 132
ought, 237–238, 245
our [ours (ourn)], 109, 175
ourselves, 178
out/outer/outermost, 257
over, 297
oversee, 297
ovum/-a, 140
owe, owed, 237–238
own, 237
ox/oxen (oxes), 132

pains, 136
pajamas, 136
palm, 89, 99

pants, 136
papoose, 115, 132
parachute, 298
paradigm, 298
paramedic, 298
paramilitary, 298
paraphernalia, 298
parasol, 298
parenthesis/-es, 141
parliament, 82
parson, 93
particular, 87
pass, 54, 105
pastoral, 114
path, 135
patient, 96
patriot, 113
pea, 138
peasant, 90
pen, 103, 111
penniless, 304
per, 278
percolate, 105
perfect, 81, 261–262, 295
performance, 87
pericynthion, perilune, 298–299
person, 93, 178
perspiration, 115
petunia, 72
phenomenon/-a, 141
phon-, 75
phone, 301
physics, 136
picture, 26, 95
pin, 103, 111
pincers, 136
pizza, 118
placate, 304
plead/pled/pleaded, 197
pleasantest, 259
pleasure, 97
plenty, 270
pliers, 136
pneumonia, 72
police, 75
poor, 104
poorly, 266
potato ('tatoes), 301
powerful, 270, 303
powerful/-est, 259
premiere, 117
presidential, 114
prettiest, 259
pretty, 115, 268, 271
priesthood, 302
pro-, 297
proceeds, 136
prognose, 312
propitiate, 96
protégé, 118
prove, 265
psalm, 99
psalter, 100
pulp, 98–99
puny, 104
pure, 104
push, 57, 59
put, 195–196

qualify, 304
quick, 267
quinine, 114
quit, 197
quite, 263, 268, 271–272
quorum, 140

radiator, 113
radio, 113
radius/-i, 139
raise, 223
-rama, 313
rancid/rancor, 310
rather, 54, 167, 248, 263, 268, 271
ration, 112
read/read, 197
real/really, 270
rebellion, 295
recognize, 115
redness, 304
refectory, 295
regardless, 302
region, 97
reindeer (*see* deer)
religious, 70
remain, 265
rend/rent(-ed), 197
request, 183
res, 139

reservoir, 87
ribald, 82
riches, 136
rid/(-ed), 195, 196
riddle, 138
ride/rode/ridden, 204
right, 261, 267, 270, 295
righteous, 95
rigmarole, 89
rigor/rigid, 309–310
ring/rang/rung, 208–211, 232
rise/rose/risen, 204, 223
roof, 103
room, 103
root, 103
rostrum, 140
rouge, 41
rough, 267
round, 261–262, 301
ruin, 108
ruinate, 311
run/ran/run, 210, *213*, 225, 232–233, 265

sailor, 82
saith, 187
salmon, 100
salmonella, 100
salve, 99
same, 328
sauerkraut, 118
save, 166
savings, 136
saw/sawed/sawn, 219–220
say/said (says, saith), 186, 199
scales, 137
scarce, 267
scarcely, 346
scare/scared (scairt), 198
scarf, 135
scavenge, 312
schedule, 26
schmoo/schmoon, 133
scholarly, 264
scissors, 136
scrutable, 300
secret/-est, 259
secretary, 87
see/saw/seen (seed), 9, 183, 216, 222, 225, 229, 233
seek/sought, 194
seem, 264–265
seethe/sod/sodden (seethed, soddened), 221–222
self, 99, 135
-self, 176
sell/sold, 198
senator, 82
senatorial, 114
send/sent, 197
sentence, 85
seraph/-im, 141
sergeant, 93
sermon(t), 90, 93
set, 195, 198, 223
seven, 85
several, 88
sew/sewed/sewn, 219–220
shake/shook/shaken, 217
shall, 183, 234–235, 240, *242–249*
shambles, 136
shan't, 86
shay, 138
she, 150–168, 328
sheaf/-ves, 135
shear/-ed/shorn, 137, 215–216
sheath, 135
shed, 195
sheep, 133
shelf/-ves, 99, 135
sherbet, 114
sheveled, 299
shine/shone/(-ed), 207
-ship, 303
shit, 195
shivers, 136
shoe/shoon, 133
shop, 105
shorts, 136
should, 100, 183, 234, 236, 238, 240, 244, 248–249
show/showed/shown, 219–220
shred/-ed, 197
shrink/shrank/shrunk (-en), 209–211, 232
shrive/(-ed)/shrove/shriven, 205–206
shut, 195
sickness, 303
sidewise (*see* -wise)
silk, 99
sin/-ful, 295

sine die, 120
sing/sang/sung, 182, 200, 209–211, 232–233
sink/sank/sunk(-en), 209–211, 232
sinus, 140
sipid, 300, 307
siren, 115
sister/sistern, 133
sit/sat, 216, *222–224*, 265
sixths, 109
skate, 138
sky, 292
slacks, 136
slay/slew/slain, 217, 219–220, 232
sleek, 102
sleep/slept, 193
slick (*see* sleek)
slide/slid/(slud), 203–205
slime/-y, 295
sling/slung/(slang), 212–213, 232
slink/slunk, 212–213, 232–233
slow, 17, 267–268
slow/(sloth), 304
sly/sleight, 304
smell/smelt/smelled, 198, 265
smite/smote/smitten, 204, 232
so, 286–287
sod, 105
soda, 72
sofa, 115
soft, 267
soldier, 95
solecism, 82
some, 124
somebody, 74
something, 271
sometimes, 292
somewhat, 263, 268, 271–272
soon, 248, 267–268
soot, 102
sore, 269
sorrowful, 304
sorry, 105
sort of, 271
sounded, 91
sow/sowed/sown, 219–220
speak/spoke/spoken, 216–217, 221, 232
special, 96
specially, 301
speed/sped, 197
spend/spent, 197
spill/spilt/spilled, 198
spill/spilth, 304
spin/spun (span), 212–213
spirit (spirt), 70
spit/(spat)/spitted, 195, 197
splendor/-id, 309–310
split, 195, 197
spoon, 104
spoonful, 142–143
spouse, 132
spread, 195
spring/sprang/sprung, 209–211, 232
sputnik, 294
squalor/-id, 309
square, 261
squaw, 115
squire, 301
stadium, 140
staff, 135
stairs, 136
stand/stood, 75, 222, 226, 265
star, 93
stardom, 303
stark, 270
status, 112–113
stay, 265
steal/stealth, 304
steal/stole/stolen, 215–216
stigma/-ata, 141
stimulus/-i, 139
sting/stung, 201, 212–213, 232
stink/stank/stunk, 209–211, 232
stolid, 307
stomach/tummy, 301
stratum/-a, 112, 140
stride/strode/stridden/(-ed), 205–206
strike/struck/stricken, 20l, 203–206
string/strung, 208, 212, 232
strive/strove/striven, 205–206, 232, 292
strong/strength, 304
stupor/-id, 309
succumb, 70
sugar, 96
suggest, 83
suggestion, 95
sumac, 96
super-, 297
superintendent, 88
supervise, 297

suppose (spose), 300
supposed to, 84–85
supreme, 261
sure, 96
surprise, 87
survey, 297
swang, 19, 233
(*See also* swing)
swear/swore/sworn, 216
sweat/-ed, 197
sweep/swept/(swep'), 193
swell/-ed/swollen (swoled), 198, 213–214
swim/swam/swum, 209–211, 232
swine, 133
swing/swung/(swang), 212–213, 232
swooned, 91
syllabus/-i, 139
symposium/-a, 140
synthesis/-es, 141

taco, 118
take/took/taken, 199, 201, 217, 232, 292
talc, 99
talisman, 132
talk/-ed, 98, 201
tarnal, 93
teach/taught, 193–194
team, 332
tear/tore/torn, 215–216
tedious, 95
telegraph, 298
telephone/'phone, 298, 301
telescope, 298
television, 298
tell/told, 198
teraph/-im, 142
-teria, 313
terrible, 270
terror, 308–309
terrorize, 304
than, 166–167, 262
thanks, 136
that, 124, 285, 322, 329–331
the, 124, 154, 253, 316, 322, 329
theater, 26, 76, 82
thee, 158–159
their, 109
-s, 175
them, 157–171, 322
theme, 141
themselves, 176
then, 280
there, 109
thermometer, 87
these, 316, 322
thesis/-es, 141
they, 151–159, 178, 328, 334
they're, 109
thief/-ves, 135
thief/theft, 304
thimble, 90
thine, 91, 175
think/thought, 194
this, 124, 316, 322
those, 322
thou, 151–153, 159
thrive/throve/thriven/(-ed), 205–206
throw/threw/thrown, 219–220
thrust, 195
thunder, 91
thusly, 268
thy, *91*, 175
tight, 267
tights, 136
till ('til), 184, 301–302
till/tilth, 304
tissue, 96
titmouse, 132
to, *183–185,* 276–277
tobacco, 115
tongs, 136
tooth/teeth, 131
top (on . . of), 278
topless, 304
torpor/-id, 309
torso, 155
tortilla, 118
toward (*see* -ward)
tread/trod/trodden/-ed/treaded, 192, 216
221
tremble, 90
trepid, 300, 308
triphibian, 298
trot, 221
(*See also* tread)
trousers, 136
trout, 134
true/truth, 304

trunks, 136
tumble, 90
tumor/-id, 310
tune, 104
turbine, 295
turbulent, 295
turf, 135
turn, 265
tutor, 82
tweezers, 136
twelve, 99
twice (twicet), 90

umbrella, 75, 89
umlaut, 118
un-, 297
uncoil, undo, etc., 297
uncommonest, 259
uninterested, 303
unique, 261–262
university, 93, 298
unlax, 297
unluckiest, 259
up, 218
upon, 278
upright, 295
upward (*see* -ward)
us, 53, 158–170
use, 42, 104
used to, 84–85
usher/(ush), 312–313
usual, 97
usury, 97
utter/utmost, 257

valor/-id, 310–311
valuable, 88, 100
vanguard, 300
vantage, 300
vapor/-id, 310
vaquero (*see* buckaroo)
varmint, 90, 93
varsity, 93
vehement, 83
vehicle, 83
verdure, 95, 97
vermin, 93
versatile, 114
version, 97
vertebra/-æ, 139
vertex, 141
very, 260, 263, 269, 272
via, 278
victuals, 82
vietnik, 294
viewpoint, 104
virgin, 97
virtue, 94–95
virtuous/-est, 95, 259
vision, 97
vortex/-ices, 141
vouchsafe, 3

wages, 136
wagon, 108
waistcoat, 73
wake/woke/waked, 217–218
waken/-ed, 218
walk, 98, 182
wampum, 115
want, 70, 239
-ward, 292
warm/warmth, 304
was, 40, 42, 53, 84
(you was), *326–327*
wash (warsh), 59, 106
we, 169, 178–179
weal/wealth, 304
wear/wore/worn, 216
weariness, 303
weave/wove/woven/(-ed), 216–217
wed/-ed, 197
weep/wept, 193
well/better/best, 254, 266
wend/wended/went, 198
were (. . if I were . .), 234–236
wet, 197
what, 330
which, 329–330
while/whilst, 89–90
who, 104, 159, 161, 171–174, 329
whom, *161,* 165, 329–331
whose, 171
wicked, 69
wiener, 118
wife/-ves, 135
wilful, 99

will, 125, 183, 234, 236, 240, *243–249*
willy-nilly, 340
win/won, 212, 227
wind/wound, 209
window, 290–291
wisdom, 303
-wise, *273*
wish/t, 90
wit/wot, 237
with, 277, 296
withdraw, 296
withhold, 296
within, 278
withstand, 296
witless, 304
wolf/-ves, 135
woman/women, 131
won't, 86
wooden, 304
work/-ed/*also* wrought, 194
world, 155
worse, 254
  (worser), 260
worst, 254
would, 100, 183, 234, 236, 240, 244, 248–249
wouldn't, 86
wreak/wreaked, 194
wring/wrung, 212, 232
write/wrote/written, 202–203, 204, 210, 232
wrong, 261, 267

yacht, 115
ye, 152, 158–159, 322
ye (the), 41*n.*
yelp, 213
yolk, 98
you, 150, 178, 322
you all, 153
your, yours, 175–176

subject index

Absolute adjectives, 261–262
Absolute genitives, 174–176
Academy, French, 7
Accusative case, 158–159, 168, 320–321
Adams, Henry (1838–1918), 151
Addison, Joseph (1672–1719), 146
Adjective derivations, 304, 307–309
Adjectives, 88, 155–156, 175, 191, 251–273, 317, 325
Adverbs, 143, 244, 251–254, 263–273, 292, 340
  dangling, 272–273
  flat, 267, 292
Advertising, 105, 282–283
Affixes, 294–295, 304
Affricates, 37, 94
Afrikaans, 342*n.*
Agreement, 316–317, 324–325, 328
Alfred the Great (849–899), 74*n.*, 345
Alger, Horatio (1832–1899), 124*n.*
Allomorphs, 126, 129, 189–190
Allophones, 49
Alphabet, phonetic, 27–28, 45–46
Alveolar consonants, 33, 36–38, 43
Ambiguity, 93, 143, 158, 188, 265, 321, 328
American English, 12, 18–20, 58–59, 97, 110–111, 113, 178, 227–228, 231
Ampersand, 85, 281
Anacoluthon, 349–358
Analogy, 138, 226
  constructions, 166, 167, 278
  Latin, 8, 162
  leveling by, 215
  pitfalls of, 204
  pronunciation, 57, 114
  spelling, 100
  verbs, 201
  word forms, 78, 87, 89, 90, 98, 105
Analytic language, 157, 258, 316
Anglo-Saxon, 41, 74
  (*See also* Old English)
Anomalies, 121, 198, 202, 325
  (*See also* Verbs, anomalous)
Antecedents, 328, 331–332
Apheresis, 300–302
Apostrophe, 146–147, 301–302
Appositive, 143, 170
Arabic, 55, 115, 296
Archaic inflections, 133, 134, 197, 203, 256, 260
Archaic participles, 204, 206, 207, 212, 214
Archaic poetry, 158, 175
Archaic preterites, 213
Archaic spelling, 352
Archaic style, 146, 193–194
Archaic subjunctives, 236, 241

Archaic substandard speech, 176, 265, 266
Archaic words, 237, 257, 269, 270
"Areopagitica," 353
Arizona Highways, 284
Articles:
  definite, 144, 154–155, 157, 171, 253–254, 316–317, 321–322
  indefinite, 83, 253, 317
Articulation, 34–36, 56
  (*See also* specific type)
Artificial language, 76, 101, 130
  (*See also* Esperanto)
Ascham, Roger (1515–1568), 7
Assimilation, 84–87, 94, 99, 109
Attributive, 174–175, 264, 310
Authoritarian, 3, 239
Authority, 62, 349–350, 353
Auxiliaries, verb, 182–183, 190, 199, 234–249, 340–343

Back formation, 84, 137–139, 299, 300, 311–313
Back vowels, 52–54, 93
Backing, 54, 92–94, 106
Bad English, 3, 13, 20, 98, 107–115
Base:
  noun, 129, 132–133, 135, 146
  verb, 182–183, 186–187, 189, 191, 229
  word, 290, 292–295, 304, 325
Beckett, Samuel (1906–), 348
Bennett, James Gordon (1795–1872), 137
Beowulf, 7, 44*n.*, 244, 260, 349
Bible (*see* King James Bible; Revised Standard Bible)
Bierce, Ambrose (1842–1914?), 243
Bilabial consonants, 36–39
Black speech, 23, 342*n.*
Bloomfield, Leonard (1887–1949), 12
Bloomfield, Morton (1913–), 202*n.*
Boas, Franz (1858–1942),12
Bradley, Henry (1845–1923), 243
British pronunciation, 26, 43, 75, 90, 93, 95–97, 103
British words, 178, 227, 243
Brown, Goold (1791–1857), 211, 213, 232
Bryant, Margaret M. (1900–), 16
Bunyan, John (1628–1688), 195
Burns, Robert (1759–1796), 170, 236
Byron, George Gordon, Lord (1788–1824), 237

Cæsar, Gaius Julius (100–44 B.C.), 151
Canterbury Tales, 109, 175, 269, 346
Capp, Al (Alfred G. Caplin) (1909–), 133
Careful pronunciation, 84, 97
Careless speech, 9, 81, 84
Carroll, Lewis (Charles Lutwidge Dodgson) (1832–1898), 258
Cases, 156–177
  (*See also* Accusative case; Dative case; Genitive case)
Causative verbs, 196, 215, 223–224, 342
Caxton, William (1422?–1491), 41*n.*, 350
Central vowels, 53–55, 68
Century Dictionary and Cyclopedia, 13*n.* 211–212, 232–233
Chaucer, Geoffrey (1340?–1400), 6, 7, 51, 81, 109, 175, 269, 296
Chinese, 44–45, 48, 315
  (*See also* Mandarin)
Chomsky, Noam (1928–), 277
Churchill, Winston (1874–1965), 169
Cockney, 82, 344
Coke, Edward (1552–1634), 293
Coleridge, Samuel Taylor (1772–1834), 341
Collective nouns, 332–337
Combinative sound change, 79, 92, 98
Command, 169
Comparative degree, 167, 253–263
Complement, 281, 321
Compounds, 73–74, 142–144, 269
Concord (*see* Agreement)
"Confederate" vowel, 54, 110
Congruence, 322–327
  (*See also* Agreement)
Conjugation, verb: irregular "strong," 191, 206, 213–215
    one-part, 225
    regular "weak," 191–193, 201, 208, 216–218, 220–221, 227
    two-part, 204, 226
Conjunctions, 164–166, 276–277, 280–287
Connectives, 263, 276–288
  paired, 286–288
  (*See also* Relatives)
Consonants, 36–45, 50–51, 56, 104
  alveolar (*see* Alveolar consonants)
  bilabial, 36–39
  defective, 108

Consonants:
 resonant, 42–43
 retroflex, 34, 43
Constitution, United States, 261
Content words, 276, 294
Continuant, 35, 42
Contractions, 199, 228, 344–345
Copperud, Roy (1915–), xii, xiii
Copula, 152, 162, 181, 187, 290, 325–327, 341–342
Copulative verb, 174, 265–266, 281
Correctness:
 problem of, 1–5, 7
 standards of, 11–12, 23, 75, 78, 120, 165
 and usage, 78, 168, 243, 249, 335
Count nouns, 256
Cummings, E. E. (1894–1962), 165

Dangling adverbs, 272–273
Dangling comparatives, 262–263
Dative case, 171, 267, 292, 320–322
Davenport, John (1904–), 70
Dean, Jerome Herman ("Dizzy") (1911–), 204
Declension, 145, 156, 253
Defective consonants, 108
Degree, adjective, 254, 256–258, 260–264, 268–271
Degree words, 259, 260, 268–271
Demonstratives, 170–171, 321–322
Dental articulation, 36
Dependent clause, 330–331
Derivations, 127, 289–314
 adjective, 304, 307–309
 (*See also* Prefixes; Suffixes)
Determiner, 124–125
Diacritics, 27, 64, 67–68
Dialect, 13, 17–20, 57*n.*, 77, 101–102, 112, 122, 195
 prestige, 20, 106, 203
Dialect surveys, 17–19, 212
Dickens, Charles (1812–1870), 269*n.*, 344
Dictionaries, xii, 56, 61, 113, 128, 261, 275
 pronunciation and, 62, 64–68, 71, 81
 strong verbs, 210–212, 232–233
Diphthongs, 44, 55–59, 65, 101–106
Dissimilation, 86–87
Distribution, 129, 200
Divided usage, 76, 78, 83, 112, 243
Donne, John (1573–1631), 153*n.*
Double comparative, 260
Double conjunction, 282
Double negative, 345–349
Double plural, 133
Downgrading, 69, 82, 85
Downtoners, 268, 271–272
Dropped "g," 38, 107–108
Dropped "h," 82–83
Dropped "r," 53, 87
Dryden, John (1631–1700), 7, 279, 298
Dual number, 279
Dual pronouns, 150
Dutch, 39, 40, 132, 138, 294, 296

Edward VIII (1894–), 331
Eisenhower, Dwight D. (1890–1969), 356
Eliot, T. S. (1888–1965), 137, 170
Elizabeth I (1533–1603), 7
Ellipsis, 166–167
Ellis, Alexander J. (1814–1890), 29, 79*n.*
Empirical, 3, 12
Enclitic negative, 237–238, 340, 342, 345, 348
Encyclopædia Britannica, 27*n.*, 31*n.*
English Vowel Shift, 79, 95*n.*
"Eneydos," 350
Epenthesis, 89
Esperanto, 76, 101
Establishment, 109, 185, 349
Etruscan, 36*n.*
Etymology, 77, 83, 86, 89–90, 103, 105, 114, 119, 193, 195, 203–204, 240–241, 261, 264, 289–290, 297–299, 310, 312
 folk, 146, 194, 206
Euphemisms, 222, 257
Evans, Bergen (1904–), xii
Excrescence, 89–90

Feminine gender, 97, 154–155
Fiction writers, 81–82, 104, 349
Five-vowel system, 111–112
Fixed stress, 74–75
Flap articulation, 35
Flat adverb, 267, 292
Flat infinitive, 184, 235, 238
Flesch, Rudolph (1911–), 353*n*
Folk etymology, 146, 194, 206

Follett, Wilson (1887–1963), xii
Ford, Henry (1863–1947), 21
Foreign accent, 38, 108
Foreign words, 115–121
(*See also* specific language)
Form, xii, 25
case, 144, 156–162, 165–168, 171–172, 174–175, 277, 322
matching, 315, 323
number, 132–133, 136, 154
tense, 183, 198–200, 203, 231, 247
Form class, 127–128, 181, 293, 316
Fowler, Henry W. (1858–1933), xii, xiii, 85, 166, 243–244
Franklin, Benjamin (1706–1790), 27
Free variation, 49
French borrowed words, 41, 75, 86, 90, 94, 96, 100, 116–118, 136, 194, 206, 227, 268, 289, 298, 301
French constructions, 144, 316, 324
French scribal practice, 198
French suffixes, 292, 304
Fricatives, 35, 39–43
Fries, Charles C. (1887–1967), 16, 124, 158*n.*
Front vowels, 52, 55–56
Function:
grammar as, 9
grammatical, 157, 159–160, 182–191, 200, 235, 252–253, 263, 276
Function words, 127, 276, 318
(*See also* Structure words)
Functional shift, 220, 293–294
Funk & Wagnalls *Standard Dictionary,* 64*n.*, 211–212, 233, 312, 344
Future time, expression of, 70, 242–249

Gender, 154–156, 328–329
Genitive case, 129, 144–147, 158, 174–176, 267, 318–320
George I (1660–1717), 7
German borrowed words, 91, 116, 118, 131*n.*, 244, 289, 296–297
German grammatical features, 132, 154–155, 316–317, 324
German phonological features, 40, 50–51, 74
Germanic, 74–75, 87, 191, 204, 235–236, 244, 253, 279
Gerund, 162, 183, 188
"Gettysburg Address," 330
Gil, Alexander (1565–1635), 352*n.*
Gimson, A. C. (1917–   ), 69*n.*
Glides, 42–44
Glottal fricative, 40
Glottal stop, 32, 48
"God Bless America," 155
Good English, xi, 3–5, 8, 11, 13, 20–21, 23–24
Gowers, Sir Ernest (1880–1966), xii, 244
Gradation, 68, 82, 201–202
(*See also* Umlaut)
Grammar, xi, xii, 3–9, 18, 24
Grammarians, 8, 16, 123, 156, 181
eighteenth-century, 15, 162–163, 165, 210, 233, 249
structural, 13, 153, 338, 353–354
transformational, 259
Grandgent, Charles Hall (1862–1939), 97
Greek borrowed words, 30, 87, 281, 292, 296–298
Greek grammatical features, 141, 315
Greek philosophers, 4, 156, 275
Greek phonological features, 74–75
Greeks, 4, 5, 37*n.*, 275
Grimm, Jacob (1785–1863), 191, 201, 253
Grimm, Wilhelm (1786–1859), 191, 201, 253
Gullah, 6

Haldeman, Samuel (1812–1880), 46
Hall, Joseph (1574–1656), 312
Hamlet, 69, 153, 157*n.*, 184, 235, 244, 266, 306, 341–342
Harding, Warren G. (1865–1923), 305
Headword, 143–144, 251, 253
Hebrew, 141–142
Hemans, Felicia (1793–1835), 166*n.*
Hemingway, Ernest (1899–1961), 349
Hendiadys, 270
Hesitation sound, 53, 357
Higgins, Professor Henry, 46
High vowels, 52, 111
Holmes, Sherlock, 105
Hollywood, 117
Homograph, 258
Homophone, 48, 109
Howe, Julia Ward (1819–1910), 175

Hypercorrection, 22, 70, 84–85, 100, 105, 108, 113–114, 161, 172–173, 188, 233, 248, 266, 268, 306
(*See also* Overcorrection)
Hyperforms, 106, 195
Hyperstandard, 62, 95, 98, 137
Hypocorism, 108, 230, 302

Iambic, 67
Indefinite pronouns, 177–179, 333
Infinitive, 183–184
(*See also* Flat infinitive; Split infinitive)
Infix, 226
Inflection, 25, 77, 125, 156, 159, 254, 290, 315–317
adjective, 253
noun, 125, 129, 133, 144, 146
verb, 182, 191–192, 230–231
Initial Teaching Alphabet (ITA), 27
Intensifier, 176, 260, 268–272
Interdental fricative, 39–40
International Phonetic Alphabet (IPA), 27, 64
Intransitive, 214–215, 223
Intrusive, 90–92
Inversion sentence, 161, 163, 337
Inverted plurals, 136
Inverted spelling, 100
Irregular inflections, 130–133, 189–190, 193–198, 213–214, 254
Irregularities, 8, 76, 121, 182, 290, 306
Isolative sound change, 78–79
Italian, 118

Japanese, 58
Jefferson, Thomas (1743–1826), 293, 299
Jespersen, Otto (1860–1943), 17, 69*n.*, 79*n.*
Johnson, Samuel (1709–1784), 8, 12, 205, 210, 212, 231–232, 249, 278
Jones, William (1746–1794), 77
Joos, Martin (1907–), xiii

Keats, John (1795–1821), 104, 227*n.*
Kennedy, John (1917–1963), 92
Kenyon, John S. (1874–1959), 17, 64*n.*, 69*n.*
King James Bible (KJV) (1611), 64, 153 157*n.*, 158, 161–162, 164, 172, 186–187, 194, 244, 279, 329–330
Knott, Thomas A. (1880–1945), 64*n.*
Krapp, George Philip (1872–1934), xii, xiii, 14*n.*
Kurath, Hans (1891–), 19*n.*, 57*n.*

Labial, 44, 98–99
Labialization, 98–101, 108
Labiodental, 39–40
Language change, 77–78
Lateral, 42–43
Latin, 6–8
affixes, 281, 295, 304
borrowed words, 91, 93, 96, 140, 142, 193, 280, 289, 302
grammatical features, 140, 235, 251–252, 317, 323, 338
phonological features, 74–75
pronunciation of, 119–121
scribal practices, 42, 100
Lenneberg, Eric H. (1921–), 30*n.*
Leonard, Sterling A. (1888–1931), xiii, 14–18, 233
Letters, 34, 45–46, 50, 146, 295
silent, 64
Leveling, 159, 186, 198, 203–206, 211–213, 215, 217, 225, 227–230, 232, 325
Levels of usage, 13–14, 17, 20–21
Lexicology, 25
Lincoln, Abraham (1809–1865), 330
Linguistic Atlas, 18–20
Linguistic science, 4, 13
Linking *n* and *r,* 91
Linking verb (*see* Copulative verbs)
Liquid, 42–44
Lisp, 108–109
Liverpudlian, 101*n.*
London English, 69, 187, 203
Long vowels, 51–52, 55–56, 59, 65, 101*n.*
Longfellow, Henry W. (1807–1882), 207
Lost positive, 299–300
Low vowel, 52–55
Lowell, James Russell (1819–1891), 262
Lowth, Robert (1710–1787), 8, 12–13, 15, 146, 205, 210, 231, 249, 279–280, 285

McDavid, Raven I., Jr. (1911–), 57*n.*, 188*n.*
Malaprop, Mrs., 306

Mancusan, 101*n.*
Mandarin, 48, 58, 315
(*See also* Chinese)
Manutius, Aldus (1450–1515), 350
Marckwardt, Albert H. (1903–), xiii, 15, 17
Masculine gender, 154–155
Mass noun, 140, 256
Mayer, Milton (1908–), 348*n.*
Meaning:
figurative, 261
versus function, 127, 276
shifts in, 236, 238–239, 303, 309
Mencken, Henry L. (1880–1956), 188*n.*
Metathesis, 115
Meter, poetic, 69
Mid vowel, 52–54
Middle ages, 6, 93
Middle English, 74*n.*
inflections, 145, 146, 184, 192, 202, 267, 268
negation, 340, 345–346
phonology, 94
vocabulary, 96, 230
Midland, United States, 57, 99, 103, 153, 229, 239
Midwestern United States, 78
Milton, John (1608–1674), 159, 204, 210, 219, 259, 353
Minimal pairs, 41, 110
Mitford, Nancy (1904–), 21*n.*
Modals, 183, 185, 235, 237–240, 244–245, 247, 249, 324
Mode, 235
adjectives, 73, 254–263
adverbs, 263–268, 272
degree words, 268–271
function of, 250–251
participles, 190, 271
Moffett, Harold Y. (1888–), 14*n.*, 15
Moore, Julia A. (1847–1920), 343
Morphemes, 125–127, 129, 146, 181–182, 290, 293, 295, 313
Morphology, 25, 146, 182
Morse, Samuel F. B. (1791–1872), 194
Movable stress, 74–75
Murray, James A. H. (1837–1915), 14*n.*
Murray, Lindley (1745–1826), 232
Mutation, 133, 143
(*See also* Umlaut)
Nasals, 35, 38
National Council of Teachers of English, 15–16
Native, 48, 75–76, 109, 292, 294, 299, 309
Natural language, 76–77, 101
Navajo, 291
Negation, 263, 339–349
multiple, 345–349
Negative:
comparison, 286–287
enclitic, 237–238
(*See also* Double negative)
Negative prefixes, 126, 297, 299
Neuter gender, 154–155
Neutral vowel, 53, 68–69, 81
New Yorker, 70*n.*, 345
Newmark, Leonard (1929–), 202*n.*
Nicene Creed, 269
Nicknames, 82, 138
Nominative case, 144–145, 156–159, 162
Noncommital, 177
Nonfinite verb, 183
Nonstandard, 17, 24
Nootka, 47
Norman Invasion, 41, 74*n.*, 317*n.*
Norman scribes, 42, 44*n.*, 198
Norse, 217
Northeastern United States, 11
Northern England, 48, 69, 79, 184, 187, 199
Northern United States, 57, 78, 105, 207, 229, 238
Notional definition, 263
Notional plural, 332, 334
Notional subject, 335, 337
Nouns, 123, 126, 128
collective, 332–337
function of, 252–253
genitives, 144
morphology of, 129
person distinction, 151
plurals: irregular, 131–144
regular, 130
verbal, 181, 187–189
Nucleus, 51–58, 191, 193
Null (*see* Zero inflection)
Number, grammatical, 129, 152–154, 323–327

Objects, 144, 158–166, 168–172, 190, 252, 277, 320–321
  complement, 252
  direct, 160, 172, 176, 252, 320–321
  genitive, 174, 319
  indirect, 144, 160, 176, 252, 320–321
  of preposition, 160, 172, 252
Oblique, 156
Old English, 74, 77, 145, 191–192, 200–202, 253, 259–260, 294, 323, 340
Old High German, 44*n.*, 131*n.*, 273
Overcorrection, 38, 42, 97, 100, 267
  (*See also* Hypercorrection)
Oxford English Dictionary, 14*n.*, 70, 83, 177–178, 192, 236, 243, 269*n.*, 276, 296, 311–312, 336, 343

Palatal consonants, 37, 39–41, 43–44
Palatalization, 94–97
Panini (*c.* 350 B.C.), 4
Paradigm, 152, 182
Paradise Lost, 159
Parallelism, 281
Parsing, 184
Participles, 38
  past, 182, 190, 200–201, 231–233, 242, 259, 271–272, 326
  present, 182–183, 187–189, 200, 259, 326
Particle, 276
Parts of speech, 123–124, 127–128
  (*See also* Form class)
Passive voice, 161, 179, 190, 326
Past participle (*see* Participles, past)
Past tense, 181, 189
  (*See also* Preterite tense)
Paul, Saint (died *c.* 67), 260
Perelman, Sidney J. (1904–), 306
Perfect tense, 190
Periphrastic comparison, 258–260
Periphrastic genitives, 174, 318–320
Periphrastic plurals, 154
Person, 150–152, 323
Phone (phonetic unit), 49
Phoneme, 47–50
Phonemic principle, 47, 49
Phonetics, 27–29, 32*n.*, 45, 47
Phonologist, 51, 53–58, 121
Phonology, 25, 28, 47, 121
Pidgin English, 6, 291
Pitch, 66, 354
Plato (427?–347?B.C.), 4
Plurals, 40, 129–144, 152–154, 316, 322
Poetic, 198, 260
Pooley, Robert C. (1898–), xiii, 14
Pope, Alexander (1688–1744), 146
Position, 48, 159, 161–162, 268
Positive degree, 97, 253
Possessive case, 129, 144, 319
  (*See also* Genitive case)
Possession, 147, 174, 228, 319
Powell, John Wesley (1834–1902), 13*n.*
Predicate, 325, 351
Predicate adjective, 325
Predicate noun, 265, 325
Predicative position, 264–265
Prefixes, 75, 295–299, 302–303
Prepositions, 160, 164–165, 183, 276–280
Prescriptive grammarians, 205, 211, 243
Present participles (*see* Participles, present)
Present tense, 182–183, 201, 231, 235, 244, 323–326
Preterite tense, 182, 189, 191–201, 231–233, 244, 326
Priestley, Joseph (1733–1804), 162–163
Principal parts, 182
Prior, Matthew (1664–1721), 146
Proclitic elements, 340
Productive affixes, 259, 296–297, 304
Progressive tense, 187, 326
Prokosch, Eduard (1876–1938), 202*n.*
Pronouns:
  case, 156–176
  gender, 154–156
  indefinite, 177–179
  number, 152–154
  person, 150–152
  reflexive, 176–177
Public speakers, 99, 173
Punctuation, 350–352
"Pure" English, xiv, 7, 227, 292
Purists, language of, 178, 211, 243, 268, 298
Pyles, Thomas (1905–), 165*n.*

Quakers, 158, 168
Quantifier, 137
Quantitative approach, 16

Quintilian, Marcus Fabian (First Century, A.D.), 319
Quirk, Randolph (1920–), 191*n.*

Radio announcers, 26, 99, 104, 106, 173
Random House Dictionary, 26*n.*, 27*n.*, 65, 83, 128, 312–313
Redundancy, 141, 201, 228, 232, 323–324, 345
Reference, 327–333
Reflexive pronouns, 176
Regular nouns, 129–130
Regular verbs, 189–193
Relatives, 329–331
Remodeling, 193, 340
Resonant consonant, 35, 42–43
Revised Standard Bible (RSV)(1946, 1952), 67, 246, 248
Retroflex consonants, 34, 43
Rhythm, 66
Roman, 36*n.*, 37*n.*, 275
Romance languages, 235
Root syllable, 75
Rounding, lip, 39, 44, 52
Rules, xii, 1, 6–8, 14–15, 73, 129, 224, 242–245, 247
Russian, 294
Rustic, 193, 210, 214, 225, 226

Salmon, Daniel E. (1850–1914), 100
Sanskrit, 4, 5, 12
Sapir, Edward (1884–1939), 12, 47
Scandinavian, 157*n.*, 171, 187, 217, 236, 291, 294*n.*, 331
Schoolmastering, 92, 195, 205, 233, 240, 327, 343
"School of speech" pronunciation, 93
Scott, Walter (1771–1832), 237, 300
Scottish, 40, 170, 199, 236–237
Scouse, 101*n.*
Semivowels, 44, 56–59
Sentence, complete, 349–355
Shakespeare, William (1564–1616), 26, 69, 70, 78, 89, 91, 146*n.*–147*n.*, 157*n.*, 158, 162–164, 167, 235, 237, 244, 259–260, 306, 346
Shaw, George Bernard (1856–1950), 21, 46*n.*, 147, 284
Sheridan, Richard Brinsley (1751–1816), 306
Short vowels, 51–52
Sibilant, 35, 130
Singular, 129, 152–153
  third-person (*see* Third-person singular)
Sledd, James (1914–), 125*n.*
Slurvian, 70
Smith, Henry Lee, Jr. (1913–), 125*n.*
Smith, Logan Pearsall (1865–1946), 262
Smith, Thomas (1513–1577), 352*n.*
Social science, 3, 21, 121
Sociologists, 20, 22
Sound change, 77–80
Southern United States, 54, 75, 78, 91, 97, 99, 105, 153, 213, 229, 235, 284
Southey, Robert (1774–1843), 134
Southwestern United States, 97, 193, 216
Spanish, 35, 39–40, 44–45, 58, 193
Spelling, 26–27, 36, 38, 64, 129
Spelling pronunciation, 69, 72–73, 81–83
Split infinitive, 184–185
Standard, 7, 11–12, 14, 16–17, 26, 61–63, 102, 243
Status, 21–22, 81, 122, 166, 179, 182, 225, 233, 249, 272
Status symbol, 22
Steele, Richard (1672–1729), 195
Sterile affixes, 297, 304
Stops, 35–38
Stress, 66–76
  fixed or movable, 74–75
  (*See also* Accent)
Strong verbs, 191, 199–234
Structural linguistics, 13, 124, 338–339, 352–354
Structure words, 127, 276, 339
  (*See also* Function words)
Subject, 144, 159–165, 167–168, 252, 323–327, 351
Subjunctive mode, 200, 235–236
Subordinator, 166
Substandard, 62–63, 111, 171, 176, 229, 255
Suffixes, 137, 176, 292, 295, 303–314, 340
Superlative degree, 253–260
Sweet, Henry (1845–1912), 46*n.*, 74*n.*, 191*n.*, 276
Symmetry, 42, 54, 202
Syncopation, 69–70, 87–88

Syntax, 25, 77, 315–358
Synthetic language, 157, 258, 316

Taste, grammar as, 9
Tautology, 186, 260, 285–286, 302–303, 347
Telescoping of constructions, 285–287, 302
Ten Commandments, 246
Tenses, verb, 181–183, 186–187, 189–190, 244, 342
Third-person singular, 186–187, 200, 325
Time, 85, 235*n.*, 300*n.*
Trager, George L. (1906–), 126*n.*
Transformational linguistics, 173, 259, 339, 354
Transitive verbs, 167, 215, 223, 281
Trill articulation, 35, 43
Trochaic, 67
Trubetzkoi, Nikolai (1890–1938), 47
Truman, Harry S. (1884–), 93
Twain, Mark (Samuel Clemens) (1835–1910), 96*n.*, 153, 305
Tyndale, William (1492?–1536), 320

Umlaut, 84, 131
  (*See also* Mutation)
Understatement, 270, 348
Universal grammar, 7
Unreleased stops, 48
Unstressed vowels, 66, 68, 81–83
Upgrading, 82, 105, 108

Variants:
  archaic, 197
  humorous, 204
  hyperstandard, 95
  morphological, 126
  phonetic, 35, 38, 39, 43, 57, 59, 62, 71, 85
  positional, 48–49
    (*See also* Phoneme)
  spelling, 89, 100, 344
Velar articulation, 36–38, 40, 44
Verb auxiliaries (*see* Auxiliaries, verb)
Verb-noun congruence, 322–327, 334
Verbs:
  anomalous, 198–199, 220–230
  copulative (*see* Copulative verb)
Verbs:
  regular, 189–193
  strong, 191, 199–234
  weak, 191–199
Vikings, 171, 187, 331
Voiced articulation, 35–37
Voiceless articulation, 35–37
Voltaire, François Marie Arouet (1694–1778), 77
Vowels, 50–59, 64–74, 101–106
  (*See also* specific type)
Vulgar English, 85, 111–112, 114, 117

Walcott, Fred G. (1894–), xiii, 15, 17
Wallis, John (1616–1703), 243, 247*n.*, 249
Watts, Isaac (1674–1748), 249
Weak verbs, 191–199
Webster, Noah (1758–1843), 11, 83, 162, 226*n.*, 327
Webster's, 11
  American Dictionary (1864), 13*n.*, 212–213, 232
  First New International (1909), 233, 311–312
  Second New International (1934), 64*n.*, 112, 192
  Third New International (1961), 26*n.*, 65, 83, 112*n.*, 128, 192, 313
Welsh, 43
Western European, 36, 39–40, 43, 48
Whatley, Richard (1787–1863), 343
Whitney, William D. (1827–1894), 13*n.*
Whittier, John Greenleaf (1807–1892), 103, 241
Williams, John (1904–), 235
Word order, 77, 157–159, 172, 254, 268, 293, 315–318, 321, 324, 327, 338–339
World War I, 13, 21, 124*n.*, 301
World War II, 13, 23*n.*, 124*n.*, 298
Wrenn, C. L. (1895–1952), 191*n.*
Wulfila (311?–381), 235

Yiddish, 294

Zamenhoff, Lazarus L. (1859–1917), 76
Zero inflection, 133–134, 221, 227